THE
FATHERS
OF THE
EASTERN
CHURCH

THE
FATHERS
OF THE
EASTERN
CHURCH

ROBERT PAYNE

DORSET PRESS
New York

formerly published as *Holy Fire*

This edition published by Dorset Press,
a division of Marboro Books Corporation,
by arrangement with Sheila Lalwani Payne
1989 Dorset Press

ISBN 0-88029-404-3

Printed in the United States of America
M 9 8 7 6 5 4 3 2 1

MIREILLAE

OPTIMAE ATQVE CARISSIMAE

CVI MULTA DEBEO

SACRUM

Fire is in all things, is spread everywhere, pervades all things without intermingling with them, shining by its very nature and yet hidden, and manifesting its presence only when it can find material on which to work, violent and invisible, having absolute rule over all things. . . . It comprehends, but remains incomprehensible, never in need, mysteriously increasing itself and showing forth its majesty according to the nature of the substance receiving it, powerful and mighty and invisibly present in all things.

DIONYSIUS AREOPAGITA,
De Caelestia Ierarchia, XV

Contents

Introduction

Too often in our modern eyes the Fathers of the Eastern Church remain shadowy and mysterious, their names forgotten, their long battles with emperors and heretics remembered only as footnotes, their works gathering dust. We remember Athanasius because he held the world at bay, and John Chrysostom for the golden words that poured from his golden mouth, but we rarely pay attention to Basil, the defender of the faith and the founder of organized monasticism, or his saintly brother Gregory of Nyssa, the first to map the pathway of the soul in its progress toward the Heavenly Mountain. We forget Gregory Nazianzen, who changed the course of Christianity in the East with five sermons delivered in a private house, though we sing his hymns. Macarius, Simeon the New Theologian, Nicholas Cabasilas, Gregory Palamas, John of Damascus—we remember them rarely, yet they were men of astonishing intelligence and virtuosity. In their own time the Fathers of the Eastern Church were regarded as only a little lower than the apostles. They fought battles with superb courage, lived lives rich in emotion, and wrote magnificently; and since for nearly two thousand years the Eastern Fathers have dominated the eastern Mediterranean, where Christianity began, it is strange that we should so often forget them.

Perhaps the fault lies with the Eastern Church, which never propagated the faith with the vigor of the Western Church and rarely sent missionaries abroad. Toward the West they showed, not indifference, but the desire to hold the watchtowers they had won. They had little desire to go beyond the places where early Christianity flowered: Alexandria, Constantinople, Athens, Antioch, Thessalonica, Jerusalem, Asia Minor. In the fourth century they sent missions to the Scythians, but we have few records of their missionary spirit until Cyril (*d.* 869) and Methodius (*d.* 885) conquered the Slavs for Christ. The profound impress of the Eastern Church on the Russian mind, extending over a thousand years, has not ceased; and even now, though Russia is offi-

On Greek

cially godless, we shall understand the Russians better by understanding the springs of their religion, in which early Christian communism and the ruthless laws of the Basilian monastic system have always had a place.

There are other reasons why the Fathers of the Eastern Church sometimes seem remote from us. Above all, they spoke and wrote in Greek. This beautiful language, of immense vigor and sweetness, was the perfect vehicle for the Christian message; no language was ever so evenly balanced between action and thought. Greek was the language of the Gospels, of the early Church, of the early liturgies, of the first Christian missionaries to Rome, and the names of all the early bishops of Rome before the time of Victor, who died A.D. 198, were authentically Greek. Greek was Paul's mother tongue; all his early education was Greek in form and language. In those days the Greek language ruled the world, and we forget our debt to Greece at our peril—the Greece of the classical period, and for two thousand ensuing years. The King James Version of the Bible retains to an extraordinary degree the original rhythms of the Greek text, and words like *Christ, church, angel, priest, eucharist,* are Greek to the core. The Fathers of the Eastern Church never forgot that they were speaking in Greek, the language which Alexander the Great had imposed on all his conquered territories. As they defied Emperors and fulminated against the heretics, they were perfectly aware they were employing a language rooted in an ancient past, and many, like Justin Martyr, confessed themselves disciples of Plato. They gloried in Greek, and some believed that Greek—a language that ripples like water and flashes like dancing flames—was spoken by the angels. Others believed it was spoken by Christ.

To understand the Eastern Fathers, we must sometimes put aside our prejudices. Their Christianity is not the same as ours. They were a people of warm imaginations, more incandescent than the Fathers of the Western Church, fiercer in denunciation, quicker in anger, more sudden to praise. They stressed many things we have left unstressed. For them Christianity was "the imitation of the divine nature"; it was not so much a way of life as a fierce effort toward perfection. They took quite seriously the text: "Be ye therefore perfect, as also your Heavenly Father is perfect," and they seem to have believed that perfection was within the grasp of mankind. According to Gregory of Nyssa the profession of Christianity was nothing less than to restore man to his lost paradise, and so they went on to explore the utmost possibilities of man's likeness to God, for God was in all things, pervading all Creation, and since God was so close to them, so was the Paradise He had promised to His children. According to some Fathers, even the Devil would one day make his peace with Heaven, his sins all pardoned and his beauty restored.

We shall not understand the Eastern Christians unless we see them, as they saw themselves, in the light of the Apocalypse or the blaze of the Transfiguration. They lived at white heat, when Christianity was still fresh as the morning dew, a thing which had come to birth only a few moments before. And so they did not dwell very much on the Crucifixion or on the youthful Christ who walked in the cornfields: the Christ who haunted their dreams neither suffered excruciating pain nor gathered the husks in His hands. For them the lightning struck and the earth trembled, and in a moment of vision they saw the image of God towering against the golden heavens, wearing on His head the diadem of an Emperor. So in Constantinople they painted Him in a glitter of mosaics, a vaster Emperor than any known to them, seated in majesty above the rim of the world, so old and wise beyond all knowing that it was enough to contemplate the divinity streaming down from Him; and their fiercest disputes were against those who would lessen His majesty, His absolute dominion over mankind, His absolute mercy, His perfect divinity.

Today they seem to have faded into the distance, those Fathers of another time. It was not always so. St. Thomas Aquinas once said he would give all Paris for a homily written by St. John Chrysostom, and is forever quoting from the Eastern Fathers. John Donne from his pulpit at St. Paul's quotes from them endlessly, assuming in his audience a knowledge of them almost as extensive as his own. There was a time in the fourteenth century when English poetry was saturated with a visionary quality derived from Dionysius the Areopagite, whose real name no one knows. Words first spoken beside remote rivers in Cappadocia and in long-vanished churches in Alexandria and Antioch still affect our lives, though we are hardly aware of it. Chance played its part. The great Western Fathers who borrowed freely from the East sometimes mistranslated, and occasionally they attached more significance to a lesser theologian than to a major, with the result that Dionysius the Areopagite was quoted far more extensively than Gregory of Nyssa; yet Gregory was the greater man and the greater saint and possessed a greater understanding of the mystery. John Damascene, who wrote his *Exact Exposition of the Orthodox Faith* in a monastery overlooking the Kedron valley around A.D. 700, came at a time when Western Christianity was going through a period of sterility and possessed no influence upon the West until Aquinas rediscovered him five hundred and fifty years later. Such things may happen again. Eastern Christianity, which remains faithful to an earlier Christian tradition, may again invigorate the West.

There is a sense in which it is true that we cannot understand Christianity unless we come to terms with the Eastern Fathers. Like Ambrose, Jerome and Augustine they helped to build the foundations. They laid a pattern which was to have profound effects on the nature of Christianity itself; theirs was the writ by which the Church achieved its unity and its truth. Though they fought heretics to a standstill and argued interminably, truth for them was not something to be approached by argument and seized upon by disputatious men. Truth was absolute and imperial. She came from Heaven, with the scepter of power in her hands, and her name was *hagia sophia,* the holy wisdom. So she remained always, undivided and indivisible, to be observed in the Sacraments which were enjoyed by the whole congregation acting together, the gift of the spirit to the community of worshipers. Here there was no room for differences of opinion: the congregation itself was a unity, molded by God and His priests, the congregation a thing of splendor while the individual was no more than a speck of dust. Yet by a supreme paradox, though the Eastern Church insisted so strongly upon the unity of the congregation, regarding the assembled worshipers as a community endowed with great spiritual power precisely because they were a community, it attached to the individual souls, those innumerable specks of dust, immense possibilities of perfection. It was not that there was any rivalry between the community and the individual. It was simply that the community represented the image of the heavenly hosts and each worshiper was made in the image of God.

Again and again in the writings of the Eastern Fathers there appears this singular devotion to the dignity of man, an attitude which survives in the Offertory in the Mass: "O God, who didst marvelously create the dignity of human nature—*Deus, qui humanae substantiae dignitatem mirabiliter condidisti.*" In the West this devotion to the dignity of man is only occasional; in the East it is perpetual. "By the honor of the body created in the likeness of God, man is higher than the angels," declared Gregory Palamas in the fourteenth century, and a thousand years before him Gregory of Nyssa, not quite so daring, wrote:

By its likeness to God human nature is made as it were a living image partaking with the Godhead both in rank in name, clothed in virtue, reposing in the blessedness of immortality, garlanded with the crown of righteousness, and so a perfect likeness to the beauty of the Godhead in all that belongs to the dignity of majesty.

[De hominis Opificio, IV, 136]

Gregory is talking about the nature of man before the Fall, but he has almost the same fervor when he talks of the living men around him. For him man is a triumph, and his triumph lies in his likeness to God. He does not share Pascal's belief in the *Deus absconditus*. God can be seen, touched and heard; a man has only to look into his soul. "Man's soul is a mirror in which he can see God," he announces firmly. Here there are no mysteries, only the terrible Mystery of God's eternal and undivided presence. Should a man desire to see the face of God, then let him look into himself:

O you who are possessed with the desire to contemplate the true good, when you hear that the divine majesty is exalted above the heavens and that His glory is unfathomable, His beauty ineffable, His nature incomprehensible, do not despair of being able to see the object of your desires. . . . You have only to return to the purity of the image established in you in the beginning: you will find in yourself what you seek, for once the spirit is cleansed and free from all wickedness, you will find the blessed vision in the serenity of your heart. There you will find purity, holiness, simplicity, all those gentle radiances of the divine nature by which God is seen.   *[De beatitudinibus, 6]*

In words not unlike these Eckhart and Tauler, the great German mystics, were to speak later. It was as though across the centuries a voice had spoken from the obscure town of Nyssa, now so unimportant a place that it hardly appears on any map.

What is most astonishing in the Eastern Church is this gentle visionary quality allied with a conception of God as the *mysterium tremendum,* the starlit flood of power sweeping across the heavens, God as the brute energy of Creation, the judge and sole Emperor through all eternity. In themselves they combined gentleness and strength; in God they saw gentleness and strength magnified to infinite dimensions. Sometimes they saw Christ as though He were all flaming fire, a thing that leaped and tossed in the winds of God, never still, never to be pinned down, and in the ever-changing shapes of the flames they seem to see the face of the flame-lit God, as in the great basilicas we see the stern and terrifying Pantocrator arising from a nest of flame. And then, after so much violence, the winds of heaven die down and the Christian sees only the calm blue sky; and there too the face of God is written. Sometimes as you read the Eastern Fathers you will find yourself entering a strange landscape, such a landscape as you might expect to see on the eve of the Day of Judgment: a great valley, flowering trees on the slopes, the sheep in the meadows and the white peaks of mountains looming beyond; and there is nothing strange about this valley except that it is simultaneously drenched by summer sunlight and split by storms of lightning, at once noon and midnight, terror and peace. It is a landscape you will see painted in their basilicas, with the ceilings of flame and the spring flowers twined around the slender columns: the Garden of Eden and the Day of Judgment, the first day and the last, alpha and omega wedded together.

So in those fine-spun imaginations lit with the orient sun Christ is seen more clearly and more sharply than in the West. It is not only that they were nearer to Jerusalem and Nazareth, but they were closer to the habits of thought of the earliest Christians. They knew, as we shall never know, how men went about their affairs when Christianity was no more than a young shoot, though from the tree of Jesse. The face of Jesus had left a shining on the air; almost they could see His face; and in His pathways they walked in fear and trembling, for almost they could see His shadow at the turning of the road. And perhaps this is why, when you are reading the Eastern Fathers, you are aware of a freshness which is lacking in the Fathers of the West, who never saw the snows of Mount Hermon or drank the thick red wine of the Syrian innkeepers or fished in Lake Galilee.

The Eastern Fathers shared with the earliest Christians the knowledge of Christ's imminent return: He had gone from them for so short a time it was easy to think of Him returning soon. For them there were no archways down the years, no sense of Christ's mission as something that happened in a remote, irrevocable past, no haunting suspicion that divinity vanished from the earth when Christ ascended into Heaven. After the first World War the German poet Rainer Maria Rilke said that "the world has passed out of the hands of God into the hands of men." The Eastern Fathers would have denied it firmly; and they were not ignorant of war and the misery men create for themselves. For them the evidence of God's presence lay in flowers, in trees, in animals, in the faces of children, in people going about their daily affairs; and it was present in the thunder and the sword blade. And for them, too, the person of Christ was incomparably greater than the person we are accustomed to represent to ourselves in our prayers. Origen and Gregory of Nyssa and many others among the Eastern Fathers believed that He came to save all spiritual creatures, not men only. He did not shed His blood on earth at Jerusalem for sin alone; He offered Himself as a gift on the high altar in Heaven, to save the angels and all the universe, of which this little corner of earth is the smallest part. His mission was the restoration of God's peace through all time, through all eternity, through all the spaces of the universe, in every heart and every sentient thing; and so they claimed of Christ more than He ever claimed of Himself, and in so doing they made His sacrifice more comprehensible.

For us the greatest virtue of the Eastern Fathers lies in their sense of the sanctity indwelling in all things. All that was made by God, all that was touched by His hand, was holy. The stars were sacred, and so were spider webs, and so were grasses waving in the wind; and man too was sacred, for did he not possess a body capable of resurrection and transfiguration? All men were revelers before the throne of God, partaking in a holy festival. Clement of Alexandria believed that all life was one perpetual holy feast—Ἅπας δὲ ὁ βίος πανήγυρις ἁγία. Holiness was something you could almost gather in your hands, as the Israelites gathered manna in their wanderings. And since "all things are administered from above for good," there is no reason to despair: holiness will say the word, and evil will be scattered away.

They did not, of course, always possess this serenity: they were sometimes plagued by doubts, and occasionally lost themselves in the vast complications of faith. Doctrinal quarrels flared up; harsh words were exchanged; and the great Arian controversy of the fourth century showed they could behave with human forthrightness and very human temper. Yet, as we look back, it is their serenity which shames us. Where we stumble, they walked sure-footed. We lack their urgency as we lack their subtlety, their fire, the brilliance in their eyes. Too often they knew in their hearts the things we can only guess at.

All these Fathers lived in the small corner of the world which borders on the eastern Mediterranean. They came from Alexandria, Antioch, Damascus, Constantinople, and obscure towns in the wilds of Cappadocia. Many of them were originally wealthy and belonged to powerful families. The family of Basil possessed estates in three provinces of Asia Minor. John Damascene, before he entered his mountain cave, was a high official in the court of an oriental Caliph. John Chrysostom was the son of a general, Gregory of Nazianzus the son of a bishop. Most of them could have risen to high positions; instead they chose lives of austerity, prayer and obedience. They were men of diverse gifts, but the pattern of their lives was singularly uniform. We can trace in nearly all of them a common evolution: a sheltered childhood, and then at some period in their youth a profound spiritual shock followed by a long withdrawal from the world. They go to the mountains or the desert, mortify themselves, rejoicing in their complete isolation and living on a few grains of barley a day; then, having lived with angels, they descend from the mountain or wander across the desert to the market place, to rejoin the world of men and to enter the Church. Usually they produced their best works when they were about forty, and they died worn out by their continuing dedication to asceticism at about sixty. To the end of their lives they bore the marks of the early years of mortification. They were often ill. Basil suffered from violent attacks of malaria; John Chrysostom seems to have been tubercular, suffered from a disease of the kidneys and was an invalid through the last twenty years of his life; Athanasius suffered from continual infirmities; Gregory of Nazianzus was frail, and Gregory Palamas is known to have died of a long lingering illness. Their physical frailties may explain some of the excitement and glitter in their writings, but not the divinity which hangs over them. They wrote like angels, with sudden visionary gleams of startling clarity; we cannot explain it away by blaming the flesh. And though their writings are unequal, there is hardly a page without some brightness somewhere. Even Clement of Alexandria, who gathered so many odds and ends in his ragpicker's basket, the author of a famous *Quilted Bag for Stuffing Bedclothes,* wrote when he chose divinely. In an English translation we cannot guess at the vividness and vitality of their writings. Greek flows; our poor English syllables are leaden-heavy in comparison. All translations fail, but translations from the Eastern Fathers fail more than most. It is something we must put up with until the flames of Pentecost descend upon us.

What did these Fathers look like as they walked down the street? We know them well, and would easily recognize them. We have their letters, their sermons, their homilies, the broadsides they delivered against their enemies, their accounts of one another. Of most of them we know as much as we know about the men who inhabited Elizabethan England. Important works are lost; only the wreck of Origen's writings is left to us; many of the manuscripts of Gregory Palamas lie in the Bibliothèque Nationale in Paris uncopied and untranslated. An amazing amount of detailed information remains. The church histories of Eusebius and Socrates fill in the gaps. The nearly four hundred surviving letters of Basil tell us as much as we can reasonably want to know about his movements and his relationships with his friends, and they reveal his private character. Together the orations and songs of Gregory of Nazianzus reveal the man, so that we seem to see him in depth. It is the same with Gregory of Nyssa, whose treatises, letters and mystical writings curiously complement one another. John Chrysostom's voluminous homilies are sufficiently autobiographical to allow us to invade his privacy. It would be pleasant to have the letters of John Damascene, but he seems to have foreseen the need of a closer view, and provided in *Barlaam and Joseph,* the first Christian novel, the outlines of a spiritual biography. Though we know almost nothing about the events of the life of Clement of Alexandria, we have his scrapbook, that vast compendium into which he wrote his ideas on all subjects under the sun: the scrapbook reveals the man so completely we would recognize the tone of his voice before he entered a room. Dionysius the Areopagite alone escapes us completely: he is all flame and mystery, and so he will remain until the Day of Judgment. Yet sometimes, browsing among the dusty volumes of the Fathers, observing them at intervals in their unguarded moments, his is the face we most hunger to see.

It is not astonishing that none of them wrote down their confessions; they would have asked what there was to confess. They lacked the desire, common in the West, to explain and justify themselves. When they were egotistical, it was not for themselves. Their task as they saw it was to celebrate God, to inquire into His nature, and to pursue the doctrine of man, glorified by the Incarnation, possessing a body capable of resurrection and transfiguration. St. Augustine's *Confessions* would have amazed them, and they would have been amazed still more by *The City of God,* where Heaven is depicted in terms of civic splendors. For them Heaven was a blinding light, a dark corner where a man can rest, a face, a throne, a quiet flame feeding eternally on the Body of Christ. They were aware that God is One, but only because He is multitudinous.

In the West there is the need for hard outlines and clear definitions: the long straight Roman roads still haunt our minds. In the East men's

Plato

minds moved like mountain trails, following the shape of the earth, not cutting through obstacles, and if there were palm trees to rest under, there they would rest. Though they lived in the blinding sun, they knew that all outlines softly recede and there is a point beyond which all definitions fail. It follows that they were perfectly capable of believing in two mutually contradictory statements. They believed for example in the nearness and the otherness of God. They believed He could be seen by mortal eyes, and at the same time (because the mere statement of such a belief took their breath away), they believed He was entirely inaccessible and no mortal man had ever bathed in the Light that shone on Mount Tabor. They wrote endlessly about the vision of God, and those like St. John Chrysostom and St. Gregory of Nyssa who spoke most triumphantly about His invisibility are precisely those who have seen God most clearly. They thrived on paradoxes. Nicholas Cabasilas wrote that God is "at once the inn upon the road and the end of the journey." It is a simple statement, and one reads it on the wing, without realizing how many complexities are concealed in it. One should remember always that the Greek Fathers had sharpened their wisdom teeth on Plato. They were all humanists, and unlike St. Jerome and St. Gregory they did not ban profane learning as offensive and abominable. They gloried in their Hellenist traditions, and saw Plato as a precursor of Christ.

The greatest age of the Eastern Fathers was crammed into a single generation. Antony, Athanasius, Basil, Gregory of Nyssa, Gregory Nazianzen, were contemporaries, living at a time when the Eastern Empire was ruled by a succession of despots, whose deaths, coming in quick succession, inevitably involved war and bloodshed. It was the time of Ambrose and Augustine, who died with the Vandals at the gates. Chrysostom was exiled twice by imperial decree, dying at last in an obscure region near the shores of the Black Sea. Athanasius was exiled five times; he wandered over half Europe and hid in the caves of the desert of Nitria, a hunted refugee. Athanasius, Basil, Chrysostom and John Damascene all defied Emperors to do their worst. Famine, war, terror, violence, were their familiars, the air they breathed. They lived in heroic times, rising as we must from a world in ruins.

During this period the split between East and West had already taken place. Historians profess to see the break between the Eastern Church, represented by the Patriarchate of Constantinople, and the Western Church, represented by the Papacy, as occurring A.D. 1054 in the reign of the Emperor Constantine IX Monomachus, but there had been divergencies from the beginning. The marriage between Greece and Rome was never consummated. The Greek imagination was winged, the Roman mind closer to the earth. Should those two giants ever come together, one would be more hopeful of the enduring power of Christianity to conquer the world. Long ago, at the very beginning of Christianity, the Christian communities of Lyons and Vienne in the south of France sent messages of affection "to their brothers in Asia and Phrygia," as though Asia and Phrygia were on the other side of the garden fence. One can only pray that this time will come again.

But though there are divergencies, there is a vast common ground where the Eastern Church meets the Western Church. The doctrines first announced by the Eastern Fathers are indissolubly ours, their hymns are sung by us, their quick imaginations have fed the flames of the West. Mysteriously, invisibly, often when we are least aware of them, they affect our lives. And if they seem to us ghostly, vanishing into the airy distance, it is only because we have the habit of forgetting our own past. Though dead, they live so prodigiously that life still flows from them; they live and breathe; they are a part of us; we cannot escape the freshness and heroism they brought to the world. In one of the old French cathedrals may be seen the Crosses of the Eastern and Western Churches standing at opposite ends of the altar: there is a sense in which the Eastern Cross still stands on our altars, though we do not see it with our eyes.

In the following pages I have endeavored to show the Fathers against the background of their times. I have attempted to show them as dramatic characters in the long drama of Christianity, and to strip them of the pedantry which is too often associated with the examination of Christian origins. So there is little or nothing about the remoter details of the Arian controversy of the fourth century or the Hesychast controversy of the fourteenth. I have thought it better that the Fathers should be shown as living persons of great relevance to our time, rather than that they should be smothered in footnotes. Though they are saints, I have drawn them as men.

The book begins at the moment when the apostles, after witnessing the Ascension, withdrew to Jerusalem. I have ended it with the astonishing figure of Gregory Palamas, who defended the mystical observance of the Prayer of Jesus in the years when the Byzantine Empire was falling into ruin. In those catastrophic days, when an Empire which had endured for a thousand years was about to perish, the spirituality of the East showed itself at its best, in the last upflare of a flame before it was quenched, and yet not quenched, for the flame which was put out in Constantinople still shines powerfully today. So this is the story of the Fathers of the Eastern Church, told as a continuing history from the beginning to the fall of Constantinople: a story of learned men, devoted to a sacred truth, walking with their heads held high in an enviable assurance, afraid of no man and in love with God.

The Forerunners

When on the Mount of Olives Jesus ascended to Heaven after blessing the disciples for the last time, the disciples trembled. He had returned from the dead, only to vanish again, so quietly and with so little warning they were bewildered by the strangeness of the event. The curtains of the Temple had been rent, the graves had given up their dead, a rock had been rolled away, Thomas had placed his fingers in a wound, and in Emmaus He had spoken to them and shared their bread and wine and announced Himself the Risen Lord; and so He was, and it was beyond all understanding that He should go from them. He who had wrapped His mantle over the earth ascended to Heaven, taking His mantle with Him, and there was no divinity left on earth. He left no relics, no doctrine, no words taken down by secretaries, no letters. There was no child to assume His royal place. There was no tomb, no coffin, no funeral dirge to die in stillness on the midnight air. He left the world unencumbered by His presence, and nothing He ever possessed except the words He gravely uttered were handed down to the disciples: neither His winnowing fan, nor His carpenter's tools, nor the cloak He had worn. He left only His remembered image, and a shuddering silence; and there were some who thought He would return instantly in a consuming flame.

It was a time of legends, a time of tribulations. No one could fathom the immensity of the event. His last words were an assurance that the Holy Ghost would descend upon them, and afterward they must teach the gospel to all nations. At Pentecost came the gift of tongues, the holy flames. And still there was that sense of desperate destinies, of the whole of creation reeling toward the abyss, the end of the world so near that Peter cried out in the words of the prophet Joel that the last days were at hand. The sun would soon turn into darkness and the moon into blood, and only those who called upon the name of the Lord would be saved. A hundred and twenty people listened to Peter announcing the Second Coming, and all were afraid. They asked what they should do. They were told there was salvation only in repentance and in baptism. It was the beginning of the doctrine; and from that day until the present repentance, baptism and the calling of the holy name have remained at the heart of the mystery.

We shall not understand the beginnings of Christianity unless we remember the shuddering silence which followed the Ascension, and how Peter immersed in visions clung to the three anchors of his faith. Many years later, when the Second Coming seemed only a remote possibility, Paul wrote to the brethren in Thessalonica the first of the epistles that have come down to us, reminding them with a raw energy and a complete certainty that "the Lord himself shall descend from heaven with a shout, with the voice of the archangel, and with the trump of God: and the dead in Christ shall rise first." And then he went on to say that the living would be caught up together with the blessed dead, to meet the Lord in the air, and this was their comfort. He saw the Christians as a people set apart, living in the blaze of the Second Coming. "Ye are all the children of light, and the children of day," he wrote. "We are not of the night, nor of darkness. Therefore, let us not sleep, as do others; but let us watch and be sober." And so, to the very end, he was continually reminding the Christians that the time was short, the fashion of the world was passing away, and soon there would come the trumpet call, when the dead would rise immortal and we should be changed. And perhaps it was about this time that the elders in Jerusalem composed the strange discourse which we know as the *Didache* or *The Teaching of the Twelve Apostles*,[1] in which the doctrines of the early Church were first established, with its triumphant conclusion filled with warnings and a staggering picture of the end of the world:

Watch for your life's sake; let your lamp not go out and your

[1] The complete *Teaching of the Twelve Apostles* is found in only one manuscript discovered in the Monastery of the Most Holy Sepulchre in Constantinople by Philotheos Bryennios, Metropolitan of Serres in Macedonia, and afterward of Nicomedia in Asia Minor. The original manuscript covers only ten pages in a small thick volume containing seven separate works bound together, bearing the signature of "Leo, the notary and sinner" and the date, June 3, 1056. Bryennios made the discovery in 1873, and published his findings ten years later. Two small fragments (two parchment leaves of the fourth century) were later discovered among the Oxyrhynchus Papyri.

loins not be loosed, but be ready; for ye know not the hour in which our Lord cometh. But ye shall come together often and seek the things that befit your souls; for the whole time of your faith *thus far* will not profit you, if ye be not made perfect in the last time. For in the last days the false prophets and the corruptors shall be multiplied, and the sheep shall be turned into wolves, and love shall be turned into hate; for when lawlessness increaseth they shall hate one another, and shall persecute and shall deliver up, and then shall appear the world-deceiver as Son of God, and shall do signs and wonders, and the earth shall be given into his hands, and he shall commit iniquities which have never yet been done since the beginning. Then all created men shall come into the fire of trial, and many shall be made to stumble and shall perish. But they that endure in their faith shall be saved from under even this curse. And then shall appear the signs of the truth: first the sign of an opening in Heaven, then the sign of a trumpet's sound, and thirdly, the resurrection of the dead; yet not of all, but as it hath been said: The Lord will come and all the saints with him. Then shall the world see the Lord coming upon the clouds of heaven.   [*Didache*, XVI]

The Teaching of the Twelve Apostles is an astonishing document, compounded of many strands, bristling with complications for the scholar, but no other document shows the color of primitive Christianity so well. Here is Christianity stripped bare of all ornament: stern rules of conduct, a catechism, an introduction to the rites, solemn injunctions, complete faith in the Sermon on the Mount and utmost belief in the Second Coming. We do not know who wrote it, nor where it was written, though it is possible that it was first written down in Antioch about A.D. 90. We do not know whether it is based upon some unknown Essene treatise on behavior. It speaks of the children of darkness and the children of light, and we do not know exactly who they are. It is filled with echoes of *Matthew, Luke, St. Paul's Epistles* and *Revelation*, and yet it possesses an authority and poetry of its own, a freshness and strength which could come only from the very early days of Christianity, before the Church laid down the laws and complexity set in. Here the rites are the very simplest. The Lord's Prayer must be said three times a day. Only those who were baptised could take part in the Eucharist, where the wine was offered before the breaking of the bread. In those early days there was said a prayer of such exquisite beauty that one wonders how the Church could have forgotten it:

Now concerning the Eucharist, thus give thanks: First, concerning the cup: We thank Thee, our Father, for the holy wine of David Thy servant, which Thou hast made known to us through Jesus Thy servant. As concerning the broken bread: We thank Thee, our Father, for the life and knowledge Thou hast made known to us through Jesus Thy servant; to Thee be glory forever. Just as this broken bread was scattered over the hills and having been gathered together became one, so let Thy Church be gathered together from the ends of the earth into Thy Kingdom; for Thine is the glory and the power through Jesus Christ forever.

And after ye are filled, thus give thanks: We thank Thee, holy Father, for Thy holy name, which Thou hast caused to dwell in our hearts, and for the knowledge and faith and immortality which Thou hast made known to us through Jesus Thy servant; to Thee be the glory forever. Thou, almighty Master, didst create all things for Thy name's sake; both food and drink didst Thou give to men for enjoyment, in order that they might give thanks to Thee; but to us Thou hast graciously given spiritual food and drink and eternal life through Thy servant. Before all things we thank Thee that Thou art mighty; to Thee be the glory forever. Remember, O Lord, Thy Church, to deliver it from every evil and to make it perfect in Thy love, and gather it from the four winds, *it,* the sanctified, into Thy Kingdom, which Thou hast prepared for it; for Thine is the power and glory forever. Let grace come and this world pass away.

[*Didache*, IX, X]

Let grace come and this world pass away . . . It was the perpetual cry of the early Christians, a cry for peace, for an escape from the bondage of the flesh as it was known on earth, for the vision of Christ and the establishment of His Kingdom. He who was "the firstfruits of them that slept" would rise in the fullness of divine blessing, to gather His saints around Him, witnesses to the marriage of the Lamb and the final Eucharist. St. John in *Revelation* had described the feast, the judgment and the war on Antichrist in minute detail. Paul was continually speaking of that day which would come so much sooner than men expected. "Now is our salvation nearer than when we believed. The night is far spent, the day is at hand: let us therefore cast off the works of darkness, and let us put on the armour of light" (*Rom*. 13:11-12). It was as though they could feel on their faces the heat of the chariots of fire and the fanning of the angels' wings. At the center of all their beliefs was the *Parousia*, the Second Coming of Christ.

At this late date, after nearly twenty centuries of developing Christianity, we incline to see the Christian faith in the light of history, growing as a tree or a flower grows, and existing in time. For the early Christians the coming of Christ put an end to history. Time vanished. They watched the world go by as though their daily existence was but the brief breathless pause before the storm of the Apocalypse. It was not only that time had vanished, but it was unthinkable that time had ever possessed any place in the divine scheme of things; history was a series of absurd anecdotes strung together on the thread of the seasons. Did not the angel standing upon the sea and the earth swear that there should be time no longer? There would be a new Heaven and a new earth, a new tabernacle indwelling among men: no more tears, no more sorrow, no more death. So they believed, with half the parables of the Synoptic Gospels sustaining their belief.

Sometimes there were doubts, and Peter raged against those men of little faith who asked: "Where is the promise of his coming? for since the fathers fell asleep, all things continue as they were from the beginning of the creation" (2 *Pet*. 3:4). Peter reminded the scoffers that the world had come to an end before; strange that they had forgotten the Deluge. Where previously the world had been destroyed by water, now it would be destroyed by fire—"the heavens and the earth are reserved unto fire against the day of judgment." The day of the Lord would come as a thief in the night, there would be a thunderclap and all the elements would dissolve in the fervent heat. It is a vision which is not unfamiliar to us, and we shall understand the early Christians better when we realize that they shared our obsession with a world given over to atomic flame.

But in most other respects they were unlike us. They lived in small communities, in quiet piety, craving miracles, exchanging the kiss of peace, confessing their sins before every offering of the Eucharist and welcoming all those who came in the name of the Lord. The love feast was central to their lives, the occasion of the holy friendship they showed to one another. "This supper is made for love," wrote Clement of Alexander, "but the supper is not love: only a proof of the gentleness of our affections" (*Paedagogus*, II, i). "The kingdom of God is not meat and drink," wrote St. Paul, "but righteousness, and peace, and joy in the Holy Ghost" (*Rom.* 14:17). Yet the love feast continued, a simulacrum of the heavenly joys, to be observed, as Clement says, as an entertainment for the heart's affections as well as a demonstration of their common fellowship with the Kingdom of God. In time the love feast vanished, and something very precious to Christianity vanished with it.

So they lived in gentleness in the shadow of the flames of the Day of Judgment. Those last flames obsessed them, but it was a quiet obsession: it was as though they knew there was a great bonfire at the end of the road and knew exactly where to find it. And they saw flames where we are not accustomed to see them. Justin Martyr believed that "when Jesus went down into the water, a fire was kindled in the Jordan, and when he came up from the water the Holy Spirit like a dove fluttered over him" (Justin Martyr, *Dialogus,* 88). That the Jordan blazed with fire was an early tradition, often repeated. Origen was only continuing the tradition when he wrote: "Christ does not baptise with water; this He leaves to the disciples. He reserves to Himself the power to baptise with the Holy Spirit and with fire" (*Comm. in Joann.* VI, 13). It is a startling sentence, but no more startling than many of the early traditional sayings of Jesus. There are many sayings, quoted by the Fathers and firmly believed by them, which strike our modern ears strangely:

He who is near Me is near the fire; he who is far from Me is far from the Kingdom.

Those who desire to see Me and seize My Kingdom shall pass through tribulation and despair.

He who seeks shall not cease until he finds, and when he finds he shall wonder, and wondering he shall reign, and reigning he shall rest.

Raise up the stone, and thou shalt find Me; cleave the tree, and I am there.

When thou seest thy brother, thou seest God.

Again, I am about to be crucified.[2]

[2] The first saying comes from Origen, *in Jerem. Homil.* XX, 3; the others from *Barnabas,* VII, 11; Clement of Alexandria, *Stromateis,* II, 9, 45; *Oxyrhynchus Logia,* 4; Clement of Alexandria, *Stromateis,* I, 19, 94; Origen, *in Joann.* XX, 12.

What is strange about these sayings is their immediacy and their
peculiarly Eastern cast, but there is no reason to believe they were not
spoken: the Fathers who pondered them were closer to the wellspring than we shall ever be. Even stranger sayings were believed to
have come from the lips of Jesus. There was a saying which Jerome
recorded three times as occurring in *The Gospel of the Nazarenes:*
"Just now my mother, the Holy Spirit, took me by one of my hairs and
carried me away to the great mountain Tabor." According to *The
Gospel of Peter* Jesus said: "My Power, Power, thou hast forsaken me,"
and not: "My God, my God, why hast thou forsaken me?" These
sayings have no place in the canon, but they breathe the spirit of
early Christianity and their echoes are heard among the Greek Fathers,
who read widely in the uncanonical scriptures and were perfectly
prepared to accept them as evidence. And they were not afraid to
believe like Clement, an early Bishop of Rome, that Jesus "had no
comeliness or beauty, but His appearance was insignificant, inferior
to the beauty of men, a man of stripes and toil, who knew how to
endure pain; for his face was turned away, he was dishonored and
discountenanced." Such a belief appears to have been widely current,
and in the earliest of the apocryphal Acts, the *Acts of John,* we are
presented with a strange and awe-inspiring portrait of Jesus as he
appeared to the two disciples, John and James, the sons of Zebedee,
as they were seated in their boat on the Lake of Gennesaret. Jesus was
standing on the shore, beckoning to them.

"What does this youth want with us? Why is he calling us
from the shore?" said my brother James to me [John]. And I said:
"What youth?" He answered: "He that is beckoning to us." I said:
"My brother James, your eyes must be dimmed by the many sleep-
less nights we have spent on the lake. Do you not see that the man
standing on the shore is a tall man with a joyful face of great
beauty?" My brother said: "I do not see him like that, but let us
row ashore and then we shall know."

When we hauled up the boat, Jesus himself helped us to make
it fast. When we left the place to follow him, he appeared to me as
a bald man with a thick flowing beard, while to my brother James
he seemed a youth with but a faint down on his cheeks. And
we could not understand and were amazed. And so it often happened, and he would appear to me in forms even more marvellous,

sometimes small of stature, with crooked limbs, sometimes as a giant, reaching to the heavens.

[*Acta Joannis,* 85]

Like the author of the *Acts of John,* Origen believed that Jesus did not always have the same appearance, but altered His countenance according to the needs of the onlooker. Many of the early Fathers believed that Jesus was small and frail, with a long face and eyebrows that were joined together, dark-skinned, red-haired and a hunchback. According to the *Acts of Peter* He was both beautiful and ugly—*formosus et foedus.* It may have been so. Tertullian placed into the mouth of Jesus the words of the Psalm: "But I am a worm, and no man; a reproach of men, and despised of the people." Irenaeus said He was "infirm and inglorious"—*infirmus et ingloriosus.* In the East no one would have been amazed at the thought of His physical infirmities; prophets and saints and gods were men whose bodies cracked under the strain of vast spiritual pressures. And though they spoke often of His appearance on earth "in the former flesh," they spoke more often of His appearance at the Second Coming, when as the King of Terrible Majesty—*Rex tremendae maiestatis*—He would stand above the flames of the world.

Meanwhile they went about their lives quietly, singing hymns, not yet preoccupied by thoughts of a stable church and ecclesiastical institutions, obeying the new law announced by Jesus, in compassionate love for one another. Love was the law, celebrated in the love feast and whenever the brethren came together. St. Paul had described at length the intricacies of love; Clement expounded its all-embracingness:

> Love unites us to God, love covers up a host of sins, love suffers everything, and is patient with everything. There is nothing vulgar, nothing vain, about love. Love knows no schism, creates no discord, does everything in harmony. By love have God's elect been made perfect. Without love nothing pleases God. By love did the Lord take us unto Himself. By the love He bore for us Jesus Christ our Lord did by the will of God give His blood for us, His flesh for our flesh, His life for ours.
>
> [*First Clement,* 49]

Love was their constant theme, the subject of their sermons, their prayers and their hymns. The word would assume many disguises, so that sometimes it was almost indistinguishable from "hope," "mystery" and "Jesus." It meant a kind of blessing, an outpouring of blessedness, a delighted awareness in the presence of the brethren who were dedicated to the same tasks as themselves. With such a love may Adam have greeted Eve in the first dawn of Creation.

One approaches the minds of the early Christians with trepidation. They were aware of Jesus as we shall never be aware of Him. They had the trustfulness of children. Living in the lost world of darkness and of death, they knew that light and life entered in the person of Jesus. Because Jesus had come, none could harm them; and so they could cry defiantly: "Who can separate us from the love of God in Jesus Christ?" It is possible to envy them with the same sense of desperate yearning which comes over us when we remember the Greeks, and for the same reason: the world was still fresh for them, and they saw it with fresh eyes.

Yet, though they breathed this air of innocence and fragility, many influences were at work on them. Jewish influences predominated; so did Neoplatonism and Gnosticism; and so more subtly did the worship of Serapis and Isis. All these were to affect Christianity, to shape it, to give nourishment to the growing Church. In the first century Christianity was purest; afterward came confusions, fierce doctrinal quarrels, headlong confrontations with other religions. How could it be otherwise? They were a hot-blooded and reckless people, bright-eyed, drunk with visions. There was a hard unchanging core to Christianity, but then as now the periphery was a changing one. In those early days Christianity wore fantastic garments and sang strange songs.

We shall never know whether Paul wrote the hymns which were inserted in the Epistles, or whether they were introduced later from the liturgies. Some twenty hymns lie embedded in the Epistles. There seems to have been some doubt whether it was proper for a Christian to sing hymns, for we find St. Ignatius writing about A.D. 107: "When you have formed yourselves into a choir, you may sing praises to the Father through Jesus Christ." It was as though they had asked his opinion whether such songs were pleasing to God. At about the same time Pliny the Younger, writing to the Emperor Trajan, spoke of the Christians in Bithynia meeting together on a certain day of the week to sing a hymn to Christ. Mostly the Pauline hymns were concerned with the celebration of the purposes of Jesus, and His powers:

> *Who is the blessed and only Potentate,*
> *The King of kings, and Lord of lords;*
> *Who only hath immortality,*

Dwelling in the light which no man can approach unto;
Whom no man hath seen, nor can see;
To whom be honor and power everlasting.

[I *Tim.* 6:15]

But there were other hymns, many of them fiercely dramatic, like the dance hymn which has survived in the *Acts of John.* According to these Acts, Jesus sung the hymn shortly before the Passion, "while the disciples made as it were a ring, holding one another's hands, while He stood in the midst of them, saying: Answer Amen unto me."

Glory to Thee, Father!
Glory to Thee, Word!
Glory to Thee, Grace!
Glory to Thee, Holy Spirit!

Glory to Thy Glory!
We praise Thee, O Father!
We give thanks to Thee, O shadowless Light!

I would be saved, and I would save.
I would be loosed, and I would loose.
I would be pierced, and I would pierce.
I would be borne, and I would bear.

I would eat, and I would be eaten.
I would hearken, and I would be heard.
I would be wise, and I would grant wisdom.
I would be cleansed, and I would cleanse.
                    Grace is dancing!

I would pipe, and all must dance!
I would lament, and all must lament!
The Heavenly Spheres make music for us!
The Holy Twelve join the dance!
All things are dancing!
Ye who dance not have no knowledge of wisdom!

I would flee, and I would stay!
I would give garlands, and I would be garlanded!
I would be united, and I would unite!
I have no dwelling, but I have mansions!
I have no resting-place, but I have the whole earth.
I have no temple, but I have the whole of Heaven.

I am a lamp to thee that beholdest me.
I am a mirror to thee that perceivest me.
I am a door to thee that knockest.
I am the Way to the wayfarer.

[*Acta Joannis,* 95]

The exuberance of the dance hymn mirrors the exuberance of early
Christianity. They were influenced less by the Synoptic Gospels than
by Johannine mysticism; and sometimes the colors of early Christian
mysticism mingled with those of Gnosticism, which derived from Plato
and other sources in the Near East a peculiar portrait of the universe
fashioned by a remote breath issuing from the Heavenly Abyss. They
believed in the Heavenly Spheres. They possessed a profound trust in
reasonable magic: the fish traced in the dust with their feet represented
Jesus, so did the phoenix which rose from its Arabian ashes, and the
318 men circumcised by Abraham were to them only an anagram of
the holy name. When they sang: "I am a mirror to thee that perceivest
me," they remembered the traditional saying by Christ: "You shall
see me in yourselves as a man sees his face in water or in a mirror."
At least four more sayings lie concealed in the hymn. We should
beware of thinking these hymns strange: such passionate intellectual
dances belonged to the exuberance of the age. To the early Christians
it was a matter of indifference whether the Creator possessed three,
seven, eight or twelve manifestations. What was decisive was whether
God had spoken through the mouth of His Son and whether all of
creation was accomplished by His divine bounty or by some inferior
Demiurge.

The hymn speaks of baptism, the new birth and the Last Supper,
and how these things have their place in the sacred dance, a dance
which embraces the whole universe. In the East such dances could be
readily conceived; and though the West frowned upon them and preferred not to conceive them, some trace of the dance remains in the
Mass. When an Eastern bishop sent a copy of this hymn to St.
Augustine with an enthusiastic note suggesting that it was a matter of
some importance, the reply was brief. St. Augustine simply pointed out
that the doctrinal truths contained in the hymn were better expressed
in the canonical writings. He would have said the same of images, or
any form of religious art.

We know that these hymns were sung in the primitive churches,
but few have survived. Happily a bridal hymn written about the same

time survives in the apocryphal *Acts of Thomas*. It appears in both Greek and Syrian versions, and is one of the great glories of early Christianity:

My Bride is the daughter of light.
She has the dazzling splendor of Kings.
Proud and charming is her countenance,
Adorned with a pure grace and beauty.
Her garments are like flowers of spring
Whose odor is fragrant and pleasant.
On the crown of her head the King is enthroned
And nourishes her pillar beneath.
She sets truth on her head
And stirs up joy in her feet.
Her mouth is open and that right fitly
Since she sings only songs of praise.
Thirty-two attendants glorify her.
Her tongue is the door-curtain
Drawn back for those who enter.
Her neck is the ladder
Built by the first Creator.
Her two hands proclaim the place of the living;
Her fingers open the gates of the city.
Her Bridal Chamber is full of light,
Pouring forth fragrance of balsam and unguents,
Sending forth sweet perfumes of myrrh
And all manner of sweet-smelling flowers.
Within are strewn branches of myrtle;
The gates are adorned with reeds.
Her groomsmen attend her,
Seven in number, invited by her,
And seven bridesmaids attend her,
Leading her in the dance.
Twelve are the servants who attend her,
All expectantly waiting for the Bridegroom
That they may be illumined by His glory
And with Him attain the Eternal Kingdom,
Taking part in the Eternal Wedding Feast
To which all the righteous shall come,
And attain to the bliss

Into which they singly will enter;
And that they may put on garments of light
And be clothed with the glory of their Lord,
And praise the living Father
Because they have received the glory of the light
And have been illuminated by the Lord's brightness,
And have received His food
Whose abundance never fails,
And have drunk of the living waters
Wherefore they neither crave nor thirst.
Praise the Father the Lord and the Only Begotten Son
And give thanks to the Spirit as His wisdom.

We know a people best through their poetry: so it is with religions, the hymns sing out loudest. We must know the seedbed from which the Fathers sprang, for often as they sharpen the weapons of their spiritual understanding we are made aware by a catch in the voice, by the introduction of a new rhythm or by an unexpected joyousness that they are men who sang hymns as loudly as the rest. Here are four short hymns which may have been known to Clement of Alexandria and Origen:

I

Tell the glad tidings unto children:
Tell them the poor have received the Kingdom,
The children are the inheritors.

II

Distil thy dews upon us,
Open Thy rich fountains
And let Thy milk and honey
Be poured over us.

And let there be within Thee
No repentance.
Those things Thou hast promised
Thou shalt not repent Thee.

Was not the end revealed
Before Thy coming hither,
And what Thou gavest
Didst Thou not give freely?

III

He hath carried me to Paradise,
Into the abounding pleasure house of the Lord.

I have worshiped the glory of the Lord,
Blessed is the Lord who planted so fruitfully,
Blessed are those who have a place in Thy Paradise.

Blessed are growing things, the fruit of Thy trees!
They have changed from darkness into light!

IV

Open your hearts to the exultation of the Lord:
Let love be magnified from the mouth and the heart!

Let the living fruit be offered unto the Lord:
Let the mouth speak steadfastly in His light!

O rise and stand, you who were sometimes humble.
Announce that your mouths have hurled the silence away!

Be lifted up, you who were sometimes lowly.
Now are you exalted before the face of the Lord.

The right hand of the Lord is on you: he is your Saviour.
Peace is prepared for you; before ever war was.[3]

The early Christians, as they went about their simple lives, singing their hymns to the Risen Lord, hoping they would witness the Second Coming, seem strangely impersonal, as though they had already escaped from the world, their persons absorbed in the Person of Christ. We come closest to them during those periods when they suffered persecution: death by flogging, burning, beheading, crucifixion, the lions' jaws. Then curiously we see them as persons for the first time; and from faces wet with blood come cries of a purely human poignancy.

St. Ignatius is the first of the Greek Fathers who comes down to us as a complete person, possessing a characteristic, recognizable voice. When we see him first he is already doomed to death, a convict in

[3] The first song is taken from an Amherst papyrus of the third century, quoted by P.D. Scott-Moncrieff, *Paganism and Christianity* (Cambridge University Press, 1913). The remaining hymns are odes 3, 11 and 8 in J. Rendel Harris, *The Odes and Psalms of Solomon* (Cambridge University Press, 1909).

chains guarded by ten Roman legionaries, making his way by slow stages from Antioch, the seat of his bishopric, to the Flavian amphitheater in Rome, where he was martyred. During two pauses on the journey he wrote seven letters, full of vigorous warnings, solemn exaltations and the passionate desire to be simultaneously alive, proclaiming Christ, and to die for Christ. They are brutal letters, written in haste, with the blood pulsing at the throat and the light of dedication in the eyes. In Smyrna, he heard that there were powerful influences in Rome working to procure a remission of his punishment. At once he wrote to Rome a letter warning those who loved him to desist. The letter should be quoted at some length, because nowhere else is there to be found so complete a picture of the aroused fervor of an early Christian confronting death:

I write to all the churches and signify to all men that of my own free will I die for God, unless you hinder me. I beseech you, do not show an unseasonable kindness to me. Let me be given to the wild beasts, by whom I shall attain unto God. I am the wheat of God, and I am ground by the teeth of the wild beasts, so that I may be found pure bread of Christ. Instead encourage the wild beasts to be my sepulcher, to leave no part of my body behind, so that when I am fallen asleep, I may not be burdensome to any. Then shall I be truly a disciple of Jesus Christ, when the world shall not even see my body. Pray unto Christ for me that through these instruments I may be found a sacrifice to God. I do not command you, like Peter and Paul. They were apostles, I am a condemned man. They were free, I am still a slave. But if I suffer, I shall become the freeman of Jesus Christ, and in Him I shall rise free. And now in chains I am learning to have no desires.

From Syria to Rome I fight with wild beasts, by land and sea, by night and day, being bound to ten leopards; that is to say, to a band of soldiers who though treated with all manner of kindness are only the worse for it. Yet through their injuries I am becoming more a disciple: "yet I am not therefore justified." May I have joy of the wild beasts that are prepared for me; and I pray they will exercise all their ferocity on me. I will entice them to devour me promptly, not as they have done to some, refusing to touch them through fear. If they will not do it willingly, I will force them to it. Pardon me: I know what is best for me. I am only beginning to be a disciple. May nothing, visible or invisible, prevent me from attaining unto Jesus Christ. Come fire, and cross, and grapplings with wild beasts, cuttings and manglings, wrenching of bones, hacking of limbs, crushings of my whole body; come all the wicked torments of the devil upon me—only let me reach the presence of Christ.

All the ends of the world, and the kingdoms of this age, will profit me nothing. Better to die for Christ Jesus than to rule over the utmost ends of the earth. I seek Him who died for us. I desire Him who rose again for our sake. The pangs of a new birth are upon me. Pardon me, my brethren: do not hinder me from living; do not desire my death. . . . Suffer me to enter into pure light, to become a man, to be an imitator of the passion of my God. If anyone has God within himself, let him consider my desire; and let him have compassion on me, knowing in what straits I am.

The Prince of the World desires to carry me away and corrupt my resolution toward God. Let none of you, therefore, help him. You should join with me, that is, with God. Do not speak of Jesus Christ, and retain affection for the world. Let no envy dwell among you. No, even if I myself, coming among you, should beg you to be envious, do not hearken to me, but rather listen to what I am saying now. Writing this, I am alive, but my desire is for death. My love is crucified; there is in me no burning desire, only the living waters which speak in me, saying in me, Come to the Father. I take no pleasure in the food of corruption, nor in the pleasures of this life. I desire the bread of God, which is the flesh of Jesus Christ, of the seed of David; and the drink I long for is His blood, which is incorruptible love.

[*Ad Romanos,* iv-vii]

The blood leaps, the eyes glitter, the pulse throbs. We are in the presence of a man who had imagined everything before the event, considered his own sacrifice, measured the responsibility and found himself worthy. Earthy, and of the earth, he desires to leap into the spirit. There is no pride or extravagance in his claims, only the vivid realization of the splendor of Christ. He will say things in those last moments which will make you stop dead on your tracks. "He who really possesses the word of Jesus can truly hear His silence, that he may be perfect." "Even those things which you do according to the flesh are spiritual, for you do all things with Jesus Christ." "Our Lord

Jesus Christ was conceived by divine dispensation in the womb of Mary, of the seed of David and of the Holy Spirit; He was born and baptized so that by His suffering He might purify water." "Nothing visible is good." So he goes on, violent and tender by turns, implacably opposed to the world, in love with Heaven, urging that all men "break the same bread, which is the medicine of immortality, and the antidote that we should not die." He begs men to pray for him, to remember his church in Antioch, to obey their bishops, to believe utterly in the Incarnation. There were heretics who declared that Jesus was a phantom, who never took the flesh of men. Clement of Alexandria in the second century spoke of those who believed in the "transparency" of His body. No, says Ignatius, He *truly* ate and drank, was *truly* crucified, was *truly* raised from the dead, and after the Resurrection He *truly* ate and drank with the disciples. "I know that even after the Resurrection He was in the flesh, and I believe that He is still so." And with this violence there went an astonishing sweetness, as when Ignatius spoke of the star of Christ which had banished all the evil stars away:

A star shone forth in the Heaven above all the stars, and its light was inexpressible and its strangeness caused amazement; and all the rest of the constellations with the sun and moon formed themselves into a chorus around the star; but the star itself far outshone them all. And men began to be troubled, wondering where this strange thing arose. From that time forward every sorcery and every magic spell was dissolved, and every bond of wickedness was destroyed; the ancient kingdom utterly pulled down; and God appeared in the likeness of a man for the renewal of eternal life. That which had been perfected in the counsels of God began to take effect, and now all things were in confusion, because He designed to abolish death.

[*Ad Eph.* 19]

His last letter was written to Polycarp, Bishop of Smyrna, who received him with kindness and reverence. Polycarp had received his bishopric at the hands of St. John, and was a young man, perhaps no more than thirty-five or -six when Ignatius passed through Smyrna. Ignatius seems to have found some weaknesses in the youthful bishop and admonishes him gently to pay more heed to the mischievous disciples than to the good, not to neglect widows, and never to mention the evil arts. He urges Polycarp: "Ask for larger wisdom than thou hast. Do not look down on slaves. Hold more frequent meetings." And then, turning from the bishop to his flock, Ignatius gives his last words of advice:

Toil together, struggle together, run together, suffer together, sleep together and rise together; as the servants, and assistants, and the ministers of God. Please him under whom you fight, and from whom you receive your wages. Let none of you be found a deserter. Let your baptism serve as shield, your faith as helmet, your love as spear, your endurance as full armor. So be patient with one another in gentleness, as God is with you. Let me have joy of you always.

[*Ad Polyc.* VI]

Then Ignatius went on to martyrdom, to die under the teeth and claws of lions in a circus.

Polycarp was not of the same stern stuff. His one surviving letter addressed to the Philippians has no flashes of lightning, and there is little distinctive in his theology. Earnest, and a little self-righteous, he proclaims the faith of the Incarnate God who suffered for all of us that we might live through Him. We must serve Jesus with reverence and fear, and imitate His patience, and we should always remember not to let the sun go down on our anger. He wrote:

The love of money is the root of all evil. Knowing therefore that we brought nothing into this world, so neither may we carry anything out, let us arm ourselves with the armor of righteousness, and teach ourselves first to walk according to the commandments of Our Lord, and then our wives to walk likewise according to the faith that is given to them in charity and in purity, loving their own husbands with all sincerity, and all others alike with temperance.

[*Ad Philipp.* IV]

Polycarp's letter is a tissue of quotations from the New Testament and the Psalms, and is perhaps not characteristic of the man who was "the angel of the church in Smyrna" addressed by St. John in *Revelation* and the man whom St. Jerome called "the prince of all Asia." Of his life we know almost nothing: he may have been originally a Syrian slave, and later he seems to have possessed slaves of his own; he visited Anicetus, the Bishop of Rome; and it was said that when he met the heretic Marcion and was asked: "Do you recognize me?" he answered: "I recognize the first-born of Satan!" But if we know little of his life, we know as much as we desire to know about his death in the swift,

well-written documents known as *The Martyrdom of St. Polycarp.*
There are moments when the unknown author of this document
writes with the fire of Ignatius. He begins his description of the martyrdom with a general portrait of the martyrs:

Who can choose but admire their nobility and endurance and
love for the Master? I speak of those men who were so flayed with
whipping that their physical bodies were laid open even to the
inner veins and arteries, yet they endured it, so that all those who
beheld them pitied and lamented them. These martyrs showed such
generosity of mind that not one of them sighed or groaned, plainly
showing that at the time they were being tortured, they were
absent from the body, or rather that the Lord stood by them and
talked with them. Being supported by the grace of Christ, they
despised the world's tortures; and at the cost of a single hour redeemed themselves from everlasting punishment. The fire of their
inhuman tormentors seemed cold to them, while they hoped to
escape the eternal, unquenchable fire, and beheld with the eyes of
faith those blessings reserved for the steadfast "which neither ear
has heard nor eye seen, nor have they entered into the heart of
man." But these things were revealed by the Lord to them, as being
no longer men but already become angels.   [*Mart. S. Polycarpi,* 2]

At the time of his martyrdom Polycarp was eighty-six years old, and
had been bishop for more than fifty years. In Smyrna the Asiarch,
Philip of Tralles, had celebrated the annual games, and during the
games there was heard the cry: "Away with the atheists!" meaning
those who refused to worship the name of the Emperor. The Asiarch
decided to put the venerable bishop to the test, and gave orders for his
arrest. Polycarp wanted to stay in the city, but was persuaded to go into
hiding in a country farm. There he prayed for all men and for the
churches everywhere, according to his custom, but while he was praying
three days before his arrest he saw in a vision that his pillow was on fire.
Then he turned to those who were near him and said quietly: "I must
be burned alive!"

He was removed to a small cottage. A poor slave boy, captured by
the police, was arrested and tortured; and Polycarp's hiding place was
revealed. On a Friday they found him in an upper room of the cottage
sitting at his evening meal. Even then he could have escaped, but
refused, saying: "It is God's will." He asked that food and drink be
given to his captors, and requested from them permission to pray for

an hour. He was allowed to pray for two hours aloud, remembering everyone he had ever encountered. At last he was led out on an ass and taken to the city. There an attempt was made to make him apostatize. They asked him what harm there could be in saying "Caesar is Lord" and burning a few grains of incense on the altar, and so saving himself. As he was taken to the arena, he heard a voice from Heaven saying: "Be strong, Polycarp, and quit thyself like a man." At the arena he was brought before the proconsul, who ordered him to abjure Christ.

"For eighty-six years I have been His slave," Polycarp answered, "and He has done me no wrong. How can I blaspheme my King who has saved me?"

"Then swear only by the fortune of Caesar."

"It seems, because you suppose I should swear by the fortune of Caesar, that you do not know me for what I am. I am a Christian. If you desire to know what Christianity is about, set a day and I shall tell you."

"Then persuade the people."

"I have thought to tell you my reasons, because we are taught to honor governments and those in authority over us, appointed by God. As for the people, I do not consider them worthy that I should defend myself before them."

The proconsul was a philosophic man, determined to abstract a renunciation from the bishop. He knew Polycarp desired to die by fire, and therefore threatened to throw him to the lions. Polycarp answered that whatever happened, it would be good. He was overjoyed at the thought of his approaching martyrdom. A herald was sent into the arena to proclaim three times: "Polycarp is a confessed Christian!" A roar went up from the multitude: "This is the teacher of Asia, the father of the Christians, the overthrower of our gods, who has taught so many of us not to sacrifice nor worship!" They demanded that the Asiarch Philip should let loose a lion upon him. Philip replied that this was illegal, because the spectacles were over. Was it legal to do away with Polycarp? Yes. By fire? Yes. And because there were no faggots in the arena, the mob ran through the town, collecting sticks and firewood from the shops and bathhouses. The anonymous *Martyrdom of St. Polycarp* continues:

When the fuel was ready, he put off his upper garments and unfastened his belt, and tried also to pull off his underclothes, though he was not in the habit of doing this before, because every one of the Christians that was about him contended as to who would be the first to touch his flesh. For he was truly adorned with his good conversation with all manner of piety, even before his martyrdom. Now all that was necessary for the making of the fire was set around him, but when they started to nail him to the stake, he said: "Leave me as I am! He who enables me to endure the fire will also enable me to stand here without moving."

So they did not nail him, but only tied him up. And he, having his hands behind him, being bound as a ram chosen out of a great flock for an offering, a burnt sacrifice acceptable to God, looked up to Heaven and said: "O Lord God Almighty, Father of Thy beloved and blessed child Jesus Christ, through whom we have received the knowledge of Thee, God of angels and hosts and all Creation, and of the whole race of just men who live in Thy presence, I bless Thee that Thou has thought me worthy of this day and hour, to be numbered among Thy martyrs, in the cup of Thy Christ, for the resurrection to eternal life, for soul and body in the incorruptibility of the Holy Spirit. And may I be accepted before Thee today as a fat and acceptable sacrifice.

[*Mart. S. Polycarpi,* 14]

Soon the flames were lit, but at first they did not eat into his flesh: the flame was immensely high and formed a kind of arch, like the sail of a ship filled with wind, making a circle around the saint, "who stood in the midst of it, not as if his flesh were burnt, but as bread that is baked, or as gold or silver glowing in the furnace." Since his body refused to burn, the executioner was ordered to plunge a dagger into his side. Then, according to the writer, there came from Polycarp's body a dove and a great quantity of blood, which quenched the flames. Later his body was burned, and his bones were carried away to some safe place. He was the twelfth martyr to die in Smyrna. The date was February 22, 156. This day was afterward remembered as his true birthday.

With the death of Polycarp the persecutions ended in Smyrna, but there was never to be any end of them in the world. On the swords of the executioners the early Christians tested their faith; and other trials were in store. Christianity had to contend with the rich and seductive philosophies of Greece and Israel. In the second half of the second century she was to begin to wrest a body of intricate doctrine out of the New Testament and the remembered traditions of Christ, testing the new against the old. Step by step she was to hammer out her own philosophy. Christ was set against Moses and Plato. The battle was fought, not in Smyrna nor in any of the other seven churches of Asia, but in the theological schools in Alexandria, the most civilized city of the time, where Jews and Greeks and Christians met on an equal footing. Origen and Clement of Alexandria were the protagonists in the drama. They wrestled with angels, delved into the mysterious origins of Christianity, consulted the oldest texts, hurled anathemas on the pagans. When they completed their work, they had laid the foundations of the faith and built up its doctrinal structure almost to the height which it reaches today.

Clement of Alexandria

Out of Alexandria came the first great schools of the Church. That teeming sun-drenched city, where the merchandise of the known world gathered under the white awnings of the market place, had become by A.D. 150 the intellectual capital of the Empire.

In Alexandria were the largest and best-equipped libraries, the best museums, the biggest theaters, the longest race track, the finest craftsmen of letters, the most widely read philosophers. Shaped like the cloak which Alexander threw down on the sand, the city spread along four miles of coast. It had two harbors—Grand Harbor and the Harbor of Happy Return—and the lighthouse was one of the wonders of the world. The main avenues were thirty yards wide. Conquered by the Romans, the city was still Greek in spirit, though the Platonic wines had fermented under the Egyptian sun. Greek was the common tongue, Greek their way of thought, Greek too the impulsiveness of these dark-skinned people who moved among the marble columns; but something of Africa and the desert had entered into them. The Alexandrians detested calm. They adored processions, harsh colors, the clanging of temple bells, all that was vibrant and shrill and colloquial. The best singers came from there, and the gayest dancers. At night this seaport was given over to the wildest license.

It was a city where magicians and fakirs abounded, and spells were cast on doorsteps, and a man leaving for work in the morning might find himself assaulted by the devotees of ten religions, running the gauntlet to avoid being dragged into their processions. The Jews had their synagogues, the Persians the gardens where they adored the Sun, the Romans their temples dedicated to the worship of the reigning Emperor. But it was the god Serapis, magnificently bearded, wearing the goat horns of Ammon between the curls on his forehead, and on his head a basket filled with ears of corn, the emblem of abundance, who was especially sacred to the Alexandrians. Serapis was so powerful that

Tertullian cried out in alarm: "His worship rules the whole world." It was almost true. He answered men's needs, gave them a white-robed and tonsured priesthood, ceremonies of baptism and communion, doctrines of salvation and redemption, daily preachings from the pulpit, habits of contemplation. There were moments when Tertullian wondered whether the worship of Serapis were not a ghastly parody of Christianity.

In Alexandria all the cults were vying for supremacy. Scholars from Greece were continually extending the frontiers of Platonism and at the same time receiving influences from Egypt. Here the Old Testament was translated for the first time into Greek. Here Judaism and Platonism, Moses and Socrates, met face to face, and Christianity, confronted by the disciplines accompanying those two intellectual systems and by a host of cults, was compelled for the first time to exercise its intellectual muscles.

About 180 there came to Egypt a man who possessed all the marks of being a typical Alexandrian. He was about thirty. Born in Athens, apparently of mingled Greek and Jewish parentage, speaking Greek perfectly and ignorant of Latin, possessing Roman citizenship and in some unexplained way connected with an imperial Roman family, he bore a suspicious name. We know him as Clement of Alexandria, martyr and doctor of the Church. He was born Titus Flavius Clemens, a name which curiously commemorates the Roman Emperor who overthrew Jerusalem, an imperial Roman family and a Pope. It is possible that he assumed the name. It is just as possible that he was descended from the Consul Flavius Clemens, whose sons were declared heirs to the throne, until he became a Christian and was put to death by his cousin, the Emperor Domitian. He was saintly, sweet-tempered and garrulous, an admirable poet, the most gentle of men. His supreme virtue is that he was the first to confront Platonism with Christianity and prepared the way for Origen, his arrogant and superbly equipped successor.

We know almost nothing about the life of Clement of Alexandria, but of the man himself we know almost everything we could desire to know. We know his views on nearly all things under the sun. He resembles Montaigne in his playful pedantry, his firm prejudices, his occasional bitterness, his grave benevolence. He believed calmness to be the most prized possession of a good Christian, but he was not always calm. He detested fops, rhetoricians, men who shaved off their beards, women who wore expensive garments, all people in high positions of authority. He was curiously fascinated by sex, and spoke about sexual matters at considerable length in his three surviving works. He was like a squirrel in the way he collected tag ends of verses and inserted them in his writings, often with little excuse except his own pleasure in them. He read voluminously—there are more than seven hundred quotations from more than three hundred authors in his works. He had the academic mind, in the best and the worst sense, he was profoundly in love with freedom, and he was the first Christian writer to assert the doctrine of free will. His piety was lyrical, contemplative, never complex: the piety of a man who had no iron in his soul and never had to battle his way to Christ. He was gentle and considerate to all people, and was particularly understanding of women and children. And when we close his books after reading him, we are aware of an astonishing lightheartedness and gaiety.

All we know of his life can be told in a short paragraph. He must have traveled widely in his youth, for he speaks of his teachers: an Ionian who taught in Greece, another from southern Italy, a third from Egypt, a fourth who was born in Assyria, a fifth who was a Jew from Palestine. At last he studied under Pantaenus, an Athenian Stoic turned Christian, who was reputed to have gone on a mission to India, where he found a copy of *The Gospel according to St. Matthew* in Hebrew characters left there by St. Bartholomew. Pantaenus headed the catechetical school at Alexandria, and on his death Clement succeeded to his office. He was head of the school from 190 to 203, when the persecution of Severus broke out. He escaped from Alexandria, traveled to Cappadocia through Syria, and we hear nothing more of him except that he was the bearer of a letter to Asclepiades, Bishop of Antioch. The letter contained the words "Clement the blessed presbyter, who has become my lord, and done me benefit." He seems to have died in Antioch about 215.

We know very little about the origins of the catechetical school in Alexandria. It seems to have been conducted privately, and was never under the patronage of ecclesiastical authority. The pupils were mostly young Alexandrian Greeks, and young women were probably included in the classes. There was a library attached to the school, and there can have been no shortage of books, for the libraries in the Serapeum and the Museum contained nearly half a million volumes. The task of the head of the school was to train young Christians in the understanding of texts. Probably there were no formal classes; it is more likely that the school resembled a study circle of intense young Christians, many of them wealthy, with Clement acting as moderator and occasionally delivering sermons.

Only one of Clement's sermons has survived entire. He discusses the text concerning the rich man who seeks eternal life in *The Gospel according to St. Mark*. Clement comments on the meaning of every verse in *Mark* 10:17-31, and comes to the conclusion that the command "to sell all thou hast" was not intended to be universally applicable. It is a simple and eloquent sermon, and he concludes with a remarkable story, "which has been handed down from the past and committed to memory," concerning St. John and the Robber. The story relates how St. John, returning from Patmos to Ephesus, met a handsome youth who gave all the appearance of possessing a talent for divine studies. The saint entrusted the youth to the care of a presbyter to be brought up in the knowledge of Christ, and soon afterward went on his way:

And then it happened that some very idle and dissolute youths, who were familiar with evil, corrupted this boy and enticed him away from the presbyter by spending a good deal of money entertaining him, and soon they were committing outrages on the highways. The youth went with them . . . and in time he became their captain, the fiercest, the cruelest and the bloodiest of them all.

Some years passed, and then the presbyters of the church asked John to come to them, to discuss the matters of the church, and afterward John said: "Now, O bishop, render me the deposit which I and the Saviour have put in thy charge." The bishop was confused. He thought John was speaking about some money deposited with him, and he could not believe this, and at the same time he could not disbelieve the words of the apostle. Then John said: "I am asking for the return of the young man I left with thee, the soul of this brother." The old bishop wept and groaned, and answered: "The youth is dead." Then John asked: "How did he die?" "He died to God," the bishop said. "He became evil. He turned to robbery, and now he lives on the mountain over there, facing the church, a band of robbers with him."

The apostle tore at his own clothes and struck his head with his fists, and wept and cried out: "I left my brother's soul in the charge of a good watchman! Now bring me a horse, and let someone be my guide, and I shall go to him."

So John rode away, just as he was, riding straight out of the church. The robbers had set up outposts on the mountain, and when they saw John approaching, they captured him. He made no effort to escape, and begged nothing of them. He said: "Take me to thy captain. I have come to see him." The captain was waiting on the mountain, armed to the teeth. When this captain set eyes on John, he turned away, ashamed, and began running. John called out after him: "Son, son, why dost thou run from thy father, who is an old man and unarmed? Fear nothing! Thou mayest still enjoy eternal life! I will assume this responsibility before Christ! If necessary, I shall die for thee, as the Lord died for us! Stand, believe! Christ has sent me!"

Then the robber hung his head low and threw down his weapons, trembling and weeping bitterly, and then John embraced him and baptized him with tears.   [*Quis Dives*, 42]

The story has so much of Clement in it that if the authorship were unknown, it would be easy to guess who wrote it.

Three major works by Clement have survived, and a scattering of fragments. These three works appear to form part of a carefully constructed plan, corresponding to Purification, Initiation and Vision. In *The Exhortation* (*Protreptikos*) the Christian is purged of heathen error; in *The Instructor* (*Paedagogus*) he is initiated into the mystery; in the *Miscellanies* (*Stromateis*) he receives his final initiation and enters the presence of God. Inevitably there is some overlapping, and Clement has the happy faculty of rarely sticking to the point. At the sight of the smallest hare running across the landscape, Clement is immediately after it.

The Exhortation is a glowing appeal to the Greeks to listen to and abide by the New Song. As he exposes and denounces the ancient myths, he seems to be gathering up all the music of the ancient world. He confronts the old music with the new, rejoicing that St. John and the angels and Christ Himself were all singers, and that man is "a wonderful breathing instrument of music, formed by God in His own image." All things in Creation are listening to the New Song, which is so ancient that it came into the world before the morning star; and yet it is new, and this is the mystery: for as Word, the song is ancient, and as Christ, it is new. Christ is our singing master. Christ is our hymn and our truth.

For Clement the simple theme of the New Song rising triumphantly over the fading voices of the past is capable of innumerable variations. Some of those fading voices still exert their spell on him. He was not one of those who believed Plato an ignorant heathen; on the contrary Plato was nobly inspired, and may have borrowed abundantly from the Hebrews. As for the ancient gods, though their voices are muted, and the Castalian springs are silent, yet they can be heard singing in the distance—the sweet-tongued Muses and Demeter wandering in search of her daughter Kore: these especially have power to seduce the Christian. He knows the pagan mysteries well, too well for his comfort, for he discusses them at length, as though he could not free himself entirely from their magic. He seems to have been admitted to the mysteries in Athens, and he quotes the Orphic song of initiation:

> *I have eaten out of the drum,*
> *I have drunk out of the cymbal,*
> *I have carried the kernos,*
> *I have entered the chamber.*

Clement knew a good deal about the mysteries in which the mutilated phallus was worshiped, and how Zeus came to smell the flesh of Dionysus when it was being cooked on a spit and hurled his thunderbolts at the Titans in revenge. He recognized that many objects employed in the mysteries were sexual symbols. Pine cones, spinning tops, apples, swords, combs, sesame pies and pyramidal cakes—they all come out of the depths! Away with them! Let the fire sweep them away! And with the mysteries, which are nothing more than ritual murder, went the hoary gods—Zeus in his cups, Hercules debauching boys, Aphrodite who was no better than a common serving-wench though she rose from the sea foam:

> Now the fables have grown old in your hands, and Zeus is no longer a serpent, no longer a swan, nor an eagle, nor a furious lover. He no longer flies, nor loves boys, nor kisses, nor offers violence, though there are still many beautiful women prettier than Leda, sweeter than Semele, and handsomer boys than the Phrygian herdsman. Where is the eagle now? where the swan? where Zeus himself? He has grown old with his feathers, but he has not yet repented of his love affairs, and he has never learned continence. Zeus is dead, as Leda is dead, and the swan too, and the eagle, and the lover, and the serpent. [*Protrept.* II]

It is almost an elegy, a long look backward at the past with a hint of sadness. But with Zeus disposed of, and the obscene rites of the mystery religions, the way is clear for an examination of the lesser gods, a final valediction. For five chapters Clement surveys the departing gods, as they sink into the shadows. He knows them all by name, their many names. He knows that in Oxyrhynchus men worshiped a fish, in Thebes a sheep, in Syria a dove, in the Troad a mouse. Egyptians worship cats and weasels. Men have been known to worship men; they even worshiped King Philip, the father of Alexander the Great, when his collarbone was broken and he was lame in one leg and one of his eyes had been knocked out. Alexander himself wore the goat horns of Ammon. There was a grammarian who thought he was the sun god. And what shall we say of Artemis the Strangler and Zeus the Averter of Flies? Those who can believe in such fictions are like worms wallowing in mud, when they could be angels in Paradise, walking about the battlements of Heaven or cutting a path through the luminous clouds, "beholding like Elias the dew of salvation." Strange, impious, sorrowful and absurd are the ways of the gods! "Therefore put your faith in the Lord of the spirits, the Lord of the fire, the Maker of the universe, Him who lit a candle to the sun, and Whom I long for with all my heart!"

The concluding chapters of the work are somber with anticipation of an austere Christ. The laughing, ribald note vanishes; the demons have been exorcised; we are no longer on a familiar earth, but in the cloudy landscape in the outskirts of the Heavenly Kingdom, where Clement has his home. Men have been endowed with immortality: let them seize their endowment: let them walk the earth for a little space as though they were in Heaven:

> We do not compel the horse to plow, nor the bull to hunt, but we set each animal to the craft best suited for it. And therefore we invite man to the understanding of God, *because he is of celestial birth, being a plant of heavenly origin,* and so we counsel him to furnish himself with a sufficient provision of holiness for all eternity. So, if you are a plowman, plow; but know God while you are tilling your fields. And if you are a sailor, sail the seas, but remember the steersman in Heaven.   [*Protrept.* X]

Clement believed that man is born for the service of God, and his soul is a gift sent to him from Heaven: throughout his work the theme of man's celestial birth is continually repeated. This belief was shared by the Christians and the attendants at the Orphic mysteries. His attitude toward man remains Greek to the end: man is the master of all things, because Christ can save men at all times. Man is song, the noblest of songs:

> A noble hymn of God is man, immortal, founded upon righteousness, the oracles of truth engraved upon him. For where else save in the wise soul can truth be written? or love? or reverence? or gentleness? Those who have had these divine characters engraved and sealed upon their souls deem such wisdom a fair port of departure for whatever journey their course is trimmed to, and this wisdom is also a haven of peace and safe return. By this wisdom those who have betaken themselves to the Father have proved good fathers to their children, and those who have known the Son have proved good sons to their parents, and those who remember the Bridegroom become good husbands to their wives; and having been redeemed from absolute slavery, they are good masters to their slaves.   [*Protrept.* X]

So Clement announces the New Song, and somewhere close at hand are the Greek poets and philosophers, whose rhythms echo through his work, and whose fame he celebrates, for he finds much in common between the Christian mystery and the Greek drama. He can never quite shake himself free from Homer, Sophocles and Plato; and it seemed to him the most natural thing in the world that the Greeks should be the evangels of Christianity. He will employ Homeric phrases to lead men to Christ. "Neither childlessness, nor poverty, nor obscurity, nor want, can hinder him who strives after the knowledge of God, nor does anyone who has 'conquered by brass or iron' the true wisdom for himself choose to exchange it, since the true wisdom is preferable to all other things whatsover." The phrase "conquered by brass or iron" comes straight out of Homer. But of the Greek poets his greatest love was reserved for Sophocles. It is what we might have expected: the serene Clement, the serene Sophocles walking together. And like Sophocles Clement showed a deep affection for the old blind prophet Tiresias:

> See, the maidens strike their lyres, the angels praise, the prophets speak. The sound of music issues forth; they run and pursue the triumphant choir; and those who are called make haste, eagerly desiring to see the Father.

So come, O aged Tiresias, away from Thebes, and throw away your divinations and your Bacchic frenzies—come to the truth! I give you the staff of righteousness to lean on! Make haste, Tiresias, believe, and you shall see! The blind have recovered their sight through Christ, and he will bathe you in a light brighter than the sun; and night will go from you; and the fire will be afraid; and death will be gone. And you, Tiresias, who never set eyes on Thebes shall see the whole range of Heaven. O true and sacred mysteries! O perfect light! My way is lighted with torches, I see the heavens and my God. . . . So let us make haste, let us run, my fellow men, who are God-loving and Godlike images of the Word. Let us haste, let us run, let us wear the yoke, let us allow ourselves to be led to immortality, the good charioteer of men. Let us love Christ.   [*Protrept.* XII]

And having sung Christ in magnificent prose, Clement goes on to sing Christ in verse which is equally magnificent in the original:

> *O bridle of colts untamed,*
> *Wing of all hovering birds,*
> *Helm of the steady ships,*
> *Shepherd of royal lambs,*
> *Gather Thy children around*
> *So they may sweetly sing*
> *From holy and innocent lips*
> *Christ the Protector of children.*
>
> *O King of the royal saints,*
> *All-conquering Word*
> *Of the Most High Father,*
> *Thou who art Prince of Wisdom*
> *And Comforter of Sorrows,*
> *Ever rejoicing Jesu,*
> *Saviour of the race of men,*
> *Our Shepherd and Husbandman.*
>
> *O Helm, Bridle, Heavenly Wing*
> *Soaring over the holy flock,*
> *Fisher of those who are saved,*
> *Luring with sweetest life*
> *Pure fish from the hateful wave.*

Lead us, O holy King,
Shepherd of reasonable sheep,
Out of the sea of darkness.

Lead Thy innocent children
In the footsteps of Christ
Along the heavenly way,
There for immeasurable ages
To bathe in eternal light
Amid fountains of mercy,
With thy eternal Word
Following the pathways of virtue.

Noble is he who hymns God:
The heavenly milk is pressed
Out of the Bride's sweet breast.
Babes with their tender mouths
Are nourished by thy virtue
With a reasonable dew
Sent by the Holy Spirit.
So let us sing simple hymns.

In honor of Christ the King,
In holy fee for His teaching,
Let us sing in simplicity
Praise of the mighty child.
O chaste people born of Christ
Sing in the choirs of peace:
Let your voices ring sweetly
To honor the God of Peace.

In *The Exhortation,* and in the *Hymn to Christ the Saviour,* Clement showed himself at his most lyrical. From this time onward he seems to have been determined to put poetry away, but he can never entirely free himself from it. At long intervals in *The Instructor* and *Stromateis* poetry comes creeping in.

The Instructor is the least poetical, the most moral and opinionated of all Clement's works. The Instructor is God, the Holy Word, in His practical aspect: the professor of morals, "whose aim is not to teach, but to train men in the virtuous rather than the intellectual life." Therefore the Instructor "first exhorts to the attainment of right dispositions and character, and then persuades us to the energetic practice of our duties." These lofty aims are to be accomplished by a healing of the passions and by ordinances against sin, by exhortations and by precepts. The opening chapters are oddly Victorian, and never entirely credible. He strains after gnats. He quotes Moses: "If anyone dies suddenly by him, straightway the head of his consecration shall be polluted, and shall be shaved." (*Numbers* 6:9). Then he comments:

> This means that involuntary sin is designated by sudden death. For he says it pollutes by defiling the soul, and therefore he prescribes the cure with all speed, advising the head to be instantly shaved, thus counselling the locks of ignorance which shade the reason to be clean shorn off.   [*Paedagogus*, II]

This is so unlike the serene Clement of *The Exhortation* that we are on our guard. Happily, in the third chapter, he announces that "didactic discourses are powerful, spiritual and accurate, but let us put them aside for the present." He keeps his promise. He was never again to be quite so pontifical, nor to commit such violence on a text. The tone changes, and for the rest of the book he is at ease with himself, discoursing in his gentle haphazard manner on the subject of children, holiness, the nature of the devil, the nature of man, and whatever comes into his capacious mind, with no order except an imaginative order which is hardly imposed upon the book, for the writing flows naturally with grace and serenity. It is Clement thinking aloud, and for that we are grateful. Soon he warms to his main subject: the habits of the people of Alexandria, and whether they are truly Christian, and what exactly should be the behavior of Christians. The precepts fly out of the window, or they are reduced to gentle remonstrances; and as he describes the habits of the Alexandrians we are made curiously aware of Clement himself, with his genuine delight in life, his gentleness and garrulity and his liking for buttonholing the people he meets in the streets. He loved the world, because the world was God's; and it is a mark of his loving-kindness that though he rebukes often, he never rebukes unfairly.

And what a time he has at it! He goes about, observing everyone, painting portraits, describing the follies and foibles of his contemporaries—the wealthy upstarts, the women who paint their faces, the owners of silver urine vases and chamber pots of crystal. He is half-amused by them. There are lengthy descriptions of the *haute monde*, which read like Petronius, and he has Petronius' habit of inserting odd scraps of classical lore. He has some curious quirks about women. He is a little appalled by the Alexandrian delight in display. Clement, the gentle Puritan, decides that beardless men are a disgraceful sight, but he approves of men cropping their hair when it gets so long that it falls over their eyes. He thought mustaches should be cropped when they interfere with eating. Women should bind their hair with a plain hairpin. Gold shoes were to be avoided. Clothing was invented to cover the body: it was absurd to wear olive, green, rose and scarlet clothes. Once you wear dyed clothes, you are offering hostages to voluptuaries. He thought laughter wildly improper, and counseled "a strict discipline of smiles." There were many habits he objected to: the wearing of crowns, and all those ornaments with which women deck themselves, hairnets, girdles, shawls, chains, anklets, bracelets. He catalogues them, and shouts with derision, quoting the comic poets, whose "extravagance of statement shames the obstinacy of female impudence." And so it is that we owe to Clement the survival of a fragment from the forgotten comic poet Alexis:

> Is the woman small? She stitches cork to her shoe soles.
> Is she tall? Then she will wear the thinnest of slippers
> And hang her head low on her shoulder.
> Has she no buttocks? She will sew them on,
> And the spectators will exclaim at the beautiful curves of her
>   behind.
> Has she a big stomach? Oh, there are ways to flatten it!
> Has she blond eyebrows? She paints them with soot.
> Or are they black? She smears them with white lead.
> Is she white-skinned? She puts on rouge.
> Is part of her body worthy to be looked at? She strips it bare.
> Has she beautiful teeth? She laughs all the time,
> And if not in the humor for laughing, she spends the day indoors
> With a slender twig of myrtle between her lips,
> As the butchers put a sprig of myrtle between the lips of a dead
>   goat,
> So that she keeps her mouth open, whether she will or not.

Clement is delighted to acquire the services of the comic poets in the battle against female wiles. "In this way does the Word most strenuously wish to save us." Then Clement asks: What is the most beautiful thing of all? and answers: A thrifty wife who clothes both herself and her husband with the work of her own hands, in which all are glad—the children on account of the mother, the husband on account of the wife, she on his account, and all in God. And he follows Paul in believing that shamefacedness and sobriety should be the only adornments of women.

Sobriety: luxury. His mind swings from pole to pole, and he has a fondness for describing the chaste and sober appearance of the Christians and setting them up against the luxury-loving pagans. He can sketch a scene or an atmosphere with grace and precision. Against luxury-loving princes, he sets the example of the Scythians, the Celts and the Germans who wear their hair long, and never put on adornments; these red-haired barbarians live frugal lives, he says, and never surrender to luxury. They live close to their animals, strenuously, despising the world of the senses. And what is wrong with shaggy hair? "Lions glory in their shaggy manes, and are armed with their hair in the fight." Clement approves of the strenuous life, the body stripped naked of finery and all vanity, dedicated to the Lord.

He has a long chapter on gluttony. He makes our mouths water with long lists of delicacies, which have turned his stomach. The tender goats of Melos, the cockles of Methymna, thrushes from Daphne, the red-brown figs of Attica—the list is endless. Men who eat such dainties are "all jaw and nothing else." He offers suggestions on the proper way of eating: the chin must be kept free from stains, the countenance must be composed, and there must be no noise during the act of swallowing. No one should talk with his mouth stuffed full of food, "for the voice becomes disagreeable and inarticulate when it is confined by full jaws, and the tongue, compressed by the food and impeded in its natural energy, gives forth a compressed utterance." Nor should a well-behaved person eat and drink simultaneously. He should take sober foods; only gluttons go in for sugarplums, honey cakes and sweetmeats. Let there be no entertainments during meals, no singing, no shouting. The Christian should eat in sober quietness, far from the hissing of frying pans in which are gathered all the strange oddments swept up in the dragnets of gluttons:

How foolish are the people who raise themselves from their couches, almost pitching their faces into the dishes, stretching from the couch as from a nest, according to the saying "a man may catch the wandering stream by breathing it." How senseless to smear the hands with condiments and to be constantly reaching for the sauce, shamelessly cramming food into oneself, not tasting it so much as ravenously pouring oneself upon it! You will see such people, more like swine or dogs than living men, who are in such a hurry to feed themselves they fill both jaws at once, and the veins stand out on their faces, and they swim in sweat and pant with their exertions, as they shovel the food into their stomachs with an uncivil eagerness. You would think they were going on a long journey, not taking a meal. Excess is a very reprehensible thing.   [*Paedagogus*, II, 1]

Why excess is so reprehensible he explains later, summoning Paul and Plato to be his witnesses, remembering that Matthew lived on seeds, nuts and vegetables, and took no flesh, and John the Baptist, "though he carried temperance to the extreme," lived on locusts and wild honey. Happily he quotes Plato, who wrote from Syracuse that he was weary of being filled with two meals a day and never being allowed to sleep alone. Gluttony, sex, envy, pride—all these are a weariness; it is better to be a good Christian, and all weariness is put away.

There are moments when Clement reads like Emily Post. As he contemplates the behavior of the Alexandrians, he is half-inclined to write a vade mecum of Christian behavior. Here and there he offers excellent advice, and sometimes he sounds strangely modern. If a man comes up to a married woman and says: "You have beautiful legs," she is counseled to reply: "They belong to my husband," and if she is told she has a lovely face, she should answer: "It is for my husband alone." Clement would prefer her to hide her ankles and cover her face, and then he remembers that the women of Alexandria wore intriguing purple veils. "It would be better," he suggests sagely, "if they did not wear these veils."

Should the flesh be seen, or hidden? Clement is never quite sure. The veil hiding a pretty girl's face only makes her more desirable. A full-length gown covers a multitude of sins, but this too can be an excitement to the eyes. Then he remembers that Jesus is traditionally represented in a long gown which covered His ankles, but this, Clement announces, is something else altogether: the gown of Jesus represents the brilliance of wisdom and the all-enclosing Scriptures. The question of clothes worries him. Dresses embroidered with flowers should be left to the dancers in the Bacchanalia. Gold embroidery, scarlet dyes, mantles dipped in myrrh—away with them all! But he moderates his severity sufficiently to say of women's clothes that they might be woven smooth and be soft to the touch, and he saw no harm in allowing them to wear a little jewelry, though for some reason he abhorred earrings. "Women who wear earrings," he snorts, "have passed beyond the pale—they might as well wear rings in their noses as in their ears!"

Clement is not afraid to deal with sexual problems, and he has many things to say on the sexual behavior of Christians. He quotes from *The Gospel of the Egyptians:* "I came to destroy the works of the Female." He is quite sure this apocryphal saying was spoken by Jesus. "The Lord did not lie," he says, "for in very truth he destroyed the works of desire, love of money, love of contention, vanity, mad lust, pederasty, gluttony, viciousness and all the vices." He regarded human birth as the soul's corruption; since then we are "dead in sins" (*Eph.* 2:5). And having stated the uncompromising position of the completely dedicated Christian he is perfectly prepared to discuss the behavior of married Christians: how they should be wise and tender to one another in their sexual affairs, and long-suffering, and steadfast in loyalty. In his mind the age-old quarrel continues: whether to be an ascetic or to enjoy the gifts of God. "The world is a field, and we are the harvest watered by the grace of God" (*Puedagogus,* II, 104). Shall a man therefore not walk in the fields? So he will speak sometimes of marriage as though evil were inherent in it from the beginning, and at other times he will raise his hand in blessing on the men and women who find a holy joy in one another. And sometimes too he will talk of marriage with such bluntness that whole paragraphs and chapters are veiled in the obscurity of Latin when they appear in English translations.

The Instructor rarely comes to grips with theological problems: in a work called *Stromateis,* which originally meant "A Quilted Bag for Stuffing Bedclothes" and then came to mean simply *Miscellanies,* Clement abandoned his casual method. Plutarch and Origen both wrote works which they called *Stromateis;* their works are lost, and we do not know whether such miscellanies were intended to suggest simply a collection of casual thoughts. Clement's title, however, is misleading. Where *The Instructor* is loose-knit and often unconvincing, the *Miscellanies* is close-grained, profoundly convincing and of vast importance to an understanding of early Christianity.

From the beginning Clement disclaims any attempt to write a formal treatise. "This work," he says, "is not composed artfully for display; it is nothing more than a collection of notes stored up against my old age, as a medicine against forgetfulness." It is the typical disclaimer of an Alexandrian author. The task Clement had set himself was to make a summary of Christian knowledge up to his time. He therefore discusses a multitude of subjects, but we are aware of a common theme and a common development, a deliberate straining toward an end, that same end which was the professed goal of *The Instructor*: the attainment of right dispositions and character. But here Clement abandons any effort to discuss practical matters, except when he returns to discuss Christian marriage, and he contents himself with a long philosophical treatise. In Book I he discusses the origin of Greek philosophy and shows how the Greek philosophies form part of the divine education of man. In Book II he discusses the revelations of Christ, repentance and the holiness of marriage. Book III is entirely devoted to a doctrine of Christian marriage. Book IV is concerned with a plan of Christian apology. Book V is concerned with faith and hope. Books VI and VII are concerned with the true Gnostic, the Christian in full possession of the knowledge of Christ. And these books, which at the first reading appear to be linked together in a haphazard order, are seen at last to form an inevitable progress. He begins with Greek philosophy, because for him there can be no other beginning. Then he will go on to study various components of Christian belief. Finally he will state the nature of the true Gnostic. Occasionally he rambles and he will discuss whatever objects interest him on the way, but the main intention is an orderly progress to a known end—from the early assumption: "Philosophy is a gift, not of the devils, but of God through the Word," to the final conclusion: "The Word took flesh of the Virgin Mary and became man."

Clement has all the advantages of freshness, but in a sense he was working in the dark. He did not have a trained massive intelligence, like Origen, who was his student. He was attempting about A.D. 200 to compose a synthesis of Christian doctrine, such a synthesis as St. Thomas Aquinas composed a thousand years later. His sources were the Bible, the legends and the mysteries that have grown around the name of Jesus. He hinted that there are some mysteries which are not to be divulged except to the true followers of Christ:

> It is necessary to hide the wisdom spoken in a mystery and taught by the Son of God. For Isaiah the prophet had his tongue purified by fire, so that he might be able to speak of the vision. As for us, we must purify not only our tongues but also our ears, if we attempt to be partakers of the truth.   [*Strom.* I, xii]

But there is little evidence that Clement deliberately concealed anything he knew concerning Christian doctrine in the *Miscellanies*. Indeed, he gives a contrary impression. He seems to be saying: "I am now writing everything I know, in accordance with the injunction, 'What ye hear in the ear, proclaim upon the houses.' "

As always, Clement is halting in his beginnings. The first book wanders over Greek and Hebrew history, and in his effort to prove that Plato is a precursor of Christ, he is compelled to the belief that Plato was indebted to Moses. He finds that many Greek philosophers owed their theories to foreigners; Pythagoras learned from an Assyrian, Democritus from the Babylonians. Far from being Greek, Thales was a Phoenician "who consorted with the prophets of Egypt." All these had attained to some portion of the truth, but Moses antedates them all—to prove it, Clement embarks on long genealogies of kings. It is plodding, but it is also effective: he knows where he is going. He must lay bare the sources of Christian doctrine, the ancient laws, the long history, all those things which prepared the world for Christ; then, and only then, will he be able to arrive at the needed condition of salvation: piety (θεοσέβεια), which he defines as "conduct in conformity with God." In his desire to be fair to the past, Clement must show that this is not something new and unexpected, and he hints that these words have been used often by philosophers of the pagan past, but what a wealth of new meaning the words contain! All his striving is toward a definition of the new knowledge which has entered the world.

All through the *Miscellanies* the past is present like a beneficent shadow. He is always returning to ancient Greece for examples with which to illustrate the new knowledge. He is speaking of true piety:

> The sacrifice acceptable to God is unchanging abstraction from the body and its passions. This is the only true piety; and therefore was not philosophy rightly called by Socrates the practice of death? For he who puts away the objects of sight when he is contemplating, and also all the other senses, and with the pure mind alone reaches out for objects is the true philosopher. This is what Pythagoras meant when he recommended five years of silence to his disciples, so that, turning away from the senses, they should look upon God with the mind alone.   [*Strom*. V, xi, 67]

For Clement there are always dangers on the journey. His aim is to explain Christ to the Greek world, and therefore he must employ the lucid, but infinitely complex structure of Platonism. Sometimes he seems to fumble, as though the task were too much for him, but a moment later he shows triumphantly that the marriage between Christianity and Greek traditions can be consummated. In the following passage, he begins heavily, as though working against the current of his thought, employing Platonic definitions and a Platonic vocabulary only because this is part of the task set before him, but how adroitly, and with what intellectual vigor he comes to his logical conclusion:

We may then apprehend the way of purification by confession, and the way of contemplation by analysis, going forward to the first notion, beginning by analysis with the things that underlie it, removing from the body its physical qualities, depriving it first of the dimension of depth, then of breadth, and then of length. For the point that is left is the monad, as it were, possessing position, and then if we subtract position, we have a monad in thought. If therefore we take away all that pertains to bodies and to the things called incorporeal, and cast ourselves into the immensity of Christ, and thence by purity go on into the Void, we may come somehow or other to an understanding of the Almighty, knowing not what He is but what He is not. Form or motion or standing or a throne or place or right or left are not at all to be attributed to the Father of All, even though it be so written. But what each of these means will be shown in the proper place. The first cause therefore is not in space, but above space and time and name and understanding.   [*Strom.* V, xi, 71]

It is a passage which deserves to be read slowly, for it conceals a method which was to assume increasing importance in the development of mystical doctrine. He names the Attributes of God ("form or motion or standing or a throne or place or right or left"), and concludes that it is not by His Attributes that He can be made known; He is known by what He is not, for the limited intelligences of men cannot rise to the knowledge of what He is. We shall see again in the works of Dionysius the Areopagite how this method, in the hands of a mystic, led to conclusions which affected the course of Christianity in the West.

For Clement, God is absolute, beyond space and time, inaccessible, unapproachable, unknowable, incommunicable. Through the Word, or Logos, He creates and governs and reveals Himself to men as a personal Father, the Creator, a loving and gentle Being whose supreme care is for the salvation of men. By introducing the Logos, who enters time and space, Clement resolved for himself the problem which was to haunt nearly all the Fathers who came after him: how can God be unknown, and yet known? how can He be unapproachable, and yet approached? The solution he offered was not wholly convincing, and sometimes Clement himself seems to remain unconvinced: for by identifying the Logos with Christ, he raised a score of theological problems, not the least of them being that Christ became a certain activity (ἐνέργεια) of the Father, and therefore assumed a place below the Father.

Clement places a high value on man. "How could it be otherwise, since God became man?" he says. Man is a rational being, possessed of free will, for he would be subject neither to praise nor to blame if he were not free. The descendants of Adam preserve their liberty, they have not lost the divine image in themselves and they are still free. At moments Clement seems to be about to enlarge on the possibilities of original sin, but he cannot quite bring himself to it. The chains that bound Adam were burst asunder by the children of Eve. It is not because of the taking of the fruit of the Tree of Knowledge that man learned sin; it was precisely his lack of knowledge that leads him into sinfulness. Clement believed that all things are free: God is free to do as He pleases, and the Devil has free will, and so has man. But the greatest freedom is to love God and to have knowledge of Him, and to train oneself like an athlete in His honor.

Salvation therefore is attained, not so much by a simple faith, as by the continued practice of spiritual austerities. For him the practice of the Christian life means rigorously patterning oneself on the model of Jesus, but since no one can imitate Jesus by a single leap of the spirit, it is necessary to study the prophets and all those who have spoken worthily; in his portrait of the good Christian there are elements of the ascetic, the scholar, the philosopher:

> So he compels himself to rise to the pinnacle of knowledge, his character in order, his bearing sober, possessing all the advantages of the true Gnostic, fixing his eyes upon noble images, on the many patriarchs who have fought the fight before him, on the still greater number of prophets, on angels beyond all power to number, on the Lord who is over all and who taught him, and made it possible for him to receive that crowning life. So he loves none of the fair things of life which the world holds out to him, fearing that they may hinder him in his progress. Instead, he loves the things that are hoped for, or rather are already known, but whose possession he hopes for. In this way he endures afflictions and tortures and labors, not like those brave men spoken about by the philosophers, from hope that the present evils shall cease and that he

will in time have a share in joys—no, this knowledge in him has begotten a persuasion, beyond all hope, of the reaping of harvests to come.   [*Strom.* VII, ix, 63]

Clement does not always speak of high things in so unrelenting a manner. Sometimes the long fugues give place to simple songs: a single phrase more illuminating than all the battling with philosophy, though the battles with philosophy were necessary to give birth to these simple phrases. John Damascene preserves a sentence from the works of Clement: "The Christian is always friendly to solitude, and quiet, and tranquillity, and peace." Nicetas, Bishop of Heraclea, preserves another fragment in his *Catena*: "Jesus is the pearl of the purest ray born of the Virgin in the lightning flash of Divinity." Finally, there are the words which lie concealed in the last chapter of his greatest work: "All this life is a holy festival" (*Strom.* VII, vii, 49). It is in such simple phrases—and his works are full of them—that we find his greatest strength.

Origen

The name sounds like a rock, and there was something rocklike in him to the end. He made himself a eunuch for the Kingdom of Heaven's sake, but no one ever behaved less like a eunuch. Born of a wealthy Christian Greek family in Alexandria and given the name of Origenes, meaning "born of Horus," he was called during his lifetime Adamantius, meaning "the man of adamant." An adamantine power flowed from him: no one ever wrestled with the inner meanings of Christianity with such formidable energy, such titanic power. Where Clement seems to grope, to offer suggestions, to convey inferences, Origen walks surefooted, with fanatic and controlled energy, never resting under his burdens until he has accomplished his purpose: the prow of the ship slicing through the immense ocean and leaving a wake which still gleams in the starlit night.

There was greatness in him, but at this late date we cannot measure his greatness with any accuracy; we can only guess at it, measuring the man by the shadow he has thrown, the huge head on the puny body, the intense gaze of the eyes, the solemnity of that heavy face as he pores at night over his manuscripts, dedicated to asceticism and possessed of a towering passion to comprehend, writing his endless books, questioning, delving, searching through the mists for every ray of light; the seaman plotting uncharted oceans. There was none like him, and there will be none like him again, for he came in at the beginning, before the doctors of the Church could weigh the evidence and come to their conclusions. This eunuch was the first great doctor, the founder of scientific Biblical scholarship. He would use reason and make reason itself the servant of Christ. He would batter down the walls of Heaven by the main force of logic alone. Only a few chapters of his work have survived in the original Greek, and most of our knowledge of his writings depends upon a mangled translation into Latin, yet his influence on Christian thought was gigantic, and cannot be escaped even now. The great Arian controversy of the fourth century, which set the East against the West, and directly contributed to the dilemmas we face today, arose as a legacy of some aspects of his thought. He wrote six thousand books, according to Rufinus, the wretched translator of his surviving works; and since he was in the habit of writing letters which became treatises—and sometimes one letter would proliferate into two treatises—there is no reason to doubt Rufinus' figure. He lived by faith and reason, and died a martyr, and for his pains was called a heretic long after his death. And though he was never officially granted the title of Doctor of the Church, he was the greatest doctor of them all.

He was born about A.D. 185, the eldest child in a large family. His father Leonidas was Greek, his mother probably Egyptian. Leonidas was the owner of a library of rare manuscripts, devoted to scholarship and his family, a devout Christian who achieved martyrdom. He seems to have been particularly devoted to his eldest son, and there is a story that he would sometimes go to the bedside of his sleeping son and seeing on the boy's chest the mark of consecration by the Holy Ghost, he would kiss the mark reverently. The boy read widely in his father's library, and asked questions interminably; so full of questions that he had to be restrained and publicly rebuked. He was never satisfied with easy answers. Rebuked, he would shrug his shoulders and put the books away, but at the first opportunity he was back again, puzzling over the ancient conundrums: how was the universe created? why did God descend to earth in the shape of a man? and how many angels stand in the air around us?

Origen was about fourteen when he first attended the school presided over by Clement, and he remained Clement's pupil to the end, showing the influence of the master, though he was to use Clement's weapons with incomparably greater skill. He was a good student. He embarked on a number of projects outlined for him by Clement. He studied voraciously. He might have become a simple professor if it had not been for the persecutions ordered in 202 by the Emperor Septimius Severus. Leonidas was imprisoned. The seventeen-year-old boy wrote to his father: "Take heed not to change your mind on our account," and soon afterward Leonidas was executed by the sword. Fearless, Origen visited the prisons and consoled and encouraged those who had been arrested for refusing allegiance to the Roman Emperor, and the historian Eusebius says of him that he would station himself on the road where the holy martyrs were being led to their deaths and in defiance of the Romans he saluted the martyrs with a kiss. The boy thirsted for martyrdom. He had sought arrest. He wanted to die with his father, and in the days just before his father's death his determination was so great that his mother had to hide his clothes to prevent him from leaving the house. With the death of Leonidas, and the confiscation of all his property, the family was ruined. Clement had vanished to Cappadocia to escape the persecution. Now Origen was alone, supported on the bounty of a wealthy Christian lady, and in hiding. A year later when the persecutions came to an end he decided to continue in the path his father had mapped for him: he would become a grammarian, and then when he had examined and sifted the sacred texts he would attempt a comprehensive interpretation. All through his life he was aware of his dead father standing by his side.

He began as a tutor, belonging to no school, giving lessons to pagans in Greek philosophy and offering elementary courses in doctrine to Christians. He was bitterly attacked, and his classes were threatened by the police, but his popularity increased; soon there were more pupils than he could cope with. The bishop gave his blessing to the enterprise. He had been teaching for about a year when he realized that he was attempting the impossible; there was not time enough to teach both the pagans and the Christians. Suddenly he abandoned his secular courses, and sold the library he had collected at great expense, investing the profits in such a way that he received an income of four obols a day, equivalent to a few pennies a week. He lived precariously. He drank no wine, walked barefoot and slept on the floor. Almost his chief expenditure was for midnight oil: he had a habit, which lasted throughout his life, of writing and studying at night.

About this time, when he was living a life of strictest asceticism, he performed the act of self-mutilation, following literally the saying in *Matt.* 19:12 that "there are eunuchs who have made themselves eunuchs for the Kingdom of Heaven's sake." He may have performed the act in a sudden irrational moment, when the calm demanded by intensive scholarship was being thwarted by the invasion of sexual energy. It may have been that he regarded emasculation as simply one more of the mortifications he imposed on the body. He said later that "those who obey the teachings of the Saviour are martyrs in every act whereby they crucify the flesh with its passions and desires." If mortification was required, then emasculation was only an extreme form of mortification, to be compared with fasting. According to Origen, however, he resolved upon the act as the result of reading two pagan works: a short essay by Philo called *Evil Often Attacks*

Good and a mystical treatise by Sextus, a Pythagorean, called *The Sentences.* In both these books almost impossibly high ideals of purity were to be encountered. Later Origen was to say that "true purity does not consist in doing violence to the body, but in mortifying the senses for the Kingdom of God." He tried to hide what he had done, but the secret was soon known and brought to the attention of his bishop, who forgave him willingly, but never forgot this strange incident in the life of his most famous schoolteacher.

Deeply immersed in Greek philosophy, Origen was training himself rigorously for the task ahead. From Ammonius Saccas, a remarkable figure who rose out of obscurity to become first a longshoreman on the Alexandrian docks, then a practicing Christian teacher and finally a Neoplatonist philosopher who turned his back on Christianity, he learned how to employ the tools of Platonism. Saccas means "the sack," and the name was given to him because the longshoremen carried grain onto the ships in huge sacks. Vastly learned, the cutting edge of his mind sharpened by contact with the world of laboring men, Ammonius had two pupils whose fame soared high above his own, but only because Ammonius himself left no written records, preferring to expound his doctrines and interpretations with no stenographers present, and therefore leaving no trace of himself except the trace he imprinted on the minds of Plotinus and Origen.

In those early years Christianity and Hellenism went hand in hand. Plato had described the way, and beyond Plato were all the immeasurable complications of a theory which must be tested on the minds of all the different races in the eastern Mediterranean. Here was a form of spirituality drawn to a fine thread, almost imponderable. When the Alexandrians read Plato and his followers, they held up these theories to their own light; so did the Antiochenes; so did the Jews and Arabs, and much later the French, the Germans, the English and the Americans; and all saw in Plato something of themselves, refining the words to their own desires. There was something liquid in the Platonic theory; you could stain these waters whatever color you wished, but they remained Platonic. In the vast reaches of Plato's mind all things had been pondered, and it is not surprising that he should leave traces of himself on those who fed at the source. Like Clement before him, Origen had dipped in the springs of Neoplatonism. Living at that time, he could not have escaped it. Neoplatonism was a force, something to be reckoned with, and Origen was to fuse the theories of Plato onto the revelations of Christ.

What did the Neoplatonists believe? They had many beliefs, but their strongest belief lay in the power of the speculative mind to solve all questions except one through the quiet logic of reasoning. All things could be understood save God alone. God was incommensurable and above reason, and could be apprehended only under three forms—as the infinite, limitless and without thought or form or being; as the one and the good, the source of all that loves; and as the sum of all the powers of the universe. Out of this superabundance issues the world of ideas, radiating from God like the beams of the sun. From the world of ideas come the souls tainted with the love of sensation and mortal desires and all this world of appearances. The task of the good man is to ensure that he belongs to the world of ideas rather than to the world of matter, in which at last the heaviest souls dwell. The doctrine that God could be apprehended only under the three forms first announced by Plato was to remain; it dazzled the Christians of the East, and in their different ways Origen, the three great Cappadocian Fathers, Dionysius the Areopagite, Maximus the Confessor and a hundred others were influenced by it. The doctrine spread to the West, kept alive by the translations of Dionysius by John Scotus Erigena which influenced St. Thomas Aquinas. There were endless subtle complexities to the doctrine. Three great Neoplatonic schools were founded in Athens, Syria and Alexandria. And it was the good fortune —or perhaps the misfortune—of Origen that he studied under Ammonius Saccas at the same time as Plotinus, the most daring of the Neoplatonists, and the most singularly gifted. But it was Plotinus who relegated God to a kind of hypertranscendence. With Plotinus God became no more than a vast all-encompassing volatilized flame.

There were other influences at work. There was the legacy of the Stoics and the Pythagoreans; there were the mystery religions; Isis and Serapis still held sway. There were the Christian Gnostics who derived from Plato and the Old Testament, from Persian mythology and the Gospels, and from sources yet undiscovered, in a God called Abyss who dwelt in the Pleroma, the Fullness of Creation, a vast expanse shining with everlasting light. Here he abode for ages in solitude and silence, till at length, moved by some secret impulse, he begat of himself two intelligences. These, male and female, became progenitors in turn, until the region of light was peopled with a numerous family of blessed spirits. As these spirits drew further and further from God, in the order of birth, they gradually came to lose their powers, their knowledge and goodness. The highest of these spirits were call Aeons, or eternal beings. Then the Demiurge, having fashioned the world, filled it with men and other animals, giving them particles of the divine essence to animate their material bodies. He then threw off his allegiance to the author of his being, assumed the government of the world in defiance of the Deity, who was moved with compassion for the divine portion of man which was confined in the prison of the flesh, and sent angels, endowed with wisdom and filled with celestial light, to instruct man in the truth; but the Demiurge slew the angels and tempted men with thoughts of the enjoyments of the flesh. Only a few men were strong enough to oppose the Demiurge. These, freed from their bodies at death, were admitted at once into the realms of light; but the rest must remain in darkness until the time comes when the Deity dissolves the world and reduces it to primitive chaos. According to some Gnostics Jesus was an Aeon who returned to the Pleroma just before the Crucifixion. According to other Gnostics there were three separate Aeons called Jesus, Christ and the Holy Ghost, and all three were sent to help men in their long struggle against the Demiurge. Some believed there had been only twelve Aeons since the Creation; others that there were thirty; and theories of the relationship between the Abyss, the Pleroma, the Aeons and mortal men proliferated. Believing in the ultimate power of the Abyss, the Gnostics led intensely moral lives; and far from hurting the young shoot of Christianity, they gave it a rich, fantastic soil to grow in.

Clement had attempted to marry Christian doctrine to Greek philosophy. In a sense he did no more than sketch the complexities of the marriage. Origen went further: he bound them together with unbreakable bonds, so that even today our concepts of Christianity are permeated with ideas which he was the first to coin. Jerome called him "the greatest master of the Church after the apostles," and we have no reason to question the verdict.

Like Clement, Origen believed that all past philosophy can be, and must be, placed in the service of Christ. He once told Gregory Thaumaturgus there could be no genuine piety in a man who despised philosophy: "a gift which man alone of all the creatures of the earth has been deemed honorable and worthy enough to possess." Philosophy was the handmaiden, but he would never allow it to become the master. Clement possessed a generous faith and reveled in the delights of philosophy; Origen's faith is fierce to martyrdom, and he employs philosophy as a weapon. Yet they were men of the same age, sharing the same preoccupations, in love with the same God.

The most important and the most wide-reaching of Origen's works is the *De Principiis,* or *On First Principles,* which has except for some occasional chapters come down to us in an expurgated translation by Rufinus, the friend of Jerome. What survives is the wreck of an original text, in which we can discern the true voice of Origen at intervals, when Rufinus was either too lazy or too engrossed in the task of translation to alter Origen's theology. This shipwreck, masts and deckwork alone above the water, remains a masterpiece.

Origen does not wander, as Clement wanders. He keeps his eye on his subject. His task is systematic theology: he will attempt to erect a complete theological structure, proof against all the blows that may be struck against Christianity. He asks innumerable questions: What is God? What is the Son? What is the Holy Ghost? What is the Devil? What are the angels? To what end was the universe created? And having answered these questions he goes on, sure-footed as always, to the remoter intricacies of the faith. For him, as for St. Paul, "Christ is the image of the invisible God, the first-born of every creature." But Christ is also "the Son of God, who was in the form of God, divesting Himself of His glory." How then shall we understand the relationship between Christ on earth and God in Heaven? He answers:

Imagine a statue so vast that it filled the whole universe, and therefore could be seen by no one; and then another statue was formed, an exact model of the other in the shape of the limbs and features, in form and material, but somehow reduced in proportions, so that those who were unable to behold the vast, all-enveloping statue could still say they had seen it, for the other preserved all the features of the great statue, and its limbs and features, and its form, and it was no way distinguishable except in size. So did the Son of God divest Himself of His equality with the Father and show us the way to the knowledge of Him who is made the express image of His person; so that we, who are unable to look upon the splendor of the shining of the greatness of His Godhead, yet may behold His brightness and so, by looking upon His brightness, behold the divine light.

[*De Princ.* I, ii, 8]

This powerful image is only one of many, for power seems to come racing into Origen's mind whenever he contemplates the Father and the Son. The vast statue and its image tell only one aspect of the relationship between God and Christ. A little later he says that the perfect Godhead and the perfect Manhood of Christ are molded together in one Person, like the fire and metal in glowing iron, and the saints bathe in this warmth. But though he will sometimes return to the statue and the glowing iron, more often he thinks of the Son as "the glory of light, proceeding from the Father as brightness from the sun."

And this splendor, presenting itself gently and softly to the frail and weak eyes of mortals, and gradually training, as it were, and accustoming them to bear the brightness of the light, renders them capable of enduring the splendor of the greater light, being made in this respect also a sort of mediator between men and the light.

[*De Princ.* I, ii, 7]

Now His wisdom is the splendor of that light, not only in respect of its being light, but also of being everlasting light, so that His wisdom is eternal and everlasting splendor. If this be fully understood, it clearly shows that the existence of the Son is derived from the Father, but not in time, nor from any other beginning, except, as we have said, from God Himself.

[*De Princ.* I, ii, 11]

Origen's mind moves in vast outlines; he takes the whole of Creation in his stride. He is not trained to think in terms of exceptions. For him all who walk upon the earth, all the animals and all the winged creatures, partake of the Holy Spirit, receiving it from God. The works of the Father and the Son are communicated even to things without life, to everything in existence; but the Holy Spirit touches only the living (*De Princ.* I, iii, 5). The stars too are living and rational beings; and in time the sun itself may say: "I desire to be dissolved, to return and be with Christ, which is far better." The sun, moon and stars are obedient to God, for did not the Lord say: "I have given a commandment to all the stars" (*Isa.* 45:12)? Thus they bestow upon the world the amount of splendor God has entrusted to them, and like all other living creatures they will partake in the end of a new heaven and a new earth, "when perhaps every bodily substance will be like the ether, of a celestial purity and clearness" (*De Princ.* I, vii, 4).

Origen's mind continually revolved around the last things: he seems to be chiefly at ease only in the regions which leave men tongue-tied. He believed that ultimately, after long ages, God's love would prevail

and there would be a final *renovatio,* a restoring of the lost innocence
to its proper place in God. Just as he believed that the sun would return
to God, so he believed that even the Devil would return to his proper
inheritance, and "walk once again in the Paradise of God between
the cherubim" (*De Princ.* I, viii, 3). And why, he asks, should it not
be? Was he not once the Prince of Tyre among the saints, without
stain, adorned with the crown of comeliness and beauty, and is it to
be supposed that such a one is any degree inferior to the saints?
Sin did not brand a man eternally; the pains of Hell are disciplinary
and temporary, not everlasting, and Hell fire is no more than the
purifying flame which removes the baser elements from the soul's metal.
Not the body as flesh, but the body as spirit will rise again on that
eternal morning, of which all the ages of the world are no more than
the previous night. And that this Heaven exists, and that the end will
be as the beginning, he has no doubt, "for God would never have
implanted in our minds the love of truth, if it were never to have an
opportunity of satisfaction" (*De Princ.* II, x, 5).

A fierce and rigorous optimism breathes through all Origen's work,
and even when he discusses matters which amaze, he talks of them in
such a way that we are aware of the certainty in his soul. The mercy
of God is beyond all things unimaginable, and yet he can write of it,
in its fullness and majesty, as something which the mind can at least
approach with a sense of understanding. So he will write, like the
great rolling passages in Beethoven's *Missa Solemnis:*

> It is beyond the power of mortal frailness to understand or feel
> how the great power of Divine Majesty, the very Word of the
> Father and the very Wisdom of God, in which all things visible
> and invisible were created, can be imagined to have existed within
> the limits of the man who came to Judea. Impossible to imagine
> how the Wisdom of God can have entered the womb of a woman,
> and been born an infant, and have uttered wailings like the cries
> of little children! And that afterward it should be said He was
> deeply troubled in death, saying, "My soul is sorrowful even unto
> death," and at last He was brought to the most shameful death
> known to man, and rose again on the third day. . . . And now if
> we think of a God, we see a mortal; and if we think of a man, we
> behold Him returning from the grave, laden with spoils after over-
> throwing the empire of death. This spectacle is to be contemplated
> with all fear and reverence, for the truth of both natures may be

clearly shown to exist in one and the same Being, so that nothing
unworthy or unbecoming may be perceived in that divine and
ineffable substance, nor yet those things which were done be
supposed to be the illusions of imaginary appearances.

[*De Princ.* II, vi, 2]

In this spirit Origen continues his inquiry into the nature of God,
the world, man and the Holy Scriptures. He will not retire before
obstacles. Sometimes he comes to odd conclusions or makes curious
guesses, as when he suggests that perhaps when all the dead arise
to enjoy the eternal Sabbath, the evil ones will have darker skins than
the rest: there must be some way in which they can be distinguished
from those who led holy lives. But the suggestion is only an infinitesimal
part of his immense design: he must explore all possibilities in order
to reach certainties.

He had brooded for many years on the Scriptures, and he was not
afraid of the inconsistencies which can be found in them. He was sure
that man possessed free will. Then what should be said about the free
will of Pharaoh, when God said: "I will harden Pharaoh's heart," and
what should be said of the Pauline text: "Both to will and to do are of
God"? Origen solves the matter in a way which demonstrates his
method. Pharaoh's heart was indeed hardened; there was a suspension
of free will; the text must be read literally; but when Paul said: "Both
to will and to do are of God," he did not mean that human will was
entirely ordered by God: he meant only that the actions and desires of
men are under the sovereignty of God, as the actions and desires of a
citizen remain under the sovereignty of his king. "The letter killeth,
but the spirit giveth life."

Following Philo and Clement, Origen often interprets allegorically.
Statements which have no literal or human meaning must be interpreted
spiritually. He suggests that it is absurd to believe that a man should
pluck out his right eye, if it offends him. Why the right eye? Why
throw it away? Simple people, he says, believe that Jesus told the
apostles: "Salute no man by the way" (*Luke* 10:4). Origen suggests it
is pure nonsense to interpret the injunction literally; the Jewish doctors
fell into such pitfalls when they went to absurd lengths to define the
burdens which could be carried on a Sabbath day: a sandal with nails
was a burden, but not one without them. Origen is prepared to go
further. A vast number of important scriptural statements are literally
meaningless, spiritually of very great value:

For who that has understanding will suppose that the first, and second, and third day, and the evening and the morning, existed without a sun, and moon, and stars? . . . And who is so foolish as to suppose that God, after the manner of a husbandman, planted a paradise in Eden toward the east and placed in it a Tree of Life, visible and palpable, so that one tasting the fruit with the bodily teeth obtained life? and again, that one was a partaker of good and evil by masticating what was on the Tree? And if God is said to walk in the paradise in the evening, and Adam to hide himself under a tree, I do not suppose that anyone doubts that these things figuratively indicate certain mysteries, the history having taken place in appearance, and not actually.... The Gospels themselves are filled with such narratives. Did the Devil lead Jesus up into a high mountain, in order to show Him from thence the kingdoms of the whole world, and the glory of them? Who is there among those who read such accounts with discernment who will not condemn anyone who thinks the human eyes can see even when they are lifted high up the kingdoms of Persia, Scythia, India and Parthia, and the manner in which their princes are glorified among men? The attentive reader will discover in the Gospels innumerable similar passages, and he will be convinced that episodes which did not occur are inserted among those which are literally recorded.

[*De Princ.* IV, i, 17]

Such speculations were intended only for theologians: Origen had no desire to make light of the Bible's authority. And though he gave an impression of vast authority in his writing, he was prepared to be humble. "If anyone else can find something better, confirming what he says by clear proofs from Holy Scripture, let his opinion be preferred to ours" (*De Princ.* II, vi, 7).

Yet, though he was humble, there was arrogance in Origen. The task he set himself was nothing less than a complete examination of all the Scriptures, all that went before and all that was to come after. If there was time enough, he would comment upon every text until he had wrung its meaning out of it; he would establish each text, analyze it, relate it to all similar texts and to Christ and to the Church. The Scriptures were like a house in which all the rooms were locked, and the keys are not in the keyholes but scattered over the corridors and stairs; and none of the keys lying near the doors open those doors.

The only way to interpret the Scriptures was therefore a close, methodical study of every text, every key. Such was the story a Jewish rabbi told him, and Origen answered: "The key of David is in the hands of the Divine Word, which became flesh, and now the Scriptures which had been closed until His Coming are opened by that key." But though Origen said this, his practice was the continual study of texts until the day he died.

To prepare himself for his study, Origen compiled a long list of lexicons. There were lexicons of genealogies and of legends, studies of the opening passages of the Prophets, learned discussions on the meanings of words. Above all there was the *Hexapla,* on which he spent twenty-eight years. This was nothing less than an attempt to rectify the text of the Septuagint, the translation of the Old Testament made by Hellenistic Jews into Alexandrian Greek some four hundred years before. In one column was the Hebrew text, in the next a transliteration of the Hebrew in Greek letters, and besides these were four complete translations made at different times for different purposes by Aquila, Symmachus and Theodotion, together with the Septuagint. Of some books he gave two additional Greek versions, so that the collection which extended to nearly fifty volumes was sometimes called the *Octapla.* Through this arduous work Origen laid the foundations of textual criticism.

There was no end to his work: his commentaries are as exhaustive as his work of criticism and emendation. He regarded the whole of the Old Testament as a continual prophecy of Christ, a foreshadowing of the New Testament. It was as though the Old Testament was a strangely fashioned glass, and by peering through it the New Testament acquired increased depth and meaning. All history vanishes; time stands still; there is only Christ, that short space of thirty years which seems to leap out of history altogether. Adam is Christ prefigured; the words of the Psalms are spoken by Christ through the mouth of David; and Solomon utters prophecies. Moses and the Prophets become aspects of Christ, for did not Christ say that Moses spoke of Him, and did not the Prophets prophecy His coming and His going? The Cross of Christ is dipped in the waters of Marah; the long journey from Egypt of the tribes of the Israelites prefigures the long journeys of Christ, or of the human soul in its search for Christ. Allegory, hypothesis, prophecy, symbolism—all have their place in Origen's interpretation. He sees the relationship between the Old and the New Testaments in so many dimensions that the mind is bewildered; and always high above the complex and strenuous drama which Origen unfolds, there is the higher drama: for all the events of earth are mirrored in Heaven, and Origen strains to interpret heavenly events in human words. So he says that Christ's blood was not only shed on earth at Jerusalem "for sin" (*pro peccato*), but also for a gift on the high altar which is in Heaven (*pro munere in superno altari quod est in coelis*). (*Comm. in Philipp* II, 10.) His vision of the heavenly economy is of breath-taking splendor, for he believed that the works of Christ extended wherever there were spiritual and material creatures; all things in the universe are sustained by the grace of Christ, saved and set free from bondage. Wherever there is alienation from God, there is restoration through Christ, who offered Himself to the Father for all things: for rocks, stones, fish, tigers, angels: for the least things, and the greatest: for the best and the worst. There was no end to the charity of His grace.

In his interpretations Origen denies that the whole meaning of any passage in the New Testament is contained in the literal sense. There is depth upon depth of meaning in every statement made by Christ. Sometimes he seems to limit himself to three interpretations: a phrase uttered by Christ is seen first as an event in the history of the Jews, then as an event of the Church, finally as an event of the Kingdom— those three methods of interpretation which St. Ambrose later explained as Shadow, Image and Truth. But there were shadows within shadows, images within images, truths concealed in truths. And sometimes, but very rarely, and then only at the moments of majestic crisis, all these methods fade: there is only one unique truth, and all the images and shadows have fled away. Such a moment occurs on the Mountain of the Transfiguration, when the apostles are bathed in the light of glory:

And then the Word touched them, and as they lifted their eyes they saw Jesus standing alone, and there was no one else. And Moses (the Law) and Elijah (Prophecy) were become one with Jesus (Gospel). And everything had changed: they were not three, but one single Being standing alone.

[*Comm. in Matt.* XII, 43]

Origen saw the Scriptures as the unique Word of God. Within the Scriptures lay the truth, and beyond the Scriptures there was no truth to be found. The Scriptures are an inexhaustible well, and all its waters, even those which seem to have a bitter taste, possess a divine sweetness.

In the first, and perhaps the most brilliant of his commentaries, written at the same time that he composed *De Principiis,* he wrote:

The Word of God [*Logos*], which was in the beginning with God, is not a vast multiplicity of words, and is never spoken in the plural [*logoi*]. It is a word formed of many strands, but each one is a part of the whole, being part of the Word. . . . And beyond this Word, even when one speaks of truth, there is no truth, no unity, no harmony. . . .

What then is this unique Book? Is it not the Book which was seen by John [of Patmos], the sealed Book which was written within and without, a Book which no one could read, and only the Lion of the tribe of Judah, who sprang from David, could open the seals? For Jesus opens the Book and no one can close it; He closes it, and no one can open it. And all of the Scriptures are indicated by this Book, which is "written without," because of its obvious meaning, and "written within," because of its concealed spiritual meaning.

[*Comm. in Joann.* V, 5-6]

There was therefore no greater task than a complete understanding of the book with the seven seals. "Once the book is understood," he wrote, "then everything else is made suddenly clear." But one needed infinite patience, infinite agility, in order to understand the book clearly; and having completely understood it, a man would be like God, for all the secrets would be unfolded to him. In one lifetime one could only hope to penetrate a few of the secrets. Of his own work Origen said that it was no more than an exercise in spiritual intelligence —*intelligentiae spiritalis exercitia.* Sometimes, as he admits, he can do more than follow his intuitions, without any assurance that they are correct. Occasionally he will give three or four entirely different interpretations. He had a habit of throwing out ideas as a kind of spiritual bait, hoping perhaps that someone else might improve on them, and always with humility and grace. So in his *Commentary on the Gospel according to St. John,* he will say with assurance that Christ is not, like God, entirely free from darkness, since He bore our sins; but he is altogether more tentative when he suggests, following the apocryphal *Prayer of Joseph,* that perhaps John the Baptist was an angel disguised as a man.

Here are two short examples of his method from his homilies on *The Song of Solomon*:

The voice of my beloved! behold he cometh leaping from the mountains, skipping upon the hills.[1]

Here the Church is speaking, exhorting the young women to prepare themselves for the coming of the Bridegroom should he decide to come and speak with them. While she is still speaking he arrives, and she points to him and says: "Behold he cometh leaping from the mountains." And here we must understand the soul of the Bride, now blessed and perfect. She sees and contemplates so quickly the coming of the Word, she knows that wisdom and love are come for her, and she says to those who do not see: "Behold he cometh!" And let us pray that we too may say: "Behold he cometh!" And if I have in any way correctly interpreted the words of God, then let me say in my fashion: "Behold he cometh!" Where does he come from? Not from the valleys or from lowly places. "Leaping from the mountains, skipping upon the hills." If you are a mountain, the Word of God will leap upon you, but if you are no more than a hill, not yet a mountain, then he will skip over you. How beautiful and appropriate are these words! He leaps upon the mountains because they are the highest, and skips over the valleys because they are the lowest. He does not skip over the mountains, he does not leap upon the hills.

My beloved is like a gazelle or a young hart on the mountains of Bethel.

These two animals are frequently mentioned in the Scriptures, and what is still more to the point, they are frequently mentioned together. So it is said: "Thou shalt eat of the gazelle and the young hart." These animals are indeed very closely related and are to be seen together. The gazelle has the piercing eye, the young hart kills snakes. The gazelle is so named by reason of its intense sharpness of vision; the hart is the perpetual enemy and hunter-down of serpents: the breath of its nostrils causes them to come from their holes and with delight it extracts their poison. And perhaps my Saviour is the gazelle according to the contemplation of God, and like a young hart in his works. He kills serpents, strangles powerful enemies, and that is why I say of him: "Thou hast broken the heads of dragons on the waters."

[*Hom. in Cant.* II, 10, 11]

[1] Origen follows the Septuagint Version, which sometimes differs considerably from the King James Version.

Origen's method of interpretation is essentially poetic; his passages of commentary read like diffused and scholarly verses, and perhaps this was deliberate. These commentaries were written in such a form that long passages of them could be remembered; and since with a few exceptions they have come down to us only in Latin translations, one can only guess at the passion of the original.

Not all the days of his long life were spent in scholarship; he was a man who was always violently liked or disliked. The story is told that the mob of Alexandria once seized him, clothed him in the dress of a priest of Serapis, gave him the tonsure and placed him on the steps of the great temple, ordering him to perform the office of a priest of Serapis by distributing palm branches to the worshipers. Origen did as he was ordered, and as he placed the palms in the hands of the people and blessed them, he cried out: "Come and receive the palms, not of idols, but of Jesus Christ!" At another time he was invited by Julia Mammaea, the mother of the Emperor Alexander Severus, to visit her in Antioch. "She was a deeply religious woman, if ever there was one," wrote Eusebius in his *Ecclesiastical History,* "and she set great store on seeing him and testing his understanding of divine things, which was the wonder of all." Origen was provided with a military escort, and shown the honors due to a high ecclesiastical official. "And when he had stayed with her for some time, and shown her many things which were for the glory of the Lord and the excellence of the divine teaching, he hastened back to his accustomed duties" (Eusebius, *Eccl. Hist.* VI, 21). In 215 he visited Rome, "desiring to see the most ancient church of the Romans," but we know little of his travels in Italy, and he seems to have returned to Alexandria the same year, for we hear of him again during the massacres which broke out in Alexandria, when the Emperor Caracalla, the most bloodthirsty of the Roman emperors, stood on the steps of the Serapeum and gave the signal for the massacre of the Alexandrian youths who had been ordered to stand reverently and expectantly outside the walls. Caracalla had murdered his brother Geta. The keen-witted Alexandrian youths had composed taunting songs on the murder, and Caracalla was determined upon revenge. The Emperor gave his soldiers license to murder all the youths, and as many other Alexandrians as they pleased. The massacre went on for two weeks, with occasional days spent in digging trenches for the dead; then abruptly Caracalla marched north to Antioch, the base for the wars against the Persians.

Origen escaped from Alexandria during the massacres, and hid in

Caesarea in Palestine. He was still a layman. Theoctistus, Bishop of Caesarea, and Alexander, Bishop of Jerusalem who had long ago decided that Origen's virtues should be rewarded, suggested that he should accept high ecclesiastical honors from them. Origen refused, but when they asked him to deliver public lectures on the Scriptures, he accepted willingly. Demetrius, Pope of Alexandria,[2] heard about the public lectures and wrote angrily to the Palestinian bishops, warning them that Origen was a layman, the head of a catechistical school and therefore in no position to act as a preacher. He ordered that Origen should remain silent in public and return home. Origen obeyed. He had no alternative. His life, his books, his school, were all in Alexandria, and he possessed a deep respect for high officers of the Church. So he returned to the life of poverty and scholarship, which left him, as he complained, no time for supper or exercise or sleep: only the endless tasks of exegesis and commentary stretching to infinity. Suddenly the labor was lifted. Ambrosius, a rich Christian, offered help. He no longer had to copy out his manuscripts by hand. Ambrosius gave him seven shorthand writers, and as many copyists, as well as girls who were skilled in writing to dictation. The stenographers, writing in rotation, attended his lectures and helped him in his study. For nearly ten years Origen lived quietly in his school in Alexandria. It was the most fecund period of his life. Commentary followed commentary. Already his works formed a vast library.

He was only forty-three, famous and still young, with many years of work ahead of him, when he left Alexandria, intending to make a prolonged journey through Greece. On the way he stayed at his beloved Caesarea, and here once more the question of his ordination was discussed by Theoctistus and Alexander. This time Origen consented, perhaps believing that to refuse consent would be regarded as a mark of pride. Shortly after being ordained, he went on to Athens and Ephesus. When he returned to Alexandria in 231 the storm broke.

Demetrius seems to have been one of those bishops who cannot tolerate the brilliance of their subordinates. A synod of bishops was convened: Origen was forbidden to preach in Alexandria, but allowed to retain his priesthood. Demetrius thereupon decided to summon a second synod. This time Demetrius reminded them that Origen had mutilated himself, and this in itself was cause enough to expel him

---

[2] The title of *Papa,* or Pope, was regularly given to the Bishops of Alexandria. (Eusebius, *Eccl. Hist.* VII, 7, 4.)

from the Church. He was deprived of his priesthood, and Jerome says all the bishops endorsed the attack on Origen except the Bishops of Palestine, Arabia, Achaia and Phoenicia. With a heavy heart Origen abandoned Alexandria forever and made his way, accompanied by the faithful Ambrosius and perhaps with a small following of copyists and stenographers, to Caesarea. Here, for the next twenty-two years, except for brief visits and journeys abroad, he remained.

As always pupils flocked to him. Gregory Thaumaturgus, who stayed with Origen for five years in Caesarea, spoke of "a certain sweet grace and persuasiveness in him, along with a strange power of constraint." Origen was the liberal theologian, determined to let his pupils weigh the evidence for themselves: the whole circle of knowledge was open to them, nothing was forbidden. On Gregory the impact was sudden and all-pervading:

It was as if a spark fell into my soul, and caught fire, and blazed up, such was my love for the Holy Word and for this man, its friend and advocate. Stung by this desire, I forgot all that seemed at one time close to me, my previous studies, my beloved jurisprudence, my country, my relatives, my present mission, the object of my travels.

[Gregory Thaumat., *Panegyric*, 6]

From all over the Near East people came to the catechistical school in Caesarea to ask questions, to discuss the meaning of texts, to sit quietly at his feet. Perhaps it was at this time that the remarkable dialogue with Heracleides took place.

We would have known nothing about this dialogue if some British officers, clearing out a cave of rubbish at Tura, south of Cairo, in 1941, had not discovered the papyrus containing the dialogue. A certain Dionysius asks Origen: "Is the soul the blood?" It was not an absurd question: Jewish commentators had for many centuries debated the meaning of the text in *Leviticus* 17:11. "The soul of all flesh is blood." The discussion is taken up by Origen and Heracleides. Origen agrees that the text is a terribly distressing one, and if we take it literally, we are faced with extraordinary complications. Obviously, it must not be taken literally. What then is meant by blood? He speaks of the mysteries contained in the text: he is afraid that if he expounds the mysteries, he will be accused of throwing pearls before swine and holy things before dogs. It is an odd sentence, and it is possible that the dialogue has been amended by Origen's enemies, for he rarely speaks so emphatically of his knowledge of mysteries. Then he goes on to say that in each of us there are two men, the inner and the outer, and he suggests that the blood is the spiritual blood proper to the inner man. There is a text in *Ecclesiastes*: "The wise man has his eyes in his head." "What is the meaning of this?" Origen asks, and he suggests that the message is abundantly clear, for Christ is the head of a man, and he hints that "the soul of all flesh is Christ." The whole dialogue is curiously strained, but there are passages in it which ring authoritatively: Origen straining, flexing his intellectual muscles, determined somehow to shake meaning from an impossible text.

He did not spend all his time at the school. He continued to collate the texts of the *Hexapla*. The great bundles of manuscript were kept in the house of a certain Juliana, who attended to Origen's needs. On Wednesdays and Fridays, sometimes every day, he expounded the Bible to public congregations. These discourses would be taken down in shorthand and later revised by him. And sometimes, like modern preachers, he complained of the inattentiveness of his audience, and of the women gossiping together in the back of the hall. Once he made a journey to Jericho, where he found in an earthen jar in a cave an anonymous Greek version of the Bible, later to be added to the *Hexapla*. But he traveled little. He was content with Caesarea, a seaport, the residence of the Procurator, a town bustling with intellectual activity. There the common language was Greek, and he was at home.

To this period belongs one of the best and simplest of his works: the treatise on Prayer. Erasmus said of Origen that his spirit was everywhere aflame, a simple flame, with no raising of the voice, no rhetorical flourishes; and if there was strain, that was only the occasional crackling of the flames as they bit into a knot in the wood. He wrote once that all of Creation was no more than the interval between the clashing of the two cymbals represented by the Old and New Testaments. Those vast images were his commonplaces, but the treatise on Prayer is curiously quiet. It is grave, earnest and deliberate. He does not give the impression, as so often, of reaching out into unknown territory. The work is addressed to Ambrosius, and consists largely of a closely woven pattern of quotations from the Scriptures. Here and there he will say wise and simple things. Only occasionally do we hear the great Beethoven chords of Origen at his superb, triumphant best.

In the treatise Origen is concerned to approach prayer in the light of the Scriptures, employing his chosen texts as steppingstones. He believed that men should pray standing, with eyes and hands uplifted, the body turned toward the East, where the sun of truth rises. All the life of man on earth is temptation; therefore Jesus, speaking through the lips of the Bridegroom in the *Song of Songs,* says: "Rise up, my love, my fair one, and come away." Men should make haste to pray, and if possible pray without ceasing:

Therefore I believe the words of saints when praying are charged with great power, especially when they pray with the spirit and the understanding. This power is like a light issuing from the mind of him who is praying; and leaping from his lips such prayers by the grace of God utterly destroy the intellectual poison deriving from evil sources in the minds of those who neglect prayer and ignore the injunction: "Pray without ceasing."

[*De precatione,* XII, 1]

In a later age this "light issuing from the mind" was to become elaborated into the Light of the Transfiguration. Origen does no more than hint at the power of divine illumination which flows from prayer. He interprets the words "Pray without ceasing" as the whole life of a saint lived as "one great continual prayer." In the same way he takes the words of the Lord's Prayer and examines them closely, never attempting to strain the meaning. Gregory of Nyssa was later to interpret "Give us this day our daily bread" in the simplest possible terms. For him it meant bread, which will keep the body alive. Characteristically Origen interprets it as the bread of the angels, the supersubstantial bread which falls like manna from Heaven. "He who receives the supersubstantial bread is made strong in heart and becomes a son of God" (*De prec.* XXVII, 12). And when he discusses the text: "Forgive us our debts, as we also forgive our debtors," he remembers that we have also debts toward ourselves; we must not waste the substance of our bodies in idle pleasures; we owe it to our souls to keep our minds keen and razor-sharp, for we are "the work and image of God, and so we are under a debt to preserve a certain disposition toward Him with our whole heart, and with our whole strength, and with our whole mind" (*De prec.* XXVIII, 3). But he does not insist on this strenuous Christian athleticism. Prayer is so many things they are almost past counting: a pathway through the snares of the world, a road to God, an act of pure worship. The angels listen to prayers and attend men's needs, though the prayers are directed to Jesus. One should pray chiefly for wisdom and beauty of the soul, not for the shadows, not for prosperity or physical beauty or for wisdom in the ways of the world:

> For when the human soul has perceived, even though in bondage to the body, the armies of angels and the captains of the forces of the Lord—the archangels, thrones, dominations, principalities and superheavenly powers—and when he understands that he can be honored by the Lord as they are, shall he not, even though weaker than a shadow, despise as utterly meaningless all those things that are wondered at by fools? And even should he receive those things, will he not despise them, rather than lose his right to enter the true principality and the divine power? Therefore we must pray for the truly great and heavenly things, and leave to God what is concerned with the shadows which accompany the essential gifts.
>
> [De prec. XVII, 2]

Then it is as though we can hear across the centuries the precise accents of Origen, but the great organ notes become no more than a quiet utterance thereafter.

Origen's calm labors were interrupted in 235 by the persecutions which broke out in the reign of the Emperor Maximin Thrax, the eight-foot tall Thracian peasant who rose to the purple and immediately seized all the treasuries of the Empire. He could draw a loaded wagon, break a horse's leg with a kick, crumble rocks in his hands. He seems to have decided upon a persecution of the Christians for no other reason than that he liked the sight of flowing blood. Origen escaped from Caesarea to the mountains of Cappadocia, but Ambrosius was thrown into prison and many of Origen's friends were in danger of suffering martyrdom. To these friends, and especially to Ambrosius, Origen addressed his treatise On Martyrdom.

It is a short work of great vigor and immense assurance. He is like someone standing at the elbow of Ambrosius, saying: "The time has come. Put away all other thoughts. There is need for martyrdom." Origen regarded martyrdom as the most holy profession of the Christian. By martyrdom the Christian showed with his whole soul the desire to be united with God. It was best to die righteously, best to depart from life with the single purpose of entering the Kingdom of Heaven: all other purposes were meaningless in comparison with this. He believed the martyrs received a special and greater fullness of beatitude than any holy men; they were the elect of God, sitting by

God's side on the Throne of Judgment, and therefore themselves beyond judgment; and their blood had the power to obtain remission of sins for others. All through the book there breathes the quiet assurance in the supreme validity of the martyr:

> God once said to Abraham: "Go forth out of thy country." Soon perhaps we shall hear it said to us: "Go forth out of every country." It would be well if we were to obey, and come to see in the heavens the place which is known as "the kingdom of the heavens."
>
> [*De Martyrio,* 5]

Origen asks what greater joy there can be than the act of martyrdom? A great multitude is assembled to watch the last hours of the martyr. He stands in the circus like an athlete stripped for the battle against the powers of unrighteousness; and the world watches breathlessly, and not only the world—the angels are present to the left and to the right, and God, too, is present. If the martyr dies, the angels rejoice; if he becomes an apostate, the demons gloat. So he recites stories of the martyrs from the *Second Book of Maccabees,* and exhorts Ambrosius against apostasy, quoting the *Psalms*: "I will take the chalice of salvation, and I will call upon the name of the Lord." It is clear to Origen that "the chalice of salvation" means martyrdom; but then what should one say of the words of Jesus: "O my Father, if it be possible, let this chalice pass from me." If Jesus were afraid, how can a man be expected to remain steadfast forever?

Origen answers that at the Last Supper and in the Garden of Gethsemane Jesus was not speaking of His own martyrdom; He spoke of "this" chalice, meaning His present suffering, not the suffering on the Cross, or perhaps He was asking for a more severe martyrdom which would have the effect of doing still greater good among men. That martyrdom was in itself the highest gift a man could make to God seemed to him unanswerable. A quiet and holy death was strangely "fruitless"; but the special death of a martyr was the most fruitful of blessings:

> And let each of us remember how many times we have been in danger of an ordinary death, and then let us ask ourselves whether we have not been preserved for something better—for the baptism in blood which washes away our sins and allows us to take our place at the heavenly altar together with all the companions of our warfare.
>
> [*De Martyrio,* 39]

At times Origen seems to be deeply afraid that Ambrosius will apostatize. The haunting fear catches him by the throat; again and again he inveighs against the apostates. God is a jealous God. He is like the bridegroom who, though wise, pretends to be jealous of any other man's affections for the bride. God will not allow a man to turn away. Have faith, have courage, above all prepare yourselves for the blessedness of martyrdom. "We are the sons of a patient God, the brothers of a patient Christ, let us show ourselves patient in all that befalls us" (*De Mart.* 43). And the best that can befall us is a martyr's death.

Origen wrote these words from the safety of Cappadocia, but no one ever doubted his own thirst for martyrdom. He hungered and thirsted for that glory, as few men have hungered and thirsted for it; and he knew that he was perfectly prepared to suffer martyrdom for the glory of God.

The persecutions came to an end. Ambrosius had not died to decorate an emperor's arena. Origen returned to the safe harborage of Caesarea, and more commentaries poured from his pen. He wrote a commentary on *Matthew,* and at the urging of Ambrosius, about 248 he wrote his great defense of the Christian position called *Contra Celsum,* in reply to a brilliant pamphlet by a Greek philosopher called Celsus. It is a masterly work, but it defies the modern reader; and sometimes the huge w~·ght of it seems to have made Origen himself tremble. He undertook the work unwillingly. He was not the master of dialectics. Celsus had made a comprehensive attack on Christianity; Origen provided a comprehensive—too comprehensive defense. Celsus had pointed wittily to the inconsistencies of Christian doctrine; Origen must show that there really were no inconsistencies, that everything was logical, ordered, comprehensible. And he is so determined to demonstrate the logic, order and simplicity of Christian doctrine that he examines every word written by Celsus and demonstrates that Celsus is lacking in just those qualities which he has accused the Christians of lacking. The style is sonorous with the lawyer's pleas, and grave like a judge's summing up; and though there are flashes of the real Origen, there are long deserts where he fades from sight. *Contra Celsum* is a sledge hammer against a wasp.

Origen's heart was in his commentaries. He continued to write to the end. He did not die a martyr, as he desired, but he was so close to martyrdom that he must have felt the breath of it on his face. In 249 the Emperor Decius announced a new persecution of Christians. The persecution was directed chiefly at the spiritual leaders of the faith. Among these were the leaders of the schools. Origen was arrested, thrown into irons and tortured on the rack. According to the church historian Eusebius, his feet "were stretched four spaces." He was threatened with death by fire, and an iron chain was fastened round his neck. It was known that he desired to die a martyr's death, but this honor was refused him; repeatedly he was brought to the brink of death, and then revived.

When Decius died in a swamp, the persecutions abated. Origen was released from prison, to spend the remaining years of his life in Tyre, where he had been arrested and tortured. Worn out by sufferings, he died there A.D. 253 at the age of sixty-nine. The Tyrians refused to allow his body to be sent to Caesarea: they buried him behind the high altar of their Church of the Holy Sepulcher and marked the place with an inscription on a marble column adorned with gold and jewels. To this same church there was brought nearly a thousand years later the body of the Emperor Frederick Barbarossa, who had sought to revive the splendors of the Roman Empire. The wall of the original church has long since crumbled. Today a man may walk in the streets of Tyre and gather some earth in his hands which may, for all he knows, contain the dust of two emperors.

Athanasius

There are times when the dark and heavy syllables of his name fill us with dread. In the history of the early Church no one was ever so implacable, so urgent in his demands upon himself or so derisive of his enemies. There was something in him of the temper of the modern dogmatic revolutionary: nothing stopped him. The Emperor Julian called him "hardly a man, only a little manikin." Gregory Nazianzen said he was "angelic in appearance, and still more angelic in mind." In a sense both were speaking the truth. The small and dauntless man who saved the Church from a profound heresy, staying the disease almost singlehanded, was as astonishing in his appearance as he was astonishing in his courage. He was so small that his enemies called him a dwarf. He had a hook nose, a small mouth, a short reddish beard which turned up at the ends in the Egyptian fashion, and his skin was blackish. His eyes were very small, and he walked with a slight stoop, though gracefully, as befitted a prince of the Church. He was less than thirty when he was made Pope of Alexandria, and he seems never to have thought of himself as a human being dedicated to human ends: he was a hammer wielded by God against heresy.

There were other Fathers of the Eastern Church who wrote more profoundly or more beautifully, but none wrote with such a sense of authority or were so little plagued with doubts. Athanasius wrote directly, always cutting to the heart of a problem. He had no gift of style. He wrote Greek as though those flowing syllables were lead pellets, and though sometimes tenderness would break through it does so only occasionally, and then against the grain. His wit was mordant. He did not often employ the weapon of sarcasm, but when he did, no one ever forgot it. When Arius, his great enemy, died, he chuckled with glee and wrote off a letter to Serapion giving all the details of Arius' death, how the heretic had talked wildly in church and was suddenly compelled by a necessity of nature to withdraw to a privy, where "he fell headlong . . . dying as he lay there." As for the Arians, Athanasius hated them with too great a fury to give them their proper names. He called them dogs, lions, hares, chameleons, hydras, eels, cuttlefish, gnats and beetles, and he was always resourceful in making them appear ridiculous. Once Gregory Nazianzen said of Athanasius that he combined in himself "all the attributes of the heathens." Gregory did not mean this unkindly. He meant that the founder of orthodoxy possessed heroic strength and a wild appetite for experience. At least twice Athanasius was threatened with death, and he was five times exiled. He was perfectly capable of riding up to an emperor and holding the emperor's horse by the bridle while he argued a thesis. In the end he had the supreme joy of outliving his enemies and four of the great emperors who had stood in his path, and he must have known as he lay dying that he had preserved the Church. Hooker spoke of "the long tragedy" of his life, but this was only part of the truth. It was the long triumph of one man against the world—*Athanasius contra mundum.*

We know very little about his origins, and nothing at all about his family. He seems to have been born of Egyptian parents about A.D. 293, but it is possible there was some African blood in him, for more than one commentator refers to the unusual darkness of his skin. His name was Greek, but innumerable Egyptians bore Greek names. There is some evidence for believing that he was born in some remote desert village in Nitria—that long stretch of barren sand fifty miles south of Alexandria, where the greatest of the hermit saints lived in an abandoned fort, and he may have been one of the children allowed to attend upon St. Antony. It is almost certain that he was born in a place which escaped the persecutions of Diocletian, for he never refers to these violent persecutions, which began suddenly in 303 and came to an end only in 311, with the admission by the Emperor Galerius that the imperial policy toward the Christians had been a total failure. Perhaps— for he hints at it—he spent some weeks with Antony. When Athanasius came to write the life of Antony, he says: "I saw the saint often and poured water on his hands." And that strange book, which differs so violently in style from anything else written by Athanasius, seems to have been written with childlike worship and youthful enthusiasm which can only be explained by an early attachment to Antony. He loved Antony more than he loved any other man.

We see Athanasius clearly and for the first time in a story written many years afterward. The story may be a legend, but it is a legend which bears the mark of truth. According to the story, Pope Alexander of Alexandria was celebrating the birthday of his predecessor, martyred during the Diocletian persecution. In his palace overlooking the sea, the Pope was waiting for his clergy to attend a banquet. For some reason the clergy were delayed, or perhaps Alexander was simply idling his time away. There were some children playing on the seashore. There was nothing unusual in the fact that they were playing, but he was struck by their decorous movements, the slow grace of their processional journeys into the water. He could make nothing of it, and sent one of his prelates to discover what they were doing, and then it occurred to him that they were imitating some of the rites of the church. The prelate returned to the palace with the children. Their clothes were wet through. The Pope studied them. Alarmed, he accused them of having performed some kind of religious ceremony. At first the children denied it, but later they admitted they had elected young Athanasius their bishop and they were obeying his commands according to the prescribed ritual. "And what ritual is that?" the Pope asked, whereupon Athanasius solemnly described the ritual of baptism in all its complex details, explaining that all the necessary questions and addresses had been followed. The Pope was pleased. Throughout the Eastern Church, there was reverence for children. He smiled, blessed them, poured the consecrating oil of confirmation upon their heads, so that the baptism became valid, and later summoned the parents of the children, explained what had happened and announced that it was his desire that the children who had acted as presbyters should enter the church. As for Athanasius, the Pope determined upon firmer measures. He adopted the boy, who henceforth lived with him "as a son with a father." Within a few years Athanasius became the papal secretary, and it was with the blessing of Alexander that Athanasius wrote in 318, when he was still under twenty, the two works which contain in embryo the complete message he was to deliver to the world. These were *An Oration against the Heathen* and *Concerning the Incarnation of the Word of God.*

They are short, pithy works, filled with the evidence of a violent and controlled imagination. *An Oration against the Heathen* is a diatribe against paganism. He laughs paganism to scorn. The pagan gods are lewd, immoral, absurd, unworthy of worship, no better than dung beetles. Imagine that people have worshiped Zeus, who spends his days guzzling at the golden tables of heaven! And those goddesses, and the horrible bastard children they produce! What an absurd demonic world those ancient Greeks inhabited! How pitiable that they were lacking in the revealed truth! Out of the lips of gods made of clay— Better say that the gods flowered out of their diseased imaginations, for clay is too good for them, and what is still worse, they borrowed from the diseased imaginations of other nations, from the Egyptians and the Persians, whose gods protected them not at all when their empires were endangered. Athanasius plays the labored game to the end; we are aware of the sardonic light in his eyes. The fruits of paganism are evil; he has almost no difficulty in proving the case. Apollo and Aphrodite come crashing from their pedestals. The gilt flakes away, the bronze turns to verdigris, inside they are stuffed with straw. As for the arguments of those who permit themselves the luxury of defending paganism: well, let us hear them, Athanasius says, and convicts them of error out of their own mouths. It is an impressive spectacle, the young judge drawing up a bill of particulars and pronouncing Christian judgment, a one-sided judgment, for whatever virtues the gods possessed are conveniently forgotten. He is so eager to attack falsehood he only half convinces, but we are made aware of the muscular strength of his mind as he sweeps the old gods away to make room for Christ.

In *Concerning the Incarnation* Athanasius comes face to face with the central mystery of Christianity, and here he walks with the same extraordinary sure-footedness, but his approach is gentler and there is no scorn in his voice for those who might disagree with him, for it is inconceivable to him that there could be any disagreement. He speaks as one to whom the mystery has been revealed. Quietly, almost patiently, he takes the whole universe under advisement, beginning with the Creation, then embracing the creation of man and all man's evil fruits redeemed by the incarnate Christ. The world has been changed past any reckoning by the presence of the risen Christ. Then why do the Greeks and the Jews hold back? Surely they can see that all Judaism moves toward this end: the atoning death of Christ and the Resurrection. And surely the Greeks are aware that their own philosophical principles leave room for an incarnation. What is the mystery but the mystery of death despised by the disciples and by all Christians, who may now trample on death "as on something dead." Beyond the wastes of heathenism, beyond the barren places of philosophy, beyond the despairing cries of the Jews, and their plaintive demand for the coming of the Messiah, comes the risen Christ Himself; and shall any man not see the Crucifixion, then it is his fault alone, for the fact is so real that it blinds the eyes. And so he dwells upon the Crucifixion at length, describing that highest moment with a kind of rapture which we shall not see often in his work, though we are aware that the Incarnation was the single force which moved his inmost thoughts. Here certainties abound. Here there is no place for doubts. Why, he asks, did Christ remain exactly three days in the tomb? Why did He not die in bed? Why did He die so accursed a death, raised high above the eyes of the onlookers? To all these questions Athanasius provides certain answers. *An Oration against the Heathen* is faintly ludicrous. *Concerning the Incarnation* is a masterpiece.

It begins calmly with the Creation and the innocent children in the Garden who lived in the blessing of the God who had promised His children they should be as gods, but they transgressed, and so "they will die like men, and fall as one of the princes." By their transgression, sin entered the world. Their sins grew insatiable. They murdered, worshiped idols, practiced sodomy, surrendered to magic arts. Then "death gained a legal hold on men, and the law which proclaimed the ruin of man ended only with the coming of Christ into the body of a Virgin." So he writes with grave dignity and smoldering passion, his arguments close-packed, of how Christ renewed the image of man and accomplished the two works of love: He renewed men by destroying death and made Himself known as the King and Ruler of the universe. And this man who walked among us was God, with power over all things. He was a child in the womb, a carpenter, a crucified felon, and at the same time He was God, immortal, blazing with divine energy. While He walked the roads of Palestine, He was still "present in all things by His own power, giving order to all things, and over all and in all revealing His own providence, and giving life to each thing and all things, quickening the whole universe." And at the same time He was truly man, "having a body in truth, and not in seeming," in order that He might die and accomplish the death of all things in His own body. "For there was need of death, and death must needs be suffered on behalf of all, that the debt owing from all might be paid."

Then Athanasius asks why it was necessary that He should be crucified. Could He not simply have died honorably "in a corner" or in bed or somewhere in the desert? No, answers Athanasius: to die in bed would be to die agreeably of a human weakness, and how could He who had healed so many die of a lingering sickness? God cannot inflict death on Himself; He must die at the hands of men. If He had died in bed or in some desert place, and then raised Himself and announced that He had come from the dead, what then? Who would believe Him? Who would trust the witnesses of His death? And then again, why did

He not suffer a glorious death? Athanasius answers that such a death would have given grounds for suspicion. Men would think He was not powerful against all death, only against the special death, the heroic death; and so He did not suffer beheading like John, nor was He sawn asunder like Isaiah. He died the accursed death which was proper for Him, for it was written: "Cursed be He that hangeth on a tree." Only death by crucifixion was appropriate to God:

> For thus being lifted up, He cleared the air of the malignity both of the devil and of demons of all kinds, as He says: "I beheld Satan as lightning fall from heaven," and made a new opening of the way up into heaven, as he says once more: "Lift up your gates, O ye princes, and be ye lift up, ye everlasting doors." For it was the Word himself who needed an opening of the gates, being Lord of all; nor were any of His works closed to their maker; but it was the human race He carried up with His own body.
>
> [*De Incarnatione*, 25]

From the Crucifixion Athanasius turns to the Entombment, passionately convinced that everything was ordered, planned, divinely reasonable:

> He suffered not the temple of His body to remain long in the grave, but having merely shown it to be dead, by the contact of death with it, He raised it up on the third day, impassible and incorruptible, victorious and triumphant over death. He could of course have raised His body and shown it to be alive immediately after His death, but the all-wise Saviour did not do this, lest some should deny that He had really and completely died. He waited one whole day to show that His body was truly dead, and then on the third day showed it incorruptible to all. The interval was no longer, lest people should have forgotten about it and grown doubtful whether it were in truth the same body. No, while the affair was ringing in their ears and their eyes were still straining and their minds were still in turmoil, and while those who had put Him to death were still present, and themselves witnessing to the fact of it, the Son of God after three days showed His once-dead body immortal and incorruptible; and so it was made manifest to all that it was not from any natural weakness of the Word which dwelt within the body that He died, but in order that in it death by the Saviour's power might be destroyed.   [*De Incarn.* 26]

To this argument Athanasius perpetually returns. He speaks with entire assurance, never allowing the eyes to waver, holding steadfastly to the vision, to the knowledge that here was the central mystery and all other mysteries were as nothing compared with the Incarnation. It occurs to him—or perhaps some heretic suggested—that God could have appeared in some other disguise, in nobler garments. He could have come as sun, moon, star, fire, air. Then why as man? Athanasius answers simply: "He did not come to make a display of glory; He came to heal." And now that He has come, there is peace at last among men. Men no longer war against one another, the soldiers have become husbandmen, and the arms that once held weapons are lifted in prayer.

This short and majestic work breathes a quiet fervor: this knowledge that Christ destroyed death and trampled on it and put an end to its reign forever. Dying, He lived; living, He died; and of all imaginable blessings this was the greatest.

Athanasius had hardly finished the book when he was involved in controversy. Pope Alexander had called a meeting of the presbyters. According to the historian Socrates the aging Pope "with perhaps too philosophical minuteness" began to lecture on the theological mystery of the Holy Trinity. Alexander had been discussing the Father, the Son and the Holy Ghost for some time when he was interrupted by one of the presbyters called Arius, a native of Libya. There is no evidence that Alexander was a profound theologian. He may have bumbled, and it is possible that Arius was justified in accusing Alexander of Sabellianism, a heresy which involved a belief in the unity of God at the expense of the reality of the Trinity. But in combating Alexander, Arius fell into a new heresy, for he announced: "If the Father begat the Son, then He who was begotten had a beginning in existence; and from this it follows there was a time when the Son was not. It follows further that He received substance out of nothing."

Here, at some time in 319, the cry of the Arians—"There was a time when the Son was not"—was first heard. The words were to have an extraordinary influence on the shaping of the Church. They were dynamite, and split the Church in two; and these words, which read in Greek like a line of a song, still echo down the centuries.

Alexander was appalled by the new heresy and knew that desperate measures would be necessary to combat it. Once it is admitted that "there was a time when the Son was not," then a bewildering series of further heresies follows. High as He is, the Son is now infinitely lower than the Father. If the Son of God had no existence before He was born in Bethlehem, then it would be reasonable to say that truth did not exist until then. The words are like a wedge, splitting the monotheism of the Church. Athanasius saw the danger clearly; and he seems to have taken over from Alexander the task of refuting Arius.

We shall never know how Arius appeared when he first confronted Athanasius, for the triumph of Athanasius was complete, and there survives only a scattering of documents written by the defenders of Arianism. Yet there emerges from contemporary records a strangely compelling portrait of the man. He was neither fool nor madman. He had a keen brain, and he may have possessed an overriding ambition, but he did not assume the task of opposing Pope Alexander lightly. He was very tall, very thin and very ascetic in appearance. He was about sixty-three when he first raised his voice against the Pope. He suffered from a curious nervous ailment, which sometimes caused a spasm to pass through his body, and he had a way of contorting and twisting himself which is not unusual among tall men with nervous dispositions. The heavy face, with the downcast brow, the firm chin and the tangled hair which fell to his shoulders, would have been handsome but for the deadly pallor of his cheeks. He had weak eyes. His voice was commanding, and he talked winningly, often smiling. Sometimes his veins throbbed and swelled, and at such times the sweetness of his voice was exchanged for a harsh, almost unrecognizable screaming. Women worshiped him, but his moral life was irreproachable, for no one ever accused him of immorality. He dressed simply in a long cloak with short sleeves and a short scarf, and walked barefoot. He looked— and was—a dedicated ascetic, a man who had turned his back on learning and held firmly to a few simple beliefs. Those beliefs, in the opinion of Pope Alexander and his Archdeacon Athanasius, could destroy the Church to its foundations.

Arius neither asked for mercy, nor gave any. He arrived at his faith logically; no one accused him of being a heretic for the sake of heresy. Like Athanasius, he was caught up in one of those violent disputes which involve the whole ethos of mankind in relation to its destiny, a time not unlike our own. Christ had asked: "Who say ye that I am?" Nearly three hundred years had passed since the Crucifixion, and it was necessary to find a simple answer to Christ's simple question. It was necessary, too, to lay the foundations for an expanding Church. There had been no general councils. A hundred dissenting groups had formed, each with their leaders. The times demanded an orthodoxy. To the credit of Athanasius he saw clearly that the most dangerous of existing heresies was precisely the heresy announced by Arius. It was a very simple heresy. All Arius said was that if the Father begat the Son, then the Son must have had a birth in time and therefore there was a time when the Son of God did not exist. Born in the remote depths of eternity, He had come into existence according to the will of the Heavenly Father, and therefore He was less than the Heavenly Father, though greater than man. Christ was no more than a mediator between man and God. No, answered Alexander and Athanasius; Christ is absolute God.

In our own heretical age the dispute between Athanasius and Arius may appear to be a splitting of hairs, but it was not so at the time. The historian Gibbon was amused by the thought that Christianity almost foundered on the controversy between *homoousios* and *homoiousios,* the fate of mankind hanging on a single iota. But the difference between Christ the Mediator and Christ the God is a very real one, and whether Christ is of the *same* substance or a *like* substance to God the Father is a matter of importance to all Christians, not only theologians. Arianism brought Christ down to earth, making Him at once inferior to the Father, and more popular. Following Arius, a man could believe that Christ was no more than a great, virtuous and superbly godlike hero. Against this conception Alexander and Athanasius rebelled; and they seem to have been perfectly aware that the heresy had the power to destroy the Church as they knew it.

It is possible that Arius was moved by thwarted ambition, for at one time he was seriously considered as a possible Pope. When the see of Alexandria became vacant, Arius had been a significant rival to Alexander. In the end Arius had transferred his vote to Alexander, perhaps expecting and not receiving a reward commensurate with his gifts. Yet, as presbyter of an important church, he was considered among the elders of Alexandria, and his influence was widespread.

Alexander seems to have behaved with patience; there were long private interviews with Arius; special prayers were offered against the emerging heresy. The clergy of Alexandria were assembled to discuss the matter, and most of them signed an urgent letter to Arius, begging him to acknowledge his heresy. Arius refused. Alexander had no alternative but to summon a synod of the bishops of Egypt and Libya and depose Arius and his followers. Thereupon Alexander issued an encyclical letter, stating tersely that the quarrel had gone beyond his powers of healing and the views of Arius were anathema. The heresy, which was to grow into an immense poisonous flower, was still only a bud, and not all its implications were visible at first. In his encyclical letter, Alexander explains some of the consequences of the heresy:

The novelties the Arians have put forward contrary to the Scriptures are these: God was not always a Father, for there was a time when God was not a Father. The Word of God was not always, but originated from things that were not; for God that is has made Him that was not, of that which was not; wherefore there was a time when He was not; for the Son is a creature and a work; neither is He like in essence to the Father; neither is He the true and natural Word of the Father; neither is He His true wisdom; but He is one of the things made and created, and is called the Word and Wisdom by an abuse of terms, since He Himself originated by the proper Word of God, and by the Wisdom that is in God, by which God has made not only all other things, but Him also. Wherefore He is by nature subject to change and variation, as are all rational creatures. And the Word is foreign from the essence of the Father and is alien and separated therefrom. And the Father cannot be described by the Son, for the Word does not know the Father perfectly and accurately, neither can He see Him perfectly. Moreover the Son knows not His own essence as it really is; for He is made for us, that God might create us by Him, as by an instrument; and He would not have existed had not God wished to create us. Accordingly, when someone asked then whether the Word of God can possibly change, as the devil changed, they were not afraid to say that He can; for being something made and created, His nature is subject to change.

The Greek language is admirably suited to such discussions of abstractions, but it is also a language which gives weight and energy to purely human perturbations. It is an ideal language for theological discussion, without the stately grandiloquence of Latin. Alexander's encyclical letter, which shows signs of having been partly written by Athanasius, is a masterly summary of the heresy in its beginnings, but it suffered from one obvious fault. It was close-knit and logical. The people wanted something they could sing, and this Arius provided in abundance. "There was a time when the Son was not" became a catch phrase. There were many other catch phrases, hymns and songs, "to be sung at table, and by sailors, millers and travelers." The people took up the cause of Arius, who withdrew to Palestine and later to Nicomedia, where he was protected by the bishop. Here, in a corner of Asia

Minor not far from Byzantium, Arius continued to taunt the Pope of Alexandria, secure in the knowledge that the people were with him.

Arius possessed other advantages. Eusebius, the Bishop of Nicomedia, had friends at court and was particularly close to Constantia, the sister of the Emperor Constantine. Already the evil which begun in the church of Alexandria was running through all Egypt, Libya, Upper Thebes, Palestine and Asia Minor. Inevitably it came to the ears of the Emperor, who discussed with Hosius, the saintly Bishop of Cordova, what should be done to put an end to the quarrels among the sects. Like James I of England, Constantine regarded unity as "the mother of order," and he was not overmuch concerned with the theological truths at stake: he decided to send Hosius to Nicomedia and Alexandria with a letter written in his own hand, ordering by imperial rescript an end to the quarrel.

The letter—one of the most astonishing letters ever written by an Emperor to priests—has come down to us in a version which shows no signs of being edited. It is hot-tempered, querulous, disjointed and commanding. It is abundantly clear that the Emperor is not quite clear in his own mind what the quarrel is about. He observes that "these questions are the idle cobwebs of contention, spun by curious wits," and he asks: "Who is capable of distinguishing such deep and hidden mysteries?" He recognizes that the contestants are well-armed with arguments, but he can make neither head nor tail of them. The heathen philosophers did better: they quietly agreed to disagree. But these new philosophers are implacable and determined enemies of his peace. Let them make profession of their ignorance of God's ultimate purposes. It was precisely this profession that Arius and Athanasius were unable to make. Almost in despair Constantine concludes his letter:

> Seeing that our great and gracious God, the preserver of all, has given us the common light of His grace, I entreat you that my endeavors may be brought to a prosperous end, and my people be persuaded to embrace peace and concord. Suffer me to spend my days and nights in quiet, and may I have light and cheerfulness instead of tears and groans.

If Constantine had seriously hoped to put an end to the quarrel, he had acted too late. The quarrel was blazing furiously. "In every city," wrote a historian, "bishop was contending against bishop, and the people were contending against one another, like swarms of gnats fighting in the air." Another historian outlined the danger even more acidly: "In former times the Church was attacked by enemies and strangers from without. Today those who are natives of the same country, who dwell under one roof and sit down at table together, fight with their tongues as if with spears." When Hosius returned from his missions in Nicomedia and Alexandria, he was a defeated man, and could only report that he could see no end in sight to the blaze which had begun when an aging Pope addressed his presbyters on the subject of the Holy Trinity.

There had been bloodshed in the streets; Alexandria and Nicomedia were exchanging defiant taunts; and in the Eastern Empire there was danger of civil war. Constantine decided to throw all his influence into the battle. It was the twentieth year of his reign, counting from the day when he received the purple by acclamation in the city of York, and it was a year since his victory over Licinius which made him effectively Emperor of the East and West. He decided to call a General Council, the first of that long series of Church Councils which ended with the Council of Trent. Perhaps it was in deference to his recent victory that he chose as the seat of the Council the small city of Nicaea in Bithynia, a few miles from Nicomedia, for Nicaea means "victory." It was a city of no particular importance, surrounded by chestnut woods, lying on the shores of a lake, with mountains snowcapped even in summer rising above it, a pleasant enough place to assemble a vast retinue of bishops. Today it is a thriving village which preserves a shadow of its former name; it is called Isnik. Of the original Greek city only a few ruined columns remain.

The Council of Nicaea, held in the early summer of 325, was of prodigious importance to the history of Europe. Here for the first time the Church and the Empire met nakedly face to face. There had been councils before like the Council of Jerusalem attended by the apostles, the elders and the brethren of the church, but all previous councils were local, and without imperial authority and sanction. The Council of Nicaea, assembled by order of the first Christian Emperor, who gave it the title of "The Great and Holy Synod," accomplished many things, but not the least important of these things was that Caesar entered into alliance with the servants of Christ.

By Constantine's orders eighteen hundred bishops were invited to attend the Council. Messengers were sent to all parts of the Empire with invitations. Each bishop was allowed to bring two presbyters and three slaves in his retinue; the services of the public post stations were offered free; from all corners of the Empire the bishops descended upon

Nicaea, crowding the public roads. It was not a good time for traveling. The Eastern rivers were flooded with the rains of a late spring, and though the Empire, stretching from Britain to the borders of Persia, was nominally at peace, there were marauding soldiers and bandits along the roads. Fewer than four hundred bishops answered the imperial summons, but their numbers were swelled by a horde of attendant presbyters, deacons, subdeacons and laymen. Most of the ecclesiastics came from the East, for Europe and North Africa had not yet been corrupted by the schism. Six bishops and two presbyters represented the West. They were Hosius of Cordova, Caecilian of Carthage, Nicasius of Dijon, Domnus of Strido in Pannonia, Eustorgius of Milan and Marcus of Calabria. The two Roman presbyters Victor and Vincentius represented the old and dying Sylvester, Bishop of Rome.

From the East came bishops who had suffered persecution. There was Paul, Bishop of Mesopotamian Caesarea, with his hands scorched by flames. Paphnutius of Upper Egypt, famous for the austerity of his life, had had his right eye dug out and the sinews of his left leg were cut during the Diocletian persecution. Bishop Potammon of Heraclea, who had known Antony and lived in the deserts of the Nile, had also lost an eye. There was James, Bishop of Nisibis, who wore a coat of camel's hair, and from the island of Cyprus came Bishop Spyridion, a saintly shepherd who refused to give up tending sheep even when he was elevated to the episcopate, a man who performed miracles to the delight of the Cypriotes and to their further delight thundered against virginity, saying that it was right and proper that married people should enjoy themselves in bed. Then there was John, Bishop of Persia and Metropolitan of India, from the lands outside the Empire, and from the unknown north came Theophilus the Goth, a flaxen-haired Scythian from somewhere in Russia. Altogether perhaps 318 bishops attended; this, at any rate, is the number accepted by the Greek Church which has set aside a special feast day in honor of "the 318 delegates to Nicaea," though it is likely enough that the number was chosen to agree with the 318 armed servants with whom Abraham delivered Lot from captivity.

This motley crowd of bishops represented all the varying traditions of Christianity. There were sharp-featured intellectuals, men of abstruse book learning, capable of splitting hairs by the yard. There were wise old hermits who had spent the previous year clothed in rough goat-hair cloaks, living on roots and leaves. There were men so saintly that it was almost expected of them that they would perform miracles during the Council. There were cantankerous men, and men riddled with heresies, and men who rode to Nicaea in hope of preferment from the hands of the Emperor. There were men who came peacefully, intending only to observe and then report to their flock, and there were other men determined to wage war in the council chamber. Yet in the last instance none of these bishops except Hosius of Cordova was to have any great and final effect upon the outcome of the conference. The two chief antagonists were Arius and Athanasius, one a presbyter, the other a deacon.

Although five separate accounts of the Council have been handed down from eyewitnesses, and there are eight more accounts written by historians of the generation immediately following Nicaea, we do not know exactly where the Council took place, whether it was in a building specially erected for the purpose or whether it was in one of the imperial palaces. Tradition points to a site on the edge of the lake, a vast marble hall enclosed with columns, and perhaps open to the sunlight. In the center of the hall was a throne on which a copy of the Gospels was placed, and at the far end was another throne for the Emperor, carved in wood, richly gilt and set above the level of the unpainted thrones of the bishops. In this hall early in the morning of Ascension Sunday, while a mist was floating on the lake, the bishops awaited for the arrival of the Emperor.

Few of the bishops had set eyes upon this Emperor who had single-handedly welded the East and West into a single empire and shown himself so devout a Christian. They waited expectantly. At last they heard the tramp of armed guards, and then some high officers of the court, themselves converted to Christianity, entered the hall to announce that the Emperor was on his way. The bishops were standing. Soon an avant-courier was seen raising a torch, the signal that the Emperor was about to enter, and then like children these bishops from Syria and Cilicia, Arabia, Palestine, Egypt, Libya, Mesopotamia, Persia, Scythia, and Europe were hushed. Human majesty in the person of Constantinius Victor Augustus Maximus was about to appear before their eyes and in the history of the world only Octavian, who had ruled the Roman Empire during the life of Christ, had ever reigned over so vast an empire.

Constantine wore high-heeled scarlet buskins, a purple silk robe blazing with jewels and gold embroidery, and there were more jewels embedded in his diadem. He was then fifty-one, but looked younger, enormously tall and vigorous, with a high color and a strange glitter in his fierce, lionlike eyes. He wore his hair long, but his beard was trimmed short. He had a thick heavy neck, and a curious way of holding his head back, so that it seemed not to be well-set on the powerful shoulders, and there was about all his movements a remarkable casualness, so that when he strode he gave the impression of someone dancing. Once, as he walked slowly toward his throne, it was observed that the color rushed to the Emperor's cheeks, and the Christian commentators note that he cast his eyes down and his steps faltered when he came close to his throne and waited for a nod from the bishops before he sat down, but it is unlikely that he felt any nervousness in their presence, and if he faltered at all, it may have been that he suddenly observed someone he recognized, or he may have been lost in thought; and though he showed at all times after he became defender of the faith extraordinary respect for the bishops, it is unlikely that he sat down at their nodding.[1] Having marched slowly across the whole length of the hall, Constantine sat in silence for a while, sitting between Pope Alexander of Alexandria and his closest ecclesiastical adviser, Bishop Hosius of Cordova.[2] All eyes were fixed on him. Bishop Eusebius of Caesarea read a speech of welcome in metrical prose, and then chanted a hymn of thanksgiving for the Emperor's victories; then once again there was silence until Constantine collected himself, and speaking in Latin, which was still the language of the Court, in a voice which seemed strangely soft and gentle for a man so commanding, he bade the bishops remember that it was the power of God which had dethroned the tyrants, and worse than any battlefield was a civil war between factions of the church.

"It is my desire," he said, "that you should meet together in a General Council, and so I offer to the King of All my gratitude for this mercy which has come to me above my other mercies—I mean that there has been granted to me the benefit of seeing you assembled together and to know you are resolved to be in common harmony together."

All this was flattery, for the very purpose of the convocation was to resolve a bitter conflict, and Constantine knew well enough from the petitions he had already received from the Bishops that bitterness remained.

[1] Theodoret, who gives a slightly different picture, says that "a low footstool was prepared for the Emperor in the middle of the Assembly, and he did not sit on it until he had asked their permission."

[2] Eusebius of Caesarea twice mentions that he was sitting beside the Emperor; probably he was sitting close by.

He continued: "When I gained my victories over my enemies, I thought nothing remained for me but to give thanks unto God and to rejoice with those who have been delivered by me. But when I learned, contrary to all expectations, that there were divisions among you, then I solemnly considered them, and praying that these discords might also be healed with my assistance, I summoned you here without delay. I rejoice to see you here, yet I should be more pleased to see unity and affection among you. I entreat you, therefore, beloved ministers of God, to remove the causes of dissension among you and to establish peace."

There was now no mistaking the threat behind the words, and as though to make his threat more clear, the Emperor summoned one of his attendants and silently produced the parchment rolls and letters containing complaints and petitions which the bishops had privately sent him. A brazier was set up. The Emperor tossed the petitions into the flames. While they were still burning, he explained that all these petitions would appear again on the Day of Judgment, and then the great Judge of all things would pass judgment on them: for himself he was content to listen to the public deliberations of the bishops and had not even read these bitter messages sent to him.

The conference was now open. At once the Arians and the anti-Arians were at one anothers' throats. Denunciation and angry accusation flew across the hall. Everyone was suddenly arguing. There was a wild waving of arms. "It was like a battle in the dark," the historian Socrates said later. "Hardly anyone seemed to know the grounds on which they calumniated one another." Constantine did his best to restore order. He regarded himself as a moderator, but he also regarded himself as one of the bishops, and took part in the arguments, rebuking those who spoke too angrily and sternly silencing those whose arguments seemed to him fallacious. He had invited Arius to be present, and listened earnestly when Arius explained the nature of his beliefs; and he was not particularly surprised when Arius burst out into a long sustained chant, having set his beliefs to music. These chants and songs were sung by the people, and Arius may have thought the Emperor would listen more keenly to chanting than to a disquisition on the faith:

> *The uncreated God has made the Son*
> *A beginning of things created,*
> *And by adoption has God made the Son*
> *Into an advancement of Himself,*

Yet the Son's substance is
Removed from the substance of the Father:
The Son is not equal to the Father,
Nor does He share the same substance.
God is the all-wise Father,
And the Son is the teacher of His mysteries:
The members of the Holy Trinity
Share unequal glories.

The anti-Arian bishops were appalled, closed their eyes and put their hands over their ears. It was as though in the middle of a critical debate on the future of the world someone interrupted with nonsense rhymes or a series of perplexing and meaningless mathematical equations. Yet the heart of the Arian mystery was in these rhymes sung to a music employed by the Alexandrian dance bands. Arius, gaunt, white-faced, his stringy hair reaching to his shoulders, could repulse any theological argument by simply chanting one of these songs; and when Athanasius, who was chosen to reply, answered with a close-knit argument, of which traces remain in the long apologia he put together under the title *Against the Arians,* there was consternation, for they seemed to be talking in different languages about different things, like two men from different worlds or different universes. We have no record of the exact words spoken by Athanasius at Nicaea, but from his account of "the blasphemous doctrines of Arius" we can guess how he marshaled his forces and demonstrated step by step all the follies that result from the simple statement: "There was a time when the Son was not." Probably Athanasius was standing just behind Pope Alexander, and therefore very close to the Emperor. We know that he attracted the Emperor's attention and that his early fame sprang from his behavior at the Council. But it was not Athanasius who resolved the issue. It seems to have been Hosius who announced that the simplest way of reaching agreement would be to draw up a Creed. The first Creed presented to the Council was written by eighteen of the Arian bishops. Couched in scriptural language, this Creed stated the Arian position so offensively that bedlam broke loose when it was solemnly presented to the attention of the bishops. At this point Eusebius of Caesarea suggested a Creed which he had first heard as a child, an astonishingly beautiful Creed which was to form the basis of the Creed finally adopted. Eusebius was careful to say that he advanced this Creed only because he believed that divine things cannot be fully expressed in human language: it was not perfect: but it was as close to perfection as he ever hoped to reach. This Creed read:

We believe in one God, the Father Almighty, maker of all things visible and invisible,

And in one Lord Jesus Christ, the Word of God, God from God, Light from Light, Life from Life, the only begotten Son, the First-born of every Creature, begotten of the Father before all worlds, through whom also all things were made.

Who for our salvation was made flesh and lived among men, and suffered and rose again on the third day, and ascended to the Father, and shall come again in glory to judge the quick and the dead.

And in the one Holy Ghost.

Believing each of them to be and to have existed, the Father, only the Father, and the Son, only the Son, and the Holy Ghost, only the Holy Ghost.

As also Our Lord, sending forth His own disciples to preach, said, "Go and teach all nations, baptizing them into the name of the Father and of the Son and of the Holy Ghost." Concerning which things we affirm that this is so, and that we so think and that it has long so been held, and that we remain steadfast to death for this faith, anathematizing every godless heresy. That we have thought these things from our heart and soul, from the time when we have known ourselves, and that we now think and say thus in truth, we testify in the name of Almighty God, and of Our Lord Jesus Christ, being able to prove even by demonstration, and to persuade you that in past times also thus we believed and preached.

This was the Creed of the Church of Palestine, and Eusebius spoke of having heard those words first on the plains of Sharon in his own city of Caesarea. The Emperor accepted it; and the Arians, seeing in it nothing which specifically destroyed their position, would have accepted it if their opponents had not seen that this Creed failed in any way to resolve the conflict. It was necessary to state the Creed in such a way that the Arians would be forced to deny their essential tenets. Pope Alexander discussed the matter with Hosius. Constantine, turning against the Arians he had previously favored, suggested that Christ should be defined as *homoousios*—one in essence with the Father—and this definition should be included in the Creed. The orthodox bishops were gaining strength. The advocacy of Athanasius had succeeded in silencing the Arians. A new Creed, formed by patching together the old Creed and a new, more vigorous statement of the anti-Arian position, was finally announced by Hosius on June 19. It read:

We believe in one God, the Father Almighty, maker of all things visible and invisible.

And in one Lord Jesus Christ, the Son of God, begotten of the Father, only-begotten, that is, from the substance of the Father, God from God, Light from Light, very God from very God, begotten not made, of the same substance as the Father, through whom all things were made, both things in Heaven and things in earth; who for us men, and for our salvation, came down and was made flesh, was made man, suffered and rose again the third day, ascended into Heaven, and shall come to judge the quick and the dead.

And in the Holy Ghost.

And those who say "There was a time when He was not" and "He did not exist before He was made" and "He was made out of nothing" or those who pretend that the Son of God is "of other hypostasis or substance" or "created" or "alterable" or "mutable," the Catholic Church anathematizes.

In this form the Nicene Creed left much to be desired. It was tortured, blunt-edged, without poetry or rhythm, and without the nobility of the Creed of the Church of Palestine. There seemed no reason for omitting the enchanted words: "who for our salvation was made flesh and lived among men." But these words, and many others which gave a living significance to the original Creed—*the Word of God, the Firstborn of every Creature, begotten of the Father before all worlds*—were in fact deliberately omitted to show that the triumphant Alexandrians would allow no compromise, no loophole for the Arians, and were bent on avoiding all misunderstanding. In its original form the Nicene Creed was a weapon: it was to become a more sublime article of faith in time, when poetry and ornament and a less abrupt rhythm were fashioned for it by the simple process of adding words. These words, which gave depth and resonance to the Creed, were added at the Council of Constantinople in 381, and finally approved at the Council of Chalcedon in 431. Then the second clause came to read:

And in one Lord Jesus Christ, the only-begotten Son of God, begotten of the Father before all worlds, Light from Light, very God from very God, begotten not made, being of one substance with the Father, through whom all things were made; who for us men and for our salvation came down from the heavens and was made flesh of the Holy Ghost and the Virgin Mary, and was made man, and was crucified for us under Pontius Pilate, and suffered and was buried, and rose again on the third day according to the Scriptures, and went up into the heavens, and sits on the right hand of the Father, and is to come again with glory to judge the quick and the dead, and of His Kingdom there shall be no end.

So there came about by the slow processes of trial and error, as a poet will substitute a new word to a line or resurrect a word used formerly, continually revising his rhythms, an astonishingly beautiful summary of the Christian faith, such a summary as might have come full-grown from the mind of one of the apostles. But in fact this statement of faith came about arduously and slowly, after many bitter contests and many subtle dialectical quarrels; and in the version accepted by the West there were to be more changes. The words "God from God," omitted in the original Creed of the Church of Constantinople, were restored, and there were still more alterations in the coda, for in time the anathemas against Arianism lost their force. No one reading the Western version of the Nicene Creed today need remember that it was originally a hammer struck at heresy.

But the heresy remained. All Athanasius' diatribes, and all the decisions of the Council, were powerless to prevent it. Later Athanasius was to write to the Emperor Jovian, saying that Nicaea was the occasion for a public proscription of every heresy. For a while he believed that "the Word of the Lord, which was given at the Oecumenical Council of Nicaea, remaineth for ever." He had good reason to believe that he had won a resounding success. Constantine had been won over. Arius was publicly anathematized. According to the historian Socrates, Constantine issued an imperial rescript ordering that all the books of Arius should be burned "so that his depraved doctrine shall be entirely suppressed and so that there shall be no memorial of him left in the world." The punishment for concealing any book compiled by Arius was death! Yet some fifty-four years later, when Gregory Nazianzen was summoned to Constantinople he found only one small congregation in the city which had not become Arian. In the end Arianism was to die, and largely as the result of Athanasius' enduring statement of the orthodox doctrine, but in spite of the anathemas it was still a living force in the land.

The council came to an end on July 25, with a solemn banquet attended by the Emperor. They had deliberated for nearly seven weeks, not only about the Arian heresy. An Arabic translation of the canons discussed at Nicaea, found in the sixteenth century, shows that they debated on altogether eighty-four subjects, ranging from the date of Easter (they set the day as the first Sunday, not coinciding with the Passover, after the first full moon following the vernal equinox) to determining whether the clergy could marry (the clergy were enjoined to marry before ordination, but not afterward). Now, exhausted, the bishops prepared to make their way homeward. The last speeches had been made. There remained only the ceremonial leave-taking at the banquet, with the Emperor sitting at a table in the midst of them. Constantine, stiff with purple, gold and precious stones, was in good humor. He complimented Athanasius, gave presents to the bishops he favored, and at one point he summoned the unregenerate Bishop Acesius, who possessed a singular regard for the Novatian heresy which held that only God had the power to pardon sins and that anyone who commits sin after baptism must be permanently refused communion. Constantine reminded Acesius that the doctrine of the Church was now finally established. Acesius made a long speech in defense of his puritan interpretation of the Scriptures. Constantine guffawed: "Ho, ho, Acesius! Now plant a ladder and climb up to heaven by yourself!" And sometime later Constantine summoned the saintly Bishop Paphnutius and kissed the empty socket, and pressed his legs and arms to the paralyzed limbs, and he was especially gentle to all the other bishops who had suffered under the persecutions. Then the bishops went out through a line of imperial bodyguards with bared swords. The Council was over.

Athanasius was now a man marked with a destiny. Had not the dying Bishop Metrophanes of Byzantium pointed him out, saying to Pope Alexander: "There is your successor! Behold in Athanasius the noble champion of Christ!" Everything had happened as Athanasius desired it to happen, and almost he could believe the words which the Emperor addressed to the community of Alexandria: "What has pleased three hundred bishops is nothing other than the will of God." Athanasius was still a deacon, but he was a deacon who possessed vast spiritual powers. He returned to Alexandria in triumph. Three years later, when Alexander was close to death, he knew already that he would be proclaimed the new Pope.

It is possible that Athanasius had no desire to accept the burdensome duties of the Alexandrian papacy. Worn out by the battle with Arius, he may have preferred to disappear into the Nitrian desert with Antony. Though he was the deacon, "the eyes and ears of the Pope," and the man expected to take charge in the Pope's absence, he was not present when Alexander lay dying. Alexander called his name. A minor deacon of the same name stepped forward in answer to the call. Alexander repeated the name again, and was heard to say sadly: "O Athanasius, you think to escape, but you cannot." Pope Alexander died on April 17, 328. Seven weeks later the majority of the bishops elected Athanasius their Pope in defiance of his express wishes. For the next forty-six years except for the long intervals when he was a fugitive from the Emperor he occupied the throne of St. Mark.

When Athanasius returned to Alexandria, the people in the streets cried out: "Give us Athanasius, the pious, the devout, the true Christian, the ascetic! He will be our Pope!" In those early days of his power, the ascetic temper seems to have been uppermost. He spoke often of the desert and made many visits to the communities of monks founded by the pagan soldier Pachomius at Tabenne. On such visits the monks, wearing their sleeveless tunics, sheepskin cloaks and woolen cowls, would come running up to him in multitudes, offering him the loyalty he received less often in the great cities. They recognized him as one of themselves. Whenever he was in danger, he had only to slip out of Alexandria to find a secure hiding place in these strange and passionless communities, where sometimes he was welcomed with sudden bursts of passionate affection. Once when he saw the hermits running out of their cells to greet him, their thousands of torches blazing, he cried out: "Who are these that fly as a crowd, or as doves to their cotes?" Then, riding his ass, he was led in solemn procession to a hiding place somewhere in the heart of the community, while the saintly Pachomius hid himself, tongue-tied and ashamed to be seen in so glorious a company, and soon the blaze of torches was swallowed up in the darkness of the desert.

In those early years he seemed to have no enemies. Proclaimed Pope when he was perhaps twenty-nine, he could look forward to a lifetime of quiet ceremonial activity. But his enemies were still active, and in the same year that he was elevated to the see of St. Mark, Constantine signed an order giving Arius power to continue his preaching. Athanasius could prevent Arius from disseminating his heresy through Egypt and Libya, but he could not prevent him from spreading the doctrine in Constantinople. Arius had friends at Court. The Emperor was convinced that the anathemas and the sentence of exile were too harsh. And with Arius forgiven, the whole battle fought at the Council of Nicaea had to be fought over again.

Athanasius fought back and accused the Emperor of levity in freeing a dangerous robber from his proper prison; he reminded the Emperor of the tribulations of the bishops only three years before. It is not healthy to remind Emperors of their sins, and soon Athanasius had cause to regret his action. "The head of the Alexandrian Church," said Gregory Nazianzen with pardonable exaggeration, "is the head of the world." Surrounded by panoply, more powerful than any civil magistrate, with a huge treasury at his command, Athanasius was in a dangerous position: he was too popular and too powerful: and his enemies sharpened their swords.

In Alexandria, then as now, rumors spread like wildfire in the bazaars and the market place. It was a simple matter to invent rumors about a popular Pope. Athanasius had written a letter to the Emperor. The letter became known, a phrase would be torn out of context, or the whole letter would be garbled. It was known that Athanasius was heartbroken over the new prominence of Arius. It was said he was conspiring against the Emperor, had consecrated a church without the Emperor's permission, was levying taxes to pay for the raiment of the clergy, had given a purse of gold to the rebel Philomenus, refused to allow the export of corn from Egypt. Sometimes, as rumors do, these stories had the ring of truth in them, and sometimes too the more preposterous rumors were credited more easily than the small rumors which took wing through the market place. A strange story was being told about a certain presbyter called Ischyras, who was quietly performing his holy offices when he was violently assaulted by an emissary from Athanasius. The emissary broke the chalice and hurled down the altar, then departed. Ischyras complained that Athanasius was responsible for the sacrilege. The holy chalice had been broken in twain, and only the most condign punishment of Athanasius would serve to placate the wrath of God. Athanasius made inquiries. He learned that Ischyras had been declared only a layman by the ecclesiastical court at Alexandria: his ordination came not from a bishop, but from a schismatical priest. It was true that the presbyter Macarius had visited the remote hamlet where Ischyras lived, performing religious offices among a small group which consisted only of his own family. Macarius had forbidden Ischyras to perform these offices. There had been a violent argument, but Macarius had left the hamlet with the impression that Ischyras had sworn obedience to the Pope. Now Ischyras was traveling up and down the land, swearing that Macarius had smashed the holy chalice, the mob dogging his heels. Athanasius ordered a complete investigation. Ischyras had given the precise date and hour of the incident. The Pope's detectives went to work. They were able to prove that Ischyras could not have performed the sacrament that day, because it was a weekday, and furthermore he had spent the day ill in bed.

There were graver charges: of murder and black magic. With these the whispering campaign produced its sharpest weapons.

A certain Arsenius, a bishop of the Meletian sect calling itself the Church of the Martyrs, had disappeared. The Meletians spread the rumor that Athanasius was responsible for the bishop's death, had killed him and kept his hacked-off hand for use in magic rites. The accusation was absurd, and therefore all the more credible. Years later the historian Ammianus Marcellinus, writing in Antioch, where the Arians were entrenched, could say of Athanasius that he was "a haughty prelate reputed to have cultivated the arts of soothsaying and augury, and to have indulged in other illegal practices." It was not true. Arsenius, who had gone into hiding, wrote to Athanasius to say he was alive and regretted the atrocious rumors. There was nothing Arsenius could do. Through the streets the Arians paraded a black and withered hand enclosed in a wooden box, saying this was the hand of Arsenius hacked off at the wrist by orders of the Pope. They did not explain how they had come into possession of the hand.

When these rumors came to the knowledge of the Emperor, a council was summoned at Caesarea, but Athanasius was too ill to attend. By this time the living Arsenius had been found in a monastery on the eastern banks of the Nile. Soon the story was forgotten. Then Arsenius vanished again, and once more the Meletians charged Athanasius with his murder. It was the thirtieth year of the reign of the Emperor Constantine. He wanted to celebrate the anniversary by dedicating the Church of the Holy Sepulcher in Jerusalem, but he proposed that the bishops should first assemble in Tyre and inquire into the behavior of Athanasius before proceeding to the dedication of the Church. Athanasius was commanded to attend. He rode to Tyre with fifty of his own bishops. He must have known that his enemies would stop at nothing to defeat him. The ecclesiastical court which met at Tyre was presided over by an Arian. His enemies surrounded him. The moment he entered the court, he knew he would have to battle for his life. He was ordered to remain standing, like a prisoner, and he was introduced to the court by the registrar, though protocol demanded that a Pope should be introduced by deacons. The old matter of Ischyras was resurrected. Macarius, who had accompanied Athanasius, was dragged in fetters by soldiers into the courtroom. Except for the fact that Athanasius was allowed to defend himself freely, and was therefore able to command his audience to silence, he was in the position of a man on trial by an assemblage of bishops of an opposing sect. Someone screamed the name of Arsenius. Athanasius smiled. A dark and withered hand was thrust in front of him. "I know Arsenius," he said, "but I do not know this hand you thrust in front of me."

There was more screaming by the bishops. Athanasius stood his ground. The historian Socrates said that "he behaved very warily." There were long silences. At last Athanasius asked whether there were people in the court who would recognize Arsenius if they saw him. Many shouted that they would recognize him at once.

"Are you sure you would recognize him?" Athanasius asked.

"We recognized him well when he was alive," they answered.

Their words were taunting, but Athanasius seemed unaffected by taunts. He beckoned to a servant, who led forward the muffled figure of a man who stood before the court with his head bent down. Athanasius withdrew the mantle which covered the man's face.

"Is this Arsenius?" he asked.

There was a sudden stir in the court. Everyone was leaning forward to get a glimpse of the Bishop Arsenius, who had arrived secretly in Tyre only the day before.

"Is this the man who lost a hand?" Athanasius went on, for now it was his turn to taunt his accusers.

Some of the accusing bishops knew where the hand came from, but there were a good many who thought the muffled figure standing there would soon show the stump where the hand had been cut off. Delicately, Athanasius lifted one side of the man's cloak. They saw a whole hand belonging to Arsenius. They shouted: "What about the other hand?" Athanasius waited. He was in a mood to keep them waiting. He turned back the cloak on the other side, and exposed the other hand.

"So you see Arsenius is found to have two hands," Athanasius declared. "Let my accusers show where the third was cut off!"

From the time when the mantle had been lifted from Arsenius only a minute had passed. Three times Athanasius had shocked his audience, and with the third shock his triumph was complete. Perhaps it would have been wiser to pause at this moment, but Athanasius could not prevent himself from taunting them once more. So he said: "Observe that this man has two hands, and two only, having received them like every other human being from Him who created all things."

There was pandemonium in the court. It was impossible to continue with the accusation of Athanasius, and he was left free to go about his own affairs.

In triumph Athanasius showed himself at his worst. Deliberately and carefully he had maneuvered his enemies into a false position, but he was not content to expose them. The victory at Nicaea had been proved barren. Athanasius determined to go to the seat of power, to Constantine himself, and demand punishment for the Arians. He sailed to Constantinople, and there unknown to the Emperor he took up residence in a house which overlooked the long avenue leading to the palace. One day when Constantine was returning with his guards from a ride, a small figure darted across the road and seized the bridle of the Emperor's horse. Constantine was not accustomed to being stopped by anyone. He was startled and annoyed. At first he did not recognize the stranger. Athanasius held his ground.

"God will be the judge between me and you," Athanasius shouted at the Emperor, "since you have joined the ranks of my calumniators!"

The Emperor made a sign to indicate that he refused to listen further, but Athanasius continued: "I want only one thing. Either you must convoke a lawful council, or you must summon the members of the Council of Tyre to meet me in your presence."

In a letter written shortly afterward the Emperor said of this incident: "When Athanasius requested to be heard, I refused, and all but gave orders for his arrest."

The Emperor had heard enough. He returned to the palace, and sent for the reports from the Council of Tyre. The final judgment on Athanasius was received a few days later. Though finding him not guilty of the crime of murdering Arsenius, they found him guilty of other crimes. Athanasius then demanded that he face his accusers. Most of those who had judged him, after attending the dedication of the Church of the Holy Sepulcher, returned to their own provinces, but a handful including Eusebius of Caesarea came to Constantinople at the Emperor's summons. Once more there was a trial. Ordered to make concrete charges, they pointed to Athanasius' wealth. Once again they accused Athanasius of preventing the Alexandrian corn ships from sailing to Constantinople. He had levied taxes on the imperial fleet. He had sent his own police down to the harbor. Athanasius faced the Emperor. He was without allies. The Court had swung toward Arianism. He could only say he was a poor man, thirsting after righteousness, obedient to Caesar, and these things they accused him of were all unthinkable. He could talk to the bishops with biting irony, but faced with the Emperor he seems to have fumbled for words and felt himself powerless. The Emperor took the easier course. He decided to banish Athanasius to Treves. The Arians were happy and demanded the immediate removal of Athanasius from the see of Alexandria, but Constantine refused to appoint another Pope in Athanasius' place.

Athanasius made the long journey to Treves in northern Gaul in winter. It was a sickening defeat, but he showed no signs of accepting defeat. Treves was the seat of government of Constantine's eldest son, who was also called Constantine. The boy was then twenty years old, well-built and intelligent, a believer in orthodoxy. He bore the title of Caesar, and surrounded himself with sturdy soldiers and skilled advisers. He was especially friendly with Maximin, the Bishop of Treves, and was kind to Athanasius, who admired and loved the royal youth, and seems to have been content to live in that powerful city set among the vine-clad hills of the Moselle. Athanasius was allowed to correspond with friends in Alexandria. He had no responsibilities now, except those of friendship; and when in May, 337, the Emperor Constantine died, Athanasius remained quietly in Treves, where a new boy-emperor calling himself Constantine II ruled over the Empire of the West, which included Gaul and Africa, while his brothers Constans and Constantius ruled Italy and the East. Within a year—there is some doubt about the exact time—Athanasius returned to Alexandria, having received from the three Emperors a strangely worded pardon, explaining that it was the desire of Constantine to shield him from his enemies and this was the only reason why he had been exiled to Treves.

In his absence Athanasius' name had been kept green by the desert fathers. When he returned, it was in triumph. Gregory Nazianzen, who seems to have been present on the occasion, speaks of the whole city waiting to receive the man who had retained the papacy of Alexandria while living far away in Gaul. There was no sudden outburst of greeting. A formal entry was agreed upon. There was a solemn stateliness in the arrangements. The men and women were apart, and children formed a group by themselves, all waving green branches. The trades-men formed compact groups; so did the church officials. Athanasius stepped off the ship, was lifted onto an ass and led the procession through the city, with gay carpets spread before his feet, and more carpets hung from the windows of the houses. Little cups filled with fragrant oil hung at the doorposts. At night there were illuminations, and the richer householders provided entertainment outside their houses. It was a time of feasting and hymn singing. "Nothing can separate us from Christ," Athanasius had written in a festal letter cele-brating his return. In Alexandria there appeared very briefly one of those rare manifestations in which whole cities are given over to wor-ship. In their enthusiasm for Athanasius hundreds and perhaps thou-sands of Alexandrians became monks; the hungry and the orphans were sheltered; and every house became a church.

Gregory Nazianzen tells the story that long afterward, when a popular prefect was received with vast enthusiasm by the people of Alexandria, a young man in the crowd was heard saying: "Even if it were the Emperor Constantius himself, he would not be so well re-ceived." An older man smiled, muttered an Egyptian oath and an-swered: "Nonsense, you should not compare such a thing with the Emperor! If you are really looking for comparisons, think of the greeting we reserved for the great Athanasius!"

Athanasius had returned; Alexandria adored him; and only Con-stantius, the Emperor of the East, detested him. Constantius was a youth of twenty, red-haired and red-bearded, with the body of a young gladiator and a supreme lust for power. He had remained an Arian, when his brothers were orthodox observers of the Nicene Creed; and under the influence of Eusebius, Bishop of Nicomedia, who had been elevated to the see of Constantinople, Constantius was determined to extend the Arian heresy. For Athanasius the great hope lay in Constans and Constantine, but Constans suffered from the same lust for power which infected his brothers. He had Constantine murdered; all of Spain and Gaul fell into his hands; and he showed little real grasp of the problems of orthodoxy. Less than three years after his arrival in Alex-andria, there came to Athanasius from Constantinople the order to vacate his post in favor of an Arian named Gregory, a Cappadocian, who as a student in Alexandria had received some favors at the hands of Athanasius. Gregory brought an armed guard. He arrived on March 23, 340, and sensing the horror of the people, he immediately set about creating a reign of terror. Orthodox churches were desecrated, and their altars polluted. Monks and virgins were arrested, thrown into prison and tortured for the amusement of the guards. Orthodoxy became criminal. "We are contending for our all," Athanasius had written to the Egyptian bishops from Treves; and now once more he was to realize that against implacable tyranny there is only one weapon—the implacable knowledge of the truth. He could not fight in Alexandria, then under military occupation. From his hiding place he slipped onto a ship, accompanied by two monks, Ammonius and Isidore, and sailed for Rome, where he was received with honor by Pope Julius.

It was the beginning of his second exile, which lasted three years. They were years of incredible confusion in the East, where Arianism in the full flood of its triumph seemed to be firmly entrenched. Athanasius was orthodoxy alive, greeted everywhere in Italy with deep respect, the friend of Antony, the apostle of orthodoxy, the inheritor of the ascetic traditions of Egypt. He visited the Emperor Constans in Milan, and was received with the honors usually reserved for an imperial legate; and the little red-bearded man wandering through the black desert of exile seemed to be perfectly at home, wise above the wisdom of the Romans. From Constantinople the Emperor Constantius sent an order to the Alexandrian magistrates to behead Athanasius the moment he set foot in Egypt.

In November, 342, Pope Julius held a Council in Rome to clear the name of Athanasius. Such a council had been suggested by the Arians themselves, but they wisely refused to send their own witnesses, and when the report of the council was sent to the Arian bishops in the East, they held their own council in Antioch, formulated a new Creed and denounced Athanasius. The Church was now divided. The West declared for Athanasius, the East was against him.

Athanasius wandered over western Europe, giving sermons, addressing congregations of bishops, visiting the aged Hosius who was living out his last years quietly in Treves. Through all his journeys he was accompanied by the two monks, Ammonius and Isidore. Ammonius was one of the famous "four tall brothers," who were to confound the career of John Chrysostom, a strange burning-eyed hermit-priest who ran through the streets of Rome like a madman until he came to St. Peter's, and there he hurled himself weeping below the altar. And soon afterward, when he heard the rumor that he would be elevated to a bishopric, he cut off an ear in the hope that this would incapacitate him for office. The stern asceticism of Ammonius worked a miracle on the Roman women; they took to ascetic works with a vengeance, and

Jerome learned from Ammonius how to persuade Roman women to sacrifice themselves for the faith.

At last, in 345, a revolt broke out in Alexandria. The pseudo-Bishop Gregory was killed by the mob, and Constantius suffered a change of heart. Alarmed by the action of the Alexandrian mob, and at the urgent insistence of his brother Constans, he offered Athanasius a safe-conduct through the East. "Our clemency," he wrote, "no longer allows us to see you tossed by the wild waves and tumultuous seas, driven from your home and spoiled of your goods." At Antioch Athanasius was received in audience by Constantius, who suggested that at least the Arians should be permitted to have a church in Alexandria. Athanasius agreed on condition that there should be an orthodox church in Antioch, which was entirely given over to the Arians. Then the matter was dropped. The Emperor promised his protection. There would be no more incidents. On October 21, 346, Athanasius came home. Once more the streets were ablaze with lights; once more there were triumphal processions, the waving of palms, the streaming faces of the worshipers and the solemn declarations on the church steps. In a mood of profound tranquillity, Athanasius wrote later: "It seemed that every house had become a church, from love of holiness among the church members, and from praising God." In the churches the peace lay deep and wonderful, and the bishops wrote to Athanasius and received from him the words for peace.

But there was no peace, only a kind of counterfeit. The East was still rampant with Arianism. Athanasius had received his safe-conduct from an Emperor who delighted in intrigue. The historian Ammianus Marcellinus said of him that he was always confounding Christianity with his private superstitions. "Instead of reconciling differences by his authority, the Emperor deliberately created them out of ignorance and by making curious inquiries; and when these differences had spread, he added fuel to the flames by assembling the bishops and urging them to ponder these differences. He ruined the postal service by allowing the use of imperial carriages to the mob of bishops who were forever travel-ing to the various synods." Later Athanasius was to say of Constantius: "He is all weathercock, with no mind of his own. He listens to the advice of the eunuch who happens to be closest to him, and therefore I do not think him bad; he is merely helpless and silly."

A silly tyrant is always dangerous; and when the Emperor Constans was killed in an uprising and Constantius became ruler of the world,

Athanasius ordered the people of Egypt to pray: "O Christ, give aid to Constantius." The Emperor was determined to trap Athanasius. In 353 a curious incident occurred. Athanasius decided to send envoys to present his case to the Emperor. A few days after the envoys left Alexandria, Athanasius received a message from Constantius commanding him not to send envoys; it would be better if Athanasius came to the court in Milan. The Emperor hinted that Athanasius had made a request to appear before the throne, and the Emperor was pleased to grant it. In fact, Athanasius had made no such request. He detected in the message a deliberate attempt to remove him from Alexandria. So he replied that he had made no request, and hesitated to waste the Emperor's time with his affairs. The next year, during the Lenten season, when the churches were crowded and people were being injured in the throngs, Athanasius was asked to hold services in the unfinished and undedicated church called the Caesareum, which was a gift of Constantius. Athanasius hesitated. The church was in the possession of the Emperor, and the use of an undedicated church might be regarded as a gross ecclesiastical irregularity. Told that the people would prefer to hold services in the open country if they could not obtain the use of the vast Caesareum, Athanasius relented. The next year Athanasius was again condemned, this time in a Council held at Milan, which was held in the presence of the Emperor. There were near-riots among the bishops. Those who held out for Athanasius were marked men: altogether 147 of Athanasius' defenders were banished by orders of the Emperor. Told that Athanasius could only be judged by bishops, not by an Emperor, Constantius roared. He roared still louder when he was accused of confounding the ecclesiastical laws with imperial decrees. "Laws!" exclaimed Constantius. "What I wish, that is the law!"

That summer an imperial envoy visited Alexandria, urging Athanasius to surrender his powers. For six months he argued, threatened, cajoled, commanded, denounced. In fear of his life if he failed in his mission, the envoy begged Athanasius to think of the peace of Egypt. And Athanasius answered: "Would there be more peace if I retired?"

He did not retire of his own will. On January 5, 356, the storm broke. General Syrianus entered Alexandria at the head of five thousand troops with orders to remove Athanasius, who refused to leave his palace unless the General produced a signed letter from the Emperor ordering his dismissal. There was no letter: Constantius had not bothered to write one, or perhaps he remembered that he had once sworn on oath that he would protect Athanasius, and he hoped to remove Athanasius without being himself directly implicated. There was constant coming and going of armed soldiers. Alexandria was in a state of siege, but surprisingly there were three days of delay before the storm broke.

On the night of Thursday, February 9, while Athanasius and his flock were keeping vigil through the whole night in the Church of St. Theonas in preparation of the Eucharist the following day, they heard a tumult without. Athanasius wrote an account of those strange hours some years later:

> Then Syrianus suddenly came upon us with more than five thousand soldiers, all armed, and with drawn swords, bows, spears and clubs. With these he surrounded the church, stationing his soldiers nearby, so that no one could leave the church or pass through them. And I, having no desire to desert the people in their perturbation, remained sitting on my throne, only telling the deacon to read a psalm and the people to give the responses. It was the 136th Psalm, with the response: "For Thy mercy endureth forever." And after this I urged them to withdraw and depart for their own homes.
>
> At this point General Syrianus burst into the church, and the soldiers then surrounded the sanctuary for the purpose of apprehending us, the clergy and those of the laity who remained with us; and these cried out that we should seek our safety. I refused, saying to the laity that I would not leave until they were safely outside. Accordingly I stood up and after a prayer, I urged them again to depart, saying it were better that my safety be endangered than that any of them should be harmed. [*De Fuga*, 24]

Then Syrianus marched in at the head of his soldiers. For a moment they paused, terror-stricken by the chanting of the Psalm. Then came shouts, and the flashing of swords. The wounded fell, and were trampled on; the nuns were stripped of their veils; the gold vessels were plundered. The General appeared before the altar screen, but by this time the monks and clergy had surrounded Athanasius and lifted him from his throne. Half-fainting, he was hurried through the gates, so small a man that the soldiers failed to see him. Then he vanished into the winter night, and sometime later the bodies of the dead were carted away and secretly buried—"martyrs of the most pious Constantius." Once again Athanasius wandered into the desert.

They said afterward that he was never very far from Alexandria and sometimes made secret journeys into the forbidden city. Egypt had opened her sheltering arms, and kept him safe; a million peasants safe-guarded him. He could still write—letters, books, apologies for his flight, attacks on the Arians. His brain never seemed to stop working. He wrote an *Apology to Constantius* couched in the respectful tones of a man inquiring from his hiding place the reasons for the order of his arrest. Constantius had let it be known that Athanasius had be-haved with impropriety in using the unfinished Caesareum as a church. Athanasius had refused to come to Milan. Worse still, it was because of Athanasius that Constans and Constantius had quarreled. In his *Apology* Athanasius rebuts the accusations calmly, cooly, without passion. There is cold reserve in the short book he wrote a little while later called *Apology for my Flight*, where "apology" means simply "explanation." Here the Most Pious Emperor is hardly mentioned directly, though he is everywhere present by implication. Finally, he wrote his important *History of the Arians*, which traces the develop-ment of the controversy from 335 to 357. Here Athanasius leaves nothing unsaid. He rages with withering power and fierce contempt against the Emperor who, in the words of Ammianus Marcellinus, "possessed considerable influence over his head-chamberlain." Athana-sius calls him all the names he can think of: he is Saul, Ahab, Bel-shazzar, Pilate, Antichrist, a poor idiot with no mind of his own doomed to hell fire. But Constantius' victory was almost complete. It was of this time that Jerome wrote: "The whole world groaned, and was amazed to find itself Arian."

There was a new Pope in Alexandria, a certain George of Cappadocia. Gregory Nazianzen wrote a description of him, which is among the most virulent portraits ever penned by a Church Father:

> There came a monster from Cappadocia, born on the furthest frontier, a man of low birth and lower mind, whose blood was not perfectly pure, but mongrel, like the blood of mules. At first he waited on everyone's table, his price being a barley cake; and so he learned to perform his services with an eye to his own stomach. Then he lived for a while on the edges of public life, filling all manner of menial offices—a pork contractor for the army, among other things. And having been proved a thief, fouling his own pocket, he was dismissed from public employment and went wandering penniless from country to country, from city to city, and then in an evil hour for Christians he reached Alexandria like one of the plagues of Egypt. [*Oratio*, XXI, 16]

Six years later the people of Alexandria rose in revolt, unable to tolerate any longer the carnival of persecution which desolated Egypt. Constantius died, there was a new Emperor—the pagan Julian—on the throne, and the Alexandrians saw no reason to suffer indefinitely. George was stabbed, his body was thrown over the back of a camel and paraded through the streets. Soon Athanasius returned, and except for two brief periods of exile, he was to remain in Alexandria for the rest of his life.

In time the memory of George of Cappadocia was forgotten; he became legend, and curiously introduced himself into martyrology. St. George, a true martyr in Cappadocia, became confused with the Arian Pope of Alexandria in the Middle Ages. Even in his own time Athanasius had been accused of being an evil magician. So legend, which is history turned upside down, told the story of how St. George fought a battle on behalf of the Empress Alexandra against the wicked Athanasius. St. George rescued the Empress from the dragon, who was only Athanasius in disguise. Such was the last legacy of the Arians to their greatest adversary.

Athanasius returned to Alexandria in triumph on February 21, 362. Six years of desert exile had left their mark on him. He was an old man with a wild strength left in him, determined to maintain the faith, crying out his anathemas against the Arians, constantly repeating with unshakable certainty the arguments he first hammered out as a youth in *Concerning the Incarnation*.

As we see him in the long years when he ruled over the see of Alexandria, always in danger of banishment, walking the knife-edge of power, continually battling with the Arians and pouring scorn on other sects, we observe a gradual change in his features. Stern, he could give way to tenderness, though rarely for long. In his letters the harsh and disciplined prose marches with military precision, heavy footed. He does not talk so much of God's love as of God's complex oneness. Occasionally we see him clear, and at least once we can detect a half-amused smile of triumph. In his first paschal letter after being invested as Pope, he took the text from *Psalm* 81:3: *Blow on the trumpet in the new moon, even in the time appointed, and upon our solemn feast day.* So he wrote to the brethren:

Therefore we are enjoined to blow on the trumpet in the new moon and upon the solemn feast-day, for He hath made a solemn day wherein the moon's light is perfected to the full: and this light is like unto trumpets. And sometimes they were called to feasts, sometimes also to fasting and war. And this was not done without solemnity, for the sound of the trumpets was solemn in order that men should know what is being proclaimed. The trumpet is a wonderful and fearful thing, and more than any other voice or instrument is terrible and exciting.

As we read this long letter, full of the poetry of trumpets, it is hardly possible to avoid the suspicion that Athanasius saw himself as a trumpeter, and was a little amused by his own "terrible and exciting" trumpet. Occasionally he could be very human indeed. One day, when he was preparing a paschal letter, he must have heard some dancers or actors walking down a street, the click of their staffs on the cobbles, gay songs on their lips. He had already written down his chosen text from *Luke*: "With desire I have desired to eat this passover with you." And these two things, the strolling players and the sacred text, must have met together in his mind, for he wrote:

> O this is a wonderful text, which sets us in mind of people ready for the theater or the dance as they walk in the street with staves, and sandals, and unleavened bread. These things belong to the past, are seen as shadows, though commonplace. But now the Truth is near, the image of God invisible, our Lord Jesus Christ, the true light, who instead of a staff is our scepter, instead of the unleavened bread is the bread that comes down from Heaven, and instead of sandals furnishes us with gospels.

In that same letter, written at Easter, 342, he succeeded in marrying his Christian joy with a statement of doctrine which runs trippingly, almost gaily:

> Why therefore do we tarry, and why do we delay, and not come with all eagerness and diligence to the feast, trusting it is Jesus who calleth us? Who is all things for us, and was laden in ten thousand ways for our salvation; Who hungereth and thirsteth for us, though He giveth us food and drink as His saving gifts. For this is His glory, this the miracle of His divinity, that He changed our sufferings for His happiness. For being life, He died that we may be made alive. Being the Word, He became flesh, that He might instruct the flesh in the Word, and being the fountain of life, He thirsteth our thirst, that thereby He might urge us to the feast, saying, "If any man thirst, let him come to me and drink."

So he goes on, summoning the doctrine to reinforce the celebration of Easter in a passage which is still strangely moving, having survived translation from Greek to Syriac and so to English, for none of his paschal letters have survived in the original Greek.

Athanasius is not often joyful. Occasionally, and then only briefly, joy blazes up in a clear flame out of smoke and smoulder. The pen hurries the thought, the vision of joy seems almost to escape him as he writes, then for long moments we see the sun leaping on the granite rocks; afterward there is only the rocky landscape of doctrine and the intrepid explorer surveying the conquered land.

To see Athanasius joyful again, we must go to the life of Antony he wrote in late middle age. It is a strange work, and was evidently written hurriedly and carelessly, perhaps when he was ill and feared he would die before he could put Antony on paper. The book has fire. It is written without art, and yet with supreme conviction. It is the first Christian biography.

Athanasius' life of Antony exists on many levels: as propaganda for monachism, as an inquiry into the heroic temper of a superb Christian athlete, as a collection of fantastic stories about the devil's wiles, as a sermon on God's mercy, as a holy tribute to a friend. Antony springs alive. We see the young Egyptian born of well-to-do parents, who detested schooling, already in love with solitude as a youth, passionately in love with church services, with something of the ascetic about him from the beginning. When he was "eighteen or twenty years old" his parents died. Six months later he was standing in church when he heard a Gospel reading: "If thou wilt be perfect, go and sell all that thou hast, and give to the poor, and thou shalt have treasure in heaven." Soon afterward he sold his possessions, gave a large sum to the poor and a smaller sum to his sister, and went to live with an ascetic in a neighboring village. There were few monasteries in Egypt, and none of the ascetics had yet explored the solitudes of the desert. It was a simple beginning. Antony turned his back against the world. He lived quietly, eating only enough to keep alive, working with his hands because he remembered the injunction: "If any would not work, neither should he eat." The devil plagued him. Masquerading as a little black boy, or a woman appearing at night, or a Greek sophist or a soldier, the devil raged and tempted him. At night Antony remained awake, the better to watch the devil's work, sleeping on the bare ground, eating only bread and salt, drinking only water, while the devil whispered in his ear about companionship and money and fame and rich foods. The devil followed Antony to one of the tombs on the outskirts of the village. There, lying on the ground, speechless with pain, Antony was flogged by the devil's minions. Sometimes, even when he was not being physically assailed by demons, his mind grew bewildered and confused "like a cloud of dust." There was no rest for Antony. The devil was determined to win him. Once an immensely tall man appeared to him and said: "I am the power of God." Antony simply blew a breath at the man, intoned the name of Christ and then the devil fled. Once the devil came in the disguise of a monk carrying loaves of bread, but Antony prayed silently and "the devil vanished like a puff of smoke through the door." At another time, when he was too weak to stand and the devil was assailing him, Antony cried out: "I am here—Antony! I shall not bend to your blows, though you give me more, for I shall allow nothing to separate me from the love of Christ."

After those first combats with the enemy, Antony determined to fight the devil on more equal terms. He made his way to the desert, to live alone with the alone. "He found upon the far side of the river a deserted fort which in the course of time had become infected with creeping things. There he lived, and the reptiles departed immediately, as though someone were chasing them. He blocked up the entrance, laid in bread for six months (as the Thebans do, and the loaves keep fresh for a whole year). There was water in the fort. Antony went down as though into a shrine, and there abode alone, never going forth nor ever seeing those who came to him."

In those early years in the desert there were terrible moments of crisis. Sometimes the devil lost patience. One day Antony heard a fearful noise and clattering. "It was as though there was an earthquake, as though demons were breaking through the four walls of his chamber— demons disguised as wild beasts and reptiles. All at once the place became a mass of spectral lions, bears, leopards, bulls, serpents, asps, scorpions and wolves; and each moved according to the shape it had assumed. The lion roared, crouching for the spring. The bull seemed about to gore him. The serpent coiled, but could not reach him, and the wolf held back in the midst of leaping. The noises of these spectral animals was hideous, and their fury terrible. Antony, torn and goaded by the demons, felt an anguish through his entire body; yet he lay there watchful and fearless of soul."

This portrait of Antony at the mercy of the wild beasts fascinated Hieronymus Bosch and a score of painters. Gustave Flaubert pondered the story for nearly twenty years and rewrote it in his own terms. Even today—so well did Athanasius tell the tale—it remains curiously convincing, the incredible portrait made credible, one saint illuminating another saint, speaking of miracles before miracles became commonplace. So he will describe Antony walking across a canal brimming with crocodiles, but the crocodiles make way for him after he has prayed. And when Antony speaks of seeing a gigantic man "being like a human being as far as the thighs, but having the legs and feet of an ass," the vision remains credible. At the time he was weaving baskets. He simply looked up, made the sign of the cross, and said: "I am the servant of Christ, and if you are about to hurl yourself against me, well, here I am!" Thereupon the ass-legged monster ran so fast that it fell dead of exhaustion. Observe how carefully Athanasius prepares the scene. Almost we see Antony as he looks up from his weaving and rebukes the monster, speaking sternly and almost sorrowfully, having experienced the presence of monsters so often before and having gone beyond the stage when it was necessary to struggle with them. Even when the demons make noises "like the cat-calls of rude boys," Antony remains unimpressed. Has he not seen the demons arrayed in their most august panoply and puffed them away with the name of Christ?

Though the commentators have had a field day and proved to their satisfaction that the life of St. Antony is either a forgery or a recension of an earlier text, the vitality of the book remains to confound them. The authentic voice of Antony comes clear, not throughout the whole work but at sufficiently close intervals to justify a belief in a real Antony judiciously observed. When Athanasius relates the story of Antony seeing in a vision the Lord's Table surrounded by mules all kicking against its inner mysteries, again the vision rings true. When Antony says: "Let no man who has renounced the world think he has given up some great thing; the whole earth set against Heaven's infinite is scant and poor," we are aware of simplicities which go beyond the complex mind of Athanasius, and even today this single phrase has power to move our souls, as it moved the soul of a distinguished civil servant called Pontitianus living in a small house outside the walls of Treves. Pontitianus read the words in a Latin translation of Athanasius' *Life of Antony* which appeared in northern Gaul within thirty years of Antony's death. Pontitianus came from Africa, and when he journeyed to Milan and met the rising lawyer Aurelius Augustinus, another African, he mentioned the book and how it had given him the hope of immortality which outweighed all the honors of imperial service, and how the blessed Antony seemed to him of all men the most blessed. We know Aurelius Augustinus better as St. Augustine. It was a civil servant, fresh from a reading of Athanasius' *Life of Antony,* who was chiefly responsible for the conversion of St. Augustine.

The *Life of Antony,* then, was a formidable document, of incalculable effect on the future of Christianity. Generations of men who never concerned themselves with Athanasius' diatribes against the Arians came to know the Pope of Alexandria only through the *Life of Antony.* The simplicities of Antony cut through the complexities of dogma. In Britain, France and Germany the deserts bordering on the Red Sea were familiar, because Antony lived there; and for them the desert flowered, and was real, and it seemed to them that the miracles performed by Antony were such that any man could perform them if he had faith enough, and what greater pleasure was there than "to go on your way trusting in God and making the demons look silly"? There is joy in the heroic contest, a joy which Antony conveys splendidly:

> When you have put fear away, then there comes the most perfect joy and contentment; and courage and recovery of strength and calmness of thought and the other things I have mentioned, and stoutheartedness, too, and love of God. Therefore be of good cheer and pray, for your joy and the peace of your soul speak of the holiness of Him who is present. So Abraham, seeing the Lord, rejoiced; and John, hearing the voice of Mary, the Mother of God, leaped for joy. [*Vita S. Antoni.* 36]

And sometimes, when speaking of joy or relating some incident in Antony's life, Athanasius makes us aware that artlessness can achieve superb artistry. Athanasius is describing how, at the age of fifty-five, after twenty years of practicing solitary contemplation in the desert, Antony was forcibly removed from his cell:

> When his friends came and smashed down the door and removed it, Antony came forth as out of a shrine, as one initiated into the mysteries and filled with the spirit of God. Now for the first time he showed himself outside the fortress to those who sought him. And when they looked upon him, they marveled to see how his body remained unchanged since they had last gazed upon him, neither grown fat through want of exercise nor gaunt from fasting and wrestling with devils. He looked indeed exactly as he was before he went into his solitary confinement. His clarity of soul

shone through. Grief had not narrowed him, nor had pleasure touched him, and he showed no dejection of mind, no extremes of joy. He was not excited by the presence of the crowd, nor was he elated to see so many acclaiming him. Utterly tranquil, he seemed a man ruled by reason and shaped as nature had designed him.

[*Vita S. Antoni*, 14]

In the original Greek the sentences move with the slow triumphant stateliness appropriate to a description of a theophany; it was as though a god had appeared, someone too sacred almost to contemplate. But we are given no portrait of Antony: all we know of him is that he was tall, well-built, with keen eyes which did not dim with age, and he kept all his teeth, though in old age they were worn down to the gums. Yet this is enough. Athanasius accomplished exactly what he intended to do: he made Antony breathe again. Here was a living man who took almost no part in the quarrels of dogma, suffered no martyrdom, acquired no ecclesiastical dignities, performed miracles casually and seemed at all times in complete command of himself as he went quietly about his self-appointed tasks. And with this description of the new kind of Christian hero "ruled by reason and shaped as nature had designed him," there was to come about a subtle change in the atmosphere of Christianity comparable to the change which came with the emergence of St. Francis nearly a thousand years later.

Athanasius is at his best describing Antony, because he evidently revered Antony completely; and this reverence, which he reserved for few people on this earth, shines through. There is a classical simplicity in the last words of Antony as recorded by Athanasius:

Bury my body in the earth and let no one know the place but you alone. At the Resurrection of the Dead I shall receive it back from the Saviour incorruptible. Give away my garments. Give Athanasius my sheepskin cloak, which he gave me and which I have worn out with wearing; and to Bishop Serapion give the other sheepskin and keep the hair shirt for yourselves. And now, my children, God bless you. Antony is going and is with you no more.

[*Vita S. Antoni*, 91]

Except for the *Life of Antony* and occasional passages of the *Festal Letters*, Athanasius wrote with a somber violence. His style suggests an ironsmith hammering upon sheets of iron. The metal rings. His phrases have immense power, simplicity and authority, but we are aware that the simplicity derives from vast complex forces. He shudders, his hand trembles, his powerful mind reels with instinctive horror at the ignorance which surrounds him in the world, and so he hurls down the words on the page with rage and defiance in his eyes. There was a sect of Christians who believed that Christ suffered physical terror on the Cross. No: says Athanasius—

> The Lord did not suffer terror, He whom the keepers of Hell's gates shuddered at, and they opened the gates of Hell for Him, and the graves gaped, and many bodies of saints arose and appeared to their own people. Therefore let every heretic be struck dumb, if he dares to ascribe terror to the Lord. From Christ death fled like a serpent, and the demons trembled at him, and the sea cried out in alarm. For Him the heavens were rent and all the powers were shaken. Behold, when He says: Why hast thou forsaken Me? Then the Father showed that He was ever and even then in Him, and the earth, knowing it was the Lord who spoke, trembled, and the veil was rent, and the sun was hidden, and the rocks were torn asunder, and the graves, as I have said, did gape, and the dead in them rose.   [*Apolog. contra Arianos,* III, 56]

Athanasius had the power to say simple things simply, and complex things superbly. He wrote once against the Arians: "Those who maintain 'There was a time when the Son was not' rob God of His Word, like plunderers." The plunderers were with him to the end. Among others, there was the young Emperor Julian, the handsome apostate, with glittering eyes, soft tawny beard and exquisite features. At court he was sometimes called "the she-goat" behind his back, in reference to his beard, which was carefully oiled and trimmed. Unlike the Emperor Constantius, Julian was not an intellectual nonentity: he had vigorous opinions which he expressed with admirable force. He was chaste in an age of license, negligent of his dress in an age when emperors wore sumptuous apparel, and brave in battle, being able to endure great bodily hardships. Brought up a Christian, he rebelled against the Arians at Court, and then against all Christians, writing a lengthy, reasoned and spirited attack called *Against the Galileans*, proving to his satisfaction that the religion of the Galileans (he avoided wherever possible the use of the word Christians) was "a fabrication composed by wicked men." It is not convincing, but it showed a deep and troubled knowledge of the philosophies and sects of his time. To

him, Christianity as it existed in the Roman Empire was an absurdity of
a thousand jarring sects, but he allowed the Christians their liberty,
hoping that the internal disputes of the Church would ultimately lead
to their downfall. He loved books, and after the murder of George of
Cappadocia, he ordered that the whole contents of the Arian Archbishop's library be sent to him. And he was annoyed when he learned
that Athanasius had returned to Alexandria without waiting for an
imperial rescript. He wrote:

Julian to the People of Alexandria

A man who was has been banished by so many imperial decrees
issued by so many emperors should have waited for at least one
more decree signed by the hands of an emperor before exhibiting
the temerity and folly which led him to return to his own country.
He has insulted the laws, as though there were no laws. We have
not even now granted to the Galileans who were exiled by Constantius of blessed memory the right to return to their churches.
We have granted them the right to return to their own homes—
only that.

I have recently learned that the exceedingly audacious Athanasius,
elated by his accustomed insolence, has once more seized upon the
so-called episcopal throne, and this is not a little displeasing to our
God-fearing citizens of Alexandria. Wherefore We publicly warn
him to depart from the city forthwith, on the very day that he
receives this letter of Our Clemency. And if he remains within the
city, We publicly warn him he will receive a much greater and
more severe punishment.   [*Ep.* 26]

This edict seems to have been composed in the late autumn of 362.
Athanasius had no recourse but to withdraw from Alexandria, and
accordingly on October 24, he left the city, taking a boat up the Nile.
To the weeping monks who accompanied him to the boat, he said: "Be
of good cheer. It is but a little cloud, and it will pass." Another boat
started after him in pursuit. Athanasius characteristically ordered the
men in his own boat to swing round and make for Alexandria; and
when the imperial launch overtook them, the officers on board shouted:
"Where is Athanasius?" Athanasius himself replied: "He is not far
off." He put in at a station near Alexandria, found friends and then
went underground. Then he disappeared among the monks of the
Thebaid.

A fugitive from justice, his influence was still supreme. When it became known that he had entered Alexandria secretly, Julian was incensed. He wrote a sharp rebuke to the Prefect of Egypt, ordering the expulsion of Athanasius from the territory of Egypt before December 1. The rebuke came in the form of an official examination of the influence of Christianity in Egypt, a long letter, full of ponderous allusions to paganism and concluding with a vituperative attack on Athanasius, "the head of a wicked and impious school," the last man the Alexandrians should crave for. The Prefect had sent to Julian a plea signed by the Alexandrian Christians for the recall of Athanasius. Julian's final words to the Prefect were written in hot anger:

I say that you sent this request because you yourself are fond of the subtlety of Athanasius—and of course everyone knows the man is immensely clever—but it is precisely for this reason that he must be banished from the city. He is a notoriously meddlesome man, and therefore unfit to be a leader in the city. The truth is, he is hardly a man, only a little manikin. [*Ep.* 51]

Early in the following year Julian left Antioch at the head of his armies with the intention of destroying Persia, like Alexander before him. He crossed the Euphrates and camped under the walls of Ctesiphon, devastating the surrounding countryside, then pushing on to join battle with the main Persian army. On July 16, 363, a stray arrow from one of his own soldiers killed him. The Christian historians report that his last words were: "Thou hast conquered, O Galilean." The pagan philosopher Libanius attributed his death to an arrow shot by a soldier who was a Christian. At the moment when the Emperor Julian lay dying, Athanasius was in hiding in Tabenne, in a covered boat. The imperial police were close by and he seemed in danger of arrest. He prayed for a while, and then he said to the Abbot Pammon: "I am calmer in persecution than in peace. If I am killed—" The abbot smiled, and then another abbot, Theodore, interrupted. "You have no need to fear," he said. "At this very moment your enemy Julian has been killed in the Persian war." The new Emperor was Jovian, a jovial soldier, a handsome rake, an orthodox Christian. He lost no time in affirming Athanasius' place on the episcopal throne at Alexandria. He marched back to Antioch after making peace with Persia, and when Lucius, an Arian pretender to the bishopric of Alexandria, was presented to him, Jovian asked him how he had come to Antioch—by land or by sea? Lucius said he had come by sea, and Jovian roared with laughter. "Well, Heaven punish the sailors who missed the opportunity of feeding you to the fishes!" he said. Athanasius was invited to an audience with the Emperor at Antioch. He was treated civilly, with many marks of respect, and returned quietly to Alexandria, a frail white-haired old man who still spoke with a thundering voice. He might have thought he had earned a rest from his battles, but there was one more to come.

Early in 364 the Emperor Jovian, leading his army along the frontiers of Bithynia, went to sleep in a country house in the town of Dadastana. The walls had been recently plastered, and a charcoal fire was therefore kept burning in the bedroom, to dry them. In his sleep the Emperor was poisoned by the charcoal fumes. In his place came the two Emperors, Valentinian I and Valens, one ruling over the West, the other over the East. Valens was an Arian. He tore up the Edict of Tolerance issued by Jovian: once more the Arians were in power. They did not yet dare to exert their full power, and it was not until 367 that Valens felt he could issue an order banishing the orthodox bishops. On October 5, Athanasius suddenly disappeared to a place of concealment in the city—some said he hid in his father's tomb. That night, the Church of St. Dionysus, where he was usually to be found, was broken into and searched by the Prefect and the military commandant. They searched the church from top to bottom, but there was no sign of him. Four months later Valens reversed his decree, and the orthodox priests resumed their powers.

There remained seven years of calm, of contemplation, of quiet command over his flock. Occasionally religious quarrels flared up, but Athanasius no longer needed his trumpet notes; there is an unexpected serenity in his last letters. He engaged in a long correspondence with Basil, healed the jealousies between the monastic orders, and composed his festal letters. Then on a May morning in 373, at the age of seventy-five, after consecrating his friend and presbyter Peter as his successor, he died peacefully. He had been Pope of Alexandria for forty-six years, and had outlived sixteen Roman emperors.

It was all over, and yet it had only just begun. The man who had been exiled five times, the little red-bearded prince of the Church, quick-tempered, fiery, with the voice like clanging metal, altered the direction of history. It was not a small matter to insist that the Word was changeless, eternal and of God, and to stay the progress of Arianism which threatened to corrupt religion with the belief that the Son was inferior to the Father, no more than an angel, a standard-bearer or a mediator. It is not a small matter to defy emperors. He was a man immeasurably above his time, dominating it with the force of his passion. Even Gibbon, who detested the quarrel between Arianism and orthodoxy, thought that Athanasius by the superiority of his character and abilities would have been a better emperor than the sons of Constantine. Basil, who came to know him late in life, wrote that he was like a lighthouse, seeing with his ubiquitous eye all that was passing in the tempestuous seas below: treachery, stupidity, shipwreck; and like a lighthouse Athanasius showed them the promised land. Gregory Nazianzen was happier when he wrote that Athanasius came with the sword of a conqueror and the breath of the quickening spirit.

Once long before Athanasius had described himself best. He was describing his beloved Antony, but what he wrote was just as true of himself: "Of all things he loved life in the mountains most."

Basil the Great

Black-bearded, with bull-like head, heavy eyebrows, glittering eyes, small lips compressed tightly together, Basil stares out from the mosaics and icons. In obscure churches in Yugoslavia, in basilicas in Constantinople and Thessalonica and Mount Athos, in Russian icons of the middle ages, those heavy features can be recognized, and it is evident that there was a continuing tradition of portraiture. Of himself Basil said he was always sickly and suffered from a lifelong malady involving continual gnawing pain, but the portraits suggest a sober strength, his feet planted firmly in the ground, with no hint of the physical dejection he speaks about so often in his letters. His forehead was like the prow of a ship. He saw clearly, and he seems never to have allowed the infirmities of his body to obscure his essential sobriety. He possessed a patrician sanity. There was something of Athanasius in his robust intellectual vigor, his gift for ruling, his impatience and the firmness of his faith. Only Athanasius and Basil were granted by those who came after them the title of greatness. Basil the Great: he wears the title well, if only because he established the foundations of monasticism and threw his vast energy into the struggle against the Arian heresy.

Of the three important Cappadocian Fathers one was Basil; the other his brother, Gregory; the third was his closest friend, Gregory of Nazianzus. Basil was the man of intellect; his brother was a calm mystic, immersed in contemplation, seeking the threadlike roads which lead to the throne of God; while Gregory of Nazianzus was the impassioned orator and poet, called *Chrysorrhoas*, the "outpouring of gold." And yet with all their differences they were all recognizably Cappadocian, stern and tender like the country they lived in, a place of gaunt nightmarish pinnaclelike mountains and flowering orchards, of bitter cold in winter, of feverish heat in summer. In spring came floods, rain, hailstorms, bitter winds, and when summer came men prayed for the north wind to cool the red-hot earth.

Cappadocia is mountainous land, in those days famous for its horses and the wry humor of its people. Cappadocia, Caria and Crete were called "the three bad K's" (*tria kappa kakista*). Men who lived in more favored regions liked to tell how a viper bit a Cappadocian, and the viper died. They were a sturdy people, and under the Romans had the reputation of being good chair-bearers and bad fighters, too provincial to care what happened in other countries, and their accents were uncouth, hard on the ears of the Greeks, so that Libanius, who had many Cappadocian pupils in his great school in Antioch, said: "I am teaching pigeons to be cooing doves." At another time he said of the Cappadocians: "They smell of fish-fry and snow, and say to everyone, 'I adore you.'"

About 329, four years after the Council of Nicaea, Basil was born in Caesarea, the modern Kayseri. The city lay in the foothills of Mount Argaeus, on the ancient trade route from Sinope to Babylon and the Euphrates, on the Persian "Royal Road" which linked Sardis to Susa, and on the Roman road joining Ephesus to the East. It was an important city, once the residence of the Cappadocian kings, and in 260 was said to have a population of four hundred thousand; there is no reason to believe the population diminished in the following seventy years. Caesarea was the civil and ecclesiastical capital of Cappadocia, a city of marble colonnades, hanging gardens and palaces, with vast wealth at its command. It was a good place to be born in, for the highways brought trade and the influences of civilizations fantastically different from one another. Persia, Syria and Greece contended for the minds of the Cappadocians.

Basil, a second child, was named after his father, a rich lawyer who possessed property in three provinces of Asia Minor, a man so famous for his devotion to Christianity that it was widely believed he could perform miracles. His mother Emmelia, a woman of great beauty, produced ten children, five sons and five daughters, and of these three sons and one daughter were canonized as saints. For seven years Basil's grandfather and grandmother lived in the woods of Pontus, hiding from the Decian persecution; and on the ancestral estate at Annesi on the Iris river they built a chapel to forty martyrs.

Basil spent his early years at Annesi, dominated by his grandmother Macrina who tended the chapel and told him stories of the persecutions and of Gregory Thaumaturgus, the Wonder-worker, a disciple of Origen, who was born in Pontus and whose memory was kept green.

Then for a while he seems to have come under the influence of his elder sister, also called Macrina, a girl of vivid imagination and almost terrifying selflessness. Then he was taken in hand by his father, who intended him for the law. He studied briefly in Caesarea, and then wandered to Antioch where he studied under Libanius. Restless, he went off to Constantinople, but he seems not to have attended the colleges there for any length of time. In 351 he entered the University of Athens, where he remained for five years under the greatest teachers of his time, studying history, poetics, geometry, astronomy and the classics. Here too he met the young student Gregory, who was to become Bishop of Nazianzus. Of this encounter Gregory said later: "I sought there eloquence, and found happiness, for I found Basil. I was like Saul, who in searching for asses found a kingdom." It was perhaps a partial judgment. Basil, too, was to say bitter things about the schools of Athens, where a man learned "fire-breathing rhetoric" and it was all "a vain felicity." In fact, it was a period of great intellectual growth, and Basil never lost the love of the classics which he studied there. He met young men who possessed his own intellectual stamina and argued endlessly. Among his contemporaries at the University was Julian, afterward Emperor and called the "Apostate." And like everyone else he was in danger of "hazing," a ceremony known as "the bath," the students jeering at the novice, pushing and pummeling him, deafening him with shouts and confused orders which had to be implicitly obeyed. Gregory was a senior student, and years later, when he preached the funeral sermon over Basil, he remembered how he was able to prevent Basil being "hazed" when he was a freshman.

When Basil returned to Caesarea from Athens, he was a graduate of the best university of his time and wonderfully proficient at rhetoric, which had been his special study. In the interval his father had died; so had his saintly grandmother Macrina. He was offered the chair of rhetoric at the University of Caesarea. He accepted it, and gave some courses. He delighted in his learning and the opportunity to display it, and he might have continued as a professor of rhetoric, with a satisfactory law practice, if it had not been for his sister Macrina and the shock of the death of his brother Naucratius. Macrina accused him of "being puffed up beyond measure with the pride of oratory." She complained that he looked down on the local dignitaries and believed himself better than anyone else in Caesarea. He was always quoting the classics at her and showed no desire to follow in the Christian traditions of the family. Then the blow fell. Naucratius was the second son, a year or two younger than Basil. According to Macrina, he excelled all the brothers in physical beauty, strength and ability. He could run faster, and though reserved, he possessed a sharper intelligence. Naucratius was deeply religious. He had wandered back to the ancestral property at Annesi, and made himself guardian of it, living alone except for a servant who attended him, looking after the old villagers of the place, spending his time between hunting, fishing and good works, determined to tame his desires and live virtuously. One day he went out to fish, and was brought home dead. There was no warning sickness. He died suddenly on a clear day, like someone struck by lightning. Basil was overwhelmed, renounced his chair and sat at his sister's feet, learning from her the secret of renunciation and Christian virtue which had eluded him in all his years in Athens. A chastened Basil took the place of the imperious rhetorician.

More and more the commanding figure in the family was Macrina. Emmelia had been thrown into an endless grief, following the death of her husband and her favorite son. Macrina solaced her, made her treat the slave girls as equals and suggested that they close the house in Caesarea and move to Annesi, and then she went on to discuss the founding of a small community of religious women on the estate, dedicated to charity and the celebration of God. It was the beginning of monasticism, and Macrina was its true founder. Women, not men, were the first monks.

Renunciation! This was the word most often on Macrina's lips, and she saw vividly all the implications of the word. One must renounce the body, renounce wealth, renounce rank, renounce all things for the sake of Christ. Without property, wearing a single garment, sleeping on the ground, eating only enough to enable the body to survive, one must live for God alone, and there must be no other thoughts except the thought of God. All were equals before God, and all must share equally in the worship of God. And while Macrina traveled to Annesi and set up the first Christian monastic order, Basil, fired by her enthusiasm, set out on a prolonged tour of Egypt, Palestine, Syria and Mesopotamia, to visit the anchorites in their caves and the little huts they erected in the desert, following the tradition of Pachomius and Antony. It was true that the anchorites lived in colonies and communities, and sometimes faithfully obeyed a chosen leader; but these undisciplined and ragged hermits suffered from spiritual pride and possessed a fierce independence of spirit, without the habit of obedience or the

virtue of humility. They were lawless athletes of God—*athletae Dei*—
too often determined to take the Kingdom of Heaven by storm; and
in Egypt they formed a standing army which could be thrown into
a battle over bishoprics. It was Macrina's idea, elaborated by Basil
later, that a community of devoted Christians, living in continence
and under the strictest discipline, served God better than the wild-eyed
anchorites.

We know almost nothing of Basil's journey abroad. It was a quick
journey, and perhaps lasted no longer than six months. By the spring
of 358 he was back in Cappadocia, full of enthusiasm for the project of
setting up a community for men like the community Macrina had
already established for women. He was eager to recite the lessons he
had learned, and called on Gregory of Nazianzus to join him. There
was considerable debate as to the best site for the monastic retreat,
and at first, to please Gregory, he chose Tiberina on the Arianzus
river. Finally they decided on Ibora, a small hamlet on the Iris facing
Annesi. Gregory was easy to convince, and Basil went to some pains
to paint a picture of the place:

> There is a high mountain very thickly wooded, watered toward
> the north with cool and transparent streams. Below the mountain
> lies a plain, richly watered by the mountain streams, skirted by a
> tremendous growth of trees thick enough to form a fence; and
> so, as you see, we live on an island more beautiful than the island
> of Calypso, which Homer thought to be the most beautiful on
> earth. Indeed, this is truly an island, enclosed on all sides; and
> the earth dips away at the frontiers of the island; and the river,
> which flows from a mountain precipice, runs along one side, and is
> impassable as a wall; while the mountain, extending itself behind,
> and meeting the hollows in a crescent, stops up the path at its roots.
> There is but one pass, and I am the master of it.   [*Ep.* 14]

"There is but one pass, and I am the master of it!" It is the authentic
voice of Basil, and the first intimation of the greatness ahead.

Gregory remained unconvinced. He visited Ibora briefly in the
autumn, and afterward taunted Basil with choosing the worst possible
site for a monastery. Where Basil saw flowers, singing birds, fresh
breezes from the river and deep pools filled with fish, Gregory characteristically saw the great shadow thrown by the mountain, the
thorn bushes and the paths which were altogether too precipitous for
safe walking. Worse still, "the roar of the river drowns the voices of

psalmody." He remembered the biting winds and the cheerlessness of Basil's little hut and the poverty of their meals together and how they nearly broke their teeth on homemade bread. But Basil possessed the dominant will and though he exaggerated the delights of the place, Gregory had exaggerated its discomforts. It was a wild and mountainous spot on the very edge of Asia Minor and not far from Armenia; and Basil was supremely content there. When Gregory returned home, Basil, wrote him another letter proclaiming the delights of the monastic existence. He said that men who live in the world only exhaust themselves, their lives dedicated to desperate stratagems. "There is only one way out," he wrote. "Complete renunciation from the world." He saw it all clearly, his practical mind busy with the practical affairs of God. Even in those early years he seems to have mapped out the whole structure of monastic discipline; he knew what the monks should wear and how they should behave. An hour a day should be set aside for food, no more. The food should consist of bread, water and vegetables. Sleep should be light and easily broken, so that especially at midnight the monks would be able to rise and utter their prayers to God. Over the lives of the monks the powers of the abbot should be absolute. As for the monks, they would wear the aspect of perfect humility:

> From the humble and submissive spirit comes an eye sorrowful and downcast; appearance neglected; hair tangled; dress not carefully tended. They should wear tunics drawn close to the body: the belt should not be tied above the buttocks, like a woman's, nor should it be left slack, with the tunic flowing loose like an idler's. The stride should not be sluggish or lackadaisical, nor should it be brisk and pompous, or of a wild impulsiveness. The only object of the dress should be to form a sufficient covering in summer and winter. They should avoid bright colors and soft, filmy materials; for what are bright-colored clothes but the equivalent of women painting their cheeks and dyeing their hair?   [*Ep.* 2]

Such was Basil's first portrait of the monk; there were to be many more. In time, he was to refine the portrait: he gave it clear contours and definition, demonstrated how every waking moment of the monk's life should be dedicated to God. He compiled a voluminous series of rules: the longer rule with 55 articles, where each subject is considered at length, and a shorter rule of 313 articles, where the subjects are often considered briefly. These rules were written with the help of Gregory of Nazianzus, and were based on close experience of the monkish life. He recommended nothing he had not undergone himself. He had gathered the wood and cut stone and carted manure. Since the monastery was to be self-sufficient, he must know how to calculate profits, how many men should be busy with repairs, the best way to grow cabbages. He was surrounded with practical problems, and then there were the interminable problems of discipline. What should be done when a monk refuses to obey his superior? Basil came to the conclusion that he must first be warned privately by the superior, and then if he perseveres in disobedience, the superior may correct him sharply before all the brethren. If this fails, and there is no improvement in his conduct, then the superior "with many tears and lamentations, but nevertheless firmly, must cut him off from the body as a corrupted and useless member." It was a harsh law. It applied to those who were detected in pride, to those who murmured against the superior and even to those who woke up crossly from their beds. Punishments for minor infractions of the rules were based on simple principles. The monk who slept too much was punished by watchings with prayer. The monk who ate too much was deprived of his food. The monk who was inattentive was compelled to listen, by force if necessary. Basil was perfectly conscious of the hardness of the rule, of the iron in his own soul. He believed that all sins were capital sins, sins unto death. A single sin could provoke the wrath of God. He was determined to make every monk perfect in Christ, according to the Pauline injunction. And to be perfect they must become like children, or like soldiers, or like slaves. He wrote:

> We obey God and avoid vices from fear of punishment, and so doing we take on the appearance of slaves. We obey the laws, and since we receive recompense we take on the appearance of mercenaries. Finally, we love Him who has granted us the law, which we obey with joy at the thought of having been adjudged worthy to obey so great and good a God, and so doing we imitate the affection of children for their parents.
>
> [*Regulae Fusius Tractatae,* 329 E.]

These fantastically long rules—they fill more than two hundred closely printed pages in an English translation—grew gradually over the years. They were the fruits of experiences, the remedies for many errors. They are so detailed that they offer the reader a quite extraordinary picture of the monastery, complete down to the number of coverlets a monk may have on his bed. Every conceivable sin has its appropriate penalty, its inevitable safeguard. Boys at the age of puberty must not sleep in beds beside one another; between them there must be the bed of an old man. Medicines may be used, but sparingly. Laughter is punishable. The hours of prayer are carefully regulated. Because the Psalmist wrote: "At midnight I rose to give thanks to thee because of the judgments of thy righteousness," the monks must rise at midnight, the hallowed hour, "for what is cockcrow for other men is midnight for the practicers of piety, when the quiet of the night grants most leisure to the soul." He was determined to produce a close-knit compact factory for the manufacture of saints, as well-regulated as a beehive; and though he failed in this, as he failed in many things, it was not for want of trying. "All must remain at their appointed posts," he wrote. "None may go beyond his own bounds nor enter where he is not commanded to go, unless he has the permission of responsible authorities." It was authoritarian; it was merciless in its punishments; and yet there was the saving grace of Christian joy to temper the iron law.

Where did Basil derive this authoritarian temper? Partly it must have come from some necessity in himself, his sense of the overwhelming sinfulness of man, of the thin thread that holds him from the abyss. There was the Christian law. No evil may be done; none may be violent, or angry, or pugnacious. The human animal is tempted too easily and strays wildly from his appointed path. Then, too, this ordered community served as a challenge to the anarchy of the time, a lawless age. He hoped for permanence, and there could be no permanent community without iron laws. He demanded that the monks should be athletes. Though living in strict community, they should resemble the anchorites he had seen in Egypt:

> I admired their continence in living and their endurance in toil. I was amazed by their persistence in prayer and their capacity to triumph over sleep. Subdued by no natural necessity, they ever kept the soul's purpose high and free. In hunger, in thirst, in cold, in nakedness, they never yielded to the body, and indeed they paid not a moment's attention to the body. Always, as though they lived in a flesh which did not belong to them, they showed how a man can sojourn for a while in this life, while having his true citizenship and home in Heaven.   [*Ep.* 203]

Here Basil expressly indicates that the Egyptian anchorites provided the original source of the monastic communities; all he added was the

idea of forming them into strict communities, so that out of the in-
choate strivings of the many, there should be formed the single unified
act of worship, which was the coenobium itself. It is possible, however,
that he was mistaken in his belief that the Egyptians were responsible
for his decision to bring a monastic community about. In his journeys
through Palestine he may have encountered the legends which had
accumulated around the Essenes, that strange sect of Jews which lived
at the time of Christ on the shores of the Dead Sea. Indeed, there was a
tradition that Christ Himself had for a short period entered their
monastic brotherhood.

A reasonably complete account of the Essenes, derived from Pliny,
Josephus and Philo, has been preserved. We know that they lived
rigorously ascetic lives in organized communities. They practiced
primitive communism, ate only the simplest fare and wore their clothes
and shoes to shreds before providing themselves with new ones. When
they entered the community, they surrendered their possessions, and
there was no buying or selling among them; a steward managed their
needs and handled all the money. They paid scrupulous attention to
cleanliness and were silent at meals and worked hard, till late in the
evening. They delighted in silence, and Josephus who for a while was
a member of the brotherhood complained that "anyone coming from
outside was awe-stricken by their silence." The penalties for breaking
the Essene laws were strict and immutable: men were simply thrown
out of the community after a trial attended by at least a hundred members of the brotherhood. Junior members were compelled to show the
utmost deference to senior members, so much so that if a senior member was accidentally touched by a novice, he would immediately take
a bath. In all these things except the last there is a direct resemblance
between the Essene brotherhood and the community of monks at
Annesi.

Basil believed that this formidable discipline could be made endur-
able by the character of the Superior, who must be meek and charit-
able, an example in lowliness to all. If the Superior committed a fault,
he must be judged by his peers, the Superiors of other monasteries, who
had the power to impeach any Superior who erred in his duty. The
Superior must be grave, thoughtful, gentle and kind, an image of
Christ, and therefore entitled to demand obedience even unto death. A
conclave of Superiors from all the monasteries provided the supreme
lawgiving assembly of the order, and their judgment was final. Basil, an
aristocrat by birth, imposed his aristocratic beliefs on the order, saying as

though there could be no possibility of controversy that there were two classes of monks: those entrusted with pre-eminence and the care of the larger body, and those made only for obedience. The Superiors were chosen for their spiritual gifts, their powers of healing, the vigor of their faith, their vast humility; and they seem to have been recognized by their power to perform small miracles, to foresee the future and to receive immediate answers to their prayers.

During the early days, and perhaps throughout all his life, Basil was the Superior of Superiors, the benevolent tyrant whose will was law. He assumed the task willingly and was never happier than when assuming his responsibilities over the monks; but the hard taskmaster could be surprisingly gentle, and sometimes we can detect a generous smile on those lips which never permitted themselves to laugh. When the boy Dionysius came to the monastery, Basil sent him back to his mother with a charming note:

> There is an art in catching doves, I assure you. When the fowlers have caught a dove and have made it so tame it will eat of their hands, then they anoint the wings with perfume and send it back to join the flock. The fragrance of the perfume is such that the whole flock becomes the property of the fowler, for they come flying to him, following the scent of the perfume, only to be shut up in the dovecot. But why do I begin my letter thus? Because having received your son Dionysius, and having anointed the wings of his soul with a divine perfume, I have sent him to your worthiness, so that you too may fly with him and occupy the nest he has built with us. [*Ep.* 10]

There are many such letters: the grave implacable Basil of the *Longer and Shorter Rules* gives place to the wry philosopher who could turn a phrase with disarming eloquence. There was geniality under the thundering brow. He was not always a perfectionist, oppressed by the world's guilt. Sometimes he will even ask for pity, and so disarmingly, and with such an Athenian turn of phrase that we detect the beginning of a laugh. He wrote to his friend Olympius: "Once upon a time you wrote me brief letters, but now not even brief ones; and your brevity, as it advances with time, seems likely to become perfect taciturnity. So resume your old habits. I shall not blame your brevity any longer: I shall treasure your little letters as signs of great affection. Only please write!" (*Ep.* 12) He could be amusing when writing about himself, especially in illness. John Chrysostom once compared himself with a spider. Basil goes one better. He compares himself in thinness to a spider web, and goes even further. "My body is so wasted with fever," he writes, "that it appears to be even thinner than I. Yes, I have become thinner than myself." (Ep. 193) To Antipater, Governor of Cappadocia, he wrote:

> I hear you have recovered your lost appetite by eating pickled cabbage. At one time I disliked it for two reasons—the old saying, Twice-cooked cabbage is death, and then because it is the constant reminder of the poverty which usually goes with it. Now I must change my opinion, laugh at the proverb and regard cabbage as a splendid nourisher of men, since it has restored our Governor to health. Henceforth I shall proclaim the virtues of pickled cabbage, and I shall think nothing of any value compared with cabbage, not even Homer's lotuses, nor that ambrosia, whatever it is made of, which the gods in Olympus serve for a salad.   [*Ep.* 186]

Once, after a month's treatment at the hot springs, Basil wrote: "Warmth does the dead no good." At another time a friend sent him some sweetmeats, and he wrote back thanking his friend for his folly in making so inappropriate a gift to a toothless old man who could no longer chew candy.

Basil's humorous moods rarely stayed with him for long. The stakes were too high for levity: he was a man who brooded deeply, and he must have walked heavily if his style is any measure of his walking gait. He had a mordant wit. "If you always live alone, whose feet will you wash?" he asked once, and damned the solitary hermits as they had rarely been damned before. Often he was overbearing, and when he mingled wit with his overbearing temper, he was intolerable. A woman called Simplicia, a heretic who possessed immense wealth and innumerable eunuchs, objected strongly when one of her runaway eunuchs was consecrated by him. He thundered back at her:

> Be mindful of the last day, and if you please, do not think of teaching me! We know more than you, and we are not so choked up by thorns, nor do we have the advantage of being able to mingle a few virtues with ten times as many vices. You have roused against us your lizards and toads, which are indeed animals of the springtime, though unclean. But there will come a bird from above to feed on them. It doesn't matter to me in the least what you think: I am concerned only with God's judgments. Should

there be need of witnesses, then slaves will not step forward, nor any of those hapless and accursed eunuchs—I mean what I say— a race neither male nor female, women-mad, envious, of evil knowledge, quick to anger, effeminate, slaves of their bellies, money-hunters, coarse oafs who grumble about their dinners.

[*Ep.* 95]

There is a good deal more of it, but this is Basil in an unregenerate mood, blazing with bad temper. Usually he was stern, calm, vigorous. There was steel in him. He asked the monks to serve Christ violently, and was violent to himself, a tall man, heavy-shouldered, who must have walked the earth sometimes as though he owned it. He liked to quote *Matthew:* "The Kingdom of Heaven suffereth violence, and the violent take it by force." "Subject thy neck to the yoke of Christ's service," he wrote to his monks, "and fasten the collar round thy throat and let the yoke press down." He urged them to accept the extremes of obedience, fasting, vigils, prayers and endurance. Demons and all those things that turn a man's thoughts away from God were the enemies, and he was determined to cast them down. He was a despot, possessed of an imperious will and was sometimes kind.

In 359 he became a lector, with the right to read the lessons in church. Five years later Bishop Eusebius of Caesarea ordained him presbyter against his will. It was the end of his monastic solitude. Eusebius was strong-willed; so was Basil; they quarreled incessantly. Basil was uncomfortable as presbyter, charged with all the minor duties of the episcopate. At last there was an open quarrel—it is not clear what the quarrel was about—and Basil returned to Ibora, glad to be free of the encumbrances of a high position, for as presbyter he often acted for the bishop and made decisions for him. For a while he thought of setting himself up against Eusebius, heading a party or founding a schism, but his friend Gregory prevailed upon him to remember the text: "Blessed are the peacemakers." He remained quietly in Ibora while the Emperors went to their wars: Julian died in Persia, and soon the Arian Emperor Valens came marching through his own empire, as though he were waging war on it. With an Arian Emperor in power in Constantinople, the orthodox Bishop of Caesarea was once more in need of a capable assistant: he sent for Basil: the indispensable presbyter returned to the city.

Basil enjoyed his position in Caesarea, but it tested him to the full. In 368 Caesarea suffered a series of disasters. First there were hailstorms, then floods, then earthquakes, then a pitiless drought. Early in the summer Basil was writing that "the floods surpass everything that tongue can describe or the eye see." Food supplies were cut off, there was no communication with the neighboring provinces, the people were starving for lack of bread. Basil wrote letters demanding the immediate building of a bridge over the river Halys. The floods frightened him, but the drought frightened him more:

> All day we see the clear, cloudless skies, calm and unchanging, and because they are calm and do not change we are weighed down with melancholy. A little while ago, when clouds hung over the earth, and there was no sunlight shining down on us, and all the air was dark, then we prayed for cloudless skies; but not now. The earth is parched, empty, sterile, cracked and broken. The sunlight penetrates deep in the cracks, and our rich springs have failed us, and the river beds are all dried up. Little children and women with their burdens cross the rivers by walking.   [*In Famem*, 62 D]

All through Caesarea the peasants scrabbled among the burnt blades of wheat, groaning and weeping. Basil complained against the rich hoarders, "who let their wheat rot, while men die of hunger." For the first time Basil saw the face of starvation:

> Hunger is the most pitiable of all ills, the worst of miseries, the most fearful of deaths. The point of the sword brings death quickly, raging fire puts an end to life suddenly, the teeth of wild beasts put an end to the miseries of men much sooner. Hunger is a long, slow punishment, and endless martyrdom. It is like a creeping disease, with death ever imminent, but always delayed. It drains the natural moistures of the body, it chills the body heat, it consumes the flesh and gradually exhausts the strength. The flesh, all color gone, clings to the bone like spider webs. As the blood diminishes, the skin loses its luster, and turns black and dries up; and this poor livid body is of a mingled wanness and soot color. The knees no longer support the body: they are moved only when force is used on them. The voice grows reedy. Weak eyes lie useless in hollow sockets, like nuts in dried-up shells. The hollow stomach contracts, shapeless, shrunken, cleaving to the spine.
> What kind of punishment, do you think, is deserved by a man who passes the hungry without giving them a sign?
>   [*In Famem*, 69 C]

Basil was heartbroken. He had inherited some property: he sold it and gave the money to the hungry. He went about Caesarea, demanding of all the rich people he knew that they should collect money and bread and give it to the poor. "There would be neither rich nor poor," he reminded them, "if everyone after taking from his wealth enough for his personal needs gave to others what they lacked." But the rich were more miserly than he had ever imagined, and in his homilies from this time onward there is usually a protest against wealth. To the poor he was gentle. "Since you have nothing, lend what you have to God," he said, and he reminded them that there was more human charity and warmth among the poor than anywhere else.

If you are reduced to your last loaf of bread and a beggar appears at your door, then take that loaf from your closet and lift your hands to Heaven, and say this prayer: "O Lord, I have but this one loaf, which you see before you: Hunger lies in wait for me, but I worship your commandments more than all other things, and therefore this little I have I give to my brother, who suffers from hunger. Do you now help your servant who is in danger. I know your mercy, and have faith in your power. And do not defer your favor too long, but bestow it according to your will." And if you should say this, then the bread you gave in your poverty will be changed for an abundant harvest.   [*In Famem*, 68 E]

It was a view of Basil which few people had seen before—the tall, stern presbyter, with the dark heavy face and the quick flashing eyes, feeding the poor with his own hands, washing their feet, wandering through the barren August countryside in vestments thick with dust, a man unlike other men, larger than life. All this time he was mellowing. It was remembered that his pride was least in the year which saw the hailstorms and the famine.

Two years later, in 370, Eusebius died, and Basil decided he had no alternative but to become Bishop. An Arian Emperor reigned in Constantinople. The aged Athanasius was still alive. An Arian Pope ruled from the throne in Hagia Sophia. Antioch was divided between two claimants of the episcopal office. Rome was far away from the center of the Church, and without influence in the East. Basil saw himself as the predestined defender of orthodoxy, able to hold his own against a multitude of bishops and to withstand an Emperor. He would stop at nothing. He would become bishop against all enemies. Bishop Gregory, the father of his friend, saw clearly that there was no alternative, but young Gregory, annoyed by Basil's intransigence, held back. At last Basil issued a summary order for all prelates to attend the election. In his letter to the young Gregory he said he was dying and earnestly desired to see his friend before his death. So Gregory set out for Caesarea from Nazianzus, and he was halfway to the city when he saw that the roads were blocked with bishops riding to the capital from all directions. Sadly, the young Gregory set his horse heading for home.

It was a time of desperate travail, violent stratagems, with the survival of orthodoxy at stake. The venerable old Bishop Gregory saw the issue so clearly that he arranged to be carried to Caesarea, to take part in the election. He supplied the final vote which secured the election and with his own hands he consecrated Basil in the great church at Caesarea. Athanasius wrote from Alexandria to say that in Basil the Church possessed a bishop every province should envy.

Basil was ill, living on his nerves and his spirit. At the time of his election it was argued that he was incompetent to rule, for being so weak in health. Gregory asked whether they wanted a bishop or a gladiator. Did not everyone know that sanctity and ill-health went together? The world received both a bishop *and* a gladiator.

As Bishop of Caesarea, Basil was also Metropolitan of Cappadocia and Exarch of Pontus. His authority extended over eleven provinces of Asia Minor. Power humbled him, sharpened his wits and sometimes poisoned him. He raged against worldly presbyters and clerics in minor orders who were unworthy to serve at the altar. Abuses had arisen in the appointment of bishops, who sold "the gift of God," and consecrated men for commerce, for gold and the huckster's traffic. Some drank, others were immoral, still others made triumphant journeys through the provinces, eating up wealth like locusts. Basil had never been slow to indignation. When he discovered that the old presbyter Paregorius was living with his housekeeper, he thundered that the woman must go into a nunnery or the presbyter must suffer excommunication. Curiously, he was more lenient with a certain Glycerius, an ordained deacon of the church of Venasa, who "possessed some natural talent at manual labor." After being ordained, Glycerius neglected his work and without any authority began to train a company of youths and maidens in dancing and singing. The maidens supported him with their offerings, and praised him extravagantly. His head was turned. He paid no attention to the reproofs he received from his presbyter. He began to assume for himself the name and dress of a "Patriarch," and one night he slipped out of the town, taking his dancers with him.

The dancers wandered through the countryside like gypsies, appearing at festivals, taking part in the chorus. The parents of the girls demanded that Glycerius send them home, but the "Patriarch" refused, and so did the girls. A small army of irate parents went after the dancers, but they were beaten and driven away. It became a scandal. The whole province was in an uproar. At last Glycerius and his followers took refuge with a bishop called Gregory, who may have been Basil's younger brother, Gregory of Nyssa. Basil wrote three passionate letters on the subject to the mysterious "Bishop Gregory," full of forbearance and pleading, saying that he was being "martyred before God and man by this evil affair," but his tone is singularly gentle. Perhaps he was altogether too shocked and too hurt to feel the horror of the affair. A friend of Basil's called Macarius once spoke of "those souls which lose their natural hardness in the fire, and the longer they remain in the furnace, the more they are softened by the flame." Basil's soul was sometimes strangely softened.

Again and again in those early years of his episcopate Basil threw up his hands in weariness and defeat. He was often ill, suffering torture from a disease of the liver, unable to rise from his bed. "Terrible among us," he wrote, "is the famine of love" (*Ep.* 91). Two years after becoming bishop, he wrote:

> The teachings of the true faith have been overthrown. . . . Gone is the dignity of the priesthood. None tend the flock of the Lord with wisdom. Proud men squander the money intended for the poor on their own pleasure and in the giving of gifts. No longer is there the strict observance of the canons. License to commit sin has spread through the land; and those who have entered office by favor reward their masters with the gift that pleases them most—license to commit any sin they please. Just judgment is dead. Everyone follows the whims of his own heart, and wickedness has no bounds at all.   [*Ep.* 92]

The situation was so bad that he calmly compared it to the time when Jerusalem was being ringed by the armies of Vespasian: chaos within the walls, and armed enemies without.

In the intervals when he could rise from his sickbed, Basil fought back. The hard taskmaster made hard rules. He refused to be defeated. He had ruled his flock in Ibora with an iron hand, and he was determined to rule Caesarea in the same way. When in 371 the Emperor Valens ordered that Caesarea should be divided into two separate provinces, Prima and Secunda, Basil's power was severely limited. He lost so many bishoprics in the territorial change that he was compelled for reasons of prestige to elevate village churches to bishoprics, and unable to find enough bishops to fill the new episcopates, he compelled his closest friend, Gregory of Nazianzus, and his closest relative, his brother, to fill newly created sees. Acting abruptly, he lost their friendship. He was harshest when he was ill, and this was the year when he lay for two months on his sickbed, complaining of nausea, terrible pains in the liver, insomnia, debility. From his sickbed he wrote that he had no desire to recover and wondered why God kept him alive. Yet he simmered with energy. Somehow he administered his diocese, preached, fostered monasteries, prepared plans for the huge hospital he proposed to build just outside the walls of Caesarea, wrote innumerable letters and published a small flood of books. He wrote letters to governors, tax collectors, widows, generals, to the churches in Gaul and Armenia, to the clerics of all the Near East; most of them are long, carefully considered and written in that hard-driving brutal style which is characteristic of everything he wrote; a style compounded of nervous energy, a fierce strength, desire for affection and overwhelming love. As he grew older, he grew gentler, but the hard outlines remain.

He needed to be hard: Valens was determined to crush him. At some time in 372, the Emperor sent the prefect Modestus to Caesarea with orders to make Basil conform to the Arian heresy or resign from the management of ecclesiastical affairs. Modestus, who bore the title of Count of the East, possessed only a little less power than the Emperor. He summoned Basil before a tribunal in Caesarea.

"Basil," he shouted, omitting all titles and honors, "how dare you defy our great power? How dare you stand alone?"

Basil hesitated. He needed time, and he was perfectly prepared to hedge. He asked Modestus what he meant: he had shown no defiance, and did not regard himself as someone standing alone.

"You know perfectly well what I mean," Modestus replied. "Everyone else has yielded, and you alone refuse to accept the religion commanded by the Emperor."

The religion of the Emperor was the worship of Jesus, created by God at the beginning of our era: not the worship of the Jesus who has stood eternally by God's side.

"It is not the will of my Emperor," Basil answered with superb courage. "I cannot worship anything that has been created, since I am myself created by God, and have been bidden to be a god."

Modestus was incensed. "What do you think of us?" he roared. "Are we then nothing?"

"You are a prefect, and one of the illustrious, but I shall not honor you more than God."

There were people who said Basil should have escaped from the city when it was known that Modestus was on his way. He knew he was in danger of being struck down by a dagger, but he was deter-minded to uphold his faith and his authority.

"Do you know what I can do to you?" Modestus roared. "Don't you fear my power?"

"What can you do?" Basil answered quietly.

"What! You dare to say that! There are many things I can do!"

"Then name them!"

"I can confiscate your possessions, banish you, torture you, put you to death?"

"Is that all? None of these things trouble me! You cannot confiscate my possessions, for I have none, unless you want to take the threadbare clothes I am wearing, and the few books in my library. Banishment— exile—what have these to do with me? Everywhere on God's earth I am at home! You cannot exile me from the grace of God, and wherever I am cast forth, there I am a stranger and a pilgrim. Torture cannot touch me, for I have no longer a body to torture; and is there any torture in being put to death with a single blow, for that is the only power you have over me. As for death, it is welcome to me, for it will bring me sooner into His blessed Presence, close to Him whom I serve. Furthermore I am for the most part already dead and have long been hurrying to the grave."

Startled, the prefect said: "No one ever addressed Modestus in such manner till now."

"No doubt," retorted Basil. "Probably you never met a bishop until now, otherwise you would surely have come upon people who speak in this way. In all other matters, we are humbler than anyone, ac-cording to our duty, and we show no arrogance to the very least of people, and still less do we show arrogance to the strong. When God is at stake, we despise all else! Fire, sword, wild beasts have no terror for us: indeed we delight in them! Insult us, threaten us, do as you will, exercise the magnitude of your power! But let the Emperor hear my words! You will never persuade us to join forces with impiety, though you threaten your worst!"

Basil's defiant rejection of Modestus did not recoil on his head. The tall, gaunt bishop, white-bearded at the age of forty-two, succeeded in awing the prefect, who changed his tone and began to argue that nothing more was demanded of Basil than that he should surrender the single word *homoousios,* meaning "consubstantial"; and he promised that if this word was surrendered, the Emperor, who was approaching Caesarea, would enter into his communion. But it was precisely this word which concealed the true majesty of God, and Basil rejected the plea outright, saying: "It is worth much to save an Emperor's soul, but I can no more add or subtract from the Nicene Creed than I can change the order of the words."

"I will give you until tomorrow to think it over," Modestus said.

"Tomorrow you will find I have not changed," Basil answered, and then he was allowed to go.

Modestus reported to Valens that Basil showed an unholy obstinacy. "He is too strong for persuasion, and will yield to nothing but force!"[1]

The Emperor was determined to make an Arian out of Basil. He sent Count Terentius, one of his best generals, to try the effects of flattery. When these failed, he sent Demosthenes, his eunuch chamberlain and *chef de cuisine.* Demosthenes had a reputation for finding quick solutions to pressing problems. Demosthenes embarked on a learned disquisition on the nature of God. Basil simply turned away, and refused to listen to the simplicities of the eunuch. Defeated, Demosthenes summoned the Bishop before the tribunal, and in the presence of Modestus, flashed a sword in Basil's face. And when the Bishop failed to show any signs of fear, Modestus, in a temper, threatened to take out his liver. Basil answered with a smile: "Then I shall be grateful to you, for I have even now no ordinary pain in my liver. Take it, and you will relieve my suffering!"

Early the following year, at the Feast of the Epiphany, the Emperor himself, escorted by spearmen, entered the church in Caesarea. The congregation must have known he was coming. His entrance was accompanied by a thundering roar, for they were singing the psalms at the top of their voices. According to the custom of the time, Basil was standing behind the altar, facing the congregation. He wore his splendid vestments as he celebrated the Eucharist, paying no attention to the Emperor. The church historians say that the Emperor trembled

[1] In Basil's surviving works there are no references to the meeting with the Prefect Modestus. This account is based on Gregory Nazianzen, *Oratio,* XLIII, 48-52, and Gregory of Nyssa, *Adv. Eunomium,* I, 59-66.

before the fervor of the celebrants, and that his hands shook and his knees buckled as he offered an oblation.

After the service, the Emperor was received in private audience, the Bishop remaining behind the sacred veil. As always, the Emperor was accompanied by his chamberlain. Demosthenes could not keep silent, and began to argue theology. Basil turned on him, smiling, and said: "It seems we have a Demosthenes who does not know how to speak Greek! He had better attend to his sauces!" The Emperor was amused. The meeting was cordial. At one point Basil referred to the hospital he was building outside the walls of Caesarea: a large hospital, with dispensaries and dormitories, a church, workshops for the laborers and artisans, and a special building for lepers. To this hospital the poor, the sick and all wayfaring travelers would be admitted free. The Emperor was sympathetic, and promised Basil the income from his estates in Cappadocia to provide upkeep for the hospital, which threatened to be so large that it was called "our new town."

Valens was a weathercock, ignorant and conceited, at the mercy of his eunuchs and generals. Suddenly there came the order for Basil's arrest and banishment. Basil was prepared to obey. He decided to flee at night, secretly, afraid that his going would be accompanied by disturbances, even by civil war. His carriage was waiting for him, and Gregory Nazianzen was by his side, when a messenger came and announced the sudden illness of the six-year-old Galates, the only son of Valens and the Empress Dominica. The Empress believed her son's illness was a punishment from God, a sign of displeasure at the threatened exile. She begged Basil to pray over the boy. He prayed, and the boy speedily recovered, only to die, according to the church historians, a little while later, when being baptized by an Arian bishop. The same historians say that when the Emperor sat down to sign a second order of banishment, his pen split three times down the middle in his trembling hands, and he was unable to make a mark on the paper. Basil's imperious will had conquered the Emperor.

He had seven more years to live. He lived them to the full, forever writing or dictating, or visiting churches, or thundering in defense of orthodoxy, or quarreling with his enemies. As he grew older, he became more gaunt, more like a wraith. He had lost all his teeth by the age of forty-six. He complained as early as August, 372, that "my body has failed me so completely I can make no movement at all without pain." He continued to drive himself hard, as he had always done. He developed a passion for embracing lepers. Like all solitaries who jump when they are unexpectedly interrupted, he was accused of being nervous. His archenemy, the Arian Eunomius, accused him of living "alone in a cottage, behind a close-shut door, and he is terribly flustered when people enter unexpectedly." Then for a moment we catch a clear glimpse of him, the spasm on the splendid face, the lips trembling.

From all over the Empire letters came to him, demanding advice and assistance and help in the interpretation of the Scriptures. He was asked to interpret the strange text: "Whosoever shall kill Cain shall discharge seven times the thing to be expiated." (*Gen.* 4:15). In an enormous letter Basil replied that the reason must be that Cain's sins were seven in number: envy, guile, murder, fratricide, evil manners, wrongdoing, lying—in that order (*Ep.* 260). It is not convincing. He is more convincing when he wore the disguise of a Jeremiah and thundered at the evils of his time:

> Let sword flash, let ax be whetted, let fire burn fiercer than that of Babylon, let every instrument of torture be brought against me! To me there is nothing more fearful than failure to fear the threats which the Lord has directed against them that blaspheme the Spirit. [*De Spiritu Sanctu,* 75]

At such times Basil does not seem to belong to his age. He belongs to the great period in Hebrew history when the Spirit of God spoke through the Prophets. He is carved out of granite, whereas his younger brother Gregory is carved out of translucent marble and his friend Gregory Nazianzen seems to be carved out of many-colored alabaster. It is recorded of Basil that his speech was slow and deliberate, but sometimes one doubts whether he measured his words, for so often in his letters excitement seizes him by the throat. The man who faced Modestus could speak recklessly at times, knowing that God was by his side.

His greatest work is the *Longer and Shorter Rules,* that huge compilation of ordinances by which monasticism came into existence. As a theologian he is remembered chiefly for a book of homilies on the *Hexaemeron,* or *The Six Days of Creation,* in which he described the works of God at the very beginning of the world, omitting to mention the creation of man—an omission which his brother Gregory artfully observed and characteristically described as an oversight. Rufinus explained the matter better when he wrote that "Basil is humble before God, but Gregory is humble before men also." Gregory wrote

an important work *On the Making of Man* in affectionate rebuttal of
his brother's theology, though he never ceased to admire the passion
which lay behind *The Six Days of Creation*.

The book can still be read with profit. It is short, and has little of
Basil's customary prolixity. It is his testament, his solemn declaration
of God's power, His infinite mercy and brooding immensity. "When
I take this book in my hands, and hear those words," wrote Gregory
Nazianzen, "I am brought face to face with my Creator. I begin to
understand the method of Creation, and feel more awe than I ever
felt before, when I looked at God's work through my own eyes alone"
(*Oratio* XLIII, 67). We do not have to share this view. Gregory, after
all, was writing a funeral oration, and he had long ago forgotten his
occasional quarrels with Basil. *The Six Days of Creation* is a strange
hodgepodge; he wrote with *Genesis* in front of him, and Aristotle a
little to one side. But in the moments when it is most lucid it breathes
a wonderful sense of awe and mystery. At such moments he will
give you an astonishing awareness of what it was like at the birth
of Creation.

He takes the opening words of *Genesis* line by line, phrase by
phrase, word by word. The mysterious words: "The Spirit of God
moved on the face of the waters," he interprets in a way more common
to the East than to the West. With Ephraem Syrus, he reads "moved"
as "brooded," and he suggests that God covered the waters as a bird
covers her nest. When God said: "Let there be light," Basil is overwhelmed with delight:

> For the heavens until then were enveloped in darkness, and
> now quite suddenly they appeared in the beauty they still wear
> in our own eyes; and all the air was lighted up, light and air
> commingling together, and splendidly and speedily did they dis-
> perse in all directions, as far as they could go. Light sprang up
> to the very ether and the heavens, and all the extent of the world
> was suddenly bathed in light, north, south, east and west. And
> the waters shone, glittering, sending forth quivering flashes of
> reflected light from their clear surfaces.   [*Hexae.* II, 7]

For a while he stumbles over the firmament "which divided the
waters which were under the firmament from the waters which were
above" and he is not too happy when he describes the emergence of
dry land, but the sight of foliage springing up all over the earth
throws him into ecstasy:

And God said, Let the earth bring forth grass. Then in a moment did the earth flower in obedience to God's laws, and all the stages of growth were instantaneously completed, and all the seeds gave fruit. The meadows lay deep in grass, the fields were like waving seas of harvest, and the wheat shook on the stem; and every little herb and shrub and flower arose out of the earth in abundance. There was no failure at the first harvest; neither the farmers' ignorance nor the weather's rages injured it; nor was there any sentence of death upon fertility. All this was in the days before men were condemned by sin to eat their bread by the sweat of their brows.   [*Hexae.* V, 5]

Basil always delighted in trees and herbs—his long letters on the delights of the wild forests of Ibora testify to his eye for nature. Now his delight knew no bounds. The virgin earth, the birds in the green shade, sheets of flowers—there, *there,* he seems to be saying, is the handiwork of God. The flowers are innocent like the stars; there is no guilt on them, no mark of Cain. He will defend flowers and plants to the uttermost. Do you say some are poisonous—hellebore, monkshood, mandrake, poppies? He answers that the plants have their own purposes and were not created for the sake of men's bellies. People say that the blood of a bull is poisonous, but should the bull have been created bloodless? No; the wild starlings feed on hemlock, and the happy quail on hellebore, and there is a nectar in poppies which dulls pain. So he celebrates, before men had ever set eyes on them, those roses without thorns, the magnificent black poplars, the acorns and the dogwood and the fig trees, which have bitter sap and sweet fruit, all admirable things, in the untouched splendor of Creation.

For some reason he is less happy when he talks of the creation of the heavenly luminaries; he turns to Aristotle, and speaks learnedly of the moon's tides, and how the sun can be seen at one and the same time in Britain and India. The stars give him occasion to inveigh against astrologers. What nonsense it is! A King's son is born at the exact time a beggar-woman gives birth to a child: is the beggar-child therefore to be made King? And as for those old wives who will tell you how to conjure the moon out of the sky— It is enough to ponder the heavens, he says; better not to attempt to penetrate their mystery. "If such is the beauty of visible things, what shall we say of invisible things? If the grandeur of Heaven exceeds the measure of human intelligence, what human mind will ever be able to trace the features

of the everlasting?" (*Hexae.* VI, 1). It is a little lame, and you have
the feeling that he could have done better with the sun, the moon, the
planets and all the stars.

He has surprising comments about fish. To him they have a special
nature, behave queerly, have a nourishment of their own, live a life
apart. They cannot be tamed and cannot bear the touch of a human
hand: which is odd: for one of the most perfect paragraphs of Gregory
Nazianzen is precisely about the joys of scooping up fish from a pool.
He adds a brief note on pearls and the long golden beard of the sea
pinna, and then mysteriously the sea reminds him of marriage and he
tells a horrifying story of a viper which crawls to the seashore, hisses
and invites the sea lamprey to embrace him. A shutter has opened, to
be closed a moment later. So quickly have the words escaped from
him, he seems hardly aware of the visionary horror which occupies
only two startling lines in the Greek text.

We do not forget the embrace of the viper and the sea lamprey
easily: it comes from the stuff of nightmares, which even the Fathers
must suffer because they are men. Innumerable paragraphs in the
Longer and Shorter Rules inveigh against sex: the young must not
approach too close to one another, they must talk to one another with
downcast eyes and never touch one another. The fires of the young
must always be banked down. Once Basil said the greatest of all
crimes was gluttony: that gluttony which led Adam to eat from the
forbidden tree. There are fourteenth-century English penitentials which
follow this tradition, but the more heinous sins of pride and sex are
more frequently mentioned. Nearly always, when he is discussing sin,
Basil agrees with the majority of the Fathers: the sexual act is exceedingly sinful.

Meanwhile Basil refused to rest. He wrote innumerable letters, and
their strange prefatory words—for he had the habit of his time of
addressing letters to Your Patience, Your Forbearance, Your Modesty,
Your Humility, Your Incomparable Nobility—do not conceal the hard-
bitten sober strength of the words that follow. He wrote to Ambrose
in Milan, who had requested the bones of St. Dionysius the Milanese,
martyred in Cappadocia. For some reason he felt compelled to insist
on the authenticity of the relics—"One coffin received that honored
body; no one lay beside him; his burial was glorious, and the honor
given him was worthy of the martyr" (*Ep.* 198). He wrote a long
letter to a calligraphist who annoyed him by writing slantwise across
the page—"When I read your writing, and find myself passing from

one line to another, then I am bewildered, because I cannot see where the line begins and like Theseus following the thread of Ariadne, I must retrace my steps and 'follow the furrow'" (*Ep.* 334). He wrote to the bishops of the West, begging them to make issue with the Emperor Valens and so defend the orthodox faith. He asked Valens to summon a council at Tarsus, so that the unity of the Eastern and Western Church might be discussed. There was no answer from the West, and Valens was silent. In one of his letters to the West he quoted from the Psalm: "I looked for someone to take pity on me, but there was no man, neither found I any comfort in me." At last in August, 378, Valens died at Adrianople, and less than five months later Basil followed him. He was only fifty, but he looked like a man who had died of old age.

Stern, ruthless, inflexible, Basil stands with Athanasius as the hero of his time. It is almost unthinkable that anyone else would have been able to stand out for the orthodox faith against the power of Valens. Almost singlehanded he held the enemy at bay, so that orthodoxy could be re-established in a happier age. Jerome said of him that "he ruined many gifts of continence and intelligence by the single evil of pride." Everything he wrote and did bears the stamp of his vast pride, which was pardonable and necessary, for otherwise he could hardly have survived. In history he stands at the head of the great list of Cappadocian Fathers, which includes Gregory Nazianzen and Gregory of Nyssa; but both of them exceeded Basil in humanity. Yet there are times when humanity is not enough: the will must rule, or everything perishes.

One day when the saintly Ephraem Syrus was wandering through Cappadocia, he heard a voice saying: "Rise, Ephraem, and feed upon intellect." "Where shall I find it, Lord?" he asked. "Go toward My church, and there thou shalt find a royal vase full of the nourishment that is good for thee." He entered the church and saw a priest standing at the altar, a tall man with stooping shoulders; on one of those shoulders a snow-white dove sat, whispering in Basil's ear.

Only of the kingly Basil and the aristocratic Thomas Aquinas is it recorded that the dove whispered in their ears.

Gregory of Nyssa

Usually the great Fathers of the Church were men of commanding presence afraid of no one, least of all afraid of Emperors. They were often small men, and some suffered from physical deformities, but in their presence men were aware of the power streaming from them and of their vast intellectual stature. Against the heretics they hurled their judicious thunderbolts with unerring aim; over the orthodox they cast the mantle of their mercy. Pitiless in their demands upon themselves, they were still more pitiless against "the servants of this world." In their hands the Holy Spirit was a singularly sharp and two-edged sword.

Yet not all the Eastern Fathers are larger than life. Basil and Athanasius might be brothers, both stern and unyielding, with the look of fire in their eyes, never plagued by doubts, the light of certainty glowing in them. Basil's younger brother Gregory was of a different order of beings. He never raised his voice; no thunderbolts escaped his hands; he walked with tenderness through a world which seemed to him too beautiful to be real. Basil sometimes gives the impression of a man who despaired of men; Gregory loved them, and thought they were too like angels for comfort. A strange undercurrent of mystical excitement flowed through him. And to the end he persisted in seeing all things in the mirror of God, a mirror of crystal purity, tenuous and dazzling.

Sometimes, reading his works, it is possible to have for St. Gregory of Nyssa something of the same affection one has for St. Francis of Assisi. Like St. Francis, he is contemplative and joyful, and believed that God moves all things simply by being desired of them. Like St. Francis, too, he came to Christianity late in his youth and had some knowledge of the ordinary human enjoyments of this world. He married, and we know that the woman was beautiful. He was so human that he even forged a letter, and he never seems to have regretted the forgery. He detested living under his brother's shadow. According to the custom of his time, he wrote the usual attack against heretics—a work of enormous length and prolixity and masterly dullness. In all his other works there is a sense of joy, a delightful welling up of excitement. Sometimes he seems not to belong to his time, but to an earlier period of Christianity, when innocence abounded. "You see that patience is sweet, more so than honey, and useful to the Lord, and He lives in it," wrote Hermas, the author of a popular book of devotions in the early part of the second century (*Mand.* V, 1, 6). "The Spirit of God which was given to the flesh cannot endure sadness or restraint" (*Mand.* X, 2, 6). It is that spirit which breathes through the writings of Gregory of Nyssa.

At first there was little to suggest he would become a saint. He was born A.D. 335, and was therefore five or six years younger than Basil. As a child, his health was weak, and his schooling seems to have been irregular. He read widely in his father's library. Mostly he read the Greek classics, and he had no particular fondness for the intense Christianity of his mother Emmelia. When his father died, he lived on his share of the paternal estate and refused to adopt a profession.

He was about twenty, a reluctant Christian, when his mother announced that the relics of the forty martyrs, which had come into the possession of the family, would be solemnly translated to a chapel especially erected on the family estate at Annesi in Pontus. Gregory was ordered to attend the translation of the relics and take part in the night long vigils. He arrived at Annesi in a furious temper. He was annoyed with the long journey and the prospect of interminable psalm singing, and he shared with many other people of his time a contempt for the worship of relics. The Emperor Julian called the Christians "bone-worshipers"; the sophist Eunapius spoke of "the martyrs, before whose bones, salted and pickled, the monks and bishops lie groveling in the dust." In a fury of annoyance, Gregory slipped away from the garden where his mother was superintending the psalm singing. In another garden he fell asleep. He dreamed that he was suddenly overtaken with a great desire to take part in the ceremonies, but when he attempted to make his way into the garden, forty armed martyrs stood in his way, threatening him, and they would have crushed him if one of the martyrs had not shown him mercy. The dream was so vivid and so harrowing that he woke up weeping. He made his way back to where the relics, gathered together in an immense urn, were being worshiped by the virgins of Annesi, entreating

God to pardon him and the armed martyrs to forgive him. It was the first crisis in his life: there were to be many more.

For a while he became a practicing Christian, and even undertook the office of a lector, reading the Bible lections to the congregation, but he had little heart for it. His father had been a great lawyer and rhetorician, and he began to think again of following in his father's footsteps. He threw up the office of lector and became a teacher of rhetoric. Gregory Nazianzen, who came to know him well about this time, heard the news and wrote a vigorous letter in protest. "So you are determined to be called a rhetorician rather than a Christian," Gregory Nazianzen wrote. "Well, my friend, do not continue for long in this way, but awake to soberness before it is too late, return to yourself and demand pardon from God and all the faithful." There is no evidence that the command was immediately obeyed. Basil and Gregory Nazianzen had long ago bound themselves to vows of chastity, and about this time the younger Gregory married a girl called Theosobeia. We know almost nothing about her. When she died, some twenty years later, Gregory Nazianzen called her "the glory of the Church, the adornment of Christ, the helper of our generation, the hope of womankind, the most beautiful and glorious among the beauty of Brethren" (*Ep.* 197). They seem to have lived together as man and wife only for a short while, and sometimes Gregory would find himself regretting his loss of virginity. Thinking of the great celibates whose lives were dedicated to God, he wrote later that he felt like the confectioners and servants who prepare a rich banquet which they will never be allowed to taste.

Married, with a small patrimony, possessed of a desultory education, a talent for speaking and a desire to write, full of self-doubts, with no great desire for traveling abroad, he remained in Caesarea with his books and disquieting thoughts. Once he wrote to Gregory Nazianzen that he felt like a piece of driftwood floating down a stream. He was still the reluctant Christian, temporizing with his doubts, and uncertain where the future lay. Then Basil invited him to the retreat at Ibora, in the wooded hills of the Iris, and he seems to have joined Basil only because there was nothing better to do. Here his religious temper quickened, and there began to flower in him the sense of God's abiding goodness and the transience of all things.

His first book written at Ibora, was *On Virginity*. In this work his style is already formed: quick, lucid, searching, contemplative, and always with the sense of the beauty of the world. For him the ideal in life consists in *theoria*, the contemplation of God by the soul which has stripped itself of everything except the love of God. Therefore to be married, to be entangled in the worldly cares which accompany marriage, is a threat to the purity of the soul. Celibacy, as a thing in itself, he does not defend; he knows the pride of "monkish" virgins. Characteristically, it is the pain and suffering accompanying marriage which he dwells on: the woman in labor, her despair when she loses her child, the husband's despair leading to madness if his wife perishes. The transience of marriage is sufficient reason for putting it aside. The lover gazes upon the beloved, and at that very moment he knows her beauty will perish—"the bright eyes beneath the lids, the arching brows, the cheeks dimpling into smiles, the red bud of her lips, the tangled gleam of her golden curls, and all those other embellishments which have been granted to her for so short a while, all these will one day melt away and become as nothing, and she will be transformed into noisome and unsightly bones" (*De Virginitate*, 3). So the years passed in a kind of waking dream, while he prepared himself slowly and awkwardly for the tasks ahead.

All through his life there were signs of this awkwardness, which Basil called "his complete simplicity of mind." He could never be expected to see problems as others saw them. Basil became Bishop of Caesarea, a potentate of the Church, a man of vast responsibilities and (as he grew older) unenviable rigidity of mind. The huge shadow of the elder brother fell on the younger, and Gregory seems to have walked uncomfortably in the shade. When he heard that Basil was quarreling furiously with an uncle who was a bishop in Pontus, Gregory decided to act. He simply forged three letters from the uncle to Basil, desiring reconciliation. Nothing could be simpler. It seemed to Gregory astonishingly stupid that these quarrels should be allowed to continue. Basil sent copies of the letters back to Pontus, and when the uncle angrily repudiated the forgery, the fat was in the fire. Basil wrote angrily to Gregory:

> It is impossible to argue with you in a letter. How can I chastise you, as you deserve, for your complete simplicity of mind? Three times altogether you fell into the trap. You allowed yourself to be snared three times. You actually forged the letter and brought it to me as from the most reverend bishop, our uncle, and you did this to deceive me! I haven't the faintest idea why you do these things! I received the letter as though it came from the bishop

and was delivered through you, and how could I have done otherwise? I was so delighted I showed it to friends, and I thanked God for this blessing. Now the forgery is exposed, and the bishop himself has repudiated it. . . . So I am writing to upbraid you for your remarkable simplicity, which I consider unbecoming in a Christian and especially inappropriate at the present time. I beg you in future to watch over yourself and spare me—I am speaking very frankly—because you are unworthy to attend to great affairs.

[*Ep.* 48]

Gregory seems not to have been unduly perturbed by the pompous letter; he remained in his monastic solitude; and he might have remained there forever if the Emperor Valens, on coming to the throne, had not decided to divide Cappadocia into two parts, with the result that Basil was compelled to appoint bishops at various outposts of his diocese to protect the see of Caesarea from the encroachments of Bishop Anthimus of Tyana, who now ruled over a larger ecclesiastical domain than Basil. Basil decided to appoint his brother to the bishopric of Nyssa, a small town ten miles from Caesarea, which survives today as an obscure village and horse station. Gregory was bitterly disappointed. He had hoped to spend many more years in contemplation, and he knew himself to be unfit for the charge. He was unhappy in the company of men. He detested giving orders. He was in no mood for offering continual obedience to his elder brother. He therefore rejected the command, and was consecrated bishop only because he was forced by Basil. He said afterward that the day of his consecration was the most miserable in his whole life, and he had known many miseries.

As Basil must have known, Gregory was completely incapable of administering his tiny diocese. He had no tact, no knowledge of human behavior and no sense of the value of money. He had been bishop three years when Philochares brought against him a charge of embezzling church finances. Gregory was ill, suffering from pleurisy. The charge was debated at a provincial synod meeting in Ancyra in Galatia, and orders were given for Gregory's arrest. Bound in chains, he was carried away by the imperial guards, and then characteristically escaped. He went into hiding, while another synod composed chiefly of Arian bishops and court prelates met at Nyssa and solemnly deposed him. He remained in hiding until the death of the Arian Emperor Valens at Adrianople; and though he complained sometimes in the letters he wrote during this period of eclipse, he was happier in hiding that when he wore the robes of a bishop in his church at Nyssa.

Yet Nyssa held him. He had gone there for the first time in a raging fury, but in exile he regretted the loss of his small house, with its humble furniture, the fire and the table and the rows of books, even the benches and the sacking on which he slept. Now he was a wanderer, "embraced by the cold and the dark." Occasionally the sunlight gleamed through the clouds. It may have been about this time—for there is no date on the letter—that he stayed on the estate of his friend, the lawyer Adelphius, and one evening, as the sun was going down, he wrote enchantingly of the delights of the countryside:

> The river Halys gleams like a ribbon of gold through a deep purple robe, and scarlet sand is washed down from the bank to touch the river with redness. High up lie the oak-crowned ridges of the hills, all green, and worthy of some Homer to sing their praises; and as the oaks wander down the slopes they meet the saplings planted by men. All over the foothills are vines, some green, others ripe with grape clusters. Here at Vanota the fruit is ripe, but it is otherwise in the nearby villages. . . . Homer never saw the apple trees with such gleaming fruit as we have here, the apples themselves almost the color of appleblossom, so white and shining. Have you ever seen pears as white as newly polished ivory? And what shall we say of the immense heaps of peaches? And what of the pathways beneath the climbing vines, and the sweet shade under the clusters of grapes, and the new wall where the roses climb and the vines trail and twist and form a kind of protecting fortress against invaders, and what about the pond which lies at the very top of the pathway and the fish that are bred there?
>
> [*Ep.* 15]

Then he goes on, delighted with all the scents and sounds of the place, to tell of the boy who dived into the deep pool "like a conjuror" and brought up fish in his hands, surprisingly tame. These fish rising from the depths "leapt into the air like winged things, as though deliberately mocking the creatures of earth; and having shown themselves—or rather one half of themselves—they tumbled through the air and dived once more into the depths."

This letter marks a moment of quite extraordinary importance in the history of literature. In the fourth century Gregory is describing nature in almost the same terms as the romantics of the eighteenth century. He describes nature simply, accurately, penetratingly, with a superb awareness of atmosphere, the air which bathes and hovers over all things seen. The scarlet sands washed into the river, the white pears hanging from the trees, the boy with the fish in his hand— no one had attempted such things before, in such profusion. Now listen to him again as he returns from his exile to his bishopric at Nyssa after the death of Valens:

> There was a chill wind blowing through the clouds, bringing a drizzle, which hit us with its dampness. The sky threatened such rain as no one had ever known, and to our left lay the thunder— unending thunder—and quick flashes of lightning, thunder and lightning in hurried succession, and all the mountains in front of us, behind us and on every side were shrouded with clouds. . . . And later the rain fell, but only a little. It was not unpleasant, just enough to moisten the air. We were close to home when the cloud bellying above us suddenly emptied, and because of the storm our entrance was very quiet, no one being aware of our coming.
>
> And then, as we reached the covered porch [of the bishop's palace], the sound of the carriage wheels along the hard dry earth was heard, and the people poured out to meet us, as though they had been mechanically expelled from nowhere, I know not how or why it came about, but they were all there, flocking round us so closely it was not easy to descend from the carriage, for there was not a foot of clear space anywhere. So we persuaded them, though with some difficulty, to allow us to alight and let the mules pass, but the crowd surrounded us and would have crushed us with excessive kindness, and I was near fainting. When we were well within the covered porch, we saw a river of fire pouring into the church, and this came from the choirs of virgins carrying wax candles in their hands as they marched in file through the open doors of the church, kindling a blaze of splendor. Then I went into the church and rejoiced and wept with my people—for I wept and rejoiced as they did—and after I had said prayers, I hastened to write this letter to Your Holiness, being myself exceedingly thirsty, but determined to write to you before surrendering to my physical wants.   [*Ep.* 3]

This is Gregory at play, delighting in words and their power to convey meaning. Almost alone of the Fathers, he could convey delight in life. "The fountain of blessing wells up unceasingly," he wrote once; and that gay, awkward, intractable spirit within him is continually bubbling with joy. It is the mark of the joyful man that he tells stories well. Sometimes Gregory told stories very well indeed. Once he complained against the Christians who only act out their parts. He said they reminded him of the ape belonging to the Alexandrian juggler. The juggler carefully trained the ape to imitate professional dancers, gave it a costume and a mask, and arranged that it should join the dancers. A man in the audience saw through the ruse. He tossed some almonds into the orchestra. The ape's greed betrayed it, for it tore off its mask and went running after the almonds, while the audience roared with laughter. Gregory points the not very interesting moral: "for many are the Christians who remove the mask of temperance or meekness or some other virtue" (*De Professione christiana*, 6). It is clear that he liked the story for its own sake.

But Gregory could be dull, too. He wrote against the Eunomians an enormous tract, full of cogent and well-marshaled arguments against the heretic. The humor is heavy-handed and the argument is endless. No holds are barred. Everything Eunomius ever said is examined in the microscope and seen to be an absurdity; and by passing from one absurdity to another, Gregory gives the impression of some beetle-browed clerk deliberately jumping up and down on some worthless pieces of paper. Occasionally the familiar Gregory peers through the murk. Eunomius contended that "the same energies produce the same kind of work." He was speaking about the energies of God. "Yes," says Gregory, "the house-breaker and the well-digger move their hands, mining and murder are the work of hands, the soldier wields his spear and the husbandman follows his plow, and the same energies produce the same work!" He gleams with malice when he discusses the early life of his enemy. Eunomius was the son of a poor farmer, who lived the farmer's life during the greater part of the year and carved out wooden alphabets for children in winter. The implication is clear—Eunomius is still carving out wooden alphabets for children! He is equally unfair, but considerably more amusing, when he discusses Aetius, who belonged to the Eunomian faction. "They say he began life as a tinker and had the grimy trade quite at his fingertips, sitting under a goat's hair tent, with a small hammer and a diminutive anvil, and so earned a scanty and laborious livelihood" (*Contra Eunomium*, I, 6). But there are few passages like this. The heavy guns are marshaled, and every inch of the enemy territory is spattered with slow-dropping shells; it is all weariness, immensity, desert.

Gregory never repeated the crime. He wrote enchantingly about divine things, and just as enchantingly about the nature of man, which he was continually celebrating. No other Father had so much faith in man. Origen had spoken of an eternal Sabbath when all men would find themselves at last within the Kingdom of God, but Origen's Sabbath consisted of an eternal quietness and repose. Gregory's Sabbath was like a triumphant chorus, an endless celebration, an eternal feast accompanied by ever-increasing joys. In his treatise called *On the Making of Man* he wrote of Adam at the dawn of Creation:

> By its likeness to God human nature is made as it were a living image partaking with the Godhead both in rank and in name, clothed in virtue, reposing in the blessedness of immortality, garlanded with the crown of righteousness, and so a perfect likeness to the beauty of the Godhead in all that belongs to the dignity of majesty.   [*De hominis Opificio, IV, 136*]

Corresponding to the vision of man in his innocence was the vision of man in glory when "Paradise is restored, and the tree of life is restored also, and the grace of the image, and the dignity of sovereignty" (*De hom. Opificio*, XIII, 8). Here he is speaking in poetic terms; later he will say the same in more reasoned terms, putting the words into the mouth of his sister Macrina as she lay dying in a blaze of philosophy. Then he said, in words that sound so final that one can hardly dispute with them, though some have found them heretical: "The Resurrection will bring about the restoration of our human nature in its original form"—ἀνάστασίς ἐστιν ἡ εἰς τὸ ἀρχαῖον τῆς φύσεως ἡμῶν ἀποκατάστασις. (*De An.* 100). It is a sentence which crystallizes the wildest hopes and the most profound beliefs, and all the sorrow and all the gaiety, of the Eastern Church. It is also the sentence which divides them most completely from the beliefs of the Western Church.

Gregory held firm to the belief in the final restoration of the image of God in man, that time when human souls will become "like celestial palm groves, the perfume of their flowers giving off the sweetest scents." He believed that at the Resurrection men will adopt the image of God in themselves, become deified, having put away those "dead animal skins" which were bequeathed to them when the first sin was committed. He believed that men are punished in the afterlife for their sins, but their punishment is not eternal:

The soul of the dead man will be brought before the judgment seat, it will hear the sentence on its past life, it will receive punishment and reward according to its desert, either to be cleansed by fire according to the word of the Gospels, or to be blessed and comforted in the dew of grace.   [*Patrologia Graeca*, XLVI, 167]

This, then, is our glory: to be clothed again in a renewed body, to come to God, to live in His eternal presence beyond sin and suffering and all the travails of the flesh. So, as always, Gregory celebrates the grandeur and nobility of men, and with such charity that he could bring himself to believe that even the Prince of Darkness would once more be restored to his seat beside the throne of God. For Gregory, as for Origen, there is universal salvation, but with what a difference! For Gregory the salvation is accomplished in the joyfulness of God; Origen sees it in the light of an abstract idea.

Gregory's joy, his sense of delight in the human soul, is manifest again in a work known variously as *The Great Catechism* or *An Address on Religious Instruction,* which is no more than a simple address to some catechists. It is a quiet inquiry into the nature of God and Man. It happens on a summer afternoon, and the catechists are gathered around him as he asks questions and suggests answers, pausing, digressing, at ease with himself. Two or three hours pass. When the talk was over, the catechists may hardly have realized that something of supreme importance had occurred: it was a voice they had heard many times before, saying very much what he had said previously. Only this time he spoke with immeasurable authority and grace.

He begins a little haltingly, with a discussion on the nature of faith and how Christianity stands at the point midway between Hellenism and Judaism. But Christianity has added a new dimension: the Trinity, where all is mystery, yet the human soul of its own accord half-divines the mystery. Man is created in the image of God, in the image of the Trinity. At this point a catechist interrupts with the question: Why on earth did God go to the trouble of making man? Gregory answers sagely that God was driven by no necessity. It was simply an act of charity: man was formed out of the abundance of God's love, "for it was not right that light should remain unseen, or glory unwitnessed, or goodness unenjoyed, or that any aspect of the divine nature should remain idle with no one to share it." (*Oratio Catechetica,* 5). A catechist observes that this is all very well, but there is so much evil and suffering inherent in man that it would have been better perhaps if man had not been created at all. Where is the soul's likeness to God? Where is the body's freedom from suffering? Where is eternal life? Man's life is fleeting, mortal, so frail, so twisted with pain it is astonishing he claims to be created in the image of God.

Gregory replies that man was endowed with the gift of liberty and free will, and brought this suffering on himself. It is not God's fault. "If a man in broad daylight of his own free will closes his eyes, the sun is not responsible for his failure to see." Man was truly made into an image of God. Before the Fall, he possessed a beauty like unto God's, and was full of candor, reveling in the direct vision of God. He was free from passion and possessed rulership over the earth and all the creatures. But all this was tinder for the adversary's passionate envy. Yet Satan could not fulfill his purpose by force or violence, for the power of God's blessing was superior to such force. It was man who destroyed man, and therefore God came down in human form to rescue him.

Then a catechist asks why it was necessary for God to come down to earth in the form of a man, to suffer birth and growth, eating and drinking, weariness, sleep, grief, tears, false accusations, the trial, the Cross and the tomb. Why go through it all? Human nature is so small a thing, and God so infinite. And Gregory answers, as Athanasius had done before him, that a single grace extended through all Creation and a man is worthy to be saved; he needed God, and therefore God came. "Man was sick and needed a doctor. He had fallen and needed to be raised up. He had lost his life and needed his life restored. He was shut up in the dark and needed the light. He was the prisoner and needed to be ransomed. He was the slave and needed to be free." (*Oratio Catechetica*, 15). Then why, suggests a catechist, was it necessary for God to take this long, tedious, circuitous route? He could have saved man with a shout, a command. And Gregory answers that perhaps nothing would have been simpler, but in the economy of God the assumption of human flesh was the most desirable way, because it effectively shamed the devil. God veiled Himself in human flesh so that the devil "like a greedy fish might swallow the Godhead along with the flesh which was the bait." And in His coming, there was all the evidence of His divinity. What more marvelous than that a virgin should suckle her child? Heavenly voices announced His eminence. He raised the dead, walked on the waters and healed the sick with a mere word. From the secret granaries of God He made bread, and

Himself sowed the sea with fish. The adversary, "seeing this power softly reflected more and more through the miracles," took heart. He was not aware that he was in the presence of God, and little did he realize the power of Jesus to drive him out of the universe. Gregory admits that there was some element of fraud and deception involved. If He had shown Himself as God naked, God divested of human flesh, how would He have escaped recognition by the devil? "You must admit," says Gregory, "that in acting in this way God showed a crowning example of justice and wisdom." And when a catechist returned to the question of why God should assume human form, Gregory answered:

There is no reason why anyone should be surprised because He took on human form. Only fools refuse to see the divinity which informs, pervades, embraces and has its dwelling place in the universe. For all things depend on Him who is, and nothing can exist which does not have its being in Him who is. If, then, all things exist in Him and He exists in all things, why should people be shocked at a process of revelation which teaches that God became man, when we believe that even now He is not outside us? For if the divine presence is not the same as He was when incarnate among us, yet it is agreed that God is among us today as He was in a former time. Now He is united to us as one who embraces nature in His being, but then He had united Himself with our being, so that men might be rescued from death and delivered from the tyranny of the adversary; and by union with the divine becoming themselves divine. *For His return from death was for the mortal race the beginning of our return to eternal life.*

[*Oratio Catechetica,* 25]

Gregory had spoken about the restoration of the image of God in man before, but never so succinctly, or with such quiet assurance. Here is the heart of *The Great Catechism*: the rest embroiders on this main thesis. The catechists, or Gregory himself, ask questions, but they cannot shake him from this truth. If he is asked why the Incarnation was so long delayed, Gregory answers that it had to be: it was necessary that evil should come to its full before God descended to put an end to it. And when a catechist says: There is still evil in the world, nothing has changed, the very air smells of evil, Gregory has his characteristic reply. He says evil and death have come to an end, Christ has killed them, and what we observe is merely the twitching of the serpent's tail after it has received a mortal blow on the head.

There are more questions—endless questions. Gregory leans back, closes his eyes as he listens, and then opens them wide. It occurs to him that it is astonishing that there should be unbelievers for all the accomplishments of Christ were so godlike, and He was never so godlike as when He rose from the tomb:

He did not remain dead, and the wounds the spear inflicted on His body did not prevent Him living. After the Resurrection He appeared at will to the disciples. Whenever He wished, He was present with them, though unobserved. He came into their midst without needing doors to give Him entrance. He strengthened the disciples by breathing on them His Spirit. He promised to be with them, and nothing would ever separate Him from them. Visibly He ascended to Heaven, and to their minds He was everywhere present. [*Oratio Catechetica, 32*]

They ask about baptism: how was it possible that water could acquire the healing energy of God? What has water in common with life? a drop of moisture, is that the image of God? And Gregory answers cheerfully that seed is also a drop of moisture, but it bears within it the image of man, who is like unto God in all things, even to possessing immortality. For Gregory seed, like water, is sacramental. It is not by the eye nor the ear nor the tongue nor any of the senses that the race is constantly carried on, but it is the generative organ which preserves the immortality of the human race, keeping death at bay. Did not God's seed enter the Virgin? And should we think it strange that God was united with human life in the same way that nature wars on death? It is all done so gently and calmly that we are hardly aware of the dazzling impropriety.

There is nothing ponderous in *The Great Catechism*; he moves so lightly, so easily among the abysses and the quicksands that he gives the impression of dancing. He has the grace of St. Francis. A trained theologian, he tosses the theological books away.

Oh, be purified in water, and then you will have a share of that purity which is most perfect in God. Observe how simple it is in its beginnings, how easily accomplished—just faith and water: faith which is a matter of our own choice, and water which is natural to our life. And what blessings spring from these—nothing less than kinship with God Himself! [*Oratio Catechetica, 36*]

It was not, of course, always as simple as this. There are terrible things: holy utterances which make the hair stand on end, nightmares and cruxes on which the baffled mind batters relentlessly, without coming upon any solution. Gregory was perfectly aware of the two-edged knives. There were texts in the New Testament which left him giddy, like a man standing on a high beetling cliff looking at the sea below. He wrote a brief commentary on the Beatitudes, and when he came to the words: "Blessed are the pure in heart, for they shall see God," he confessed himself in a quandary. How shall God be seen? God said to Moses: "There shall no man see me, and live." In the *Gospel according to St. John,* it is written: "No man hath seen God at any time." St. Paul said: "Whom no man hath seen, nor can see." But if God is life, then not to see Him means to be deprived of life, and the hope of all mankind is obliterated, annihilated, utterly destroyed. Then how shall a man go about being a Christian?

This preoccupation with the vision of God is central to the Eastern Church, and some of Gregory's greatest writings are concerned with it. It would be simple to compile an anthology from the Fathers, setting in one column all the proofs that God cannot be seen and in the other all the proofs that He is visible to the mortal eyes of the mystic; sometimes the same Father would appear in both columns. The most authoritative texts said that God remained eternally invisible, yet it was not certain that they meant exactly what they said. How should one read the words of Habakkuk: "His brightness was as the light; he had horns coming out of his hands; and there was the hiding of his power." Was this the vision?

Like other Fathers Gregory is never sure: he seems to hover between the belief that God may be visible to the elect, and that he hides permanently behind the cloud of unknowing. He says in *The Life of Moses:*

> The vision of God consists in this: that He cannot be seen, since what we seek is beyond all knowledge, being wholly concealed in a cloud of incomprehensibility. Therefore St. John, who also entered into this bright mist, says that no man has seen God at any time, meaning by this denial that the knowledge of the divine nature is impossible not only for man but for every intelligent creature.   [*De Vita Moysis,* 376 D]

But this is not final: he will go on, and like the young prince from Egypt who ascended Sinai, he will attempt to grapple with incomprehensibility, wrestling with angels.

Gregory's *Life of Moses* and *Commentary on the Song of Songs* are his two great mystical works. Neither has been translated into English, though indirectly they have contributed to the great stream of English mysticism, for he clearly influenced Dionysius the Areopagite, through whom Oriental mysticism entered the West. Here he writes as a contemplative mystic, tossing dogma aside, no longer concerned with controversies, desiring only the knowledge of God. Reading him, we are aware of a man employing all his forces and faculties in an attempt to describe the indescribable. He was the first to speak of "the dark night of the soul," the first to describe in any detail the complex workings of the mystical consciousness. He is like a mountain climber, moving slowly at first, consolidating his ground, taking the easier slopes wherever he can, resting sometimes, until at last on some high pinnacle he feels strong enough to launch himself at the summit, at the ultimate mystery. He often stumbles, but never falls. So, in strange composure, he spurs himself to relentless efforts to approach the majesty of God, charting the dark and chequered spaces immediately below the throne, those places where everything is precarious, because the nearer a man comes to God, the greater the dangers. Here the lightning flashes, the thunder rolls, and the voice speaking out of the burning bush may be a man's own whispers or the voice of God Himself.

Gregory seems to have written *The Life of Moses* in his old age, for in the introduction he speaks of his white hair. But it is just as possible that he wrote the book early in his life, his white hair being no more than a figure of speech. It is the prose of a comparatively young man, with grace and muscle in it, and he had been reading Plato not long before, for the rhythms of Plato joined with the rhythms of the Old Testament dominate it. At the beginning he pretends not too successfully to have put Plato aside. "What have I to do with the pagan philosophers?" he asks; and he answers that they are full of enigmas and seductive theories and half-truths. They teach the immortality of the soul, but not content with the soul's immortality, they must go on to elaborate theories on the transmigration of souls. They teach the existence of God (so far so good), but explain Him as a physical being possessing physical appetites. They teach that God created the world, and then look around for matter, since God could not have made the world without matter. They teach that God possesses divine goodness and power, and then insist that He is chained to fatality. They have corrupted true doctrines with absurd additions. No; it is best to be done with them! And having tossed Plato abruptly away, he seems unaware that Plato continues to stand by his side.

The meat is in the last chapters; the first two-thirds of the book are no more than a preliminary survey, a climb over the foothills. As the Alexandrian Jewish philosopher Philo had done before him, and sometimes in almost the same words, Gregory describes the life of Moses and the exodus of the Israelites as an allegory of the human soul. Sometimes he borrows from Origen, who had also spoken about the soul's mysterious journeys and about the exodus, paying strict attention to the hardening of Pharaoh's heart, which Gregory for some reason omits altogether. There are echoes, too, of St. Paul, who spoke of how "all were baptized unto Moses in the cloud and in the sea." Philo had compared the Logos with Moses, standing at the frontiers of the natural world and the celestial order, and interceding for mankind, the young lawgiver appareled in the robes of the mediator. It was the custom to see allegories in all things. The raised hands of Moses represented the Cross. The Passover represented the blood of the Lamb. Manna was the Word of God. The twelve springs were the twelve apostles, and the seventy palm trees were the seventy elders of Jerusalem. The cavalry archers and slingers who tumbled over one another in the waters of the Red Sea were the turbulent passions of men. There is a good deal more of this. It is written elegantly, but we have the feeling that Gregory is not altogether convinced by his own interpretation, and he even admits that there are considerable dangers in "explaining mysteries by mysteries." But as the Israelites approach Sinai, the prose quickens, the shadows darken, the pulse throbs, the air flashes with lightnings. No longer concerned with the easy solutions of allegory, he darts forward toward the ultimate mystery. Did not Moses confront God face to face on Sinai? Did not the hunter seize upon his quarry? There, in a cloud, mysteriously hidden for forty days, Moses saw into the blazing eyes of majesty.

But before Gregory assails the inmost recesses of the shrine, he makes one last survey, one last careful circumambience of the territory to be conquered. He asks himself what is the nature of the pursuit. What powers must Moses possess to burst upon the treasure house? He must be perfect, but what is perfection? It is, he says, an unyielding dedication to the tasks of God, a movement ever forward and yet so paradoxical that it is no movement at all. Perfection does not consist in accomplishment; it is not like the stone carved by the sculptor; the perfect act consists in performing a perpetual flight toward the throne of God. In these realms the unerring flight is itself the goal. To seek is to find, the desires of the soul are fulfilled because they are insatiable, and the soul of the devout man goes beyond itself and yet remains unmoving. It is a landscape of paradox. Here men plunge into the heights. God is not found; He is flown to; and to perform the flight is to perform a divine act, to become like God.

So the eternal pursuit, endlessly renewed, is the discovery of God. The endless desire for Him is itself the sight of Him. And in the flight toward God there is no fluttering of wings, only an unmoving motion, an enraptured progress around a center. When Moses is seen climbing over the foothills of the holy mountain, Gregory puts into the mouth of God the words:

O Moses, because you are straining with so great a desire for that which is before you and there is no weariness in your progress, know that the spaces around you are so vast you will never reach the end of your journey. Here there is only motionlessness. I set you on the Rock; and now there occurs the most astonishing thing of all: for here to be in motion, and to be unmoving, are the same thing. Here he who advances stops, and he who stops advances, and he advances by the very fact that he is motionless.

[*De Vita Moysis*, 405 B-C]

Here in this world of fantastic dangers, at the cliff's edge, where a man is safest only when he is standing at the very rim of the abyss, the natural law is exchanged for heavenly law. Later, borrowing from Gregory, Dionysius the Areopagite was to employ the same image of the God who is at one and the same time in movement and motionless, and he was to color this strange progress with the light of an overshadowing love:

We dare to assume and affirm (for it is the truth) that the Creator of the Universe in His beautiful and tender yearning for the Universe is through the excessive yearning of His goodness transported out of Himself in His providential activities toward all living things; and He is touched by the sweet spell of goodness, love and yearning, and is drawn from His transcendent throne above all things to dwell within the heart of all things through a superessential and ecstatic power whereby He yet remains within Himself. [*De divinis Nominibus*, IV, 13]

But this ecstatic language is foreign to Gregory, who remains calm and in complete control of his vocabulary when he approaches Sinai. With Dionysius the words tumble over one another; Gregory simply seeks for some human analogy, and he finds it in the man climbing a deep sandy slope. "Watch him," he says, "as he makes great commotions with his legs, but all to no purpose, for the sand keeps falling and he remains at the bottom: there is wasted movement, and no progress. But if in the words of the Psalmist a man lifts himself from the pit and sets his feet upon the Rock—here the Rock is Christ—then his progress will be sure, speedy and steadfast and anchored in goodness." So Moses advances into the cloud by remaining spiritually motionless; he expends spiritual energy, but his spiritual energy increases the more he expends it. Then he approaches the ultimate mystery, the invisible sanctuary.

Gregory describes the stages of the ascent in terms as far removed from abstractions as possible. He asks questions, suggests answers, hints at the vast glories of God, but in the end he discovers that the face of God remains hidden, and by being hidden is revealed. Many times in *Exodus* the Lord is said to speak face to face with Moses, but Gregory accounts these statements as exaggerations. Moses did not see the face of God in the burning bush, "which was no more than a simple thorn bush, yet it glowed more splendidly than any stars." No, the true confrontation occurred when Moses cried: "I beseech thee, show me thy glory." Thereupon God answered: "Thou canst not see my face; for there shall no man see me, and live." But God said that His Glory would pass by, and Moses will be placed in a cleft in the rock and covered with God's hand. "And I will take away my hand, and thou shalt see my back parts; but my face shall not be seen." (*Exod.* 33:18, 20, 23).

For Gregory these are the supreme moments of the life of Moses; beyond this no man except Christ can ever go until the Resurrection. It would seem that Moses is defeated in his endeavor. On the contrary, says Gregory, this is the moment of his greatest triumph:

> For how did it happen to him who had seen so many appearances of God, according to the Holy Scriptures, which say that he "spoke face to face with the Lord, as a friend talking to a friend" —how did it happen that when he came to Sinai he who had so often found God should demand to see God again at this time? The heavenly voice announced that God would show Himself and

not refuse Moses this grace, and yet he must be shown that his desire exceeded all the desires of human nature; and so Moses was led to despair.

But God said: "There is a place by me," and there Moses would find a rock and a hollow within the rock, where Moses was to stand; and God said He would cover Moses with His hand as he passed by; and Moses would see the back of Him whom he had summoned; and so he would believe at last that he had seen what he desired to see, and the promise of the Lord was not in vain.

[*De Vita Moysis,* 400 A-B]

There follows one of the most extraordinary passages ever written by one of the Fathers. After the intense investigation of the character of the young Moses, after describing in detail the circumstances of the journey which led to Sinai, after preparing the reader for all the paradoxes which will confront Moses as he climbs the mountain, Gregory describes the ascent in short, quick sentences which glitter like fire leaping off the tesserae of an immense mosaic:

He sees the flame springing out, and lightly climbs toward it, removing his shoes. He claims the same liberty for his family and his friends. He has seen his enemies drowned beneath the waves. He remains in the cloud. He quenches his thirst on the Rock. He gathers bread from Heaven. And stretching out his hands, he triumphs over the stranger.

Then he hears the trumpet blasts, and enters into a dark place, penetrating into the secret heart of the uncreated tabernacle. He learns the secrets of the priesthood. He hurls the idols away. He begs God's mercy. He re-establishes the Law, which has been broken by the Jews. He shines with glory, and having reached this high summit, he burns even now with an insatiable desire, and he thirsts for that which already fills him; and as though he had not yet entered the place, he demands that God should appear to him not in the measure which is permitted to him, but to see God as He is. . . .

So he desires, not the reflection or the mirrored image of God, but God seen face to face. And the divine voice, by refusing, offers him what he desires: a few words which open out into an immense abyss of thought, the magnificence of God fulfilling his desires, but never promising either peace or satiety. For this is the true vision of God: that those who lift their eyes toward Him never cease to desire Him. And that is why God said: "Thou canst not see my face; for there shall no man see me, and live."

But the Scriptures do not mean by this that the face of God is a cause of death to those who see Him; for how could it be that the face of Eternal Life could cause death to those that come near it? The divine being brings life, but it is beyond our understanding, and yet Moses came to learn from God's words that the divine being is infinite, boundless, beyond anything hoped for. . . .

What then is the Rock and the cleft in the Rock? What is the hand of God which stops up the orifice in the cleft in the Rock? What is meant when God says: "All my goodness shall pass before thee?" And what are those shoulders which God promises to show Moses, who demanded only to see God's face?

[*De Vita Moysis*, 401 A-D]

For Gregory the answer is simple: all these things denote the presence of Christ, just as the tabernacle and all its furnishings denote aspects of Christ. So he returns to a familiar conclusion by way of the forbidding landscape in which the soul makes its ascent to God. Until Gregory, no one had ever described the mystical ascent so well, or invaded its mysteries with such assurance of victory. Dionysius the Areopagite, St. Bernard, a hundred others, were to describe this same movement of the soul, often employing the same terms, nearly always borrowing directly or indirectly from Gregory. The *De Vita Moysis* was the first great mystical treatise; and the speech which Gregory puts into the mouth of God as Moses climbs the mountain and the long passage describing the Ascent are among the most brilliant of Christian inventions.

Gregory never quite reached these heights again. Toward the end of his life, while staying in Constantinople, he was prevailed upon by the deaconess Olympias, the friend of Chrysostom, to write a *Commentary on the Song of Songs*. It is a brilliant, but uneven work. Like Origen, pursuing the same allegorical method, he will say dull things on dull texts. Commenting on the words: "If thou know not, O thou fairest among women, go thy way forth by the footsteps of thy flock," he merely insists that men should know themselves, avoid carnal pleasures, set their minds upon God. On such occasions he seems to be talking without conviction, saying something that has been said so many times already it is a weariness to continue. But there are texts which set his mind on fire. Like many Fathers he believed that the

Song of Songs was a mystical treatise, a veiled description of the mystical process leading to ultimate union with God. A man who had pondered the mysterious cleft in the Rock at Sinai might be expected to pause when he reads in the *Song of Songs*:

O my dove, thou art in the clefts of the rock, in the secret places of the stairs, let me see thy countenance, let me hear thy voice; for sweet is thy voice, and thy countenance is comely.

[*Song of Songs*, 2:14]

What is God saying? Surely He is offering some mysterious clue to the nature of the vision at Sinai. So Gregory reads the *Song of Songs* with Moses continually in mind. For him it is not a poem celebrating the fidelity of the Shulamite for her shepherd lover; it is a poem written with all the authority of King Solomon who purified his heart before setting down, to the honor of God and of Moses, a description of the soul's entrance into the divine sanctuary.

The Shulamite rises from her bed, and calls upon the watchmen to tell her where her lover can be found. There is no answer from the watchmen. Soon she finds her lover, holds him and will not let him go, "until I had brought him into my mother's house and into the chamber of her that conceived me." Gregory writes:

The watchmen were silent when she spoke, and showed by their silence they were powerless to seek Him whom her soul loveth; and she, abandoning herself, came to know that Him whom she was seeking was someone unknown to her. And so she says: "It was but a little that I passed from them," meaning that she had passed beyond created things and everything known in Creation, abandoning everything except her faith, and so she came to the Beloved. "I would not let him go": meaning that she held onto Him by the bridle of faith, until He entered into her chamber, that chamber which is the heart made into a habitation of God, as in the days when human nature was first known. [*In Cant. Hom.* 893 B-C]

In the same way, throughout the whole commentary, Gregory sees a divine outpouring of mystical love and a strange identity between sexual symbols and the symbols appropriate to Sinai, the shrine on the mountain and the dark cloud. The night of the *Song of Songs* is the night of Moses. When the Shulamite says: "I sat under his shadow with great delight, and his fruit was sweet to my taste," then she is speaking the same words which are spoken in a mystical sense by Moses in the cleft in the Rock; and the shadow of the apple tree is brought into the service of a mystical inquiry:

> For when the soul is removed from her attachment to evil, she desires that her mouth shall be close to the source of light, receiving the mystic kiss which will render her beautiful. And then having passed through all the world of appearances and having flown above the world as the dove flies, she will take shelter in the shadow of the apple tree—and here we must understand the shadow of the tree to be the image of the dark cloud—and then at last she enters the divine dark where her lover approaches, but is nowhere seen.   [*In Cant. Hom.* 1001 B]

This is the spiritual world of St. Teresa of Ávila and St. John of the Cross, a world where sexual images are employed deliberately, because no other images are appropriate; these images are employed with a full consciousness of their physical meaning in order to map out the Kingdom of Heaven. Here there is no shame, no petulance, no perplexity. The theme of sexuality is stressed, not thrust aside, but only in order that the perfection of mystical love shall be made known. We should beware of thinking the mystics consumed with sex. The sexuality of women in the complete abandoment of love is tinged with mysticism; more than men they are aware of the cleft in the Rock, the mysterious sanctuary in the divine dark, the burning bush, the fountain of living water. For the mystic the marriage with God assumes to a terrifying degree a likeness, lifted to heavenly dimensions, of an earthly marriage. "There are some who seek salvation out of fear," wrote Gregory. "There are others who are virtuous, not because they despair of physical love, but in hope of recompense. Those who aspire to perfection must be without fear, disdain recompense and love with complete abandonment. Such is the salvation by love taught in the *Song of Songs*."

For Gregory it is almost as though all the secrets of the universe were contained in the *Song of Songs*. His mind hovers over immense fields of vision. The Shulamite is the Church, she is Christ, she is whatever he desires her to be; and her beauty is a temptation which all good men will run to, or a reminder of blessings in another age. So, as he describes her beauty, he is tempted once more to think of man at the dawn of Creation before he was encompassed in sin:

Now of all things that were very beautiful one was man; or rather man was adorned with a beauty so great it was above that of beautiful things. For what else is so beautiful as the likeness of perfect beauty? For if all things were very beautiful and among all things man was pre-eminent, death was not at all in man, for he would not be a thing of beauty if he bore within him the mark of degradation which is death; but being the image and likeness of eternal life, he was truly and exceedingly beautifully adorned with the joyous seal of life. *[In Cant. Hom.* 1020 C]

Joy, beauty, delight, desire—few others have spoken of these things with such knowledge, and such intimacy. Sometimes he was a little troubled at the thought of using these words. "It is very strange," he wrote, "that we should be teaching the annihilation of the passions with words which are so very passionate." But he was never troubled for long when he was writing about the divine spirit in man, and we find him again and again soaring to these dizzy heights in celebration of man's deathlessness, his eternity, his likeness to God.

Drunk with God, rejoicing in the ultimate restoration of man, Gregory had no illusions about man's impermanence, his pride, his endless follies. The restoration is not yet. Now we live on an earth which is like a cemetery. He speaks of the giddy triumphs of youth with sorrow, for it is all so fleeting:

You are pleased because you are handsome, because your hands move quickly, because your feet are nimble, because your curls are tossed by the wind and your cheeks show a downy beard. You are proud because your clothes are dyed a deep purple and on your silken robes there are embroideries of war and hunting and great deeds. And perhaps you look down at those black leather sandals you are wearing, with their elaborate needlework. You look at such things, but you do not look at yourself. Let me show you as in a mirror your true image.

Have you ever witnessed the mysteries of the cemetery? Have you seen the heaps of bones tossed hither and thither? Skulls without flesh on them, fearful and ugly, the sockets empty. The grinning jaws and the limbs strewn about. Look at these things: there you will find yourself. Then where is the flower of youth? Where the lovely color of your cheeks, the fresh lips, the splendid shining of the eyes gleaming under arching brows? Where the straight nose set so wonderfully between the cheeks? Where the hair falling to the neck and the curls at the temples? Where the hands skilled with the bow, and the feet which so ably master the galloping horses? Where the purple, the fine linen, the mantles, the girdles, the sandals? Where, in all these bones, are the things that make you proud? What fleeting dreams, what hallucinations, what shadow is this dream of youth which vanishes as soon as it appears?   [*De beatitudinibus,* 1]

Only one thing astonishes us in this familiar graveyard catalogue: the skill with which Gregory suggests the delights of being young. If he intended to frighten, he failed. He was too much in love with the spectacle of joy to be entirely overwhelmed by the transience of joyous things. In the same way he speaks of the pleasure enjoyed by animals. "The horse prances, the bull kicks up dust, the boar's bristles stand on end, the puppies play and all the calves are leaping" (*De beat.* III). It is the ascetic speaking, but it is an ascetic who has never frowned on our innocent earthly joys. To him we are like those children who clutch at sunbeams, "but when they think they hold the sunbeam fast in their hands and then unloosen their fingers and see the sunbeam slip away, they laugh and clap their hands." (*Contra Eunom.* I, 239). He loved children, and hated only lawgivers and magistrates and those who stand in judgment over men, thus intruding themselves into God's authority.

For himself he asked little. It was enough to attend to his duties and spend the rest of his life in communion with God in prayer and thankfulness. He attached overwhelming importance to prayer. "Prayer is the delight of the joyful, the consolation of the weary, the crown of the bride, the feast on the birthday, the shroud that covers us in our graves" (*De precatione,* I). To pray, asking nothing in return, to serve the Lord, to avoid temptations, to touch the earth but lightly with the tip of the toes, to be joyous always—he asked for nothing more, and he knew it was more than any man has a right to demand.

Joy came rarely in his last days. When Basil died, he felt like someone who had received a blow from which he would never recover. A few months later his beloved sister Macrina lay dying at Annesi, where she superintended the community of nuns. As he hastened to her, he was terrified by a thrice-repeated dream, in which he saw her carrying in her hands the relics of the forty martyrs: the relics gleamed like sunlight flashing in a mirror. The monks of the monastery flocked out to meet him, and the virgins were awaiting his arrival in the church. He knew she was very ill when he observed that she was not among the nuns who took part in the church service: he had thought her only suffering from a fever. He had always felt very close to his beautiful sister, who at the age of twelve had refused all offers of marriage after the bridegroom chosen for her died. All those years she had spent in the nunnery, living in poverty and chastity, sleeping on the ground, possessing only a homespun cloak, a hood, a pair of worn-down shoes, an iron cross on her breast and on her finger a hollow ring which contained a splinter of the True Cross.

Gregory hurried from the church. He knew by the expressions on the faces of the nuns that there was little hope left. He was taken to Macrina's cell. He found her choking with asthma, lying not on the bed, but on the floor, her head propped up by boards. She had changed remarkably. At first he could hardly recognize her. She made an effort to conceal her sufferings, smiled at him tenderly and somehow muffled her fits of coughing; and seeing Gregory so grief-stricken she reminded him cheerfully of the apostle's words, forbidding Christians from taking comfort in grief. And soon, telling him that he must take refreshment after so long a journey, she dismissed him.

When Gregory returned to her cell, a change seemed to have come over her. She was very composed, and fully in command of herself. They spoke together in hushed voices. They did not talk about their childhood memories; their subject was the nature of death, and of the soul, and of the Resurrection. Gregory believed that around the freshly dug graves shadowy phantoms of the departed could often be seen, and that a peculiar sanctity hovered over the dying; so now, confronted with the sight of his sister wasting away before his eyes, he was concerned to fix in his mind the shape of her beauty, and of her sanctity, before she became the nesting place of phantoms. Some time later Gregory, remembering this conversation vividly, wrote it out at length in a treatise he called *Concerning the Soul and the Resurrection,* where Macrina appears sometimes under her own name, but more often under the name of "the Teacher." He was to say that from her dying lips he learned more than anyone else ever taught him.

Why do we grieve for them that sleep? Why do all men suffer from a deep-seated and instinctive horror of death? Why do we honor doctors, and wear armor, and build immense fortifications around our cities, if death is but the gateway to an eternal feast? And how shall the body be resurrected, when it has fallen into the dust? And what is the nature of hell? Shall the eyes of the rich man be lifted up in hell, when he has left his bodily eyes in the tomb? How can a disembodied spirit feel the flame? These, and a hundred other questions they debated together calmly, as if they were two young students hot for certainties. Gregory asks her what is the purpose of life. She answers: Love. And what is love? She answers:

Love is the foremost of all excellent achievements and the first of the commandments of the Law. Love is the life of God, and it cannot be otherwise, since perfect beauty is necessarily lovable to those who recognize it; and out of this recognition comes love. The insolence of satiety cannot touch this perfect beauty, nor can satiety ever put a stop to man's power to love what is entirely beautiful; and so the life of God consists in the eternal practice of love; and this life is wholly beautiful, possessed of a loving disposition toward beauty and never receiving any check in the practice of love. And because beauty is boundless, love shall never cease.   [*De Anima et Resurrectione*, 8]

So through the day and part of the next day, they talked in a state of calm exaltation concerning eternal things, Gregory shuddering at her approaching death, Macrina rebuking him, saying that in the end all things shall be restored, and even the devil will return to his place in Heaven: a belief to which Gregory was to hold firmly, though it was sometimes pronounced a heresy. Toward the end of the next day she was lifted onto a couch facing the East, and there she died in his arms with the prayer that God would send her "an angel of light who will lead me to quiet pastures and the waters of peace and the bosom of the Holy Fathers." The thought of the angel of light in her dying moments led her to think of the angel with the flaming sword, and then to the restoration of all things in a final Eden. So she prayed:

O Thou that didst break the flaming sword and didst restore to Paradise Him who was crucified with Thee and implored Thy mercies, remember me, too, in Thy Kingdom; for I, too, am crucified with Thee. I have nailed my flesh to my fear of Thee, and of Thy judgment have I been afraid. Let not the terrible abyss separate me from Thy elect. Nor let the Slanderer stand against me in the way; nor let my sin be found before Thy eyes, if in anything I have sinned in word or deed or thought, led astray by the weakness of our human nature. And may my soul be received into Thy hands as an offering unto Thee.   [*Vita S. Macrinae,* 33]

Then she sealed her eyes, mouth and heart with a cross; her voice died away; she prayed silently; and when someone brought in a lamp, all at once she opened her eyes and looked toward the light and made signs that she wanted to sing the Thanksgiving sung at the Lighting of the Lamps, but there was no strength left in her, and a little while later she died. Gregory closed her eyes. Later he performed the funeral offices. Previously he had searched for funeral clothes to bury her in, and asked the deaconess Lampadia to let him see his sister's cupboard. "There is no cupboard," the deaconess answered. "All she possessed is in front of you. A cloak, a hood and her worn shoes."

The funeral of so great a saint brought mourners from all the provinces around. They wailed interminably. "I had to shout," Gregory reported, "to be heard above the noise of the mourners." He had no high opinion of their behavior. They sang the Hymn of the Three Children, and Gregory helped to carry her to the Chapel of the Forty Martyrs and then to the grave where her parents and her brother Naucratius, Macrina's favorite, were buried.

With the death of Basil and Macrina, Gregory seems to have had little to live for. We catch occasional glimpses of him. In 381 he attended the Second Ecumenical Council of Constantinople, where he was greeted with high honors and regarded as "the common pillar of the Church," the foremost Cappadocian, the man who had stepped into the shoes of Basil. Meletius, the beloved Bishop of Antioch, presided, dying a few days after the Council came to an end; and Gregory who had been happy to see Gregory Nazianzen elevated to a bishopric, wept as he delivered the funeral oration over Meletius. He had long talks with St. Jerome and the deaconess Olympias, the friend of Chrysostom, and he may have added the words which the Council ordered to be attached to the Nicene Creed, for they are in Gregory's style. Then he hurried home, for he had no great liking for Constantinople. Once in a mood of petulance and overwhelming irony he wrote a famous description of the city:

A city full of profound theological disputes, everyone talking and preaching in the squares, in the market places, at the cross-roads, in the alleyways: old clothes men, money-changers, coster-mongers: they are all at it. If you ask a man to change a piece of silver, he informs you wherein the Son differs from the Father; and if you ask for the price of a loaf, you are told by way of reply that the Son is the inferior of the Father; and if you inquire whether the bath is ready, the man solemnly informs you that the Son was made out of nothing.   [*Oratio, de deitate filii*, 4]

There is reason to believe that Gregory meant precisely what he said. A few months later we see him in the company of prelates attending the Synod of Antioch. The Emperor Theodosius had recognized him as the supreme authority in all matters of theological orthodoxy, and once more he was treated with extraordinary respect. The Synod charged him to report on the Church in Arabia and Babylon, and so he set off in an imperial carriage, with all the facilities generally offered to an imperial legate. "For us," he wrote, "the carriage was as good as a monastery, and we spent the whole journey singing psalms and fasting unto the Lord." He was happy on the journey, but exploded when he came to Jerusalem and watched the seething mass of the pilgrims. It made no sense. They were dirty, and their habits in the inns shocked him. He found Jerusalem a filthy, adulterous and poisonous city; there was no other city in the Empire where people were so keen to murder one another. "I cannot imagine that the Lord is living there in the body today, or that there is an abundance of the Holy Spirit in the place," he wrote, but those were his gentler words. He fumed over Jerusalem. He could remember no passage in the New Testament which suggested that Christians should go on pilgrimage; the invitation to the Kingdom of Heaven did not include the miseries which attend the innyards of Jerusalem. He wrote:

> If a man changes his place, he is no further from God; wherever you may be God will come to you, if your soul's lodging is such that the Lord may dwell in you and walk among you. If you are full of evil thoughts, even though you be on Golgotha or on the Mount of Olives or under the Chapel of the Resurrection, you are as far from receiving Christ within you as those who have not acknowledged His sovereignty. Accordingly, beloved, advise the brethren "to journey to the body of the Lord," but not to make the journey from Cappadocia to Palestine.   [*Ep.* 2]

He was in good heart; the roads were excellent; he was greeted everywhere with the respect due to a man of his attainments; and he seems to have settled the affairs of Babylon without any great delay.

He was back in Constantinople in 383 when he preached a sermon on the Godhead of the Son and the Holy Ghost. Then, except for one last glimpse of him, he vanished from sight. And this last glimpse is terrifying.

All his life Gregory had celebrated the dignity of man and the dignity of God. A short, slight, slender man, contemplative and sensitive, withdrawn from the world but intoxicated by the world's beauty, he suffered no man to slight him. Almost his spirit had been destroyed by the hard irritability of his brother, Basil. There was worse to come. It happened that the Emperor Theodosius held Basil's successor to the see of Caesarea in high regard. Bishop Helladius was the pure courtier, a man who had achieved the undying hatred of Ambrose and Chrysostom for appointing the quack physician called Gerontius to the bishopric of Nicomedia. Gerontius was a famous liar; Helladius a famous simoniac. Gregory detested the Bishop of Caesarea, although he had several times attempted to make peace with him. Our last glimpse of Gregory is as he shivers in the rain after a long and desperate interview with Bishop Helladius, in which neither spoke more than a few troubled words.

It is one of the classic confrontations of early Christianity, and it is described with amazing force and skill. Gregory has Proust's gift of describing the silences which sometimes settle between men, those silences which have all the power of self-perpetuating explosions. In a letter to his friend Flavian, the Bishop of Antioch, Gregory tells of how one evening he was concluding services in honor of the martyrs of Sebaste and about to return to Nyssa when he heard that Bishop Helladius was in the town of Andumokinoe some fifteen miles away over the mountains. Gregory rode on to Nyssa, thinking it better that the meeting should take place later in Caesarea, but a messenger came from Halladius urging an immediate meeting. The messenger said that Helladius was gravely ill. Immediately Gregory left his carriage and hurried across the mountains, sometimes on horseback, sometimes on foot, the roads almost impassable at night, the sheer mountains on one side and precipitous cliffs on the other. He traveled part of the night and most of the next morning. It was about eleven o'clock on the Sabbath when Gregory looked down from the foothills and saw Helladius with two more bishops holding an assembly in the open air. The Bishop showed no signs of illness; on the contrary he looked remarkably well. Dragging his feet, Gregory came down the hill in the blazing summer heat, only to discover that Helladius had observed him and disappeared in a nearby house. Gregory could not help feeling depressed. The congregation had not yet dispersed. They crowded around him as he sat at the gates, trembling with heat, having sent a messenger into the house, asking to be admitted into the presence of the Bishop of Caesarea. Listen to Gregory as he recounts with mingled pride, exasperation and terror the events of that strange afternoon:

So I remained there, sitting at the gate, waiting to be invited into the house, the time unseasonable and the crowd gaping. The time was long, drowsiness came on, and a great weariness made all the greater by the fatigues of the journey and the fierce heat of the day; and all these things, the people staring at me and gaping and pointing me out, were so distressing to me that the words of the Psalmist were realized in me: "My heart within me was desolate."

I was kept waiting in this state till noon, and heartily did I repent this visit, for having brought upon myself so great a discourtesy; and my own reflections vexed me worse than the injuries done by my enemies, for I was now warring against myself and bitterly regretted that I had made the journey. At last "the gate to the altar" was thrown open, and we were permitted to enter the sanctuary. There I was confronted with His Lordship. I stood there for a moment, expecting an invitation to be seated, but none came, and so I went to one of the chairs on the other side of the room, and rested, and I still thought he would utter some friendly words or give me a nod of recognition.

But not a word was uttered. There was a silence as of the night, a tragic darkness of countenance, amazement and astonishment, and the most absolute dumbness. As in some midnight gloom, a long and speechless interval passed. I was so struck by this reception, in which he accorded me not the least sign of civility—not even a "welcome," or "where do you come from?" or "to what am I indebted for this pleasure?" or "what business brings you here?" —and so it came to me that I was spellbound in the silence of Hell; worse, for in Hell all men are reduced to an equality of misery and none of those things which disturb our earthly existence happen there. Into Hell go the souls of men who suffered from pride, conceit and petulance; but they enter the place naked and unencumbered, and none of the horrors of life await them there. To me it was like being in the underworld, in a dark dungeon, a gloomy torture chamber, the more so because I was reflecting upon the treasures of social courtesies we have inherited from our ancestors and those records of civilities we leave to our descendants. . . .

The truth was, I could see no difference between us. From the wordly point of view, where was the height from which he had descended, where was the dust in which I lay? And seeing that the vastness of his conceit and his overweening pride were so great that the height of Heaven were too narrow for it (and yet I could see no cause or occasion whatever for this diseased state of mind, such as might make it excusable for a man to contract the disease; when, for example, rank or education or pre-eminence in dignities of office may have happened to inflate their tender minds), I had no means whereby to advise myself to keep the silence, for my heart swelled with indignation and the absurdity of it all.

So at last I said: "Does my presence hinder some of the things required for your comfort, or is it time we withdrew?"

"I want no refreshment," Helladius answered, and then there was silence again.

Then I asked him what the matter was, and he spoke briefly about the injuries he said he had received at my hands, and thereupon I answered: "Lies possess an immense power to deceive mankind! At the Last Judgment no doubt these misunderstandings will cease; and for my part I am bold enough to believe I shall obtain forgiveness for all my other sins, but if I have acted in any way to harm you, then let this sin remain unforgiven forever!"

[*Ep.* I P]

But these words did nothing to calm Helladius, and they continued to stare uneasily at one another. An hour passed, and then another; the bath was being prepared, and a banquet was being made ready, for the day was a martyr's festival. Gregory had hoped he would be invited to the bath and to the banquet, but the stern silence of the Bishop of Caesarea was as unyielding as his own. At last, around six o'clock according to Gregory, he escaped from the spell and abruptly left the house. That night a storm came up: the ragged little company traveling the precipitous road to Sebaste was soaked to the skin, while

Gregory reflected in the misery of injured pride that Christ, who received the kiss of Judas and entered the house of Simon the leper, would not have treated him so ill.

For many reasons it is a terrifying story: it revealed his weaknesses and strengths, the strange terror with which he regarded the formal world of high ecclesiastical authority, his perpetual hatred of being watched, his horror of himself. That long silence, like the infinite reflections in two parallel mirrors, is something to ponder at: it reverberates still, so that we feel his anger and share his awkwardness, and are no nearer the solution of the mystery. But there is another reason for regarding the story as profoundly significant of the man. Many times he had spoken of the mysterious moment when Moses enters the dark cloud on Sinai and meets God face to face. Gregory was obsessed with the mystery of the ultimate confrontation with authority. In the obscure town of Andumokinoe it was as though, on a blazing summer day, there was given to him a mysterious and shadowy foretaste of the terror which lies in the heart of God's power.

Of the three Cappadocian Fathers Gregory of Nyssa is the one closest to us, the least proud, the most subtle, the one most committed to the magnificence of man. That strange, simple, happy, unhappy, intelligent and God-tormented man was possessed by angels. A bishop, he hated power, but hated indignity still more. He never saw himself as the little leader, vaulted high in air, exerting a brief and illusory authority; it was enough to be a man, to wander, to praise God, to delve into the mystery. He employed all the resources of Greek philosophy to help him in his task, but he also employed those resources which are given only to the shivering contemplatives overwhelmed with the majesty of God. Once Gregory wrote: "The totality of humanity is God." No one else ever dared to say the thing so simply. And while he lived, no one would have dared to believe that this man would come to exert on the Eastern Church so great an authority. In Eastern Christianity his *Great Catechism* follows immediately after Origen's *On First Principles*. These were the two seminal works, close-woven, astonishingly lucid, final. But unlike Origen, Gregory possessed a deep-rooted pity for men.

Athanasius was the hammer, Basil the stern commander, Gregory of Nazianzus the tormented singer, and it was left to Gregory of Nyssa to be the man enchanted with Christ. For him the Passion was like a dazzling cloud of blood veiling the glory to come; he seems to stand not before the veil, but behind. His very humanity made him more godlike. Four hundred years after his death, at the Seventh General Council held A.D. 787, the assembled princes of the Church granted him a title which exceeded in their eyes all the other titles granted to men: he was called "Father of Fathers." It was an odd, yet singularly appropriate honor to bestow on a man who went through life as though it were a troubled dream, hardly touching the earth, lonely, thirsty, weary of this wandering life below. He had no need to be weary; he had touched the wellspring.

Gregory Nazianzen

In the great mosaics of Palermo, Ravenna, Cefalú and Constantinople the saints stand out in frozen splendor. They stare from the honeycombed walls with no shadows on their august faces, eyes wide open, lips pursed, wearing miter and alb and halo, black crosses slashed across their tunics, books open in their hands. No winds have ever lifted their stiff garments, and no breath of summer ever touched those winter faces. They seem encased in ice, or like those saints in the Cathedral of the Holy Apostles in Thessalonica, where the walls have been chipped by Turkish picks, they seem to stand in an eternal storm of snowflakes. Prematurely old, they are marked with the wisdom of the ages: old, and ageless, and worn down until the flesh has almost left them, and only the spirit remains. Among these saints you will come upon Gregory Nazianzen, with his immense domed forehead, accusing eyes and long white beard—the oldest, the most superbly dignified, the most august of them all.

But the portraits of Gregory have only the faintest relation to the man who lived on earth. He was a small shrunken vivid man, bald-headed, with a long red beard and red eyebrows like Athanasius, wrinkled, nearly always in pain, haggard with vigils and fastings. Throughout his life he was poor and ill-clothed, and he was unpolished and abrupt in his talk. He feared no one. He had an unruly humor. He is the only man who is known to have dared to laugh at Basil. He was quick-tempered, sullen, unhappy in the company of most people, strangely remote from the world. Appointed to the Patriarchate of Constantinople against his will, he found it Arian and in a few swift months converted it to the orthodox faith. He was the first Christian poet, and wrote prose angelically, and throughout his life gloried in the Greek poet Pindar, who celebrated athletes and spoke only of human glory. He loved God, and then the art of letters, and then men—in that order. He was not a great theologian, but of all the Fathers of the Church he was the only one to be granted after his death the title "The Theologian," which until this time was reserved for an apostle—John of Patmos.

He was born about A.D. 330 in the obscure town of Nazianzus in southwest Cappadocia. According to Gregory, it was a dull and unpleasant place with few inhabitants. His father belonged to the sect of "illuminated priests" who called themselves Hypsistarians, a sect which reserved its worship for "the Highest" (ὕφιστος). They placed the symbols of light and fire on their altars, and seem to have been influenced by the Zoroastrian religion of Persia. While Gregory's father was a heretic, his mother Nonna was an orthodox Christian, praying for her husband's salvation. One night the father dreamed he was singing the first verse of the Psalm: "I was glad when they said unto me, We will go into the house of the Lord." Soon he exchanged heresy for orthodoxy, and in time he became Bishop of Nazianzus. He built a church and was noted for his gentleness and geniality.

Nonna was of sterner stuff, a dominating woman with a passion for reform. Gregory speaks of her affectionately, but of his father he speaks more tenderly, with greater passion. It is recorded of Nonna that she never spat in church, never kissed pagan women, never entered a theater, averted her eyes from pagan temples and sat entranced before the Christian altar. When Gregory was born, she dedicated him to the service of God and consecrated him by placing his hands on the Bible in the church. Gregory said that she was like Hannah giving Samuel to the Lord at Shiloh.

A red-haired boy with a dwarfish body, he grew up under her stern commandments. He was about seven when he dreamed that two beautiful women had come to his bedside, dressed in long white robes and wearing veils which did not conceal the brightness of their eyes. They announced that their names were Purity and Chastity, the companions of Jesus, and after bidding him join his spirit with theirs, they vanished. The dream affected him profoundly. He consecrated himself afresh, and had visions of becoming a great Christian orator. He was about thirteen when he went to Caesarea to study. He may have met Basil there. Studying in Caesarea under Carterius, the teacher of John Chrysostom, he made great progress in rhetoric. A few years later he went to study in Neocaesarea in Palestine, and from there went on to Alexandria, where he may have seen Athanasius being carried in procession through the streets. Alexandria was the nerve center of Christianity, but Gregory was already dreaming of a literary career, and so he decided almost at a moment's notice to set sail for Athens, a place which Basil always detested, calling it "the empty blessedness," while Gregory called it "the golden city" to the end of his life. He set sail during the equinoctial gales and his ship was nearly lost in a tempest off the coast of Cyprus. The storm lasted for twenty-two days. When they ran out of fresh water, the terrified passengers gave themselves up for lost. In those days baptism often came late in life: it was not unusual for a man to wait until he was thirty, since it was remembered that Christ was baptized in the Jordan when He was thirty. Gregory was in mortal terror of dying before being baptized. Almost insane with agony, he tore off his clothes, threw himself down on the deck and vowed with a flood of tears to devote his life to God if only he were saved. Weeping and groaning, he begged God for the gift of "spiritual water from the deadly waves." Soon a Phoenician ship hove to and provided them with fresh water and food, and the storm ceased. A Christian boy on board told Gregory he had seen Nonna running over the sea to take the vessel in her hands and lead it to a safe harbor. Gregory was deeply moved by the dream, and remembered it often in the years to come. He had left Alexandria in November, but it was December when the ship, battered by heavy seas, sailed into the harbor of Aegina, fifteen miles from Athens. Gregory was sixteen or seventeen when he arrived in Athens, and he was thirty when he left.

The schools at Athens had been famous for nearly a thousand years. Here a man might leisurely bring himself to know all that was known. There was a mania for triads: everything was taught in threes. Physics comprised theology, mathematics and the theory of ideas. Nearly every student was required to learn the rudiments of medicine. Here rhetoric and the study of the classical authors were the main ingredients of Athenian education, and into these Gregory threw himself with the same impetuous energy as his friend Basil, who seems to have arrived at the University at exactly the same time. They met, and were thereafter inseparable, and both of them were on terms of friendship with the young Prince Julian, who could be counted among the Cappadocians, for he had spent the years before coming to Athens with his tutors in the imperial hunting park at Macellum in southwest Cappadocia.

In those days Julian was a Christian; later he was to become the most famous of apostates. Gregory fell under the spell of his charm. Years later, when Julian was dead and Gregory's memory of the man had soured, the Prince took on the aspect of another Monsieur de Charlus, a strange dominating prodigy of evil, larger than life. Gregory's description of him is brilliant, but it suggests an early affection concealed by accretions of hate, and we can almost discern the features of the elegant Prince beneath the handsome caricature:

There was nothing good, I argued, about that loosely jointed neck, the shoulders continually shrugging as if the man were a human weighing scale, the eye rolling from side to side with that insane glitter in it, the stumbling, unsteady feet. Then his proud disdainful snorting, his whole countenance conveying a ridiculous impression of disdain—then the violent, staccato guffaws of laughter, and his unwarranted nods indicating assent and dissent, the halting speech, the long pauses for breath, the disorderly unintelligent questions with the answers that were no better, pouring out in an incoherent stream—it boded no good. [*Oratio,* V, 23]

It was a good portrait, but Gregory went on to spoil it, talking of "that dragon, that apostate, that artful schemer, that Assyrian, that common enemy and corrupter of all." Julian did not attack the Christians; he simply despised them, knowing only the argumentative power-loving Christians at court. He wrote that "the majority of Christians are more savage in their fights among themselves than wild beasts." He refused to call them anything but Galileans when he became Emperor, and tore off their insignia from the standards of the Empire. There was no bitterness in him, only weariness and distaste for the quarreling prelates, Arians and orthodox alike. So in the eyes of Gregory Julian became Antichrist, an unexpectedly complex Antichrist, for "he persecuted without appearing to do so, even his humanity was inhuman and his courtesies were cruelty in disguise." In his hatred of Julian, Gregory found himself in the astonishing position of defending and exalting the incompetent Emperor Constantius, describing him as "the most divine and Christ-loving of Emperors." This was a view not shared by Athanasius.

There were coteries among the students in Athens, waging an endless intellectual warfare among themselves. Students from Cappadocia would debate with students from Palestine, Boeotia, Sparta, Egypt and Armenia. The guild of young Armenian students decided upon a debate with the Cappadocians. Some of them had studied under Basil's father in Caesarea, and were determined to show they were not awed by the rhetorical powers of the son. We do not know what they debated about, but we do know that Basil scored a triumph and that Gregory then went to the assistance of the routed Armenians, perhaps afraid that

Basil's pride, already notable, would receive too great a celebration of itself. His assistance was so powerful that Basil began to lose ground, and then Gregory had to come once more to the help of his friend. It was characteristic of Gregory that he should attempt to be the moderator, standing quietly between the two opposing sides. His affection for Basil, whose tactlessness made him a trial to his friends, remained unshaken. "In Athens I sought for eloquence, and I found happiness, because I found Basil," he wrote afterward; and he complained of being restless and miserable when Basil left the University and returned to Caesarea.

In Greece Gregory lived by John Colet's motto: *Fide et litteris,* "by faith and by letters." He had no particular yearning for the priesthood, but he was consumed with a desperate desire to live the Christian life and to become a good writer. The seeds of his prodigious capacity to write ringingly were sown in Athens, and toward the end of his life, speaking briefly about his ambitions, he pointed to one talent which he would cling to to the end—his power over words:

> I tossed to the winds all other things: those who want them can have wealth and high birth, fame and the power to govern other men, all those earthly pleasures which pass like a dream. But there is one thing I cling to—my power of words, that alone, and so I do not grudge the vicissitudes by land and sea that gave me this. May the power of words be mine, and may it belong to him who calls me friend. I cherish it deeply, and so I shall always, placing it first except for that which is the very first—I mean all holy things and the hopes which stretch beyond the tangible world. [*Oratio,* IV, 10]

For the rest of his life he would always turn toward Athens and the Greek poets after turning toward Jerusalem and the Cross.

So he remained in Athens, a small red-bearded man with a strange pallor and a scar over his right eye, with the Bible in one hand and Pindar's poems in the other. He seemed to be the perpetual student, the man who spends his whole life quietly studying, with no desire for action. Suddenly, at thirty, he left Athens and made his way back to Cappadocia, passing through Constantinople, where his younger brother Caesarius, after a brilliant career in medicine, had been appointed physician-extraordinary to the Emperor Constantius. Caesarius was trained in Alexandria. He was a man of the world, efficient, capable, delighting in his worldly success, delighting above all in having the ear of the Emperor. Gregory was suitably impressed. He knew his brother to be a good Christian. He stayed for some months in Constantinople and then the brothers decided to visit Nazianzus. Their parents were growing old. Gregory remained quietly in Nazianzus, eating his heart out for Athens, staying in this obscure town out of loyalty to his parents, with no desire to settle down and at odds with the world. Asked what he proposed to do with the fruits of his prolonged years of study, he simply shrugged his shoulders and said he had a lot more studying to do. He was asked to give a few public addresses. He agreed, but without enthusiasm. "I performed my little dance for them, and then quit the stage," he said. He wanted to live quietly, in holiness, with his books by his side.

He had made the vow of chastity, now he made the vow of poverty and lived a life of rigid asceticism. He slept on the ground, clothed himself in rough clothes, lived on bread and salt, and drank only water. He spent half the night in prayer and meditation. During the day he managed his father's estates and complained bitterly against having to manage the slaves. He was not a particularly skillful overseer. His heart was not in it. There were other worries. Julian became Emperor in 361, and Caesarius was still at the Court. It was rumored that Caesarius had obeyed the young Emperor's order and turned apostate. The rumors reached Nazianzus, but were carefully kept from the aging Nonna. Gregory, almost beside himself with worry, wrote angrily to his brother:

I am thoroughly ashamed for you! I wish you would hear what others are saying—neighbors and strangers alike—anyone who knows us at all—not to speak of my own disappointment in all these stories about you. . . . Our venerable Father is distressed by all he hears, and is weary of life. I try and console him as best I can by making promises on your behalf. I've told him that you won't cause us any further pain. As for Mother, if she were to find out anything about you (we have tried by every means to keep it from her), you know she would be utterly inconsolable. . . . I warn you solemnly: you have only two alternatives. Either be a Christian and range yourself with the despised Christian community, though you risk your career and all your ambitions, or enjoy your honors and lose the most important thing of all. You will have a share in the smoke, if not the fire.   [Ep. 7]

Happily, the rumors from Constantinople had been exaggerated: Caesarius had not compromised his faith. Summoned by the Emperor before an assembly of courtiers to apostacize, Caesarius bluntly refused, saying: "I am and remain a Christian, and so I shall always be." According to Gregory, Julian thereupon exclaimed: "O happy father! O unhappy sons!" But the threat, if it was a threat, was never carried out. Caesarius remained in Constantinople, and Gregory continued to superintend his father's estates.

There were occasional moments of respite. Gregory and Basil had continued to correspond, and when Basil decided to found a monastic retreat, Gregory suggested that his father's estate at Tiberina on the Arianzus river would be a perfect place for it. Basil was staying at Caesarea, about twelve miles away, and rode out to inspect the estate. It was winter, and the fields were deep in mud. Basil was annoyed. He saw nothing whatsoever in Tiberina to commend it. It was dirty, muddy, unappetizing; it would even be better, he suggested, to have the retreat in Caesarea itself. It was perhaps Gregory's fault, for he speaks of racing Basil across the muddy fields until he was out of breath. A little later Gregory wrote: "I will not have you talking about *our* mud, and instead of that mud you talk of I will fling in your teeth the swindlers of Caesarea and all the other nuisances of the city." It was the villager's protest against the city dweller, and there may have been some reason for it: then as now Caesarea was renowned for its sharp-dealing merchants and for sharp practices of all kinds. The story is told that the devil once challenged a merchant of Caesarea to a duel. The devil, having choice of weapons, picked the longest pole. The merchant, having choice of battle ground, placed the devil in front of a hidden well and quickly backed him into it.

Gregory had a fondness for Tiberina, and he was angry when the offer was so cavalierly refused. Basil, however, had the stronger will, and when he decided to found the retreat at Ibora, opposite his mother's retreat at Annesi, Gregory was invited to stay there, seduced by Basil's long letter describing the beauty of the place. But before leaving for Ibora, Gregory, who must have known something about the Pontine landscape, wrote mockingly:

> I really don't mind when you attack Tiberina: I revel in your command of language and enjoy everything that comes from you, come what may. I see you are jesting, but not for the sake of jesting: you are like those people who dam up rivers to force them in another channel, and that is how it always is when you are talking.
>
> Well, I will admire your Pontus, and the Pontine mists, and those habitations exquisitely prepared for our exile, and the heights

of those precipitous mountains which are not adorned with flowers but are like heavy curtains, and the air which must be carefully measured, and that sunlight you yearn for, which you see as though through a chimney. Poor Pontine Cimmerians devoid of the sun, condemned to the six months' night, and never free from shadow, your lives are no more than one long darkness, and truly they are passed "in the shadow of death." Therefore I praise your narrow and precipitous pathways, for I do not know whether they lead to the Kingdom or to Hell, but for your sake I shall prefer they lead to the Kingdom.

And then that central place you speak of—shall we call it Eden, the fountain branching into the four rivers which water the earth? or shall we call it a dry and empty desert, which no Moses will ever conquer, striking water from the rock with his staff? That wild place of yours is all rock, and where there is no rock, there are gullies, and where there are no gullies, there are thickets of thorn; and all above the thorns is precipice; and the road over it is precipitous and slopes both ways, terribly annoying to travelers who must take lessons in gymnastics before committing themselves to this road. And the river roars below, having more stones than fishes, and it does not spread itself into a lake, but dashes over a cliff, O my grandiloquent friend and framer of beautiful words! And this river is great and fearful and drowns the voices of the choristers with a sound like the roaring of the Nile cataracts, and there is no end to it—it goes on all day and night. You cannot ford this river. There is only one morsel of kindness about it: it does not sweep your dwelling places away when torrents and storms drive it mad.

This is what I think of your Isles of the Blessed, and the blessed people who will live there, living in the high winds among singing birds (who sing of famine) while fanning you with their wings (as they would fan the desert air). No one, you say, visits the place except for hunting. You might have added—no one comes at all except to view your dead bodies.   [*Ep.* 4]

After visiting Ibora, Gregory developed an affection for the place. He continued to mock gently at Basil's pretensions: the place was never so beautiful as Basil claimed. It was a rough, ugly, dark-shadowed hostile place, with no more to commend it than its vivid and austere character. It was frontier life, with all the advantages and disadvantages of living on the edge of nowhere. The handful of dedicated spirits who founded the retreat toiled continually at woodcutting and stone-carving, planting, irrigating, building huts, cutting down thornbushes. In the evenings, worn out with labor, Basil sat under a golden plane tree and gathered his flock around him. Reluctantly at first, and then with increasing delight, Gregory became a member of the community. He half-worshiped Basil. Once he wrote to Basil: "You are my breath, more than the air, and so far only do I live as I am in your company and with your image." In those early days Basil's furious determination to dominate each situation as it arose had not yet made him that marvelously efficient machine he was to become later. Together, they compiled from the writings of Origen an anthology they called *The Philokalia,* which still survives. Almost two years passed before Gregory returned to Nazianzus.

Nazianzus had changed. Schisms rent the air. Julian was Emperor now, indifferent to the Arians and the orthodox alike, with the result that heresies were rife and heretics were at one another's throats. Gregory's father, once a Hypsistarian, now the orthodox Bishop of Nazianzus, was accused of departing from the true faith, and when Gregory returned home, he was confronted with a seething mob of monks thirsting for his father's blood. He made a speech defending his father, for no one had ever accused him of being lacking in knowledge of the orthodox doctrine; and he seems to have defended his father so well that peace returned to Nazianzus.

At Christmas, 361, there occurred an event which struck terror in Gregory's heart. It came like a sudden thunderclap, depriving him of reason. It was something very simple, and had happened to many people before him, but Gregory never entirely recovered from the blow. What happened was that he was suddenly seized, carried to the church and compelled to become a priest. The congregation acclaimed him, and he could no more refuse the priesthood than a general could refuse to become Emperor if he were acclaimed by the army.

Gregory took his elevation to the priesthood with bad grace. He was not prepared for it. He had no desire for it. He felt singularly unworthy of the responsibility. He felt he was being submitted to "spiritual tyranny." At the Feast of the Epiphany, twelve days later, he fled to Basil at Ibora, and there he remained until Easter, still shuddering, still convinced of his unworthiness, hurt and bleeding from an internal wound. For Gregory these were months of pure terror. His soul was a City of God in violent disorder, full of merciless street warfare against the weeping army of the damned, and among the damned he included himself, the unworthy incumbent of the priesthood. Basil argued and cajoled and threatened, and then at last Gregory grew quiet. He returned chastened, prepared to take his punishment, claiming that he was not rebellious, he had simply taken refuge in Pontus to console himself with his grief. Then he delivered his *Apologia,* which is the first of the great sermons on "the despair of being a priest," ranking with Chrysostom's *De Sacerdotio* as among the greatest of all works on the priesthood.

Gregory's *Apologia* was carefully prepared and brilliantly constructed. He knew his flight had been misinterpreted. It was whispered that he despised the spiritual office, that he was afraid of Julian, that he was annoyed because he was not offered a bishopric. Gregory answered that all these things were untrue: he despised no one, was afraid of no one, had no desire for a high ecclesiastical position, for there was sufficient terror in the lowliest church office to make a man tremble in his bones. What is a priest? He is a servant of God, and no one is worthy of God unless he has offered himself completely as a living and holy sacrifice. A man must possess almost supernatural powers before being ordained into the priesthood:

A man must himself be cleansed before cleansing others; himself become wise, that he may make others wise; become light, before he can give light; draw near to God before he can bring others near; be hallowed, before he can hallow them; be possessed of hands before leading others by the hand, and of wisdom before he can speak wisely. [*Apologia,* 71]

And it was not enough that a priest should possess these incalculable virtues, he must be so worthy of God's grace that he can commune with God's majesty. Because he is, in some sense, the mediator between the people and God he must be like Moses climbing the mountain of Sinai:

It is not anyone who may draw near to God, one must be like Moses, one must be able to bear the glory of God. Remember how, when the Law was first uttered, there were trumpet blasts and lightning and thunder and darkness and the smoke pouring from the whole mountain, and there was spoken the terrible threat that if even a beast touched the holy mountain, it must be stoned to death, and there were many other things like this preventing the people from approaching—those people for whom it was a great privilege, after purification, merely to hear the voice of God from a distance. But Moses—Moses actually climbed the mountain and entered the cloud and was charged with the Law and received the tables! [*Apologia, 92*]

Gregory explained that the knowledge of his own unworthiness was the most critical reason for his flight, and he had returned to accept the priesthood, not because he now thought himself worthy, but because he yearned for the people of Nazianzus and for his aged parents, and because no one had a right to resist a call of God. So he remained, working quietly, until he seemed to have lost himself within this remote and ugly little town, "the least among the townships of Cappadocia," as Gregory called it. He was content to practice his quiet austerities while the great world went by: while Basil became a bishop, and an Arian Emperor, Valens, came to the seat of power.

When Basil became Bishop of Caesarea A.D. 370, the iron entered his soul. He was forty-one, an age when men with firm beliefs grow harder. He was the champion of orthodoxy, "the keeper of the lion," the lone outpost against the state religion. He owed his election partly to the exertions of the two Gregories, father and son. Basil invited the younger Gregory to attend the solemn enthronement, and when Gregory suggested it would be better if he remained in Nazianzus because people would say that Basil was being surrounded by his partisans, Basil took umbrage. "It seems to me," he wrote, "that you have no further interest in my affairs—I am no more than gleanings abandoned on the roadside!" Gregory wrote back in mingled pride and anger:

O divine and sacred Master, how dare you say your affairs to me are no more than abandoned gleanings? How could these words have escaped between your teeth? How could you have let yourself say such things? How did your mind countenance these words, or the ink write them, or the paper tolerate them? O speeches! O Athens! O virtues! O literary labors! By the way you write, you make me into some sort of tragedian. O eye of the world, great voice, great trumpet, palace of eloquence, have you forgotten what manner of man I am? So I have no further interest in your affairs! How can anyone admire anything on earth, unless Gregory admires you! There is only one Spring among the seasons, only one Sun among the stars, one all-encompassing Heaven, one voice among all—yours, if I am any judge at all, and if—which I do not believe —my love for you does not deceive me. [*Ep. 2*]

It was a letter calculated to make Basil speak in sweeter tones, but it was not wholly successful. Basil was offended, perhaps thinking there was laughter concealed beneath the oratorical periods. A little while later Gregory was offered the position of chief presbyter in Caesarea, but the offer was rejected. A few months passed. Basil remembered Gregory again when Cappadocia was divided by the Emperor Valens into two provinces. According to the new arrangement all the cities of southern and western Cappadocia formed the new province of Cappadocia Secunda, leaving only Caesarea itself and the imperial estates in Cappadocia Prima. By the canon of Nicaea civil provinces formed ecclesiastical units, headed by the bishop of the metropolitan city. Valens' order was interpreted by Basil and his friends as a deliberate attack upon himself, as a leader of orthodoxy.

Basil decided to act quickly. Obscure villages became bishoprics. He appointed his brother to the see of Nyssa, and he ordered Gregory to become bishop of the town of Sasima, some twenty-four miles from Nazianzus, on the very edge of Cappadocia Prima. Sasima was a horse station where three roads met, "a detestable little place without water or grass or any mark of civilization," Gregory wrote. "Here is nothing but dust, noise, screams, groans, petty officials, chains and instruments of torture, and the population consists entirely of commercial travelers and strangers" (*Carm*. XI, 439-46). Gregory hated the place, and accused Basil a little unfairly of choosing the most damnable spot on earth for the new bishopric—"Sasima the illustrious," filled with hucksters, ostlers, drivers, people rubbing down their horses, setting up their paltry stalls, the dregs of humanity. "So you have given me this place," he wrote to Basil. "Is that the reward of our days in Athens together, when we studied and lived together as though we were one person? Is this the reward of our marvelous friendship and our common vows? Must all this be scattered to the winds and dashed to the ground? Then let me fly to the wild beasts; for they, I believe, are more to be trusted!" (*Carm*. XI, 476-86).

Gregory was in agony, and his friendship with Basil was at breaking point. Basil was like a general throwing his reserves into battle, desperate to defend orthodoxy. For him affections and friendship were of small account compared with the duty of maintaining the power of the Metropolitan. He charged Gregory with sloth and cold-bloodedness for refusing the proffered honor, and Gregory replied bitterly that Basil was sweeping everything into his own lap, like the rivers and the mountain torrents, to swell his own glory.

As it happened so often before, the will of Basil prevailed. Gregory was consecrated Bishop of Sasima in his father's church at Nazianzus. It was a strange consecration. Gregory felt crushed and cowed, with no will of his own, blindly obeying the orders of Basil, who took complete command. Gregory was anointed, clothed with the ephod, sanctified and mitered, and led to the altar of the spiritual holocaust, like a sheep led to the slaughter. Force—the force of Basil's driving will—led him to make this sacrifice, and forever afterward he regretted it. And when the consecration was over and Gregory was compelled to address the congregation, he said in a voice trembling with agitation: "Look upon the man who is consecrated, upon whom the Spirit has descended, and watch him as he goes on his way weary and dispirited." A few weeks later, in reply to one more of Basil's corrosive letters, he answered with his tongue in his cheek:

> How hotly and like a colt you skip in your letters! It does not surprise me that you must display the glory you have recently acquired, to make yourself more august. But then, if you continue to show such ostentation and such vast ambition, discoursing to me condescendingly, like a great Metropolitan talking to someone of small moment, well, I too can oppose pride with pride. And this, of course, is in everyone's power, and is perhaps the most reasonable course to pursue. [*Ep.* 50]

Gregory possessed a timid character, but the trappings of his timidity were wrapped around an iron core. He would not budge, if he had made up his mind. Out of a sense of duty, thinking of himself as "a bone flung to the dogs," he took up his episcopate at Sasima with the intention of staying only as long as he thought he could do any good. There was little good he could do, and soon he returned to Nazianzus, working as coadjutor bishop to his father, saying nothing to Basil, and not caring whether Basil was indignant. His father was over ninety. Caesarius, who had been appointed by the Emperor Valens Imperial Treasurer of Bithynia had fled from his post after an earthquake shook Nicaea. He had believed the earthquake a sign of God's anger, and returned to live quietly in Nazianzus where he died suddenly after a short illness, leaving one of the shortest wills on record: "I give all my possessions to the poor." His death was followed by that of his sister Gorgonia, who lived the life of a dedicated Christian matron, bringing up her five children in fear of the Lord. Shortly before her death, she was warned in a dream of the time when she would die. She gathered her relatives round her bed, and took leave of them. Her last words were: "I will lay me down in peace, and sleep."

These deaths shook Gregory to the quick. He had never possessed any earthly ambitions; now the mere thought of himself as a bishop with power over his flock drove him into panic. Disaster followed disaster. The year 373 was one of those terrifying years when disasters became commonplace. It began with an epidemic among cattle, and was followed by a devastating hailstorm, which ruined the crops. Then the taxgatherers came and the farmers revolted against them. The revolt was put down. The governor ordered Nazianzus to be struck off the list of imperial cities; henceforth it was to be known only as a town, and since it had never been anything else, the Nazianzenes suffered a vast blow to their pride. Finally there came news that the governor was threatening to level the town to its foundations. In anger and perplexity the townspeople appealed to their bishop for protection, as the Antiochenes were to look to St. John Chrysostom for protection a little later; and both saints gave the same advice—Beware, fear the Lord, out of the vials of His wrath still more terrible things may come! Gregory reminded them that they had seen the smoke of His anger, but they had not yet seen the torrents of His flame:

> I know the glittering sword blade, the sword made drunk in Heaven and commanded to slay, to annihilate, to make childless, sparing neither flesh nor marrow nor bones. I know Him who is free from all passion, and yet He comes to meet us like a bear robbed of his whelps, like a leopard in the way of the Assyrians. I know there is no one who can escape the mighty quickness of His wrath when He watches over the evils we commit, and His jealousy, which pursues His enemies to death and utterly devours His adversaries. I know the emptying, the making void, the making waste, the melting of the heart and the knocking of the knees.
>
> [*Oratio*, XVI, 7]

The governor's troops were called off, but disaster continued to pile upon disaster, while Gregory reeled. His old father, who had spent forty-five years as Bishop of Nazianzus, died, and shortly afterward Nonna died, clutching the altar and gasping: "Lord Christ, be merciful!" as she fell to the floor. The next year Gregory fell ill, and was himself close to death. For him, as always, there was escape in solitude, and so he wandered into Isaurian Seleucia, living quietly, apart from the world as in a grave. He was in Seleucia when he heard of Basil's death. Remembering how their broken friendship had never been repaired, he collapsed, took to his bed and sobbed out his grief. Then he wrote to the rhetorician Eudoxius the most terrifying of his letters:

> You ask how I am. I will tell you—I am a cup overflowing with bitterness. I have lost Basil. I have lost Caesarius, who was my brother of the flesh and my brother of the spirit. I say with the Psalmist: "When my father and my mother forsake me—"[1] I am in feeble health, and old age hangs over me, and I am overwhelmed with cares and interruptions, and my friends are faithless, and the Church has no shepherds. All honor has perished; evil lies naked before our eyes; we journey into the dark; and there is no beacon anywhere. Christ lies sleeping. What will happen to us? I look for no relief from these disasters except the relief of death; and if I am to judge by things here, I am terrified by the things beyond the grave.   [*Ep.* 80]

It was a time of upheaval and terror, with the Goths battering at the doors. In 378, the year before Basil died, the Arian Emperor Valens died at Adrianople on a moonless night after being wounded and carried by eunuchs and guards to a country cottage, which the invading Goths surrounded and set on fire. Then the smoke began to clear, and the young Theodosius came into the purple, leaving his peaceful estate near Valladolid in Spain for an uneasy throne in Constantinople. For a few brief years there was peace in the Empire.

Gregory had withdrawn from the world, and was in no hurry to return. He lived quietly on his father's estate in Arianzus, composing poetry, practicing austerities, sitting in the sun. A stream flowed through the estate, and he spent his waking hours brooding by it. In his reserve and retirement he had become like a Chinese philosopher, his senses dulled, his mind preoccupied with thoughts of the transience of things. "Who am I?" he wrote. "What shall I become? I do not know, nor does He know who is far wiser than I. I am like a man enshrouded in mist, wandering hither and thither, without desires, not even those desires which spring out of dreams." He wrote of himself as a dead leaf floating in the stream. He was on the eve of becoming Patriarch of Constantinople.

We do not know how Gregory made his way from the quiet of his

---

[1] "When my father and my mother forsake me, then the Lord will take me up" (*Psalm* 27:10).

country estate to the turmoil of Constantinople. Perhaps the new Emperor commanded him; perhaps he was invited to Constantinople by a ruse. Suddenly, around Easter, 379, he appears there, living in the house of a kinsman and in one of the large rooms in the house he delivers his sermons and homilies to a small group of orthodox Christians. He is in command of himself; he has thrown aside his private melancholy; he talks like a man on fire with the love of God, in a city where it was still dangerous to pronounce the orthodox faith, for all the hundred churches of Constantinople were still occupied by Arian priests. Orthodox Christians hid in the remote corners of the city.

It was a new Gregory, a man who thought lucidly, with a fervor he had never shown before. He had passed through the dark cloud into the sunlight of God. Men said of him that his voice was clear and his eyes were beautiful, and they forgot that one of his eyes was dulled and blinded by trachoma, that his shoulders stooped, that he was prematurely aged and that the points of his beard were turning gray. He was fifty years old, sickly, dwarfish, his skin astonishingly pale, and still wore a livid scar over his eye. He dressed like a beggar, for he had never cared for clothes. His red beard spattered with gray, he looked like a small and formidable tiger as he thundered against the evils of the capital, where all life revolved around the Hippodrome. His life was often in danger. Stones were thrown at him. His one-room church was profaned. Bands of heretical monks, accompanied by screeching women, tried to waylay him with sticks and firebrands. "They throw roses at other people," he wrote. "At me they throw stones."

It was not only the Arians who filled the churches of Constantinople; strange prophets, bearded philosophers, dervishes, entertainers, cried out to be heard from the pulpit. Among these was a certain Maximus the Cynic, who came to Constantinople from Alexandria. He seems to have been a religious adventurer of remarkable talents. He curled his hair and dyed it yellow, so that he resembled a Goth. He wore the loose cloak of the Cynic and claimed to be related to many martyrs, and there were bruises on his body which he claimed he received in defending the orthodox faith. Gregory regarded this Maximus as a paragon of virtue: excused his foppery: spoke of the man's virtues in the presence of the whole congregation. The ladies were impressed. "Gregory is a good preacher," they said, "but Maximus has such darling curls" (*Carm.* XI, 751-52). Maximus increased in power, and continually plotted against Gregory. There came to the church a presbyter from Thassos, bearing a large treasure chest to buy marble to decorate a church. Maximus somehow obtained possession of the money, and one night, when Gregory was ill in bed, he entered the church accompanied by some Egyptian presbyters who solemnly proceeded to consecrate Maximus bishop. The ceremony was half-completed when the faithful heard of it. They gathered in the church and booted the pretender out. Taking his treasure chest with him, Maximus took refuge in a flute-player's shop, and there his golden curls, which reached down to his shoulders, were ceremonially cut off and his consecration was completed. Then Maximus went off to Thessalonica, where the new Emperor Theodosius was in residence, preparing for his entry into Constantinople. He offered himself to Theodosius as Bishop of Constantinople, but Theodosius saw through the disguise, and sent Maximus on his way. In Milan the saintly Ambrose, in Rome Pope Damasus, in Alexandria Pope Peter, vowed that Maximus was the rightful bishop. Gregory seems not to have been disturbed. He was biding his time.

We do not know when he made the five speeches concerning the Trinity, on which his fame as a theologian rests. It was probably about the same time that he was contending with Maximus. These five speeches, or orations, are unlike anything else he wrote. They are mannered, but they are also crystal-clear; they move as the spirit moves them; there is no stumbling. Gregory had delivered funeral orations, long and bitter invectives against the Emperor Julian, immense letters concerning points of dogma, but always there had been the sense of strain, a seeking for effect, a curious cloud of melancholy. Now, through all the intricacies of a debate concerning the nature of the Trinity, he moved at last with the appearance of effortless strength and an easy grace. It is a work to be compared, though on another plane, with the *De Incarnatione* of Athanasius. For the Eastern Church, he spoke the final word on the Trinity in those five long orations.

Today, we have to set these orations against their own time. He was battling not only with Arians, but with the sects among the Arians—the Eunomians, who believed the Son to be unlike the Father, and the Sabellians, Marcellians, Photinians, Macedonians, who believed in the Arian creed with minor reservations. He took as his text the words from *Jeremiah:* "Behold, I am against thee, O thou proud one," and then attacked their arguments, and held them up to scorn. These attacks have little relevance today. But the orations remain important because Gregory had many positive things to say. His chief argument is a simple one: God is incomprehensible, He is Father, Son and Holy Ghost, and this is a mystery, and yet nothing could be so logical. If you ask whether the Father generated the Son, you are asking a question which is essentially absurd, for this happened in the time before time; and if you ask how the Spirit assumes a part in the Trinity, this too is absurd, for this holiness is something which is known, cannot be argued about, is altogether necessary, final, beyond our human apprehension. The divine nature cannot be apprehended by human reason. The darkness of the body has been placed between us and God, like the cloud between the Hebrews and the Egyptians. Something in the environment of man is forever creeping in to prevent a clear vision of God. We must accept Him as mystery, and regard ourselves as "darkness in a secret place." What then of those who say they have seen God? What of Isaiah and Ezekiel? He answers:

> One of them saw the Lord of Sabaoth sitting on the throne of glory, encircled and praised and concealed by the seraphim with six wings, and he was purged by a live coal, and he was made worthy of his prophetic office. The other described the cherubic chariot of God, and the throne upon it, and the firmament over it, and God who showed Himself in the firmament amid voices and powers and great deeds. But whether this was only an appearance by day only visible to His saints, or an unerring vision of the night, or an impression of the mind holding converse with the future as though it were the present, or some other strange form of prophecy, I cannot say. The God of the Prophets knows, and they know who are thus inspired. But neither these of whom I have been speaking, nor any of their fellows, ever stood before the secret heart or essence of the Godhead, or saw, or proclaimed the nature of God.   [*Oratio*, XXVIII, 19]

Then he asks where we shall find God, and he answers that God is present in the vast intricate design of living things: all is miraculous, beyond being comprehended, unless we believe in God's goodness and mercy. How is the body nourished by food? How is the soul nourished by reason? How is it that children and their parents are chained to one another with adamantine chains of love? A child is born, an old man dies, but the river of life continues tranquilly under the blessing of God. The eye is a miracle, settling with lightning speed on the thing it perceives. We sleep. Is that not God's blessing? And then perhaps remembering his small estate in Arianzus, he speaks of God moving through the splendor of birds and peacocks and fishes:

Look at the fishes gliding through the waters, as though they were flying through the liquid element, breathing the air of water, but coming into danger when they breathe our air, as we fall into danger when we breathe theirs. Watch their habits and demeanors, their intercourse and their births, their variety and their beauty, their affection for places, their wanderings, their assemblings and departings, and their behavior which so nearly resembles those of the animals which dwell on land, some living in community, possessing all things together, and others possessing their own private knowledge of property.

And then look at the birds, how many there are, and their colors and their varied shapes, those which sing and those which are voiceless. Whence came their songs? Who gave to the grasshoppers the lute strings in their breasts? Why do they sing and chirrup among the branches when the sun bids them play music at noon. Why do they sing in the groves, comforting the wayfarers? Who wove the song for the swan when he spread his wings to the wind? Who fashioned from their rustling feathers so sweet a music? I am not speaking of the voices that are sometimes tortured out of birds, but of their true voices. Where did the peacock, the boastful Persian bird, derive his love of beauty and of praise, for I assure you he is fully conscious of his beauty. Watch him when he sees anyone approaching, or when he would make a show before the hens—see how he raises his neck and spreads his tail in a circle around him, glittering like gold and studded with stars, aware of his beauty, and striding with pompous steps in front of his lovers.   [*Oratio*, XXVIII, 24]

God rejoices in splendor, and what is more splendid than air? Gregory goes on; for now the mood of praise is in him, and he will not be thwarted. How miraculous is air! It is like the sea, unfathomable, vast, sufficient for all, falling like an abundance of manna on young and old alike. It is the chariot of birds, the home of the winds, the conveyor of the seasons. Where are the storehouses of the tempests? Where are the treasuries of snow? Who gave forth the drops of dew? Out of whose womb came the ice? God made these things, and shall you dare to ask God how He gave birth to His Only-begotten Son?

There is irony here, and sometimes more than irony: a hint of
savagery. According to the Arians the Son was inferior to the Father
because he was created in time, not in eternity. "I marvel," says
Gregory, "that they do not conceive of marriage and pregnancy and
the dangers of miscarriage." Would you desire to know how God
was born? "I will tell you. It was in a manner known to the Father
who begot, and to the Son who was begotten. Anything more than
this is hidden in a cloud." Then what is God? There follows a famous
statement of the paradoxes of Jesus, the divine antitheses:

He was born, but he was already begotten; he issued from a
woman, but she was a virgin. . . . He was wrapped in swaddling
bands, but he removed the swaddling clothes of the grave when
he arose again. He was laid in a manger, but he was glorified
by angels, and proclaimed by a star, and worshiped by the Magi.
He had no form nor comeliness in the eyes of the Jews, but to
David he was fairer than the children of men. And on the mountain he was bright as the lightning, and became more luminous
than the sun, initiating us into the mysteries of the future. . . .
He was baptized as man, but he remitted sins as God. He was
tempted as man, but he conquered as God. He hungered, but he
fed thousands. He thirsted, but he cried: "If any man thirst, let
him come unto me and drink." He was weary, but he is the peace
of them that are sorrowful and heavy-laden. . . .
He prays, but he hears prayer. He weeps, but he puts an end to
tears. He asks where Lazarus was laid, for he was a man; and he
raises Lazarus, for he is God. . . . As a sheep he is led to the
slaughter, but he is the Shepherd of Israel and now of the whole
world. . . . He is bruised and wounded, but he heals every disease
and every infirmity. He is lifted up and nailed to the tree, but by
the tree of life he restores us. . . . He lay down his life, but he has
the power to take it again; and the veil is rent, for the mysterious
doors of Heaven are opened; the rocks are cleft, the dead arise.
He dies, but he gives life, and by his death destroys death. He is
buried, but he rises again. He goes down to hell, but he saves the
damned.   [*Oratio*, XXIX, 19, 20]

Gregory's purpose is to show that the Father, the Son and the Holy
Ghost are three Persons, one Godhead, undivided in honor and glory
and substance and kingdom; and it must be admitted that he fails
to prove his case completely, for the Holy Ghost, who is discussed

in the last oration, is introduced perfunctorily. Little mystery attaches to Him. He is the breath of holiness which accompanies the Father and the Son. And the final mystery of the Trinity is explained in terms of the familiar pun on the word *ophthalmos*, which means an eye, a fountain, a river. "In these there is no distinction in time, nor are they torn away from their connection with one another, although they seem to possess three separate personalities." Yet all through the five theological orations there is vigor and truth and a kind of dancing gaiety. He is not angry with the heretics who deny the equality of the Father and the Son; he dances over them. The river, which is also an eye, a fountain and perhaps many other things, is colored with silver fishes and the reflections of the dancing peacocks on the river bank. So gently and graceful, and with prodigious authority Gregory introduced the orthodox faith again to Constantinople.

Those evenings when he delivered his orations in a private house were precious to him. He has left an account of one of them. He sits on a bishop's throne, while the elders are grouped around him, below the dais. The deacons and the ministers of the church are robed in white, and from a hundred candles the light blazes. The congregation hums like bees, everyone busily attempting to reach a place close to the chancel, some even clinging to the holy gates. An overflow congregation forms outside the house. The virgins and matrons listen from an upper gallery, and there are four or five young students surreptitiously taking down the sermon in shorthand. As he describes the nature of the Trinity some are bewildered, some are sunk deep in meditation, others are openly opposed to him, still others are shouting; and as the shouts and murmurs increase, the whole congregation begins to resemble a tumultuous sea. And Gregory adds with pardonable pride that as he entered deeper into his oration, "he called across the tumult, and the tumult quieted" (*Carm.* XV, 35).

In these days he was at the height of his powers. He had no title except the title Basil had given him, Bishop of Sasima. He had no church, except the large room belonging to his kinsman. But he possessed authority and the respect of Theodosius, who had already marked him out for preferment. On November 24, 380, Theodosius made his formal entry into Constantinople. Almost his first command was to order the Arians out of the churches. He expelled the Arian Bishop Demophilus, who quoted the Saviour's words: "When they persecute you in one city, flee to another," and sadly departed. Two days later the Emperor escorted Gregory to Hagia Sophia. They walked together, while the imperial troops rode before and behind. It was a gray day, with a bitter wind coming from the Black Sea, and half the inhabitants of Constantinople regarded the evil weather and the raging winds as ill omens. Rain fell, and the Arians screamed abuse, and they walked on, across the vast square of the Augusteum, the red-faced and handsome Emperor accompanied by a dwarf with a beard which was now half silver and half auburn. Gregory was always pale; now he was pale to astonishment. As he walked, he gazed upward at the lowering heavens. A ray of sunlight shone at the exact moment when Gregory took his seat in the chancel. Then, because it seemed a miracle, and the light was magnified by the immense banks of candles, the people shouted: "Gregory for Bishop! Gregory for Bishop!" The Emperor turned to address the congregation, and said that this was his opinion also. Then it was Gregory's turn, and he rose slightly from his seat and begged them not to be hasty in their judgments, for he was unworthy; and let them decide upon the bishopric in their good time. He would accept the charge only in the canonical manner. Usually such ceremonies were accompanied by bloodshed, but this time among the ten thousand people in the Cathedral, only one drew his sword and this was immediately sheathed in its scabbard.

A few months before, in the lonely wilds of Arianzus, Gregory had despaired of the world. Now wealth and power were his. He no longer spoke in a room in a private house,[2] but in the largest and greatest church in Christendom; and all its revenues and treasures were his. Orthodoxy had triumphed without bloodshed. The ghost of Athanasius presided over Hagia Sophia. But power and wealth and the company of Emperors meant little to Gregory. He was in ill health, yearning for the quietness of Arianzus, and when a council of bishops was convened in Constantinople the following spring, he had already decided to retire from the scene. As usual, there were doctrinal quarrels; there were also personal quarrels. The bishops Meletius and Paulinus both claimed the see of Antioch. Their claims were hotly debated. Meletius had formerly belonged to a semi-Arian sect; Paulinus

[2] On the site of the house belonging to Gregory's kinsman the Church of Anastasia was built later. Anastasia means "the Resurrection," and the name of the church was intended to convey the resurrection of the orthodox faith after Nicaea. The Mosque of Mehmet Pasha, overlooking the Marmora, today marks the site of the church where Gregory first preached in Constantinople.

was orthodox. Suddenly Meletius, "the honey-tongued," died, and it was decided to appoint Flavian instead. The battle raged furiously. Gregory compared the assembled bishops—they included Gregory of Nyssa, his brother Peter of Sebaste and Cyril of Jerusalem—to a flock of chattering jays, and to a storm of stinging wasps. He was president of the assembly, but felt powerless to control them. Meanwhile Timothy of Alexandria arrived, and began to challenge Gregory's position as uncanonical. Was Gregory Patriarch of Constantinople, or was he the titular bishop of the obscure township of Sasima? He could not be both, and in any event, according to rules laid down at the Council of Nicaea to prevent ambitious men from striving for position, he could not be transferred from one see to another. Gregory offered to withdraw from the Council and from Constantinople. He said he was not responsible for the tempest, but if they thought the ship too heavily burdened with him on board, well, he would throw himself overboard and lighten it: the friendly fish would come to his salvation. Then the bishops debated whom they would appoint in Gregory's place, until Theodosius took the matter out of their hands by putting Nectarius, the mayor of Constantinople, in Gregory's place. Nectarius had not even been baptized. He was amiable and easily swayed, and for sixteen years, until the eunuch Eutropius summoned Chrysostom to Hagia Sophia, he retained his throne in the Cathedral.

Gregory was delighted to return to Arianzus, but he was understandably bitter. He had held his office for only a few months. At first he decided to slip away unobserved, but the clamor of the people demanded a farewell oration, and this he delivered from the high throne of Hagia Sophia:

No one told me I was to contend with consuls and prefects and the most illustrious generals, who hardly know how to relieve themselves of their abundance of possessions. No one told me I was expected to put the treasuries of the church to the service of gluttony, and the poor-boxes to the services of luxury. No one told me I must be equipped with superb horses and mounted on an ornamental chariot, and there should be a great hush during my solemn progresses, and everyone must make way for the Patriarch as though he were some kind of wild beast, with the people opening out in great avenues to let me pass, as I came like a banner seen from afar. If these things offended you, then I say they all belong to the past. Forgive me. . . .

And now farewell! Farewell, Church of Anastasia, and this great Church which takes its greatness from the Word, and all those other Churches so beautiful and so splendid! Farewell, apostles, who have led me into so many wars! Farewell, my bishop's throne, that dangerous and enviable chair! Farewell, assemblies of bishops! . . . Farewell, O modest virgins and noble matrons, and you hordes of widows and orphans, for the eyes of the poor are always upon God and us! Farewell, hospitable houses, and lovers of Christ, and those who helped me in my infirmities! Farewell, you who loved my sermons, you who thronged the Church, you who took them down in shorthand surreptitiously or openly, and farewell to these gates which you so often crowded against! Farewell, O ye Emperors, with your attendant courtiers; and whether they are loyal to you I cannot tell, though I know they are disloyal to God. Clap hands, applaud your orator as he says farewell! My busy and insolent tongue will sink to silence, but it shall not always be silent—I shall fight by your side with all my strength and my power of words. Farewell, O great and Christ-loving nation, for I will speak the truth, though your zeal offend your knowledge! This parting has made me kinder. Come to the truth! Change yourselves, though it is late! And honor your God more than you are accustomed to do. . . . Farewell, O ye angels, who preside over the Church and over my person and my departure, so long as my fortunes are in the hands of God. Farewell, O most blessed Trinity, my meditation and my glory! Mayest Thou be preserved by these, and mayest Thou preserve my people! Mine they are, though others rule them! And may the good news always come to me that Thou art being exalted and uplifted by them! So, my children, keep what is due to you, and remember my stonings! The grace of the Lord Jesus Christ be with you all. Amen.

[*Oratio*, XLII, 27]

A few weeks later Gregory closed his residence in Constantinople, and left the city forever.

Sometimes, as he meditated on his estate in Arianzus, there would be little flares of bitterness, curious moments of self-assertiveness when he reflected on the mistakes of others, but those moments were rare. He told himself he would not talk about these affairs, he would offer the sacrifice of silence, but he could not forbid himself to write letters.

He wrote ceaselessly, sometimes complaining a little, more often describing the joys of retirement. Once he wrote that he had been cast away from an ungrateful city "like a fleck of sea foam or a shred of seaweed." He still took part in controversies, and wrote a long letter against the spread of the doctrine of Apollinaris, who rejected the complete humanity of Christ, saying that "God was made flesh, but not man." God was not really born; he merely passed through the Virgin's body. Gregory insisted that God was born and grew and was in every aspect humanly formed, and at the same time He was divine; and to deprive God of His manhood was to deprive Him of every reason for coming to earth. Meanwhile he took little part in public life. Sometimes he retired to a mountain cave, and there withdrew from the world, sleeping on some sackcloth stretched over the earth, friendly to the beasts who penetrated his hiding place. At last, in 389, at the age of about sixty, he died in Arianzus on his father's estate. Except for a few small bequests, he left everything to the poor.

Once he wrote: "I am small, and I come from a country of no repute." But the divine passion in him was immense, and he was one of the three Fathers who gave meaning to Cappadocia. Frail and wise and weak, a man who sometimes shed tears of anger and gave way to sardonic laughter, he accomplished more in the few weeks of his episcopate in Constantinople that he accomplished in twenty years in Caesarea. He published no formal treatises, occupied no formal position in the Church, made no deep study of the Scriptures, changed nothing except the hearts of men. A spirit blazed in him which men recognized, as they recognized the spirit blazing in Athanasius. But in the Eastern Church no one called Athanasius "the Divine" or "the Theologian." Those were titles which were given to Gregory Nazianzen alone among the Fathers of the Church.

Shortly after his death, his remains were taken to Constantinople, where they remained until the Crusaders besieged the city A.D. 1204. Then his body was taken secretly to Rome. Today his relics rest in the Vatican, in the Chapel of St. Gregory designed by Michelangelo.

John Chrysostom

In the fourth century Antioch was one of the three great cities of the eastern Mediterranean, rivaling Constantinople and Alexandria. Here the Sun-God had touched the earth, and everything glittered. Here were great palaces, theatres, racing stables, market places where one could buy silks from China and furs from Russia and amber from the Baltic. Running from east to west across the city was a broad avenue four miles long, with marble colonnades paved with red granite, and a host of gold-plated statues in the avenue. Here, too, beside the river Orontes lay the Grove of Daphne, a forest of laurel and myrtle, cypress and scented shrubs, dark and mysterious, and somewhere in the grove lay a temple dedicated to Apollo who pursued the nymph Daphne until she cried out to the earth to open and shelter her, and where she disappeared a laurel tree sprang up. Where there was once a laurel tree now stood a gigantic statue of Apollo in gold and ivory, glowing with jewels. Antioch the Great, with the pale green waters of the Orontes flowing through it and high mountains protecting it, glittering in the sun, rich beyond any city of the known world except perhaps Seleucia on the Tigris, was a place given over to pagan luxury. People said: "It is better to be a worm and feed on the mulberries of Daphne than to be a King's guest." They meant that of all the places in the world Antioch was closest to Paradise.

About A.D. 347 there was born in Antioch, to a Christian mother and a pagan father, a son who was baptized John. His father, the descendant of an illustrious Greek family, bore the title *Magister Militum Orientis,* which may be translated: General in command of the Eastern Army. Of the father we know almost nothing except that he died shortly after the child's birth. Of his mother we know little more than her name Anthusa, which means "flowering," and that her piety was unexcelled among the women of Antioch. There was one other child, a daughter, some years older than John. Anthusa had married young, and she was only twenty when her husband died.

Of his early years we know little. He seems to have lived quietly and happily, surrounded by private tutors, on a large estate. He must have visited the theatres, for he shows a surprisingly detailed knowledge of them. Brought up as a Christian in a city where nearly half the population were Christians, he was fourteen when the Emperor Julian removed his capital from Constantinople to Antioch. Julian was now sole Emperor of the Roman Empire, his power stretching from Britain to the borders of Persia, and Antioch was now the center of the world, a city of panoply, of unbelievable luxury. Julian had apostacized. He attended the great ceremonies at the Temple of Apollo, and it is related that one day, when he went to consult the oracle and found it dumb, he was told that Apollo was silent because the grove was polluted with the presence of a dead body. These words pointed to the relics of the Christian martyr Babylas, who was buried nearby and whose fame in Antioch exceeded that of the apostles. Julian gave orders for the removal of the body of Babylas and the destruction of the small chapel erected over it. The order was obeyed. The Christians poured out of the city and bore the body to a church, making a fierce display of their affection for Babylas and their hatred for Julian. That same night the Temple of Apollo was struck by lightning and burned to the ground. John, who took part in the great processions through the city which attended the worship and translation of the remains of Babylas, hurried to see the flames. For the first time he saw what flames could do to places he hated; it was not the last. All through his life there were to be these sudden explosions of flame, always mysterious, for no one was ever able to decide whether they were miracles caused by divine intervention or the work of incendiaries.

In those days a boy of fourteen was ready to attend the university. He may have gone briefly to Athens to study, but it is more likely that he remained in Antioch, where we know that he studied under the Neoplatonist philosopher, Libanius, a man with a somber talent for depicting the evils of his time. Libanius taught rhetoric and violently opposed Christianity; he was responsible for turning the young Prince Julian against Christ. He was ponderous and brilliant, full of human sympathy, and without guile. He wrote of Antioch: "It is a city where you can tell the difference between night and day only by the *quality* of the illumination. The work goes on at night, and at the same time the singers and dancers continue their performances: Hephaestus and Aphrodite share the night between them." Libanius had a particular liking for John. It was said he wanted John to succeed him as head of the school, "had not the Christians stolen him." But John had already encountered the monk Diodorus, whose pale face, sunken cheeks and emaciated appearance once aroused the ridicule of the Emperor. Diodorus lived in a monastery in the mountains, and John frequently visited him.

At the age of eighteen John suddenly turned against the teachings of Libanius. He decided to become a monk and put aside all "this debauchery of learning," remembering the words of St. Paul: "All these things I set aside, with all outward adornment." He was baptized, but Meletius the Confessor, Archbishop of Antioch, refused to allow him to live the anchorite's life. For three years he was an acolyte attached to the Archbishop's palace, and later became a lector. All this time he was kicking against the pricks. Finally the Archbishop relented. John went out in the mountains and began to live a life of self-discipline in the company of an old Syrian called Hesychius. The name of the Syrian means "quietness." And it was quietness that he wanted, to deaden the pain of his mother's death, to put away the temptations of Antioch, to bury forever his love of physical pleasure. He had wanted to become a hermit long before, following his friend Basil, his closest companion at college, who "accompanied me at all times, studied by my side, walked to lectures with me and returned with me, so close to me that we were always discussing the way of life we would adopt together." For a while he lived in community, practicing asceticism moderately. Later, he decided to practice self-mortification. He retired to a cave, denied himself sleep, read the Bible continually and spent two years without lying down, apparently in the belief that a Christian must stand in order to obey the injunction: "Be ye watchful." The result was inevitable. His stomach shriveled up, and his kidneys were damaged by cold. His digestion permanently impaired, unable to doctor himself, he came down the mountain, walked to Antioch and appeared before Archbishop Meletius, who immediately sent him to a doctor and sometime afterward appointed him to the office of attendant upon the altar.

His health ruined, John had learned his lesson. Like Buddha, he now set himself against the life of self-mortification, though he never lost his admiration of the monk's eternal contemplation in a monastery. Years later he wrote: "The monks in their monasteries live lives suitable to heaven, and no worse than those of the angels, free from quarrels and anxieties." And he said it was absurd to ask an ordinary man to take to the mountains or the desert. "We ask that he shall be good, and sweetly reasonable, and sober, while dwelling in the midst of the city." Henceforward he was to be good always, sweetly reasonable nearly always, and if he was rarely sober, it was because he was drunk with God, or with rage against men's follies and with joy in their joys.

For six years John remained a minor deacon under Meletius, and almost nothing is known of him during this period. Six years later, in 386, when Meletius was dead and Flavian had been ordained Archbishop, he was appointed presbyter, and then the active work of his ministry began. Now for twenty years he was to write angelically, saying the things that needed to be said, in a time when the major heresies had died down and the theologians were free once more to speak of the things closest to their hearts.

As presbyter, John's task was to mount the pulpit and encourage and admonish the worshipers. In this he had no help from a commanding presence. We know a good deal about his physical appearance. He was a small, bald, slender, hollow-cheeked man with deep-sunken eyes and a huge wrinkled brow and a beard which turned gray when he was young. His voice, though sweet, had little strength, and he was constantly calling upon the worshipers to draw nearer to the pulpit. He was awkward in his movements and called himself "spidery." He had the emaciated frame of the ascetic and the ascetic's light step and suffered horribly from a disease of the kidneys, taking food with difficulty. He hated noise, broken plates, the clink of armor, the painted faces of women, the simpering of some priests and acolytes. He could be astonishingly lighthearted, and the thin voice could sometimes explode in thunder. He was careful with his dress, and when he was appointed to the see of Constantinople, he was occasionally stiff and formal, determined that the Emperor should bow before him as the representative of Christ. Quite deliberately in his sermons he used the language of the stews to frighten his audience into righteousness, with the result that some of his homilies cannot even now be published in English. He spoke once of God desiring a harlot, giving to the image of Christ desiring the salvation of the human race all the free scope and imagination he could contrive; and evidently the lesson went home. He was profoundly concerned with practical morality. He had a mind like quicksilver, a prodigious sense of drama, a grim humor, a desperate sympathy for his fellow men and the passion of a social reformer. So many things were mixed up in him that it is not surprising that he seems to have a modern temper, and there is no greater authority for the lives of ordinary people in fourth-century Antioch and Constantinople than the sermons he delivered. And no one has ever inveighed with such violence against the greed of the rich.

This strange spidery prelate had no care in the world except that Antioch should be brought to Christ. He could look forward to a life spent in reasonable quietness. In the midst of his preaching came the crash of tragedy. Antioch revolted, tore down the statues of the Emperor Theodosius and the Empress Flacilla, and waited breathless for the punishment—the destruction of the city.

In the tenth year of the reign of Theodosius, and the fifth of that of Arcadius, his son—the same year that Augustine received baptism from the hands of Ambrose in Milan—an imperial edict announced a forced levy on behalf of the army. The army claimed a donative of five gold pieces for every soldier. In Antioch the edict was proclaimed during the morning of February 26, 387. When the proclamation was read outside the praetorium, it was received for a moment in stunned silence, broken by the wailing of women. In the crowd, according to Libanius, who discussed the incident afterward, were some professional agitators, the same men who were hired by the officials to applaud them during processions and by actors to applaud them on the stage, "the kind of people," according to John, "who earn their livings off the the dancers and sell their voices to their bellies." The crowd was surging against the praetorium when one of these agitators, or perhaps an officer of the guard—for no one knew exactly what happened—uttered the cry: "To the bathhouses!" Immediately the mob surged in the direction of the Baths of Caligula, while a few Christians went hurriedly to the palace of the old Archbishop Flavian to seek his advice: there was no sign of him: he was in fact sitting by the bedside of his sick sister in another part of the city. In their rage the crowd smashed everything they could lay their hands on in the Baths of Caligula, cutting the chains which held the bronze lanterns and then letting them crash on the stone floor and hacking down the trees in the gardens. The professional agitators were enjoying themselves, but they failed to canalize the emotions of the crowd. The mob swung back to the praetorium, rushed past the guards and demanded the abrogation of the levy. There was no sign of the prefect—he had slipped away, over the garden wall. The mob rushed through the great marble audience hall, where the prefect was accustomed to sit in state, wearing the robe and the slender silver crown of his office, under the statues of the Emperor and Empress. There was no prefect they could shout to. They had exhausted most of their energy and they might have gone quietly and sullenly from the palace if a small boy, clutching a stone in his hand, had not suddenly decided to throw the stone at the statue of Theodosius. The equestrian statue of gilded bronze represented everything the crowd detested. Soon they were all hurling stones at the statues. There were altogether five statues, representing the old Count Theodosius, the father of the Emperor, the Emperor himself, the Empress Flacilla, who had recently died, and the two princes, Honorius and Arcadius, who bore the titles of Emperor of the West and Emperor of the East respectively. The statues of the Emperor and the Empress were torn down, smashed, mutilated and led in triumph through the streets. Rain had fallen. The streets were thick with mud. The mob, insane with fear and joy, was chanting: "Try to defend yourself now, proud horseman!" Meanwhile there were some who remained behind in the praetorium, busily smearing mud on the Emperor's tablets and setting fire to the heavy silk curtains hung between the marble pillars.

Three hours later the prefect led the archers into the city and the mob dispersed. Then there was only a deathly silence, and pieces of twisted bronze in the mud in the streets. No one moved. The clouds hung heavy and low over Antioch, and the city seemed to have given itself up for dead. Everyone knew that in the eyes of the Emperor the whole city had committed the crime of *laesae maiestatis*. The penalty was death.

That day the punishments began. Men arrested by the archers and the praetorian guards were summarily executed. The executions went on for days. The prefect sent a messenger to Constantinople, to report the crime. Fortunately the messenger was detained by a fall of snow in the Taurus Mountains. Archbishop Flavian, a man of eighty years, slipped out of the city and made his way through the snow to Constantinople, to plead for mercy at the feet of the Emperor. The ringleaders of the assault on the Baths of Caligula had been put to death; most of the professional agitators were rounded up; then came the turn of the leading citizens, now made hostages of the praetorian guard, examined in the torture chambers, their wealth confiscated, their wives and children thrown out onto the streets, to live as best they could. "There is a silence," said John, "huge with terror, and utter loneliness everywhere."

All hope for the city depended upon the intercession of the Archbishop, and hardy anyone believed he would be able to cross eight hundred miles of barren countryside deep in snow, and return alive.

For seven days John remained silent, while the executions went on. Then he could contain himself no longer. He began to deliver to the people of Antioch that long series of sermons which is known as *On the Statues*. In these sermons he said very little about the statues. Most of all he spoke of God's mercy, and how there are things far more dreadful than death or slavery. He spoke too of his fond hope in Flavian's intercession and his desire that the people of Antioch should embrace death, if they had to, or life, with equal courage. He talked gently, in tones of lament, and sometimes in paradoxes, as when he said:

> Strip yourselves, for it is the season of wrestling. Clothe yourselves, for we are engaged in a fierce warfare with devils. Whet your sickles which are blunted with long surfeiting, and then sharpen them with fasting. [*On the Statues*, III, 3]

He reminded the worshipers that Abel was murdered and was happy, while Cain lived and was miserable. John the Baptist was beheaded, Stephen was stoned, yet their deaths were happy. No one should fear death at the hands of the Emperor. Slavery? Why should a man fear slavery so long as he was free to worship his God? Have faith in Christ and in His servant Flavian:

> I tell you, God will not suffer this errand to be fruitless. The very sight of the venerable Bishop will dispose the Emperor to mercy. This is the holy season. In such a season Flavian will show the Emperor the blessedness of forgiving sins, for this is the season when we remember how Christ died for the sins of the world. The Emperor will be reminded of the parable of the ten thousand talents. Flavian will put fear into the heart of the Emperor. He will add the prayer which the Emperor was taught when he was admitted into Holy Communion. "Forgive us our trespasses, as we forgive them who trespass against us." He will bring to his memory that in this city the faithful were first called Christians by name. And the Emperor will listen to him. Let us assist him with our prayers; let us supplicate; let us make an embassy to the King who reigns above, an embassy of tears. And remember how it is written of repentant Nineveh, "God saw their works,"—not their fasting, not their sackcloth; nothing of this kind. "They turned every one from their evil ways, and the Lord repented of the evil that he had said he would do unto them."
>
> [*On the Statues*, II, 39]

At this time John was forty-one years old; he looked sixty, and resembled an Old Testament prophet, breathing forth fire and thunder, excoriating the people for their past vices, their addiction to wealth, their love of the theater, their sensual enjoyments. If they had lived more strictly, they would not have behaved like wild beasts as they raced through the praetorium, and if they were true Christians, they would not have possessed this abject fear of the Emperor, and his power over them. A king is only a man. Why fear him? No kings ever entertained angels, but the Heavenly King is forever attended by them. Again and again, on these strange days when destruction hung in the air, he inveighed against wealth and luxury:

> Abraham was rich, but loved not his wealth; he regarded not the house of this man, nor the wealth of another; but going forth he looked around for the stranger, or for some poor man, that he might entertain the wayfarer. He covered not his ceilings with gold, but placing his tent near the oak, he was content with the shade of its leaves. Yet so bright was his dwelling that angels were not ashamed to tarry with him; for they sought not splendor of abode, but purity of soul. So let us, beloved, imitate Abraham and bestow our goods on the needy.   [*On the Statues*, II, 15]

John believed that it was the desire for luxury which precipitated the rebellion. The mob rebelled for the sake of a few gold coins; and if the gold coins had been taken from them, what then? Surely they would have spent the money in the theaters, on horse races, on dancing girls, on still more sumptuous houses. Their desires dwelt on the things of earth: perhaps the visitation of destruction was deserved. Sodom and Jerusalem had been destroyed, and now there was God's vengeance on Antioch! So he goes on, exhorting, threatening, consoling, conjuring up visions of Paradise if the Antiochenes should imagine themselves about to be martyred, and offering his own firm faith to those who desired only to live in Christ on earth.

These staggering sermons, which were delivered to the people daily in church, kept the flock together. After the first day there was no more panic, though the tortures went on and day by day the people could see the senators of Antioch, and everyone else thought guilty by the praetorian guard, dragged through the streets to prison. Yet hope filled the air. Rumors reached Antioch that Flavian had been successful in his mission of mercy; these rumors were followed by others protesting the direst punishments. In fact Flavian had reached Constantinople a full week before the messenger sent by the prefect. On the orders of the Emperor he delayed his return. It was Easter before he returned in his triumph.

About the middle of Lent two imperial commissioners, Hellebicus and Caesarius, reached Antioch with orders to make a complete report on the rebellion. They were both Christians, and possessed friends in the city. They were empowered to hold a public inquiry and to put the highest citizens on trial and to execute summary judgment. The old scholar Libanius pleaded for the life of the city, and was given a special place on the tribunal beside the judges. Others came to plead, among them some wild hermits from the mountains, saintly men who walked barefoot, with tattered clothes and ragged beards. Crowds followed the hermits, and John especially delighted in them, pointing to their frugal lives, their asceticism, their avoidance of the temptations the world sets in front of them. The commissioners must have regarded the hermits privately as an unspeakable nuisance, for they were hammering at the doors of the praetorium, continually begging for mercy. In public, as good Christians, the commissioners were apt to regard them with veneration.

The story is told of the aged hermit Macedonius the Barley-Eater, who subsisted on only a few grains of barley a day. He had no other name. He was the most ragged of all the hermits. One day the imperial commissioners were riding through the street when they saw the wild hermit approaching them. "Who is that mad fellow?" they asked, and when they were told it was a most saintly ascetic, they dropped off their horses and went down on their knees. According to Theodoret, who tells the story rather wistfully, as though he did not quite believe it, the hermit regarded them sternly and gave them a lesson in Christian behavior. "My friends," said the hermit, "go to the Emperor and tell him from me: 'You are an Emperor, but you are also a man, and you rule over beings who are of a like nature with yourself! Man was created after a divine image and likeness! Do not then mercilessly command the image of God to be destroyed, for you will provoke the Maker if you punish this image!' And tell him to reflect that it is easy to build statues, but he can never create again a single hair of a man he has put to death" (*Theodoret*, V, 20).

These hermits, who fell upon Antioch like a plague of locusts, begged for mercy for the city and martyrdom for themselves. When John discovered that the caves they had abandoned were now being filled with the scholars who scattered from the city in the time of danger, he was happily ironical:

Tell me this: Where are those long-bearded, cloak-wearing, staff-bearing fellows—those cynical lickers-up-of-crumbs-from-be-low-the-table, those gentlemen who work so hard on behalf of their bellies? I will tell you! They have scurried away and hidden them-selves in the caves and dens of our hermits who walk boldly about our forum as though no calamity had ever threatened!

[*On the Statues,* XVII, 1, 2]

In Constantinople Archbishop Flavian had presented the case for the city with great dignity and sweetness. He reminded Theodosius of a similar event that had happened during the reign of the Emperor Constantine. A stone had been thrown at his statue, the face of it was disfigured, and the Emperor had asked to be taken to the statue. Then he stroked his own face and said laughingly: "I do not find the mark of any wounds." Flavian reminded the Emperor that it was in his power to create the most splendid statue in the world. "If you will pardon the offense of those who have done Your Majesty injury, if you take no revenge upon them, then they will build for you a statue neither of brass, nor of gold, nor inlaid with jewels, but one adorned in a robe more precious than any costly silks: the robe of humanity and of tender mercy: and every man will erect this statue of you in his own heart." Before such an advocate the Emperor was helpless. He pardoned the city: there would be no general massacre. Instead he gave orders that Antioch should be degraded from the rank of capital of Syria. The metropolitan honors were transferred to the neighboring city of Laodicea.

On the day when the news of the pardon finally reached Antioch, John gave the last of his sermons *On the Statues.* "Today," he said, "I shall begin with the same words I spoke in the time of danger. So say with me: May God be praised, Who enables us this day to celebrate our festival with so light and joyful a heart. May God be praised, Who is able to do exceeding abundantly above all that we ask or think!"

On Holy Saturday Flavian returned to the city, an old man with almost no strength left in him. Lamps were lit; torches shone in daylight; spring flowers and green leaves covered the shops; the forum was decorated with garlands. The Archbishop made his triumphal entry, while the crowds gathered round him, eager to touch his garments or to stand in his shadow; and then he blessed the crowd and entered into the basilica.

The strain of those long weeks when the survival of the city hung in the balance fell heavily on John. For many days he was ill. When he recovered Antioch seemed hardly to have changed: evil was still abroad: the hermits had returned to their caves: and though there were no more places of amusement (Flavian had extracted from the Emperor a ban against theaters and horse racing), there was God's work to be done. For nearly ten more years he was to remain in Antioch, delivering his sermons and writing his occasional books, and sometimes there would come to him in the middle of a phrase the sudden recollection of those terrible days when the faggots were lit in the market place. He lived two lives, one contemplative, one active. The measure of his active life lay in the torrent of sermons and homilies he delivered to an enthralled congregation, speaking outward, exhorting his flock and explaining the Scriptures. The measure of his contemplative life is revealed in his books and those occasional passages in his sermons where he gives evidence of wrestling with angels, speaking inward, continuing that dialogue which the saints maintain with God. He has one speech for his flock, another for God; and sometimes, but very rarely, they were the same speech.

Shortly before the riots in Antioch, beginning in September, 386, John delivered a series of five sermons on the incomprehensibility of God. It was, of course, a theme which fired the imagination of the Eastern Church, and Gregory of Nyssa had concluded that the vision of God was perpetually obscured by the cloud that reposed on Sinai, and at the same time he had suggested that the appearance of God was such that the eyes of the soul could perceive Him. But Cappadocian mysticism was foreign to the sober Antiochenes, who did not share the worship of asceticism and allegory which Gregory of Nyssa derived from the great Alexandrians. In Antioch men were aware of the physical and palpable earth, of a visible and palpable flesh. Ignatius was the forerunner, thirsty for glory, for martyrdom, for the sober lion's tooth. And John was the child of Ignatius concerned with heroism and martyrdom, and so certain of his faith he had no need to penetrate step by shadowy step up the slopes of Sinai. To the question whether God can be comprehended, he answers with a shuddering No. God is altogether too great, too majestic, to be contemplated by human eyes, and for him it is the wildest absurdity to suggest that the immensity of God can be comprehended by the limited intelligence of men. He who has no beginning or end, or any birth, whose powers are limitless, whose ordinances circumscribe every man, whose peace passeth all understanding—how dare men say they can comprehend Him? Taking as his text: "He dwells in an unapproachable light" (*I Tim.* 6:16), John surveys, like a man looking over some mist-enshrouded mountains where only a few shadowy outlines suggest the presence of peaks and valleys, the known landscape of God; and where Gregory of Nyssa and later Dionysius the Areopagite will seek to find some entrance somewhere, some means of mapping the mountains, John surveys the mist in shuddering awe and cries out: "What can I know except His majesty and power?" More than any of his other writings, the five sermons on the incomprehensibility of God are like a direct and fearful prayer. What it man? He is earth and ashes, blood and flesh, smoke and shadow, a vain thing. Look at man, he says; then look at the splendors of creation:

> Look at the sky, how beautiful it is, and how vast, all crowned with a blazing diadem of stars! For how many ages has it existed? Already it has been there for five thousand years, and shows no signs of aging. Like some young creature full of sap it preserves all the shining and the freshness of an earlier age, and manifests the beauty it possessed in the beginning, and time has not wearied it. And this vast, beautiful, ageless sky, unchangeable and gleaming, with all its stars, having existed through so many ages—this same God, whom some profess to be able to see with mortal eyes and comprehend with their own pitiable intelligences—this same God created it as easily as a man, throwing a handful of sticks together, creates a hut. And this is what Isaiah meant when he said: "He stretches out the heavens as a curtain, and spreadeth them out as a tent to dwell in."
>
> Look at the great mass of the mountains, and all the innumerable people who dwell on earth, and the plants, all so rich and wonderfully varied, and the towns and the vast buildings and the wild animals, and all these the earth supports easily on her back. And yet with all its vastness, it was fashioned by God "as though it were nothing." So speaks for us Isaiah, searching for a phrase which will explain the ease with which God created the earth. . . . And then look at the inhabitants of earth, of whom the prophet said: "He sitteth upon the circle of the earth, and the inhabitants thereof

are as grasshoppers," and a little while earlier he said: "Behold the nations are as a drop of water falling from a bowl." Think of all the peoples who inhabit the earth: Syrians, Cilicians, Cappadocians, Bithynians, those who live on the shores of the Black Sea, in Thrace, in Macedonia, in all of Greece and the islands and in Italy, and beyond the places well-known to us, think of the islands of Britain, Sarmatia, India, and the inhabitants of Persia, and then of all the innumerable other peoples and races, and all these are "as a drop of water falling from a bowl." And what small atom of this drop of water thinks he can know God?   [*De Incomprehensibili*, II, 6]

For John it is all mystery, power, the terror in the heart of terror. He quotes from the *Psalms*: "He looketh on the earth, and it trembleth; he toucheth the hills and they smoke." He quotes *Job*: "He shaketh the earth out of her place, and the pillars thereof tremble." He quotes *Isaiah*: "He saith to the deep, Be dry." All those texts which reflect the shuddering immensity of God are brought into play. Man is clay, God is the potter, and think what vast a distance separates mute clay from the living hands of the potter? The praises of men add no substance to the unimaginable glory of God, whose radiance has never been seen by mortal eyes.

What then of those who say they have seen God? He quotes the famous vision of the seraphim in *Isaiah*:

In the year that King Uzziah died, I saw also the Lord sitting upon a throne, high and lifted up, and his train filled the temple. Above it stood the seraphims: each one had six wings; with twain he covered his face, and with twain he covered his feet, and with twain he did fly. And one cried unto another, and said, Holy, holy, holy, is the Lord of hosts; the whole earth is full of his glory.

[*Isa.* 6:1-3]

John almost laughs the vision to scorn. He refuses to believe that God sits on a throne, and he notes that the seraphim cover their faces with their wings because they dare not look upon the brightness of God; and if the seraphim dare not look, how dare Daniel see? No; what Daniel has seen is only the faint image of the invisible glory, such as God might offer in His mercy to one He loves; no more than a shadow, the same kind of shadow which Daniel thought he saw when there appeared to him a jewel-encrusted angel; and having seen the vision Daniel says: "My comeliness was turned in me into corruption, and I retained no strength." John asks how it was that Isaiah could look steadily upon God, while at the sight of a mere angel Daniel was utterly cast down. "No one has seen God," said St. John. "No man shall see me, and live," God said to Moses. "He dwells in an unapproachable light," Paul wrote to Timothy. With these bricks John, with fear and trembling, builds his prayer.

Where Gregory resembles a mountaineer, carving his dangerous way up the steep slope of Sinai, John flies straight up the mountain and announces boldly the presence of the *tremenda maiestas*. God is there, invisible, not to be approached, and we shall know Him only by our perfect fear, by an agony of soul, such as one experiences when looking down from a high cliff at an immense sea. "Thereupon, seized with vertigo, terrified and awe-stricken, we try to turn back." And then it is too late. We stand; we watch; and we are aware in the depths of our being of a terror so great that no one dare put it into words, and on these matters it is best to preserve a holy silence.

John does not talk often of the terror of God. His rich and fertile mind was more concerned with the riches and fertility which poured down from Heaven. But sometimes, and then with a violence which is overwhelming, he will speak of the terrors he has known intimately. Something of the terror he knew is conveyed in his book *On the Priesthood*, where he discusses the terrible responsibilities which weigh upon the priest, who must act at all times in conformity with God's law. At the thought of surrendering himself to the spiritual combat, he writes with shuddering awe and a fierce brilliance:

> Imagine, then, the daughter of the King who rules over the whole earth is betrothed to a certain man. Imagine that this virgin is possessed of perfect beauty and is far superior to all other women in beauty, and imagine too that she possesses virtues of soul greater than those possessed by men in the past and in all the time to come, and that in grace and gesture she rises above all art, and that the loveliness of her person is eclipsed only by the beauty of her countenance. Imagine that her betrothed loves her more deeply and passionately than any lovers ever loved before. And then imagine, while he is burning with love for her, he hears that some mean, abject, low-born cripple is about to wed her. Then you will understand my grief. . . .
>
> Or imagine an army composed of foot soldiers, horsemen and

sailors, with the ships out to sea and the columns of infantry and the horsemen careering over the plain and on the spurs of the mountains, armor gleaming in the sun, helmets glittering, shields throwing off flashes of blinding light. Imagine that the sound of the clashing spears and the horses neighing is borne up to the highest heavens, and imagine that the land and sea are so thick with brass and iron that they cannot be seen. Imagine a savage enemy drawn up in his battle lines, and let the time of the engagement be at hand. And then imagine some shepherd boy, fresh from piping, whose only knowledge consists of knowing how to lean on his crook, is suddenly brought forward, thrust into armor, introduced to the army, the captains and high officers, the bowmen and the slingers, the spearmen and the horsemen, and the ships and the ships' commanders, all that thronging mass of soldiers and sailors and all those multitudes of engines of war. And then imagine that the boy is shown the enemy's battle lines, sees their fierce and warlike countenances, their vast destructive engines, their accumulation of weapons. And in his sight all the valleys and ravines and sheer precipices are obscured, and the dust and the darkness bewilder him.

Imagine the torrents of blood, the groans of the dying, the shouts of the survivors, the piled heaps of the dead, wheels dripping with blood, horses with their riders thrown headlong because there were so many dead bodies in their way, and all the earth is confusion, and everywhere it is spattered with blood, bows, arrows, hoofs, piles of heads, human arms, chariot wheels, helmets, brains still attached to swords, and the point of a lance broken off with an eye transfixed to it.

Let the boy imagine all this: the sufferings of the soldiers and sailors, and the ships burning on the waves, and sinking with their heavily armored crews, the screams of the sailors and the mountains in flames. Let him imagine further that by some enchantment the horses and the foot soldiers are borne through the air, and there is sorcery and witchcraft at hand. Let him consider those evils of war: the clouds of spears, the hail of arrows, the thick darkness which comes from deathly weapons, and the blood-red waves crashing against the ships; and when he has been carefully instructed in all the horror of warfare, let him be told too about the further horrors of captivity and slavery, which is worse than death;

and when he learns all this, order him immediately to mount his horse and take command of the army. Would not he be dismayed?

[*De Sacerdotio*, VI, 12]

It is not often that John writes like this. The vast collection of his homilies spoken at Antioch consists largely of the careful elaboration of selected texts. They were delivered before Mass, taken down in shorthand and then revised. He comments sensibly, rarely seeking for allegorical meanings, with a superb sense of authority, in a rich prose which flashes like the prose of John Donne, who was forever quoting him in his sermons. He has Donne's wit, and Donne's power of rising straight off the earth. And if in his wit and soaring imagination he is most like Donne, there is something of Dostoevski's Father Zosima in his sweeping passion, in the transparent goodness and sobriety of his faith. He is wonderful in his denunciations against luxury. He has no patience with painted women: "mouth like a bear's mouth dyed with blood, eyebrows blackened with kitchen soot, cheeks whitened with dust like the walls of a tomb." He will interrupt a sermon to inveigh against those who come noisily to Mass. "The table," he thundered, "is not for chattering jays, but for eagles who fly thither where the dead body lieth." He never forgot that to be a Christian was to be a hero, and he was determined to shock the people of Antioch out of their complacency.

These homilies gave him the opportunity to discuss all subjects under the sun. In the Eastern fashion he discusses the most intimate things of life openly: stews, bathhouses, theaters, race courses, he knows them all. Usually it is a dry and sober brilliance, but if a thought occurs to him on the wing, he will follow it wherever it leads him. He was not afraid of blind alleys, and he was perfectly capable of imagining the whole human race as a harlot desired by God. Something of his temper can be gauged by these five extraordinary improvisations taken almost at random from the three thousand pages of his surviving homilies:

God desired a harlot

God desired a harlot, and how doth He act? He doth not send to her any of His servants. He doth not send any angels or archangels, cherubim or seraphim. No, He Himself draws near to the one He loves, and He does not take her to Heaven, for He could not bring a harlot to Heaven, and therefore He Himself comes down to earth, to the harlot, and is not ashamed. He comes to her secret dwelling place and beholds her in her drunkenness. And how doth He come? Not in the bare essence of His original nature, but in the guise of one whom the harlot is seeking, in order that she might not be afraid when she sees Him, and will not run away, and escape Him. He comes to the harlot as a man. And how does He become this? He is conceived in the womb, He groweth little by little, as we do, and has intercourse with human nature. And He finds this Harlot thick with sores and oppressed by devils. How doth He act? He draws nigh to her. She sees Him and flees away. He calleth the wise men, saying, "Why are ye afraid? I am not a judge, but a physician. I come not to judge the world, but to save the world." Straightway He calleth the wise men, for are not the wise men the immediate first fruits of His coming? They come and worship Him, and then the harlot herself comes and is transformed into a maiden. The Canaanite woman comes and partakes of His love. And how doth He act? He taketh the sinner and espouseth her to Himself, and giveth her the signet ring of the Holy Ghost as a seal between them.   [*Eutropius,* II, 11]

On the Resurrection of the Flesh

If God had not intended to raise us up again, if it was His desire that we should all be dissolved and blotted out in annihilation, He would not have wrought so many things for us. He would not have spread out the heavens above, or stretched out the earth beneath. He would not have fashioned this whole universe, if it were only for the short span of our lives. The heavens and the earth and the seas and the rivers are more enduring than we are; ravens and elephants live longer, and have a longer enjoyment of the present life, and they are more free from griefs and cares. What then? you ask. Has God made the slaves better than the masters? I beseech you, do not reason thus, O man; nor be so ignorant of the riches God spread out before you. From the beginning God desired to make thee immortal. Ah, but thou wert unwilling!

[*In I Corinth. Hom.* xvii]

Pentecost

This day the earth became Heaven for us. Not because the stars descended from the heavens to earth, but because the apostles ascended to Heaven by the grace of the Holy Spirit, which was now abundantly poured forth, and so the whole world was transformed into heaven; not because human nature was changed, but because there was a change in the direction of the will. For there was found a taxgatherer, and he was transformed into an evangelist. There was found a persecutor, and he was changed into an apostle. There was found a robber, and he was led into Paradise. There was found a prostitute, and she was made the equal of virgins. There were found wise men, and they were taught the Gospels. Evil fled away, and gentleness took its place. Slavery was put away, and freedom came in its stead. And all debts were forgiven, and the grace of God was conferred. Therefore Heaven became earth; and from repeating this again and again I shall not cease.   [*Hom. in Act* 2:1]

The Night

The night was not made to be spent entirely in sleep. Why did Jesus pass so many nights amid the mountains, if not to instruct us by His example? It is during the night that all the plants respire, and it is then also that the soul of man is more penetrated with the dews falling from Heaven; and everything that has been scorched and burned during the day by the sun's fierce heat is refreshed and renewed during the night; and the tears we shed at night extinguish the fires of passion and quieten our guilty desires. Night heals the wounds of our soul and calms our griefs.

[*Hom. in Psalm* VI]

The Tomb of Alexander

Tell, me, where is the tomb of Alexander? Show it to me, and tell me the day on which he died. Even his own people know not where his tomb may be found, but the place of Christ's tomb is known everywhere in the world. The tombs of the servants of the Crucified are more splendid than the palaces of kings, not because they are beautiful or of vast extent, but because of the great concourse of fervent people who attend them. The Emperor himself, wearing the purple, embraces these tombs, lays his pride aside, begs the saints to be his advocates before God. Wearing his diadem, he implores a dead tentmaker and a dead fisherman to be his protectors.

Before these tombs all rank is turned upside down. Here kings and great ministers of state find themselves standing below the lowliest servants. But someone says: "It is a sweet sight to look on a king crowned and decked with gold, with his commanders and generals and captains of horse beside him." But I say that the spectacle presented to Christians is more awful and more splendid than that presented by earthly kings, which is no more than a child's game played before a painted curtain. Step on holy ground. Then immediately a flight of angels soars to the throne of God, to the unapproachable glory, with the news of your holy coming!

[In II Corinth. Hom. xxvi]

So he spoke in those long years in Antioch, where he was so loved by the people that he had to restrain them from cheering in the middle of a sermon—a gay, passionate, brilliant, earthy people, who were continually being reminded that gaiety, passion, brilliance and earthiness were foreign to the Kingdom of Heaven. John had no illusions about them. He regarded them with something of the Emperor Julian's distaste; Julian wrote a charming book on the Antiochenes called *Misopogon*, in which he told them what he thought of their treacherous, luxurious and frivolous way of life, people who were so proud that they despised their young Emperor because he followed the ancient pagan virtues and even dared to grow a beard. John thundered at them; and the louder and more terrifying the thunder, the greater the applause. Yet there was good reason for their applause. In his homilies *On the Statues* and in the long sermons on the books of the New Testament, we hear that last echo of the great tradition of oratory which goes back to the great days of Athenian democracy.

His temper was monastic, and to the very end there was something monkish in him: the outward and the inner man fought together. Throughout his sermons we find him appealing to the gentleness of monastic life, far from the murmur of the multitude. In the monasteries there are no brilliant discourses: there is silence and profound peace of soul, and the words "mine" and "thine" are never heard. No one snores; people do not sleep like logs; at night a monk will awake instantly from sleep and surrender himself to the urgencies of prayer:

And there they stand, forming themselves into a holy choir with their uplifted hands as they sing the sacred hymns. They are not like us; they do not demand a few hours in which to shake the sleep from their eyes. As soon as they have opened their eyes, they are like people who have been immersed in contemplation for many hours; for their brains are not choked by an excess of food, and their hands too are pure, being composed in sleep in quietness.

Among the monks none snores or breathes hard or tosses in his bed or lies with his body exposed, but they sleep as decently as those who are awake, and all this is due to the orderly progress within their souls. These men are truly saints and angels. And do not wonder when you hear these things: their fear of God is so great that they do not suffer themselves to lose themselves in the depths of sleep and drown their minds. Sleep falls gently on them, giving them only a peaceful rest.   [*In I Timoth. Hom.* xiv]

More and more as he grew older this was the vision which attracted him: a life lived in responsibility only to God, solemn vigils at night, quietness. He did not know, and could not guess, that he was to spend the rest of his life warring against the principalities of this earth.

In September, 397, there died in his palace in Constantinople the loose-living Archbishop Nectarius, who had ruled his see for sixteen disastrous years. Little could be said in favor of Nectarius, and still less could be said for the strange eunuch, Eutropius, who bore the title of Consul of the East. No one was ever less like a Roman Consul. He was born into slavery somewhere near the Euphrates. Castrated as a child, he was sold to a certain Ptolemy, a brothelkeeper, who sold him to the old general Arintheus, who employed him as a pander. Then he was given as a slave or as a house servant to the old general's daughter at her marriage: his duties were to wash her hair, fan her in summer and prepare her bath. Then, for some act of impropriety, he was dismissed. He wandered in rags around Constantinople until an officer at court took pity on him. At last he reached the lowest rank of imperial chamberlains. By bribes, by favors, by pandering, by friendship with the Frankish general Bautho whose daughter Eudoxia was the Empress of the Emperor Arcadius, this strange dwarfish misshapen eunuch, whose skin under the paint was loose and wrinkled like a raisin, had reached supreme power, even erecting statues to himself in the Senate and in the provincial capitals inscribed: "Eutropius, Third Founder of Constantinople." In all history no one had risen so high so quickly with so little to commend him. He exerted his authority in all the affairs of state and had a finger in every pie— even in religious pies. The Emperor Theodosius, who developed a curious affection for him, had sent the eunuch to the hermits in Egypt before undertaking the Italian campaign in 394. Since then Eutropius had been in fact, if not in name, the civilian head of the state church, and it was Eutropius who decided that the next incumbent on the throne of Hagia Sophia should be John of Antioch. The futile Nectarius and the fearful Eutropius were responsible for the choice of a genius to the greatest and most powerful see in Christendom.

It was arranged carefully. Eutropius had guessed that John would refuse the offer, and that even if he accepted, the people of Antioch would never permit him to go to Constantinople. Accordingly Eutropius addressed a letter to Asterius, the Governor of Syria, ordering him to put John secretly out of the city and take him under strong escort to Constantinople. He suggested that Asterius should invite John to meet him at one of the martyr chapels outside the walls. Unsuspecting, John rode out of the Roman gate at Antioch, never to return. Soldiers pounced on him, he was hurried into an imperial carriage and driven to Pagrae, the first stage on the road to Constantinople, where the escort commanded by an imperial chamberlain and a high officer of the army was waiting for him.

An Archbishop or Pope can only be ordained by another Archbishop or Pope. Pope Theophilus of Alexandria was in Constantinople, and Eutropius ordered him to ordain John. Theophilus refused. Eutropius whipped out a sheet of paper containing charges so damaging that Theophilus paled. "You will ordain him," Eutropius said, "or face trial on the charges listed here." On February 26, 398, John was enthroned as Patriarch of Constantinople.[1] He who hated power was now in the seat of power. He who fought against luxury and despised the kings of this world lived in a luxurious palace close to the palace of the Emperor. Only a few years remained to him, but all of them were filled with bitter fighting.

Years before, when he was writing his book *On the Priesthood,* he had foreseen the difficulties which now faced him:

> The souls of men elected to the priesthood ought to be endowed with such power as the grace of God bestowed on the bodies of the saints who were cast in the Babylonian furnace. Faggot and pitch and tow are not the fuel of this fire, but things far more dreadful; it is no material fire to which they are subjected. The all-devouring flame of envious men encompasses them, rises on every side, assails them and searches them out more ardently than the flames

[1] It is possible that the Emperor Arcadius was more to blame for the appointment. I have followed Palladius and Sozomen. Theodoret says more simply: "On the death of Nectarius, Arcadius, who had succeeded to the Eastern Empire, summoned John, the great luminary of the world." (*Eccl. Hist.* xxvii).

searched out the young men. . . . All men pass judgments on priests: we are thought to be angels, not men of flesh. And just as all men fear and flatter a tyrant as long as he is strong, because they cannot put him down, so they flatter the priest, but when they see his affairs going adversely, they abandon him, search out his weaknesses and utterly cast him down.   [*De Sacerdotio*, III, 14]

So it was now. Almost from the moment when he arrived in Constantinople under the patronage of Eutropius, he was the unwilling victim of all those who feared his power.

There were two Johns: one was the priest of Antioch, the other the Patriarch of Constantinople. The first held his temper in check, calm and fitful and brilliant, a man who seemed like Ignatius to possess in the highest degree the spiritual excitement characteristic of the Antiochenes. From this point onward he assumes the fiercer colors of Constantinople. We see him standing against more ornate altars, with thousands of candles gleaming, surrounded by servitors, wearing the heavy silken vestments of a prince of the Church, a man given over to a holy impatience, his voice fiercer, sterner, grave with doom. He is so changed a man that we may give him a new name, the name by which he is now known to us, though it was invented for him long after his death: Chrysostom, meaning "the golden-mouthed."

Almost as soon as he became Patriarch, he began to sweep Constantinople with his broom. He emptied the episcopal palace of the costly plate and furniture bought by Nectarius and sold the marble columns recently purchased for the Church of Anastasia, to build a hospital. He reformed the life of the clergy. He discovered that they were in the habit of living with widows and consecrated virgins who were called "spiritual sisters." He forbade the practice and told a bishop who approved of the custom that he was no better than a brothelkeeper. He summoned the "spiritual sisters" to his presence and harangued them for the evil they had caused, then summoned the priests and told them they were a blight on the church. Within three months they were up in arms against him. He lacked tact. He was the dedicated saint with a tongue like a rough sword. Appalled by the expenditure of the clergy, he solemnly advised the rich not to donate to them; they should be their own almoners, giving money only where it was needed; and the priests, fearing a loss of income, began a vast rumor campaign against him. Because he lived so quietly and alone, they whispered that he spent his days in cyclopean orgies, stuffing himself with fine food. Once, when these rumors were being spread all over the city, he showed himself half-naked, gaunt rib bones showing through the starved and ravaged flesh, but his austerities only angered the luxury-loving priests he called "belly-worshipers, table giants, hawks who pounce on women." He examined the church account books minutely and ordered the bishops to list their expenditures. After a tumultuous horse race held on Good Friday, attended by many Christians, he delivered a sermon "Against the Games and the Theaters." He refused invitations to parties and banquets, and gave no official dinners; and for this he was accused of pride. He ridiculed the wealth of Constantinople: the marble floors dusted with gold, the rich carpets, the silver couches, the gold spittoons. He objected strongly to dancing girls and singers who accompanied the bride and bridegroom home after a Christian marriage, singing indecent songs. He objected just as firmly to female mourners at funerals, wailing dirges. He spoke against slavery and on behalf of the equality of women, and raised a hornet's nest. He threatened fire from heaven upon the rich: the theme of the frivolous luxury of Constantinople is constantly recurring. Why must they have doors of ivory and ceilings inlaid with gold? Why must their horses' bits be fashioned intricately in gold? Why those tables of gold so heavy that two youths cannot lift them? Why should a nobleman possess ten or twenty mansions and as many private baths? He ridiculed the clergy for their frailties, the rich for their hedonism, the people for their love of the theater; and he must have known that the weapon would one day be turned against him.

Yet he had powerful supporters during the early months of his rule. The flaxen-haired Empress Eudoxia sent magnificent gifts to the churches and the poor, and spent long hours with Chrysostom. In September, when some relics were being translated into a martyr chapel outside the walls, she followed the procession barefoot at night, without her veil and walking humbly like a handmaid of the Lord. In a sermon delivered shortly afterward Chrysostom spoke of being overwhelmed by the honor paid to the Church. "What shall I say? I exult, I am mad, and my madness is greater than wisdom! Flying and dancing I am borne on high! In a word, I am drunk with spiritual delights!"

Eudoxia, who spoke Greek with a Frankish accent, tall, slender, beautiful and strangely pale, was a woman of fire. There was no Greek blood in her. She detested Eutropius and despised her husband, and loved ceremony, and had long ago believed she had the right to be crowned Augusta. Eutropius had refused her this right, and she was determined upon his downfall. Her opportunity came when the Goths revolted on the frontiers. Eutropius put his legions in the hands of an incompetent general called Leo, a former wool carder, whose armies were destroyed at night on the great plain of the Eurymedon and Melas, while Leo himself was drowned in a bog. The Goths pushed forward, sending an ultimatum that they would seize Constantinople unless Eutropius was put to death. The Emperor was reduced to despair. Eutropius, hardly knowing what he was doing, seeing the whole world arrayed against him, chose this moment to quarrel with Eudoxia, reminding her that he had raised her to the throne and could as easily hurl her from it. Eudoxia hurried to the Emperor's chamber and bitterly complained. Eutropius was summoned by Arcadius to an audience, where he was stripped of all his honors and emoluments and dismissed from the palace under pain of death. He knew he was the most bitterly detested man in all Constantinople. He crossed the great square called the Augusteum which separated the royal palace from Hagia Sophia. With tears streaming down his cheeks, his scant gray hair smeared with dust, he slipped into the Cathedral, and pushing aside the curtain which divided the chancel from the nave, he clung to the altar, imploring protection. Chrysostom was summoned. He hid Eutropius in the sacristy, and when the soldiers entered the Cathedral, he barred the way. "You shall not slay Eutropius," he declared, "unless you first slay me! Take me to the Emperor!" Then Chrysostom was marched off between two rows of spearmen to defend Eutropius. The interview was grotesque: a Patriarch defending a wrinkled eunuch, a weeping Emperor demanding the eunuch's death. Arcadius relented. He had no argument against the argument that the punishment must come from God.

On the next day, early in the morning, Chrysostom enjoyed a moment of supreme triumph. He ordered the curtains of the sanctuary to be drawn. It was Sunday. The Cathedral was thronged. Five thousand people saw the former Consul of the East quaking in abject terror at the foot of the altar. Chrysostom pointed dramatically at the prisoner and delivered a long sermon on the vanities of power. "The altar is more awful than ever now!" he exclaimed. "See, it holds the lion in its chains!" It was as though the devil himself had been captured and put in a cage for the delectation of the multitude, and there were some who thought Chrysostom had shown no mercy to the weak. It was a charge that was remembered against him afterward.

But the sermon Chrysostom delivered over the weeping eunuch was strangely lacking in vituperation, or unkindness, or satisfaction over his fate. Occasionally, standing on his high platform, the Patriarch pointed at the man crouching and shuddering there: the real man, the real eunuch, the former dictator of the East: but in the mind of Chrysostom he was already a symbol of the vanities of this world, no more than an emblem of things passing and to come, a vain and useless thing. So he asked:

> Where now is the pomp and circumstance of his Consulship? Where are the gleaming torches? Where is the dancing, and the noise of the dancers' feet, and the festivals? Where are the garlands and the curtains of the theater? Where is the applause which greeted him in the city? . . . They have all gone like visions of the night, dreams which vanish with the dawn of day, spring flowers withering on their stems with the coming of summer, no more than fleeting shadows or bubbles which have burst or the torn threads of spider webs. Therefore let us sing this spiritual song: Vanity of vanities, all is vanity!   [*Eutropius*, I, i]

A little later he spoke of Eutropius crouching there "like a hare or a frog, chained to the altar rail not by physical chains, but by the chains of fear, repressing his arrogance and subduing his pride, according to the Scriptures which say: 'All flesh is grass.'" So he returned, as always, to the theme of vanity, and man's weakness before God, and the power of prayer. Eutropius remained in the Cathedral for some days. Chrysostom said later that if Eutropius had chosen to remain in the Cathedral indefinitely, he would never have been surrendered to the civil authorities. Eutropius escaped. He was found outside the Cathedral and taken prisoner. The Emperor had promised Chrysostom not to kill him. There was a trial. The former Consul of the East was banished to Cyprus. Some weeks later he was arrested on what must have seemed to him a minor charge, for the Emperor remembered that Eutropius had mingled the imperial insignia with those of his Consulate. Eutropius had committed many crimes, but this was almost the least of them. He was brought back to Constantinople in chains, put on trial again, sentenced to death and beheaded in Chalcedon, a suburb of Constantinople. The people danced in his blood, his wealth was confiscated by the imperial treasury, his palaces were taken over by the Emperor, his name was expunged from the lists and his statues were thrown down and smashed to pieces. And with the end of Eutropius, there began the long years of Chrysostom's martyrdom.

No one knows how it began. A thousand influences were at work. Chrysostom was a man who was always either violently beloved, or violently hated. He had brought upon himself the hatred of the clergy and many of the high ladies of the Court. Historians remembered later that a certain Acacius, Bishop of Beroea, once a warm admirer, was overheard saying: "I'll cook his goose for him!" Court ladies and court officers had sworn to put an end to him, because he spoke too often concerning luxury. There were monks who regarded his continual austerities as "a candle burning before sore eyes." When he chastised people with his tongue, there was sometimes a note of contempt in his voice.

At the beginning of the year 400 he was aware of a mounting tension in the air. Eudoxia, finally crowned Augusta, was turning against him, jealous of his influence with Arcadius. Every day his enemies were increasing in numbers, but he was still strong enough to ride the storm. In the early months of the following year he decided to put an end to the corruption of the Church in Asia, and made a three months' tour. At Ephesus he held a synod and deposed six bishops convicted of simony. He swept through Asia like an avenging storm. In his absence Severian assumed the role of acting Patriarch. Severian was Bishop of Gabala, a close friend of Chrysostom. He betrayed his trust, and attempted to turn the whole court against Chrysostom in his absence.

The most bitter of Chrysostom's enemies was the man who had ordained him—Theophilus of Alexandria. He had been the secretary of Athanasius. Jerome says he was deeply skilled in science, mathematics and astrology. He was an insatiable builder of churches. He had spent his youth in the desert and was devoted in his early days to Origenistic mysticism. Suddenly he turned fiercely against Origen, denounced the lawlessness of the communities of monks and selected the four "Tall Brothers"—Ammonius, Dioscurus, Eusebius and Euthymius—as his particular enemies. Ammonius had accompanied Athanasius in exile, and his austerities had shocked the Romans into a love of asceticism. These men he banished and excommunicated, and then sent some armed ruffians and Ethiopian slaves to attack their mountain refuges in the Nitrian desert. According to Palladius, the faggots were laid: their cells, their copies of the scriptures and their sacred vessels went up in flames. The four "Tall Brothers" succeeded in fleeing to Palestine with about three hundred of the monks. Then they went on to Constantinople, and put themselves at the mercy of Chrysostom, who gave them sleeping quarters in a church, but refused to give them any further aid. He was an Antiochene, with no particular liking for Alexandrian mysticism and no desire to quarrel with Theophilus. Scenting danger, he refused even to receive the monks in communion. He was at his wit's end. The monks were parading through the city, calling upon the Emperor and the Patriarch to punish Theophilus, showing their wounds, inciting the populace. Chrysostom wrote a pathetic letter to Theophilus, begging him to receive back the members of his flock before they could file indictments against him. Theophilus replied that the fate of the monks was none of his affair; a formal indictment was an absurdity; he could not be put on trial in Constantinople; he could be tried only by his peers, the bishops of Egypt. The monks pressed a petition into the hands of Eudoxia when she was attending Hagia Sophia. Theophilus was wrong. An imperial edict could summon him to Constantinople; another imperial edict could place him on trial; a third imperial edict could banish him to the frontiers of the Empire.

Theophilus chose the moment of his arrival well. He reached Constantinople in August, 403, when the corn ships were flocking to the Bosphorus. He came with a bodyguard of Alexandrian sailors and costly presents for the Empress, resembling, according to Palladius, "one of those dung beetles from Egypt or India which emit a sweet scent to conceal the smell of their jealousy." Chrysostom invited him to stay in the episcopal palace; instead, Theophilus accepted an invitation from Eudoxia to stay with his suite in one of the imperial palaces at Pera. For three weeks Theophilus remained at Pera. He gave banquets to the clergy and the nobility, and held conferences with unfrocked priests. Two deacons, expelled from the church by Chrysostom for murder and fornication, spent long hours in his company. One of these deacons presented the Patriarch of Alexandria with a long memorial of the crimes of Chrysostom, containing twenty-nine charges. He charged that Chrysostom had sold Church property, left the church without saying his prayers, calumniated the clergy, and despotically and illegally deposed bishops in Asia. He had struck a man in the face, he had held private audiences with women, dined on gargantuan feasts, robed and unrobed on the episcopal throne, and devoured lozenges immediately after celebrating communion. Only the last charge was true: Chrysostom had advised everyone after communion to take water or a lozenge, to prevent them from involuntarily spitting out a portion of the sacramental bread and wine. Theophilus decided to use the memorial to depose Chrysostom. It was an explosive document, and he was determined to use it to the full. The problem of the Origenistic monks was forgotten; henceforth there was only one problem—how to destroy Chrysostom.

In the Palace of the Oak Tree, in the suburb of Chalcedon where Eutropius had been executed, Theophilus convoked an assembly of thirty-six bishops. Of these twenty-nine were Egyptian bishops who had accompanied Theophilus from Alexandria, possessing no ecclesiastical authority whatsoever over the see of Constantinople. But the synod was held under the protection of the imperial family, and its authority stemmed from Eudoxia. To the original twenty-nine charges eighteen more were added, and the crowning charge was that Chrysostom had called the Empress Jezebel. He had not done so. He had said once that the clergy were like "the priests who ate at Jezebel's table." The synod passed a resolution depriving Chrysostom of all his offices.

While the Synod of the Oak Tree was in session, Chrysostom was sitting with forty of his bishops in the refectory of his episcopal palace. His nerve seems to have failed him, and the bishops were distressed, weeping and commiserating with one another. "I know the cunning of Satan," Chrysostom said, and he quoted the words of Paul to Timothy: "I am now ready to be offered, and the time of my departure is at hand" (2 *Tim.* 4:6). Shuddering, the bishops passed in front of him, to kiss him on the eyes, the head and the lips. Because he could not endure their weeping, he bade them compose themselves. He reminded them that the matter was of small importance. All life is vanity. We gaze upon a fairground, and finish our buying and selling, and then move elsewhere. One of the bishops bade him act quickly. How could he endure the terror of Theophilus, who would alter the church laws, ride roughshod over the poor and dominate the Church with intolerable presumption. Chrysostom kept tapping the palm of his left hand with the forefinger of his right hand. It was a gesture they knew well, signifying that he was in deep thought and had not heard their complaints. Then he said:

The teaching office did not begin with me, nor will it come to an end with me. Did not Moses die, and was not Joshua found to replace him? Did not Samuel die, and was not David anointed in his place? Jeremiah ended his days, and did not Baruch follow him? Elijah was lifted up, but did not Elisha assume his place among the prophets? Paul was beheaded, but did he not leave behind him Timothy, Titus, Apollos and countless others?

[Palladius, *Dialogus,* 28]

Soon messengers came from Theophilus, bishops armed with the charges and resolutions against him. He ordered that they should be admitted. "We have a letter, and we are ordered to read it aloud," they said. John nodded, listening quietly. "The Holy Synod assembled at the Palace of the Oak Tree to John—" the letter began, and none of Chrysostom's titles was included. Then it continued: "We have received certain memorials containing countless grave charges against you—" A few days later the Emperor ratified the decree, banishing Chrysostom on false charges of immorality and high treason.

With a word Chrysostom could have brought the mob of Constantinople into the streets. He despised Theophilus; refused to fight; refused to defend himself. At noon, after delivering a farewell sermon, he simply slipped out of Hagia Sophia and surrendered to the Emperor's officers, who conveyed him that evening to the harbor and put him on board a ship bound for Hieron in Bithynia at the mouth of the Pontus. Though he concealed it, his anger was real. He called the officers sent to arrest him "spiders sent by a spider." He called the charges of Theophilus "frailer than a spider web." He was like a man enmeshed in a million spider webs, concealed in their warm and gluey darkness, seeing no way out, a lost soul on his way to banishment on the furthest frontiers of the Empire, listening to the rejoicing triumph of his enemies. He must have prayed that the lightning would strike.

The lightning struck the next day. It took the form of an earthquake which shook the palace and the bedchamber of the Empress. Eudoxia was terrified. She at once wrote to Chrysostom, begging him to return, saying she was innocent, she knew nothing of what was being done, she could not forget that Chrysostom had baptized her child. A notary from the royal household was sent to restore Chrysostom to his throne. He refused to enter the Cathedral, saying that he could only be restored to power by the synod that had deposed him. But the synod was in full flight: Theophilus and the Egyptian bishops sailed away the same day, in fear of being hurled into the Bosphorus by the mob. A synod of sixty bishops was convened, and all the proceedings at the Palace of the Oak Tree were annulled. Eudoxia and Chrysostom exchanged friendly greetings.

Two months later the spiders were at work again. It was September now, the time of the imperial festival, following the return of the Emperor from his annual summer visit to the hunting grounds in Phrygia. In the midst of the celebrations over the return of the imperial family, Eudoxia erected in the Augusteum, opposite the entrance to Hagia Sophia, a silver statue of herself mounted on a high and slender porphyry column. Chrysostom was incensed. He is supposed to have said: "Again Herodias dances, again she rages, again she demands the head of John." His words were communicated to the Empress. She had destroyed Eutropius. Once before she had nearly destroyed Chrysostom. This time she was determined to act, without fear of earthquakes. Afterward Chrysostom said: "Once there was a time when she called me the thirteenth apostle; now she calls me Judas." That Christmas neither the Empress nor the Emperor communicated in the Cathedral. Once again the Emperor issued an edict, stripping Chrysostom of his powers. He refused to obey. "I have received the Church from God our Saviour for the care of the salvation of the people," he declared. "I cannot desert it unless you thrust me out by force: only then can I plead your authority in defending myself against the charge that I have deserted my post." On Easter Day, April 16, 404, the Emperor ordered four hundred newly enlisted Thracian archers to scatter the assemblies of Christians who accepted Chrysostom as their Patriarch. They polluted the churches, plundered church treasure, stripped the clothes off young girls and drove the catechumens half naked into the street. They attacked the public baths of Constans, where the clergy had taken refuge, occupying the night vigils in reading aloud. Twice Chrysostom's life was attempted. For two months he remained in his palace. Then at last, seeing that the lives of the faithful in Constantinople were in danger, he obeyed the Emperor.

On the evening of the summer solstice Chrysostom took leave of Constantinople for the last time. Wearing his white gown, he walked from his palace to Hagia Sophia, where he kissed his bishops in farewell, and then in the baptistery he summoned the women who had served the church, begging them to obey the archbishop who would succeed him. "As you have bowed your heads to John, so bow to him, for the church cannot exist without a bishop; and may you find mercy, and remember me in your prayers." Someone brought the news that there were cutthroats waiting in the public baths, who would drag him out of the church if he delayed; all Constantinople was in an uproar; it would be best to slip out of the city quietly. The women were weeping. He made a sign to one of the clergy to remove them, for fear that their weeping would be heard by his own followers waiting at the western gate of the church. The deaconess Olympias was there, and it seems to have been her weeping which affected him most. Everyone thought he would leave the church by the western gate and give a last blessing to the faithful, but instead he walked straight to the eastern gate, where the imperial guard was waiting for him. Surrendering, he was taken down into a boat and carried over into Asia.

It was a night of uproar. Guards milled about the people waiting at the western gate. At Chrysostom's orders a mule had been saddled, and left at the western gate, to give the impression that he would soon emerge through those heavily decorated gates, a necessary deception if bloodshed was to be avoided. When they realized a trick had been played on them, his followers gave a sudden roar "like the roar one hears in a theater," and then pandemonium broke loose, with the soldiers bringing their whips and cudgels down on the bewildered worshipers, and everyone was screaming. Blood flowed. The spilling of blood at the gates was followed by a mysterious fire, which originated somewhere near the Archbishop's throne. The flames leaped to the rafters and then sprang onto the roof. Soon the whole church, built by the Emperor Constantine only forty-four years before, was ablaze. The flames, driven by a violent wind, soared across the street, forming a fiery archway over the heads of the panic-stricken people below, and licked the walls of the palace where the Senate assembled. By morning Hagia Sophia and the Senate were in ashes. Some said the followers of Chrysostom started the blaze, others that the Empress had secretly ordered it, and still others spoke of heavenly intervention. Strangely, though the flames roared across the city, there was no loss of life.

Throughout his occupation of the see of Constantinople, the elements had worked for Chrysostom: the lightning had struck when it was most suitable for him. Now the elements worked against him, and for the rest of his life he was forced to contend with storms and tempests, bitter cold nights and blazing hot days, snowdrifts, barren mountains and the raging of the winds. For the rest of his life he was to be a wanderer in the power of his armed guards.

In the beginning of his exile, no one told him where he would be sent. It was rumored that his destination was Scythia, or perhaps Sebaste in Pontus, or perhaps Cucusus, a village in the Taurus Mountains on the edge of Cilicia and the Lesser Armenia. At first he was taken to Nicaea. Evidently the Empress had not yet decided on his punishment, for he remained there for nearly two weeks, writing letters, breathing the clear air below Mount Olympus, and a little surprised to find himself in good spirits, though in Constantinople an inquiry into the burning of the church had resulted in a direct accusation against him. From Nicaea he sent a letter urging that he should be allowed to plead his innocence, but he was refused a hearing. On July 3 he received his marching orders. The Empress had decided to banish him to Cucusus, a remote village which was outside Asia Minor altogether, a guard post opening out on the valley of the Euphrates, at the very limits of the Empire. His guards had orders to take him straight across the heart of Asia Minor by way of Caesarea, where Basil had preached, and Nyssa, where Gregory had spent his youth. It was high summer. They traveled at evening or at night to avoid the heat of the day. Some of the way he traveled in a sort of sedan chair hung between two mules. The going was slow; the valleys in the interior of Asia Minor were in turmoil, with the road stations deserted and the people in the cities hurriedly putting up fortifications against barbarian inroads. Chrysostom suffered from fever; the food was bad; he complained of dizziness, headaches, a strange feeling that he was adrift on a wild sea. He wrote to Olympias: "The night is moonless, the darkness thick around me, and crags and cliffs all before me." Yet in the same letter, to please her, he spoke of being in good health and in no worse case than a man tossing about in harbor. The ominous phrase "There are tempests" is continually repeated. His strength was ebbing. Ahead of him there was only some cold Chorasmian waste, a permanent exile somewhere at the edge of the world.

The news of his exile ran ahead of him. At Caesarea people came flocking to greet him. A house was put at his disposal. The horrors of exile were forgotten as sickness slowly gave way to health. There was soft bread he could chew, and clean water, and a clean bed. He complained against the heat, but that would pass. Monks, nuns and doctors attended him, and one of the doctors even offered to accompany him for the rest of the journey. For some reason he had always hated broken crockery, and he notes: "I no longer have to wash in a cracked basin, and I have even contrived some sort of bath." The only thing that disturbed him was that he received few replies to the letters he wrote to friends in Constantinople: the imperial censorship was presumably taking care of them.

As his body grew stronger, no longer "a mere cinder in the fierce flame of fever," he began to think he might be allowed to rest in Caesarea until he had fully recovered. His guards had received no orders to move on. He was settling down quietly in a house in the outskirts of the city; his visitors were overwhelming him with kindness; everyone was saying the Bishop of Caesarea was kindly disposed toward him. The Bishop, however, made no move to visit him, and gradually it occurred to Chrysostom that the Bishop, under orders from Constantinople, was deliberately plotting to do away with him. There were ominous signs. Little groups of fanatical monks, armed with clubs, were always wandering about, up to mischief. One morning at the crack of dawn a battalion of these monks surrounded the house, threatened to set fire to it and kill Chrysostom, unless he left the city at once. The mayor of Caesarea hurried to the house, but there was nothing he could do, the monks refused to listen to him, and Chrysostom was told that he must leave the city at once or suffer the consequences. Chrysostom, who was ill at the time, asked for three days' grace. This was refused, and the next day the monks came flocking round the house again, brandishing their clubs. A crowd had gathered. There was nothing to be done except to move on to the next stage of the journey to Cucusus, and to make matters worse, the Isaurians, the wild tribesmen of the Taurus Mountains, were known to be gathering along the highway. At noon Chrysostom, shivering with fever, threw himself into his sedan chair and gave orders to his guards to continue the journey. A few moments later there was a reprieve. Seleucia, the wife of one of the chief citizens of Caesarea, had pity on him, offered him the use of her fortified villa five miles out of Caesarea, and there he remained briefly, guarded by armed farm laborers who were perfectly prepared to take on the ragged battalions of fanatical monks.

He had been living in the villa only a few days when he was confronted with a danger greater than clubs wielded by monks: treachery among the people he had thought were his friends. The presbyter Evethius had shown him only kindness. Chrysostom relied deeply on Evethius' advice. But in the dead of night, when he was sleeping, Evethius awoke him roughly, shouting: "Get up, I beg you! The barbarians are coming! They are quite near!" Chrysostom's thoughts went immediately to the bishop. If the barbarians were near, then he would fare better among them than in the city. Evethius kept urging him to prepare for the journey to Cucusus. There was no moon. It was pitch dark. There was the smell of treachery in the air, but he could not trace its source. He ordered torches, but Evethius observed that the barbarians would be attracted to the light, it would be better to put the torches out. Caesarea is surrounded by mountains, and the road to Cucusus led across rocky mountain trails. His guards were useless, unable to make up their minds. Chrysostom got into his sedan chair, but one of the mules slipped and fell, and he was thrown out. He began to crawl along the path, but Evethius, who had been riding a mule, dropped down, took him by the hand and dragged him along. We know nothing more about the journey to Cucusus except that it took seventy days and the Isaurians were constantly on the watch, threatening to attack, but for some reason they failed to do any harm to the small procession winding its way along the mountain trails.

At Cucusus Chrysostom breathed again. He described the place as "the most deserted spot in the universe," but there were compensations. A strong force of soldiers guarded the overgrown village against the Isaurians. He was well-housed, had nothing to fear from the bishop or the local prefect, and enjoyed the climate, which reminded him of Antioch. He busied himself writing letters of thanks to people who had helped him in Caesarea, and spoke charitably of his enemies. He wrote to Olympias:

> After reaching Cucusus, I rid myself of the remains of my sickness, and I am now in most perfect health, and I am released too from my fear of the Isaurians, for we have a strong force of soldiers here ready and eager to do battle with them. There is abundance of everything, everyone welcomes me with open arms and the greatest kindness, and all this in spite of the great desolation of the place. My lord Dioscorus happened to be there; he even sent a servant to me for the very purpose of inviting, nay begging, me to accept his house and no other; and many others did the same. I availed myself by preference of his offer, as I felt I ought to do, and took up my abode with him; and he has been overwhelming me with his attentions, so that I am continually protesting against his lavish expenditures on my behalf. He even left his house to me and went to live in some other place, in order to show me every attention possible; and he arranged to ready the house for the winter and put himself to a great deal

of trouble. In a word, he left nothing undone which could be of service to me. Many others, too, agents and stewards, have received letters from their masters, ordering them to call upon me, as they have done continually, and in every way to study my comfort.

And now I have told you all about me, the distressing past and the favorable present, lest any friend should be precipitate in getting me removed elsewhere. If these persons who wish to be kind to me offer me the choice of a dwelling place, I shall willingly accept; but if they remove me to some other place, if they send me on another journey into another exile, then they would give me greater pain than I suffer now, and this because I could hardly endure a journey to a more distant and worse place, and because the thought of traveling horrifies me more than a thousand banishments. The miseries of my last journey brought me close to death, but here in Cucusus I am replenished with uninterrupted quiet and rest, and so by quiet nursing I hope to end my long agony and give peace to my shattered bones and weary flesh.

The deaconess Sabiniana arrived in Cucusus on the day I arrived, and she too was weary and put out, being too old to make such journeys, yet in her fortitude she behaves like a young girl, taking no account of suffering, prepared (so she says) to go on to Scythia, if need be. There were indeed rumors that I was to be sent to Scythia. She says—she insists—she will stay with me, wherever I am. The priests gave her a warm welcome. As for the most religious priest Constantius, he would have reached here long ago, for he wrote asking my permission to come, saying he could not venture on the step without my leave, much as he desired it, for he cannot, being in hiding, remain at home; he is overwhelmed with troubles. And so I beg you on no account to attempt to have me moved, for I am enjoying my peace—within two days all the horrors of the journey passed from my mind.

[Ep. 43]

This long letter—there were many similar letters—shows signs of strain. There are too many repetitions to suggest he was really at peace with himself. No longer do the phrases gleam like burnished rapiers: he was tired and old and perhaps too weary to care very much for himself; and in those letters full of gratitude to those who have helped him, we are made aware of the somber foreboding, the knowledge that time was running out. He wrote to Carterius, the legate of Cappadocia: "I shall never forget what you did for me in Caesarea, in quelling those furious and senseless tumults, and striving to the utmost, so far as your power extended, to place me in security." Perhaps the phrase is barbed: we cannot be sure. To Hymnetius, the physician who attended him during his illness at Caesarea, he wrote: "I am continually singing your praises, as the worthiest and best of doctors, and a true friend; and whenever I am called upon to talk about my sufferings, of course I bring you into the story." He wrote similar letters to all those who had befriended him. The sentences flow gently, but without fire, without passion, without the peculiar sign manual of his own style. Yet he lived in his friends, and he could not live without writing to them, without feeling that he was in some way connected with them.

So the autumn of 404 wore away, and then it was winter, with the snow on the ground and the Isaurians threatening this desolate guard post on the edge of nowhere. He caught a chill and took to his bed, and then for some reason the letters become even more demonstrative, more filled with affection. News from Constantinople was bad. The fire that consumed the church and the senate house was still vividly remembered; two of his bishops were arrested and banished; his favorite young lector was put on the rack, torn with hooks, scourged and scorched with torches until he died. Some of his followers were in hiding, others were on trial, at least thirty including an officer of the Imperial Guard were flogged, then tortured, then banished. Olympias had been arrested, though she was highborn and had powerful relatives at court: she was fined and banished. Palladius gives a long list of the punishments received by his followers. The police enjoyed themselves: they tore off pieces of skin, opened up rib cases, roasted their victims with oil lamps, flogged unmercifully. By imperial order the followers of Chrysostom were scattered to the winds, some exiled to Arabia and Africa, others to Crete, others to Gaul. They were no longer allowed to preach the gospel. Palladius reports: "As for the holy Bishop Sylvanus, he is now in Troas supporting himself by fishing."

Only one piece of news that winter may have brought a somber smile to Chrysostom's face: the Empress Eudoxia died suddenly, apparently in childbirth. His life had been inextricably involved with the life of this Frankish princess. She had been his close supporter, his confidante, his enemy, his most terrible friend. Now that Jezebel was dead, he could breathe more lightly.

When the spring came, he wrote to Olympias about the cold weather and the constant disturbances of the Isaurians; the roads, and the mountain passes, were deep in snow; brigands were everywhere; he had been ill again, but was now fully recovered. The long hibernation was over, and a new note appears in his letters. In the hot blaze of summer a persistent, irrepressible ferment seized him. He must take charge again. He writes authoritatively. The church must be put in order. We must send missionaries to Phoenicia and destroy the pagan temples. There is an outbreak of heresy in Cyprus—see that this heresy is put down. He ordered his priests to Persia and Scythia. There was no time to waste. He wrote to the Bishops of Thessalonica, Corinth, Laodicea, Jerusalem, Carthage, Milan, Brescia and Aquileia. He asked about forgotten friends in letters that smell of the lamp, for his own flame was burning low, and sometimes, as life ebbed in him, we are aware of a voice striving ineffectually for composure, a tormented countenance, all the old intolerable memories of fire and riot in dark streets lived over again. Then the voice suddenly grows clear again, strong, urgent, demanding. He will be heard. He will not stay all his life in this God-forsaken village in Armenia. He announces that, come what may, he will return to Constantinople to face his accusers. "Not even in the courts of the heathens," he wrote, "would such audacious deeds have been committed, or rather not even in a barbarian court. Neither the Scythians nor the Sarmatians would ever have judged a cause in this fashion, deciding it after hearing one side only, in the absence of the accused."

He wrote to Pope Innocent in Rome, who was sheltering some of his followers, demanding the intervention of the Holy See, but he must have known that the cause was doomed to failure. The whole court, goaded on by Theophilus, considered him an incendiary. Theophilus published a voluminous attack on him, which St. Jerome was to translate from Greek into Latin, adding his own approval to the wild charges of the Pope of Alexandria. Yet all was not lost. In increasing numbers his followers were making their way to Cucusus. He was almost more powerful in banishment than when he was sitting on his throne in Hagia Sophia. "All Antioch is in Cucusus," they said. "This formidable dead man," wrote Palladius, "was terrifying the living, and men in authority too, as bogies frighten children." The court in Constantinople was alarmed by his increasing power, and decided upon further punishment, ordering him out of Cucusus at the beginning of winter. He was to go to Aribassus, some sixty miles away to the north. It was mountain country, the mists were swirling down and the Isaurians were on the war path. The summer heat had affected his health, and he was suffering from fever. He wrote to his friend Nicholas:

> Lately I have been fleeing from place to place in the very depth of winter, now in towns, now in ravines and forests, driven furiously by the inroads of the Isaurians. When there was a brief respite from their attacks, I left these desolate places and made my way to Aribassus: not to the town, for the town is just as insecure as the wild regions I have been wandering in, but to the fortress, which is safer, though worse than any prison. And I must tell you that we faced death daily from the Isaurians, who came from all directions, putting people and houses to fire and sword. We are in dread of famine too, having little resources of food, and there are so many mouths to feed among those who have taken refuge here. Finally, I have to endure a tedious illness brought on by the winter and my incessant wanderings. I still have vestiges of illness, but I have recovered from its main violence.   [*Ep.* 69]

It was the beginning of the end. Armenia was in turmoil, and the Isaurians were pressing hard. He wrote to another friend: "The cities are but walls and roofs; and the ravines and woods are cities. We who dwell in Armenia are continually on the run, living the lives of nomads and wanderers, for fear of settling anywhere." He spoke of children who rushed out of their houses when the Isaurians came in the dead of night, and their bodies were found frozen in the snow. Blood flowed in torrents, cities were put to the flame, corpses were piled high. His letters are full of strain. He had not thought he would live through so much; and now, as he contemplated his survival, he began to think how wonderfully he had been preserved. It was all miracle, and he thanked God for the hope which sprang perpetually in his breast: that he would return soon to his beloved Constantinople. He remained in Aribassus during most of the second year of his exile, returning to Cucusus in the autumn.

He faced the third winter with extraordinary confidence. He had passed through the fires. "Never be cast down," he wrote once to Olympias, "for only one thing is fearful, and that one thing is sin." He was accustomed now to all the vagaries of Armenian winters, the blinding snows, the sudden winds, the impossibility of keeping the body warm. He had few reserves of strength. He sat huddled over a charcoal fire, wearing three or four heavy gowns, the windows closed, waiting for an Isaurian attack. Somehow he survived the winter. He was a ghost of himself. Spring came, and the days passed pleasantly with his Antiochene visitors, letters to Honorius, the Emperor of the West, and to Olympias, and to all those who still kept faith with him. Then when summer came, there were rumors that the court was hardening its heart against him. In the middle of June, 407, word came that he was to leave immediately under two praetorian guards for Pityus, a small town on the shores of the Black Sea, the farthest, the most miserable place in the whole Empire.

Pityus lay far to the east, beyond Colchis and under the Caucasus. It was on the edge of territories occupied by the Scythians, and here the laws of the Empire hardly applied. He must have known he would never reach Pityus, for he had suffered from fever during the summer and there was almost no strength left in him. The two praetorian guards harried him unmercifully. They made it clear that they wanted nothing better than that he should die by the roadside: they would receive promotion more quickly. One showed him occasional kindnesses, the other never spared him. Palladius tells the story vividly:

All this man wanted was that John should die a miserable death. He deliberately gave orders that they should start out even when it was raining furiously, with floods of water running over the bishop's neck and chest. He was pleased when the fierce sun beat down, for then the bald head of the blessed Elisha would ache terribly. When they reached a city or a village where the refreshment of a bath was available, the wretch would not consent to stop for a moment.

All these sufferings the saint endured for three months. During all these horrors he remained as one shining with the brightness of a star, his poor body burned red by the sun, like an apple on the topmost branch of a tree.

When they came to Comana they passed through it as if the main street was no more than a bridge over a river, and lodged outside the wall in the shrine of a martyr some six miles from the town.

That night Basilicus, Bishop of Comana, martyred under Maximinian at Nicomedia, together with Lucian, a priest of the Church of Antioch in Bithynia, appeared before him and said: "Be of good cheer, brother. Tomorrow we shall be together." John knew this to be a word of warning. The next day he begged his guards to remain at the shrine until eleven o'clock. They refused and marched on, and when they had gone about thirty furlongs, he was so ill they had to return to the shrine they had started from.

When they reached the shrine, he asked for white garments befitting his life and removed those he was wearing, and clad himself from head to foot, still fasting, and gave away his old clothes to those around him. Then he communicated in the Lord, said his last prayer, which closed with the words, "Glory be to God for all things," and then having crossed himself at the last Amen, he stretched out his feet which had been so beautiful in their running as they brought salvation to the penitent and reproof to confirmed sinners.   [*Dialogus,* 38]

So on September 14, 407, died John of Antioch, known as St. John Chrysostom, who defied emperors and loved God.

According to Palladius the news of his death spread like wildfire, and the burial ceremonies in the shrine of Basilicus were attended by a host of virgins, ascetics and men renowned for their devout life, flocking from Armenia, Pontus and Cilicia, and as far away as Syria. For a little more than thirty years his body remained in the shrine. Then at the beginning of 438 the relics were solemnly removed to Constantinople. Theodoret tells how the people of Constantinople gathered in close-packed boats lit with torches at the mouth of the Bosphorus to see his coming. The relics were deposited in the Church of the Apostles, with those of emperors and patriarchs; and a new Emperor laid his head on the reliquary and implored forgiveness before God for the wrongs committed by his mother and father; and after him the Emperor's sisters, the four princesses Flacilla, Pulcheria, Arcadia and Marina, prayed. There in an ornate tomb the saint remained until 1204, when the Crusaders rifled the Church of the Apostles. Soon his bones were scattered over Italy, France and Germany. Today his head reposes among the relics of the Cathedral at Pisa, and some of his bones lie in the great church which bears his name in Venice, and there are others in the Chapel of St. John Chrysostom in St. Peter's.

Of the many things that were said of him after his death, the best was spoken by his pupil, Cassian of Marseilles: "It would be a great thing to attain to his stature, but it would be hard. Nevertheless even the following of him is lovely and magnificent" (*De Incarnatione,* VII, 31).

Dionysius the Areopagite

Wwe do not know the real name of the man who called himself Dionysius the Areopagite, or when he lived, or in what country he was born. He may have been a Syrian monk, or he may equally have been a Greek ecclesiastic in high office. He may have been a brilliant youth like Pico della Mirandola who died young, having burned himself out in contemplation of a heavenly vision. We know he probably lived in the fifth century, for his influence began to be felt immediately afterward. Yet it was a quiet influence, working most on those who had retired from the world. Then in the fourteenth century his name spread like wildfire. In the age of Chaucer a chronicler said that his *Mystical Theology* "ran through England like the wild deer."

The strange and unknown theologian who chose to ascribe his work to the Areopagite, the friend of St. Paul, secured his anonymity so carefully that no one has found in his writings any trace of his history. At moments we seem to catch a glimpse of his face: the high brows and enormous eyes and sunken cheeks of the dedicated mystic so rapt in the mystery he seems hardly aware of the world where normal human behavior exists. For him there is only one world: the world of God, the celestial thrones, the seraphim and cherubim, the archangels and the angels seen against the blazing heavens, all heaven opening to reveal the majesty of God. Without affection for dogma, and in defiance of creeds, he hurls himself against the ultimate things.

When the Church Fathers speak, we are aware of their humanity. They have their foibles, and they are recognizable human beings. Across the centuries we can hear the hoarse and gentle voice of John Chrysostom complaining that God has failed to give him a throat strong enough for the torrent of words he uttered; we recognize Basil as he walks through the tangled thornbushes of Annesi, drawing a manure cart by leather thongs bound round his waist and his neck; and though we have no reliable portrait of Origen, we know the man by his tumultuous prose. Only Dionysius remains impersonal, even inhuman, as though he was half-spirit or half-angel. He stands alone in a dark cell; there is a small plain altar; and somewhere a choir of angels can be heard singing in the darkness, and a blaze of mysterious light hovers over him. He has no features, no gestures, no tricks of eloquence, nothing by which we can recognize him. Except when he dwells on the subject of fire, he betrays no excitement. He refers so often to the great darkness of God that we know he was accustomed to long nights of contemplation below the altar, but beyond this—almost nothing. He was the pure contemplative, mapping out the heavens as a mathematician or a pure physicist will attempt to map out a formula which will describe the whole of creation. Inscrutable and elusive, escaping all our efforts to place him in historical perspective, he talks with the power of tongues about those heavenly things which no other theologian had ever dared to talk about. There are times when Dionysius, rather than Origen, seems to be the greatest of them all.

Luther, who hated him, called him a liar. St. Thomas Aquinas loved him, quoted him interminably in the *Summa* and paid him the supreme compliment of writing a commentary on *The Divine Names*. John Colet, the Dean of St. Paul's and founder of St. Paul's School, translated him with the help of Erasmus, and the Italian humanists saw in him the precursor of their own attempts to impose order on the universe. He became fashionable. Tiepolo's angel-crowded heavens owe a debt to him. Dante acknowledged his debt in the *Paradiso,* and thousands who never heard the name of Dionysius know him indirectly through their reading of Milton, who wrote of

Thrones, Dominations, Princedoms, Virtues, Powers.

So, too, with Shakespeare, who spoke of the orbs of Heaven "still quiring to the young-eyed cherubim." And when Spenser described the mighty "christall wall" of heaven in *A Hymne of Heavenly Beautie,* where the angels

in their trinall triplicities
About Him wait, and on His will depend,

then again the influence of Dionysius can be felt, for more than anyone he was responsible for our knowledge of the angelic orders, the heavenly hierarchies.

When Dionysius' works first appeared in Latin, their coming was attended by miracles. The Greek text had been sent by Pope Paul to the Gallican Church in 757, but for seventy years they lay unread. In 827 the Byzantine Emperor Michael the Stammerer sent an embassy to Louis the Pious, the son of Charlemagne, bearing another copy. King Louis ordered Hilduin, the abbot of the Abbey of St. Denis, to have a translation prepared, carefully arranging that it should appear on the feast day of St. Denis, the first bishop of Paris, the apostle of the Franks and the patron saint of France, believing that Dionysius and St. Denis were one and the same man. The Abbot wrote to his King:

These authentic works written originally in Greek were given into our hands on the eve of St. Denis, when the dispenser of the Church at Constantinople and the other ambassadors of the Emperor Michael were presented to Your Majesty in public audience at Compiègne. And as though this gift, so dear to our hearts, had come down from Heaven, the blessings of God followed soon after. On this same night Our Lord, rejoicing in the praises of His Name, and having received the prayers of His glorious martyr, condescended to perform nineteen miracles on the bodies of infirm people. These miracles have been well-attested in the depositions of many people familiar with the neighborhood.

[*Patrologia Latina*, CVI, 16]

The story of the nineteen miracles which accompanied the translation spread like wildfire, and the original Greek text of Dionysius, supposed to have been written in his own hand, was regarded as a holy relic. This relic, which remained in the hands of the Kings of France until the time of Louis-Philippe, still survives in the Bibliothèque Nationale in Paris, a small quarto volume of 216 finely written pages of parchment. The original binding is lost, and the entire text of Dionysius' *Mystical Theology* has mysteriously disappeared, together with one of the letters which Dionysius is supposed to have written to Timothy; otherwise it is the same volume which was sent by the Eastern Roman Emperor to Louis the Pious.

After the nineteen miracles came a silence of about forty years. The translation of Abbot Hilduin seems to have been unsatisfactory, and on the orders of the new King, Charles the Bald, the Greek text was retranslated by the Irishman, John Scotus Erigena, who added a translation of the commentary by Maximus the Confessor and incorporated the ideas of Dionysius in his own systematic treatise called *De Divisione Naturae*. It was from the translation of John Scotus that St. Thomas Aquinas drew his knowledge of the Areopagite. These books, after their strange wanderings, became a force to be reckoned with. Hugo of St. Victor and St. Bonaventure both wrote commentaries on *The Heavenly Hierarchies*. Peter Lombard, Alexander of Hales, Albert the Great, Robert Grosseteste, Vincent of Beauvais—all cardinal names in medieval scholasticism—drew upon it heavily. Oriental mysticism had taken the West by storm.

Four of his works and ten of his letters have survived; at least six are lost. The lost works included treatises on the soul, on sacred hymns and the Just Judgment of God. Of these, beside their names, nothing at all is known.

It is best to begin with *The Celestial Hierarchies,* because it is the simplest, the most imaginative and the one with which the name of Dionysius is most intimately connected. It begins quietly, with no suggestion of what is to come. At the head of the first page comes the text: "Every good gift and every perfect gift is from above, and cometh down from the Father of Lights" (*James* 1:17). Dionysius would have us believe that the following chapters are no more than a sermon on the text. He wishes us to know that everything he is about to say is purely symbolic. The pure and tranquil eye of the Christian can at best contemplate a reflected glory; he will talk of visions, but the words are only inadequate symbols to describe the majesty of God. He will speak of ointments and unguents, of flashing torches, of imperial eagles, of heaven trembling under the paws of lions; and he will do this only because he has to, because there are not words enough to describe the heavenly splendors, and we must employ "the poetry of holy fictions" because we have no other tools at hand. An ancient tradition, long employed by the holy Fathers, has maintained that we can represent celestial beings as one might depict men shining like gold, clothed in magnificent clothes, a soft light spreading from them. He would have us believe that the angels are only fictions, but when he describes them, we are almost compelled to a suspension of disbelief. Those cherubs who are all eyes, absorbing the rays of divine light, those loving seraphs who are all wings, perpetually flying toward the Godhead, those angels, archangels and principalities arrayed in robes of glory seem only too tangible; they glitter and blind; and we hear the whirring of their wings. In the celestial world of Dionysius we are removed from the preoccupations of St. Paul; we are no longer in a world where guilt has any place. There is no God in which men live and move and are. We are in a world of mysterious emanations from a hidden center, a secret glory. Here all is holy, and everything is blinding, and yet we may discern, within that center of blinding electric force, the faint outlines of wings and the shapes of fire. Here the soul suns itself in a blaze of divine light and the angels perpetually minister to the most blessed of them; and though the radiance of God is beyond all human reckoning, yet sometimes by degrees it sinks from the heavenly summits into the earthly valleys. Dante was thinking of *The Heavenly Hierarchies* when he placed Dionysius among the great theologians of the Church and set him in the Heaven of the Sun. "He is that candle," he says, putting the words into the mouth of St. Thomas Aquinas in the *Paradiso*, "who from this world of flesh saw most profoundly into the nature of angels and their ministry" (*Paradiso*, X, 115-17).

What is astonishing in Dionysius is his assurance, the way he moves at ease among the hierarchies. Hear him as he describes the thrones, the seraphim and cherubim who together form the first of the hierarchies:

> In the first order of celestial beings are those who dwell eternally in the constant presence of God, cleaving to Him and being above all others united to Him. According to the teachings of the Holy Word, the most holy thrones and many-eyed and many-winged ones,[1] who are named in the Hebrew tongue Cherubim and Seraphim, are established in the immediate neighborhood of God, being closest to Him. . . . And they surpass all other celestial beings in their reverent desire to receive divine enlightenment, and yet they do not ask questions of God directly, saying: "Wherefore are thy garments red?" but they first eagerly question one another, showing that they seek and continually thirst for knowledge of His divine words without expectation of the enlightenment which God divinely grants to them. . . . These celestial beings are purified and illumined and possessed of perfection; and their purification arises because ignorance of the divine mysteries is utterly cast from them, and all the highest forms of knowledge have been granted to them; and they are illuminated inasmuch as they have received the quintessence of the divine illumination; and they are perfected inasmuch as they have received the luminous initiation into the divine mystery.

[1] Previously, on the basis of the meaning of the words in the original Hebrew, Dionysius described the wise Cherubim as all eyes and the loving Seraphim as all wings.

Such then is the first order of celestial beings which is established around God, immediately encircling Him, in perpetual purity encompassing His eternal knowledge in a most high, eternal and angelic dance, rapt in the bliss of their blessed and infinite contemplations, shining in the beams of a pure and perfect splendor, filled with the many foods from the table of the Divine Banquet, and living in perpetual union with God.

[*De Caelestia Ierarchia,* VI, VII]

Then come the dominions, virtues and powers comprising the second of the angelic orders. For Dionysius each order is "the herald and interpreter of the one above," and since they are further from the Godhead, they are correspondingly weaker. Yet, as Dionysius makes clear, this weakness is relative; it is as though there were various degrees of infinitude. The dominions possess freedom from all earthly ties. They are "lords, perpetually aspiring to true lordship." They represent the naked strength of rulership, while the virtues represent the outpouring of divine energy, "being possessed of unshakable virility, which wells forth into godlike energy." The powers are more ceremonial: their task is to see that due order is imposed upon the heavenly pathways.

In the third circle come principalities, archangels and angels; and now at last we are in the presence of heavenly forces which are faintly touched with earthiness, for the principalities represent "the divine princeliness" and are recognized because they lead "in princely fashion," and Dionysius knows no more about the archangels than that they stand midway between the principalities and the angels. The angels are "the interpreting order, that choir which is more intimately concerned with visible and manifested things." All of these celestial beings, according to Dionysius, "share in the participation of the divine knowledge and wisdom, but in varying degrees."

It is heady wine, and the mind reels, confronted with those angelic presences, which receive a peculiar stark reality from his description of them. We believe these wheeling Intelligences to be as he describes them, for while we read, we are under his spell. He speaks with a vast assurance, as one who has seen them with his own eyes. He is another Isaiah in the presence of the seraphim; and so he calls Isaiah as a witness, and celebrates the vision of the sixfold wings:

And when Isaiah beheld the many feet and many faces of the seraphim, and perceived that their eyes and their feet were covered

by their wings, and that their middle wings were in ceaseless movement, he was guided to the intelligible knowledge of a revelation;
and this revelation came to him through the far-seeing and far-
reaching power of the most exalted Intelligences and through their
holy awe, as in their heavenly tradition they pursue boldly and
persistently their endless search into higher and deeper mysteries,
in constant imitation of God and perpetual soaring into the heights.

[*De Caelestia Ierarchia*, XIII]

There are moments when Dionysius soars off the earth, losing
himself in a language which is almost beyond communication. Vision
pursues vision. These celestial creatures can only be described by
implication. Dionysius speaks at length of the way we envisage the
angels, as handsome youths, as furious clouds, as fleet horses; but
mostly he sees them, as Blake saw them, as winged youths whose
eyeballs are emblems of their fidelity to divine things, whose powerful
shoulders demonstrate their spiritual energy and whose loins symbolize
their immense fecundity, as their feet symbolize divine speed. Lions,
horses and eagles—he passes them all under review, and finds the
symbolism wanting. "But have we not always considered the angels as
living flames?" he asks. "Are they not fiery wheels, living creatures of
fire, men flashing with lightning, streams of flame? Surely it is best to
regard them as flames!" So at last, wearying of their complexities, he
described them magnificently in terms of fire:

For men say that the thrones are fire, and the seraphim too,
as we know from their name, are blazing with fire, and therefore
we are compelled to agree that the symbol of fire has the largest
meaning. . . . Fire is in all things, is spread everywhere, pervades
all things without intermingling with them, shining by its very
nature and yet hidden, and manifesting its presence only when it
can find material on which to work, violent and invisible, having
absolute rule over all things, violently assimilating to itself everything it triumphantly seizes, and so renewing all things with its
life-giving heat and blazing with inextinguishable light: never
defeated, unchangeable, darting upon its prey, changeless always,
as it lifts that which it gathers to the skies, never held back by any
servile baseness, self-moved, moving other things. It comprehends,
but remains incomprehensible, never in need, mysteriously increasing itself and showing forth its majesty according to the nature of

the substance receiving it, powerful and mighty and invisibly present in all things.   [*De Caelestia Ierarchia,* XV]

There is nothing ascetic in his vision of the angels; and at the very end of the work Dionysius asks himself how it could be otherwise, since they are fashioned for the purposes of divine joy, and are drunk with peace, and are perpetually celebrating the glory of God and the sinners who are saved.

In *The Celestial Hierarchies* Dionysius wrestled with the angels; in *The Divine Names* he wrestles with God Himself.

It is a strange wrestling match, and one watches with a curious sense of apprehension, for Dionysius begins by stripping himself of all his weapons. "It is impossible," he seems to be saying, "to come close to God. I have neither the strength nor the courage. I am completely ignorant of the method of attack. Here, on this terrible battleground, neither the Bible nor Plato are of much service to me. I must fight alone, depending upon my wits, upon logic, upon those rare statements of Jesus which afford occasional clues. I shall strip God of all the things He is not, and so by describing the darkness, I shall be able to hint at the light." And so without illusions, employing all the arts of implication, almost as though he were determined to astonish God into revealing Himself, he succeeds in presenting a portrait of God which is strangely convincing. His method is not that of the painter; he is the sculptor cutting away all the dead stone, all that is not God, to reveal the living image embedded beneath.

It is a singular method: no other theologian had attempted it, none won such victories, no one ever wrote in a style so impersonal, so devoid of color, so lacking in outward excitement. Yet the excitement is there. One should read him slowly. Too often he is accounted an impersonal mathematician attempting to encompass Heaven by a circle of chaste equations, but in fact there is a seething violence beneath the apparent calm. He is like the lover who says: "I adore you, I love you, I offer you everything I possess, if only you will reveal yourself." These, too, are bare statements. In Dionysius we recognize the passion by the tone of voice, the twists of emphasis, the alterations of mood. The long close-knit frigid paragraphs reveal a mind in a state of incandescence.

He begins quietly, almost formally, with the statement that nothing is known. God is beyond everything that man can think, "a Mind beyond the reach of mind, a word beyond utterance." The Scriptures themselves declare the incomprehensibility of God. Have not the Fathers of the Church declared that the understanding of the nature of God is inaccessible to human creatures, unsearchable, past finding out? None has penetrated those infinite depths; He has no name, no shape, no form, since He includes all names, all shapes, all forms. And yet some things are known about Him. We know that He stands at the beginning of all Creation, and is the fountain from which all things spring. "To them that fall away He is a Voice recalling them and a Power that uplifts them, a holy anchorage for them that are cast adrift by fierce assaults." We know that He is eternally revealing Himself by illuminations and drawing holy minds into contemplation of Himself. We know He is wise and beautiful beyond any beauty we can imagine, and He has given the promise that we shall all be equal to the angels and shall be the Sons of God, being Sons of the Resurrection. We know He is within the world and above it, the center and the circumference and all that lies between; and is everywhere and nowhere. He is Sun and Morning Star; He is Fire and Wind and the Water of Life; He is Spirit, Dew and Cloud. Men have spoken of Him as a fiery or amber shape; as a Hand, as a Face, as a Feathery Wing, as a Rock; and still He escapes them. Then where shall we find Him?

Such is the prologue, with the mysterious actor stepping out in front of the stage. Then the curtain rises, and we are presented with the flashing drama.

At first we see nothing on the stage except that naked athlete of God conjuring up visions of what God is not. Then the light begins to clear, and we are made aware of certain subtle emanations from the Godhead, certain paradoxes, unexpected concentrations of force. Somewhere there is a shrine, and we recognize the shrine by the presence of the angels, the evangelists of the divine silence; and the lights beckon. These are spiritual lights which drive ignorance and error away, "stirring and opening the eyes which are fast shut and weighed down with darkness, and these receive at first only a moderate illumination, but as the desire and taste for the light increases, then does God give Himself in greater measure and shines in greater abundance upon them 'who have loved Him greatly,' and so he constrains them according to their powers of looking upward." The light comes down from Heaven, but the prayers go up to God; and who shall measure the energy of the prayers which soar to the Holy Trinity? So we are presented on the bare stage with the descending lights of Heaven and the ascending prayers of men:

The Trinity is nigh unto all things, and yet not all things are nigh unto It. Only with holy prayers and pure minds and with souls prepared for union with the Godhead do we come nigh to It; for It is not in space, so as to be absent from any spot, or to move from one position to another, and to speak of It as omnipresent does not express this all-transcendent and all-embracing infinitude. But let us press on in prayer, always thirsting for the divine benignant rays.

As if a luminous chain hung suspended from the heights of heaven and reached down to this world below, and we by seizing it, first with one hand, then with the other, seemed to be pulling it down, but in very truth instead of pulling it down, we found ourselves carried upward to the higher splendors of the shining rays,

Or as if we were on a ship, clinging to the ropes which bound the ship to some rocks, and we were pulling on the ropes, but we would not be drawing the rocks toward our ship, but in very truth we would be pulling the vessel close to the rocks,

Or as if we were standing on a ship pushing away the rock on shore, but we would not be affecting the immovable rock, for in very truth we would be separating ourselves from it; and the more we push it, the more we would be warding it off.

So it is, before every endeavor and especially those endeavors which concern divinity, we must begin with prayer: not to pull down to ourselves what is nigh both everywhere and nowhere, but to commend and unite ourselves to God by these invocations and remembrances.   [*De divinis Nominibus,* III]

What Dionysius is attempting to do is to chart the field, moving from the known—the prayers of men, the knowledge of the heavenly illumination—to the unknown, which is God. His task is to penetrate the mystery, to give shape to the shrine, to recognize its paradoxes, never to allow paradox to win the day. He will use paradox against the paradox. "The Trinity is nigh unto all things, and yet not all things are nigh unto It." Men can be remote from God even when God is within them. It is only the first of many paradoxes; and Dionysius walks among these paradoxes with astonishing sure-footedness. God is formless, but produces all forms. He is mindless, but produces all wisdom. He is without life, but produces an excess of it. These paradoxes suggest a further dimension by which God can be known: *that which is not, is.* And so he introduces, very tentatively at first and then with complete assurance, the idea of the negation of the attributes of God, the negative way, the image of the divine darkness which an English mystic was later to call "the cloud of unknowing."

The idea was not original to Dionysius—there are hints of it in Gregory of Nyssa—but his use of the idea is original. He insists that "that which is not" shares in the Beautiful and Good, "for that which is not is itself beautiful and good when by the negation of all attributes it is ascribed superessentially to God." He is saying that the shapeless stone in which the sculptor seeks to find the hidden face is itself the face of God. But at this point incredible complications occur. According to Dionysius, all evil partakes of nonexistence. Evil is the state of not-being, possessing neither goodness nor creativity nor the power to create goodness. But he has already stated that "that which is not" shares in the Beautiful and Good. So evil can have no existence, it is not only "that which is not," but it is also something immeasurably less, something wholly removed from the world of realities—even from the perplexing realities of "that which is not." The unreal seducer lusts after an unreal flesh, but still he possesses a share in the Good because his lust is a reflection of ideal love seen in a distorting mirror. Anger, one of the seven capital sins, may even serve to remove evils; evils struggle with evils and cancel one another out. Evil is not something negative; it is simply zero. As for the devils, how can they be evil, since they sprang from God? They are evil only insofar as they are not. "What is the evil in the devils?" he asks, and answers: "Brutish wrath, blind desire, headstrong fancy." And yet these qualities are not wholly and irrevocably evil; living creatures possess them, and it happens that their possession may enable them to exist. He concludes that the devils are not evil insofar as they fulfill their natures, but only insofar as they do not. And writing of the angels who fell from Heaven, he says:

> We maintain that the angelic gifts bestowed upon them have never themselves suffered change, but remain unblemished in their perfect brightness, even if the devils themselves do not perceive it through blinding their faculties of spiritual perception. They possess their existence from the Good, and are naturally good, and desire the Beautiful and Good in desiring existence, life and imagination, and all these things *are.* And they are called evil through the

deprivation and the loss whereby they have lapsed from their proper virtues. Hence they are evil insofar as they do not exist; and in desiring evil they desire what is nonexistent.

[*De divinis Nominibus,* IV]

There is nothing cavalier in Dionysius' dismissal of evil. He pursues the argument at length; there are four quite separate discussions of the nature of evil, all leading to the same conclusion, and one has the feeling that he has not altogether convinced himself that the sum total of all evils is zero; but he must go on to the end, adding the sum up in different ways, for fear he has made an error. But there is no error: triumphantly he concludes that "good must be the beginning and the end of all evil things." And having dismissed evil, having relegated it to the status of a transitory and illusory thing, at best possessing only an accidental kind of existence, he returns to the contemplation of God, on whom no shadow of evil falls, who is and is not, one and multitudinous, superessentially present and superessentially absent, the known and the unknown, the beginning and the end. But in the interval Dionysius has entered the landscape of things which are not and has exercised his muscles upon the vast paradox, which is God, and so he returns to the task of defining God by negations, by what He is not. He speaks of the soul, becoming godlike, meeting "in the *blind* embraces of an *incomprehensible* union the rays of the *unapproachable* light." In exactly the same way, in the invocation to the Trinity with which he begins *The Mystical Theology,* he speaks of the mysteries of heavenly truths "lying hidden in the dazzling obscurity of the secret Silence, outshining all brilliance with the intensity of their darkness, and surcharging our blinded intellects with the impalpable and invisible beauty of glories beyond all beauty." At such moments he seems to be attempting to leap outside of language altogether. Under the impact of his imagination, negatives become positives, the impalpable becomes palpable; and if at times he seems to employ a language which evaporates in abstractions, self and not-self, subject and object vanishing in the unknowable mystery, he is perfectly capable of writing in a way which shows that he has this new language completely under control. What is an angel? he asks; and answers:

> An angel is an image of God, a manifestation of the invisible light, a burnished mirror, bright, untarnished, without spot or blemish, receiving (if it is reverent to say so) all the beauty of the

absolute divine goodness, and (so far as may be) kindling in itself, with unalloyed radiance, the goodness of the secret Silence.

[*De divinis Nominibus*, IV]

It is as though, long after compiling *The Celestial Hierarchies,* there had come to him quite suddenly and effortlessly the final, the perfect portrait of the angelic presences.

Again and again Dionysius complains against the paucity of words; there are not words enough to describe the paradoxes which lie close to the throne of God; and indeed there is no need for words. In the end the mysteries cannot be explained, only hinted at; and the mystic plunging into the darkness where God dwells leaves behind him, after his long ascent, all heavenly voices, all divine utterances. At this last extremity even the Bible is of no use to him. Naked and alone, in silence, in fear and trembling, he approaches the throne of God, and what he sees there is incommunicable to man.

And yet, like Gregory of Nyssa, employing the same image of Moses in the cloud, Dionysius attempts the impossible. He will come as close to God as men dare and describe what he has seen, as clearly as language permits. He wrote once that divine love draws those whom it seizes beyond themselves, so that they belong no longer to themselves, but wholly to God. So now with Moses as his guide he approaches the terrible darkness that dwelt on Sinai:

> After he was purified, Moses heard the many-voiced trumpets and saw many lights flashing forth with pure and streaming rays, and then stood separate from the multitude and with the chosen priests pressed forward to the topmost pinnacle of the divine Ascent. Nevertheless he did not meet with God Himself, yet he beheld— not God indeed (for He is invisible)—but the place wherein He dwelt. And this I take to signify that the divinest and the highest of the things perceived by the eyes of the body or the mind are but the symbolic language of things subordinate to Him who Himself transcendeth them all. Through these things His incomprehensible presence is shown walking upon those heights of His holy places which are perceived by the mind; and then It breaks forth, even from the things that are beheld and from those that behold them, and plunges the true initiate into the Darkness of Unknowing wherein he renounces all the apprehensions of his understanding and is enwrapped in that which is wholly intangible and invisible,

belonging wholly to Him that is beyond all things and to none else (whether himself or another), and being through the passive stillness of all his reasoning powers united by his highest faculty to Him who is wholly unknowable, of whom thus by a rejection of all knowledge he possesses a knowledge that exceeds his understanding.

Unto this Darkness which is beyond Light we pray that we may come, and may attain unto vision through the loss of sight and knowledge, and that in ceasing thus to see or to know we may learn to know that which is beyond all perception and understanding (for this emptying of our faculties is true sight and knowledge), and that we may offer Him that transcends all things the praises of a transcendent hymnody, which we shall do by denying and removing all things that are—like those men who carve a statue out of marble and remove all the impediments that hinder the clear perception of the latent image, and so by removing marble, they display the hidden statue in its hidden beauty.

[De mystica Theologia, I, II]

With immense learning and penetration Dionysius had described God and the angelic hosts: it remained for him to describe the ceremonial life on earth: baptism, the Eucharist, the chrism—the three visible means of grace. This he did in *The Ecclesiastical Hierarchy,* the least lyrical as it is the most baffling of his works. Here no heavenly lights flash, no burning seraphim hover around the throne of God: all is somber, majestical, curiously menacing. It is as though Dionysius has been hurled down to earth after the contemplation of the heavenly mysteries and finds himself in some strange way manacled by earthly presumptions. He no longer breathes freely. Often haltingly, perhaps no longer sure of himself, he describes the ecclesiastical hierarchies as mirrors of the heavenly hierarchies; and just as there are thrones, seraphim and cherubim around God, so there are bishops, presbyters and deacons around the altar, and beyond this holy circle lies another circle of catechumens, baptized laymen, monks. Everything is in threes. Like Dante, he sees threes everywhere, and he has Dante's aristocratic temper. Order rules, because there is always a chain of command. And the bishop, standing at the topmost pinnacle of human attainment in the divine, standing in the rays of God's light, his eyes fixed upon the sacred symbols on the altar, has only to dip his fingers in the purifying water to become "the image of pure divinity."

When he speaks of worship, Dionysius is the child of a harsh law.

For him the only power on earth is held in the sacramental hands of the bishop: through him and from him the splendors of divine clarity are reflected onto those below. Like an athlete, the bishop dispenses power. Like an earthly seraph, he conveys tribute and rejoicing to God. He belongs to the elect, and his knowledge can only rarely be transmitted to his inferiors. He is king, and his word is law. Significantly, Dionysius does not call him by the usual Greek word for "bishop"—*episkopos*—but calls him *hierarch* instead.

Just as in *The Celestial Hierarchy* Dionysius made many different attempts to describe the angelic hosts, so here he produces a number of portraits with variations of the bishop. He shows in detail how the bishop presides over baptism, the Eucharist and the consecration of the holy oil, a mysterious and sovereign figure endowed with gifts which remove him from the common lot, able with a word to drive the demons away:

> He becomes truly divine and worthy to participate in divine things, having performed the work of perfection, and so he raises himself into the greatest possible conformity with God, paying no attention to the flesh except that he obeys the demands of nature, but only as it were in passing; for he is the temple and companion of the Holy Spirit, striving by all possible means to imitate Him, preparing a worthy house for the divinity in him. And this man is never tormented by illusions and devilish terrors, but on the contrary laughs at them and fends off their assults, and toward them he is far more active than passive, for he hounds them down and triumphantly sets them to flight; and by his courage which is in no way touched by the passions he delivers his brothers from the influence of the evil spirits.   [*De ecclesiastica Ierarchia*, III, 7]

The bishop alone celebrates the most sacred mysteries, for he is the interpreter of divine judgment, the messenger of the Lord. Therefore the bishop's prayers over the dead are more likely to be answered, and when the bishop pours the holy oil on the dead, he is standing in the place of God, blessing with royal hands the Christian who stands now outside the gates of Heaven; and by that dropping of holy oil the dead are aware that their purification is complete, and their resurrection in the spirit and the flesh will come about.

All through *The Ecclesiastical Hierarchy* we are confronted with the vast sacerdotal powers of the bishop. Though Dionysius discusses the clergy and the sacraments, their symbolism and their hidden and secret meanings, the baptism of children, the reasons for triple immersion and the covering of the sacred bread with the veil, the figure of the bishop, accoutered with implacable powers, looms so large that the deacons and presbyters seem no more than small objects disappearing under the immense hem of his robe, almost forgotten, of so little importance in the divine scheme of things that he barely mentions them.

Yet there was compassion and humanity in Dionysius. The stately ceremonials, the vast processions, the superb figure of the bishop in royal vestments—these are sometimes forgotten. He will say simple things with divine simplicity, as when he says: "God is drunk with the divine essence." Or again: "God knows Himself, and in knowing Himself, knows all." He could be forgiving to heretics, and in one of the surviving letters he exhorts the presbyter not to attack those who differ from him, but simply to set forth the truth and let it speak for itself. In another letter, addressed to the monk Demophilus, he tells a story which must rank with Dostoevski's *The Grand Inquisitor* as one of the greatest stories to come out of the Eastern Church. A miserable sinner, an unbeliever, had thrown himself at the feet of a priest in the sanctuary. The monk Demophilus saw what was happening and scornfully ejected both the priest and the sinner, and afterward wrote to Dionysius, explaining proudly how he had saved the sacred place from profanation. Thereupon Dionysius rages. "No," he says, "you have not saved the sanctuary from profanation, because you have yourself committed profanation, because you showed no mercy. To the very least of beings Christ showed an infinite compassion. Must you elevate yourself above Christ?" Then he tells the story of Carpus:

> One day when I was in Crete I received the hospitality of Carpus, a man famous for the extreme purity of his spirit. He was a man of a deep religious and contemplative cast, who never celebrated the holy mysteries without being consoled during his preliminary prayers with a sweet vision. He told me how one day he had been plunged into black despair when he learned that an unbeliever had stolen into the church and converted a Christian to paganism, and this had happened during the holy feasts which followed the baptism of the Christian.
>
> So Carpus prayed for the two sinners and invoked the help of God, desiring that God should convert the pagan by His mercy, and bring the apostate back to the fold. He decided to spend the rest of his life exhorting them, putting an end to their doubts,

so that after they have been punished for their temerity and folly, they might be brought back to the knowledge of God. And when nothing of the kind happened, Carpus fell into a fierce temper of indignation.

One evening he went to sleep, still overwhelmed with bitterness. It was his custom to awake during the night and compose himself for prayer. When the time for prayer had come, he awoke from his restless sleep, utterly cast down. He gave himself to prayer, but from his lips there came only a complaint against God, an indignant challenge, saying to God that it was unworthy of Him that He allowed the unbelievers, those who crossed the pathways of the Lord, to remain alive on earth. He begged God to send the lightning, and pitilessly destroy the two sinners. And he had hardly spoken when he observed that the house, where he was praying, trembled violently and then split suddenly in two.

Then it seemed to him that a vast and dazzling flame had been let down from Heaven, to fall at his feet, and in the depths of the open skies Jesus appeared, surrounded by a multitude of angels in human form. Carpus lifted his eyes, saw the miracle and trembled. Then he lowered his eyes, and saw beneath his feet that the ground had opened, revealing a vast and shadowy abyss. The two sinners he had cursed stood on the very edge of the abyss, trembling fearfully, barely able to hold one another up, in danger of falling. Out of the abyss terrible serpents were climbing toward them, winding round their feet, coiling round them, pulling them down, now biting them, now caressing them with their tails, in every conceivable manner attempting to fling them into the abyss. And as though the serpents were not powerful enough, men came running up, and they too attempted with blows to hurl the miserable sinners into the abyss, until at last the sinners, partly out of weariness, partly out of utter weakness and dejection, were close to being overthrown. Carpus watched all this in pure tranquillity of heart, observing the miracle before his eyes while forgetting the miracle he had observed a moment ago in the heavens. And as the contest was prolonged, tranquillity gave place to rage: he asked why their ruin should not be accomplished more quickly, and himself went to assist those who were trying to hurl the sinners down. And because he failed, his anger only increased and he cursed them.

And then it occurred to him to ask of the heavens why they

were still allowed to exist on the edge of the abyss. In the heavens the miracle was being continued. Jesus was looking down from the depths of the sky, but Jesus was filled with compassion. He rose from His throne, descended toward the sinners and stretched out His hand to them. Angels came down from heaven, and they held up the sinners. And Jesus turned to Carpus, saying: "Now lift your hands and strike Me, for I am ready to die once again for the salvation of men, and it would be sweet to me if I could be crucified, though committing no crime. Which do you prefer— to be hurled into the abyss, or to live with God and the angels, who are so good and friendly to men?"

This is the story Carpus told me, and I believe every word of it is true. [*Ep.* 8]

Such was Dionysius the Areopagite, who passed across the Eastern Church like a meteor and spread his light over the West, and was especially beloved by Dante and St. Thomas Aquinas, a man of vast energy and vision, more like a great flare of consciousness than a man, the faceless saint who looked into the face of God as the eagle looks at the sun.

John Damascene

Higg up in the white cliffs of the Valley of Fire, among the wild hills between Jerusalem and the Dead Sea, overlooking a deep gorge produced by a violent earthquake, lies the monastery of St. Saba. In this desolate region where the rains stream in torrents in winter and the summer heat is like a burning glass and no grass grows, the monks live out their lives in small caves dug out of the precipitous rock eight hundred feet high. The monastery is a complex of caves hanging to the rock like an eagle's eyrie; for whole months in winter, when the steps are worn away, it is unreachable, and supplies are taken up by a long rope dangling down the cliffside. Here are domes, towers, battlements, staircases, all carved from the living rock. Here there are no trees, no shrubs, only the silence of the desert and the howl of jackals and the sound of the three monastery bells ringing over the Dead Sea. Once John the Baptist wandered through these harsh valleys, in the days before he manifested himself to Israel. Once ten thousand anchorites lived in these cave dwellings. Today only a handful of monks remain, to share their food with the strange birds who haunt these rocks, blackbirds with dark blue plumage and bright orange wings. In this monastery on the edge of the world, yet within ten miles of Jerusalem, in sight of the leaden-blue waters of the Dead Sea, there lived for the greater part of his life a Syrian of gentle blood, whose family name was Mansur, meaning "victory," whom we know as John of Damascus or John Damascene. At various times he was prime minister at the court of the Omayyad Caliph Abd-ul-Malek, a profound novelist, a great hymn writer, the defender of images in the long war against the iconoclasts and the author of the first *summa theologica*. He was almost the last of the great Fathers of the Eastern Church, and until the coming of Gregory Palamas five hundred years later there were to be no others.

He was born in Damascus about A.D. 676, the son of a certain

Sergius who had taken service in the Court. His parents were wealthy and descended from a long line of Christians. There was nothing unusual in the fact that Christians took service under the caliphs. The Omayyad dynasty was tolerant and took pains to celebrate the arts. The court poet Akhtal was a Christian; and in this tolerant age it was not thought remarkable that he should be led in a robe of honor through the streets of Damascus while a herald proclaimed: "Behold the poet of the Commander of the Faithful! Behold the greatest of all Arabian poets!" Damascus was a city which flaunted its luxury. Rich and powerful, it had only just become the seat of the Omayyad government. From the marble colonnades people looked out on vast processions led by the caliph on a snow-white horse. Flushed with victory, the Arabs were delighting in the new civilization they found all round them. Sergius, elevated to the rank of Prime Minister, seems to have been perturbed at the thought that his son John would adopt Arab ways, and placed the boy under the instruction of the Italian monk Cosmas, who retired to the monastery of St. Saba when he had taught John all he knew. Suddenly the father died. He was very close to the caliph, who was inconsolable. The caliph decided to appoint John to the high position of *protosymbulos* or chief secretary. In an Oriental court only the position of *logothete* or counselor of state was higher, and in time John enjoyed the powers once possessed by his father.

Dark-eyed, dark-bearded, possessing the elegance of the Syrians, at ease in the Court, John Mansur could look forward to long years of service under a Saracenic prince. He might have remained at the Court for the rest of his life if it had not been for the Italian monk Cosmas, who influenced him profoundly. Cosmas had been a monk and later a priest. Captured in Sicily by Saracenic pirates, he was brought to Damascus to be sold as a slave in the market place. There the old Prime Minister Sergius set eyes on him. Normally a slave would be sold to a farmer and made to work in the fields until he dropped dead. There existed laws against introducing slaves into the houses of official families. Cosmas was already an old man. Sergius pleaded with the Caliph, ransomed the slave and took him into his own home. From the old man John acquired a formidable knowledge of theology, rhetoric, natural history, music and astronomy. He possessed a vast knowledge of the world and a vast knowledge of spiritual theory, and these two seem to have existed in an easy alliance. He was deeply religious, and like his father given to good works, but his religion did not interfere with his public duties. There was a thorn in the flesh. Calmly and serenely he seemed to be living in Damascus, but in fact he was obsessed by the thought of giving up all his wealth and offering it to the poor and then disappearing to some remote monastery in the desert. He seemed to have no care in the world, but he was dominated more by the majestic figure of Cosmas than by the Caliph. When Cosmas disappeared into the monastery of St. Saba, John Mansur had only one desire: to follow him.

In 726 the Greek islands of Thera and Therasia were shaken by a volcanic eruption in the sea. The Emperor Leo III, known as the Isaurian, issued a strange decree, announcing that the eruption was due to God's wrath on the idolatry of the Greeks. The text of the decree is lost, but we know that Leo III ordered the destruction of all paintings, mosaics and statues representing Christ and His saints, and soon afterward he decreed the destruction of the great statue of Christ over the bronze gate of the palace in Constantinople. The destruction of the statue caused a riot; and the officers responsible for tearing the statue down were torn to pieces by women. Thereupon the Emperor gave orders for the execution of all those who had attempted to rescue the statue. They were the first martyrs of iconoclasm.

The Emperor's hostility to image worship has never been satis-factorily explained. Once, writing to the Pope in Rome, the Emperor said: "I am both Emperor and priest," meaning that he set himself above the Patriarch of Constantinople and the Pope in religious mat-ters. Stern, bearded, with enormous eyes, resembling in his surviving portraits a curious mixture of the wolf and the cat, he seems to have believed that he could impose his private credo on the whole Empire. Among the tenets of his private credo was a fundamentalist belief in the second commandment.

From Damascus, where he was still a high official, and perhaps the highest official, in the Caliph's government, John Mansur answered the Emperor. As images, paintings and statues were smashed, a wave of horror went through Greece. Revolts were put down by the imperial armies. All this had come to John Mansur's attention, who replied that the destruction of the images was not warranted by the Scriptures. Did not figures of the cherubim and seraphim adorn the Ark of the Covenant? Was not Solomon ordered to adorn the walls of Jerusalem with living figures, with flowers and fruit? Then how much more fitting that Christians should adorn their churches? It was a reasoned scholarly reply, filled with quotations from the Bible, and curiously without any sense of urgency; later, John Mansur spoke of this discourse as being "not very intelligible to the multitude."

The iconoclastic controversy continued, with Pope Gregory II and Germanus, Patriarch of Constantinople, throwing their influence into the battle on the side of the image worshipers, those who believed that it was perfectly proper to have statues and paintings of Christ in the churches. Leo III was determined that the images should go; and he may have believed that Christianity needed the purification that would come with the destruction of the images, if it was to survive the increasing power of Islam, which taught that "images are an abomination of the works of Satan" (*Koran,* V, 92). In 730 he called a second council and issued his second edict against the holy images, and deposed Germanus, who refused to sign it. In his place Leo appointed a certain Anastasius, whose house was thereupon attacked by image-worshiping Christians. From Damascus for the second time John Mansur issued a formidable attack, quoting the evidence of the Fathers of the Church who favored the worship of images. Had not St. Basil said: "The honor and veneration of the image is transferred to its prototype?" (*De Spiritu Sanctu,* 18, 45). Dionysius the Areopagite, Gregory of Nyssa, Chrysostom, all these had spoken openly in favor of images, and should the Emperor regard himself as more learned, and more understanding in the ways of God, than these Fathers? The iconoclasts said God cannot be circumscribed. John Mansur answered that God is not being circumscribed in the images; he is being venerated, and it is right and proper to venerate Him. Not content with a quiet and carefully composed attack on the iconoclasts, John Mansur thundered against the Emperor, and deliberately misquoting *Galatians* 1:8, he said: " 'Though we, or an angel from heaven, *or a King,* preach any other gospel unto you than that we have preached unto you'—and now, I beg you, close your ears, for I shrink from repeating the words of the divine apostle: 'let him be accursed.' " By adding the words "or a King," John Mansur had thrown down the gauntlet. From now on there could only be unbroken hostility between Leo III and the great official in the Caliph's Court.

In later years the story was told that Leo III's vengeance penetrated the courtyards of Damascus. Unable to overwhelm John Mansur by force of argument, the Emperor determined to destroy him by a stratagem. He forged letters addressed to himself, purporting to be written by John Mansur from Damascus. The letters informed the Byzantine Emperor that the guards surrounding Damascus were weak and negligent, and could be easily suborned. If the Emperor was wise, he would send an army immediately against Damascus; when the army arrived, Leo III was assured of the co-operation of John Mansur. These forged letters were sent by messenger to the Caliph. John Mansur was summoned, and asked how he could explain them; and when he offered no explanation, the Caliph ordered his right hand struck off. All that night John Mansur prayed to the Virgin, holding the severed hand to his wrist. In the morning there was only the mark of a suture to show where the executioner's knife had passed. Soon afterward he begged the Caliph to relieve him of office, and he disappeared into the monastery of St. Saba, having sold all his worldly possessions and given the proceeds to the poor, and possessing only the coat on his back.

The monks of the monastery were not prepared for the reception of so distinguished a pupil. There is a story that they tried to reject him, and that for a long while they pretended he was not living among them. At last a very old monk was found to take charge of him. John Mansur asked what was demanded of him. "Complete silence," the monk answered. "And beyond this?" "The renunciation of all secular learning." "And beyond this?" "You shall not use the pen." Some time later he was ordered to go through the streets of Damascus selling baskets made by the monks. He was to demand an exorbitant price for them, and to suffer whatever indignities the people showered on him, when they recognized in the shambling monk the features of the man who had once been the closest adviser to their ruler. About 735 he was ordained for the priesthood, and then the restrictions were removed. For the rest of his life he lived in a cell high up on the white cliffs of the Valley of Fire.

He wrote voluminously: a flood of homilies, commentaries, ascetic tracts, liturgical canons and hymns flowed from his pen. The best and most famous of his works was *The Fountain of Knowledge,* which consisted of a treatise on logic, a summary of heresies and a comprehensive *Exposition of the Orthodox Faith.*

The *Exposition* of John Damascene is an astonishing and striking document. It is not only that he wrote with great art and authority; he wrote with freshness and excitement, and with a kind of illusive calm, which never completely conceals his sense of Christian drama. The stakes are high; the imponderable powers of evil are confronted with the eternal majesty of God; the war between divinity and mortality must be fought to the end. Meanwhile, he seems to be saying, let us regard eagerly and yet calmly the vast panorama of Christian life as it is laid before us, and let us before we are too profoundly engaged in the conflict know the exact worth of the forces which are fighting on our side. So with a novelist's art, and with a surveyor's precision, seeming to stand a little apart from the conflict in order to have a better view of it, he describes the earth and the Heavens and the abysses of Hell and all the mortal and immortal spirits. His purpose is nothing less than a complete, succinct cosmology. Nothing will be left out. He will describe the nature of God and the Trinity, and from there he will go on to describe the nature of human passion and human thought. The airy demons have their place; Paradise will be charted; the seas and the mountains of the earth must also be described. What is memory? What is air made of? Who are the angels? To all these questions he provides appropriate answers. Unlike St. Thomas Aquinas, who provides arguments *pro* and *contra,* and then states his conclusions, St. John Damascene usually announces his conclusions with breath-taking boldness. Only very occasionally does he refer to his authorities. He possessed a passionate admiration for Gregory Nazianzen, and Gregory's name appears at intervals, as though John Damascene were determined that he should be remembered, but in fact all existing traditions are summed up in this extraordinary document.

Let us examine briefly the question of the angels. What exactly was their function? In what way did they act as mediators between God and men? What precisely should be the Christian doctrine concerning these creatures who are so rarely seen? It was a question of vast importance, but there was no agreement among the Greek Fathers about them. Clement of Alexandria describes them simply as "graceful spiritual beings," and refused to be drawn into any further discussion. Origen devotes a chapter to them in which he avoids the issue, saying only that he believes the souls of good men after death join the ranks of the angels. Some Fathers thought their bodies were pure fire, others believed them to be a mixture of fire and air. John Chrysostom said he was certain they were present at the Eucharist. Gregory Nazianzen said he was uncertain whether they were immaterial fire or purely intellectual spirits. Theodoret believed they were bodiless, and Dionysius the Areopagite regarded them as beings provided with intelligence, and though he discussed the angelic hierarchies profoundly and at considerable length, he was unable to determine their form. Sometimes they resembled flames, but there were angels mentioned in the

Scriptures who resembled clouds and winds and rushing rivers and colored stones. There were even angels who resembled lions and horses, both symbols of majesty. He could not say whether they communicated with one another, but he was certain that their purpose was to adore God and prosper in God's ways. Now listen to John Damascene:

They are derived from that first light which is without beginning, for they possess the power of illumination; and they have no need of tongue or hearing, for without a word exchanged between them they communicate their thoughts and counsels with one another. They are created by the Word, and by the sanctification of the Holy Spirit are they brought to perfection, and each shines in brightness and grace according to his value and his place in God's sight. Also, they are circumscribed: for when they are in Heaven they are not on earth and when they are sent by God on earth they do not remain in Heaven. They are not hemmed in by walls and doors, by locks and seals, for they have unlimited powers. I say they have unlimited powers because, when God wishes them to appear before worthy men and reveal themselves, then they assume the shape the beholder is capable of seeing. Yet that alone is perfectly unlimited which is uncreated, and every created thing is limited by God who created it. . . .

They are mighty and prompt to fulfill the desires of God, and they are endowed with such speed that wherever the divine will bids them go, there they are straightway found. They are the guardians of the divisions of earth; they are set over the nations and regions allotted to them by God; they govern all our affairs and bring us succor. And the reason surely is that they are set over us by the divine will and command and are ever in the neighborhood of God. *[De Fide Orthodoxa, III, 3]*

Here there is no stumbling: the statement is clear: and we are as close to the angels as we shall ever be. Characteristically, John Damascene has refused to enlarge on the hierarchies of angels, seraphim, cherubim and thrones, powers, dominations and virtues, angels, archangels and principalities. He is concerned with their power and origin, not with their complexity, the precise positions they occupy, their particular place in the worship of God. Dionysius the Areopagite gave special powers to the seraphim, distinguishing them from the cherubim and the thrones and all the other members of the angelic orders. John Damascene prefers to suspend judgment and says he does not know whether they are equal or whether they differ from one another. "God, their Creator, who knoweth all things, alone knoweth."

He does not often admit to ignorance, for it is not in his temper to regard Christian doctrine as a mystery: it is a thing bathed in a great light, which can be seen if the eyes are accustomed to an intense illumination. He says difficult things with fantastic ease. What is Heaven? "Heaven is the circumference of things created, both visible and invisible." It is all so quick, so effortless that the mind is almost appalled by the simplicity of the discovery. So it is again when he discusses the problem of the energy of Christ. It was a problem which sometimes weighed heavily on the Greek Fathers; and some six hundred years after John Damascene's death, in the days when Constantinople was shuddering against the onslaughts of the Turks, it revived to plague the Emperor John VI Cantacuzene and the monks of Athos. Could Christ possess two energies? Yes, answers John Damascene, and he goes on to provide in the image of the flaming sword and in the story of the raising of the daughter of Jairus the answer to those who doubted that the Son of God could possess two separate energies:

We hold that there are two energies in our Lord Jesus Christ. For as God, and being of like essence with the Father, he possesses divine energy, and as man, and like essence with man, he possesses the energy proper to human nature.

Look at the flaming sword. In such a sword the natures of fire and steel are preserved intact, and so are their two energies and their effects. The energy of the steel lies in its cutting power, and that of fire in its power to burn; and the cut is the effect of the energy of the steel, and the burn is the effect of the energy of fire; and these are kept distinct in the burnt cut and in the cut burn, though the cut does not take place apart from the burning. So there is unity in the flaming sword, and so there exists in Christ an energy which is divine and omnipotent, and at the same time He possesses a human energy like our own. And the effect of His human energy was His taking the child by the hand and drawing her to Himself, while that of His divine energy lay in His restoring her to life.   [*De Fide Orthodoxa*, III, 14]

This was not of course the end of the matter. Though John Damascene seems to speak with authority, there were many among the Fathers who would not have dared to speak with so much assurance. He spoke with the same assurance on the nature of man, but this time there is little that is original in his summary as he borrows heavily from *The Great Catechism* of Gregory of Nyssa; yet the dry, and singularly authoritative manner, is his own:

God made man without evil, upright, virtuous, free from pain and care, glorified with every virtue, adorned with all that is good, a second microcosm within the great world, another angel capable of worship, compounded of many things, surveying the visible creation and initiated into the mysteries of the realm of the mind, king over the things of the earth but subject to a higher King of the earth and of heaven, temporal and eternal, belonging to the realm of sight and the realm of mind, midway between greatness and lowliness, spirit and flesh: for he is spirit by grace and flesh by overweening pride: spirit that he may abide and glorify his benefactor, and flesh that he may suffer, and suffering may be admonished and disciplined when he prides himself on his greatness. Here in this present life his life is ordered like an animal's, but elsewhere in the ages to come he is changed and— to complete the mystery—he becomes deified by merely inclining himself toward God; and he becomes deified in sharing in the divine glory rather than being changed into a divine being.

[*De Fide Orthodoxa*, II, 12]

Here, as elsewhere, we have the feeling that the dreams and half-formed thoughts and wonderful guesses of Gregory of Nyssa have suddenly been codified. The poetry has gone: the definition of man is a tissue of sentences gathered out of the works of Gregory and strung together in due order, with a bewildering sense of proportion which Gregory would never have possessed. Here finally is man! And except for the last blazing sentence, we are aware that he has become a formula!

There were some subjects which John Damascene made peculiarly his own. Among these was the subject of images. He wrote about them in the *Exposition* briefly, and with the same finality:

It is absurd and impious to give form to God; and yet, when out of His pity for man and desiring man's salvation, God became man, not as He was seen by Abraham, nor as He was seen by the prophets, but in being truly man, who lived upon the earth and dwelt among mankind, worked miracles, suffered and was crucified, rose again and ascended to Heaven, and all these things actually took place and were seen by men, and written down for our remembrance and instruction who were not alive at that time. . . . So, when we look upon His image, then His saving Passion is brought to our remembrance, and we fall and worship what is imaged there.   [*De Fide Orthodoxa*, IV, 16]

In the monastery he seems to have taken no part in the iconoclastic controversy which raged throughout the Eastern world, to be continued after the death of Leo III A.D. 741 by his son, Constantine Copronymus, meaning "named from dung," because it was said that he fouled the baptismal font. The statues and paintings were destroyed, but John Damascene had nothing more to say about them than this brief summary in the *Exposition*. He seems to us a remote and mysterious figure, withdrawn into the shelter of his cell, his supreme task to give definition to theology. Five hundred years after his death Pope Eugenius II ordered a translation of the *Exposition* to be made into Latin. The translation appeared in time to fire the imagination of St. Thomas Aquinas, who built his own *Summa Theologica* on the foundations of the great summary produced by John Damascene.

We would know John Damascene better if it were possible to translate his hymns worthily, but no adequate translations have been made. Yet we know a great deal about his inner life as we read between the lines of his extraordinary novel, *Barlaam and Ioasaph*, which tells the story of the enduring love between the monk Barlaam and Prince Ioasaph, who are evidently Cosmas and John Mansur disguised.

The history of the novel is as strange as the novel itself. It is clearly based on an Indian fable. Once it enjoyed the popularity reserved for those rare religious novels like *Pilgrim's Progress* which take whole centuries by storm. A shorter version of the story appeared in *The Golden Legend*, a compilation of lives of the saints edited by the Dominican monk Jacobus de Voragine in the thirteenth century. It was translated by Caxton and printed in London in 1483. There were endless editions. It became a prolific source for poets, preachers, romancers, playwrights and writers of mystery plays.

At the very beginning of the novel John announces that he received the story from India, or rather from "the inner land of the Ethiopians, which is called the land of the Indians." In this imaginary country, then, he places his protagonists, the childless Indian King Abennir and the Christian monks whose virtuous lives goad him to detestable acts of savagery. The King is evidently modeled on the Caliph Abd-ul-Malek. He is "the possessor of great wealth and power, one who brings victories, brave in war, aware of his splendid stature and beauty of face, proud of those worldly honors which pass so soon away." He is a man who enjoys luxury and all the pleasant things of life, practicing vices "in the Greek way," knowledgeable and in perfect command of his faculties. We are not told why he hates the monks with a deep, savage hatred, and perhaps this is inevitable, for he is only a projection in John's mind of some facets of the Caliph's character. He is followed on the stage by the King's chief minister, a humble man of great physical beauty, evidently modeled on John's father. This chief minister, "whom the King loved so fondly," is outraged by the tortures and blood sacrifices suffered by the monks, their continual hounding by the state police. He does not protest: he simply retires across the desert and joins the monks, having studied the divine oracles and purged his senses. The King orders his arrest, and when at last the chief minister is brought to him, an old man wearing sack-cloth who once wore the panoply of power, they upbraid each other; and while the King roars against the Christians, the chief minister pronounces Christian doctrine and is summarily dismissed for his pains. And then a little while later, to the King's intense delight, a child called Ioasaph, meaning "The Lord gathers," is born to him, and to celebrate the birth of his heir there are public feasts and fifty-five Chaldean priests are summoned to foretell the fate of the child. The most learned of the astrologers announces that the child will never rule over a worldly empire; a better and a greater kingdom lies in store for him. Alarmed, the King decides to do everything in his power to prove the Chaldean wrong. The child is hidden away in a remote palace, attended by handsome youths who are enjoined to reveal nothing which could conceivably make him unhappy: he must know nothing about illness, poverty, disease and death. He must have no desire except to rule over the kingdom, and to live at ease among musicians and mimers. He must love the earth as it is, and have no thirst for a greater and better kingdom.

Suddenly the calm existence of the young Prince ends. He simply asks why he is never allowed outside the palace and sees only the people who are chosen for him. He learns from the tutor about the existence of the Christians, who have been persecuted and burnt at the stake, so that there are almost none left in the kingdom "except those who take refuge in the mountains and the caves and the holes of the earth." From the tutor the Prince hears that the Christians possess a way of life which answers men's most desperate needs. He is still forbidden to go outside the gates. When the King comes to the palace, the boy is asked why he seems to be so weighed down with melancholy and he answers: "Because I am never allowed to enjoy the company of the fair people beyond the palace walls." The King relents. The boy may go out, provided he is accompanied and shielded. One day the boy sees a maimed man, then a blind man. A few days later he sees an old, toothless, shriveled, gray-haired man, bent double and drooling nonsense. There is death in the man's face, and the boy has seen it now for the first time. He asks himself whether death will one day overtake him, and what meaning a man's life can possess, if death overtakes him in the end. Troubled to the depths of his being, pale and sickly, he renounces the world, but in his father's presence he pretends to a cheerfulness he does not possess. And when he asks the tutor how he can join the Christians, he is told that none remains, for all have been banished or killed. "So he lived in great conflict and distress of mind, and accounted all the pleasures and delights of the world as an abomination and a curse."

At this point the monk Barlaam arrives on the scene in the disguise of a merchant bearing a jewel of great price. There is no doubt that Barlaam is intended to represent Cosmas. John Damascene inserts several clues, including a pun on the name of Cosmas, who is described as "a certain monk, wise in the knowledge of heavenly things, graced (*kosmoumenos*) with an understanding of learning and the world around, and a most meticulous observer of monastic rules." Barlaam offers the boy the jewel, which possesses magic properties. It gives speech to the dumb and strength to the afflicted, and only the most virtuous can look at it and remain unharmed. The boy is overwhelmed by the goodness of the monk and by the beauty of the jewel, which he can look upon, because it is only another name for Christian doctrine; and so Barlaam launches into a long history of the world seen in the light of Providence. He tells the story of the Garden of Eden, and the devil's wiles, and the long journeys of the children of Israel, and how at last there came forth from the Virgin "a body of flesh inspirited with reason and intelligence, but possessed of one single substance, being of two natures, perfect God and perfect man."

The Prince is impressed, for the doctrine is pronounced at considerable length, and large passages of it were later to find a place in John's theological writings. But the formulas of theology are not always employed. Barlaam tells stories well. Considering the known vices of King Abennir, the stories are sometimes sharply edged:

There was a King who ordered four caskets to be made of wood. Two of these he covered with sheets of gold, and in them he placed the decaying bones of dead men; and these two caskets he sealed with golden seals. The others were smeared over with pitch and asphalt, but these were filled with precious stones and rare pearls and all manner of aromatic perfumes; and these two caskets he bound with ropes of hair. Then he summoned the great officers of his kingdom who had complained at his way of accosting men in the streets.

Now there were four caskets lying before them, and the great officers were ordered to appraise their value. They guessed the golden caskets were of greater value and probably were filled with diadems worthy of a King and jewel-studded girdles. And they said that the caskets smeared with pitch and asphalt were probably of no value at all. "Ah," said the King. "I know that such is your answer, for with the eyes of sense you have judged the objects of sense, but this you should not do—rather should you see with the inner eye the hidden worthlessness." Then he ordered the golden chests to be opened. What was inside was hideous and had a loathsome smell. [*Barlaam and Ioasaph*, IV, 43]

After long disquisitions on the nature of faith, Barlaam tells the story of the man and the unicorn. It is a good story, with an excellent moral, and since Ioasaph plainly enjoyed it, it should be repeated here.

I consider all those who have alienated themselves from the life lived in the service of God to be like the man who fled from the raging unicorn. You remember how he could not bear to hear the sound of the unicorn's roar, and its terrible bellowing, and so, in order to avoid being devoured, he ran away as fast as his legs could carry him. But while he was running he fell into a great pit, and as he fell, he stretched out his hands and clasped his arms round a tree and somehow succeeded in gaining a foothold, and for a moment he thought he was safe. But then he saw two mice, one black, the other white, and they were forever nibbling and gnawing at the root of the tree, so that there was only a slender thread holding the tree upright. And then he looked at the bottom of the pit and saw a fire-breathing dragon, with its jaws agape, exceedingly fierce and grim. And then when he looked at the place where his feet were resting, he saw four asps. Then he looked above him, and he saw there was a little honey dripping from the upper branches of the tree. At that moment he clean forgot all the troubles surrounding him: how the unicorn was raging to devour him, and the fierce dragon was yawning to swallow him, and the tree was almost severed at the roots, and how his feet rested on a slippery ledge. All these terrible things went clean out of his mind as he hung on the sweetness of the tiny drops of honey.

[*Barlaam and Ioasaph*, XII, 112]

It is a good story, comparable to the story of Carpus, and such stories were necessary to sweeten the heavy load of theology with which Barlaam addresses Ioasaph. Inevitably Ioasaph is converted; just as inevitably King Abennir is outraged. Barlaam wanders away in his hairshirt to some fastness in the desert, while the young Prince argues with his father on the nature of God and rulership. Then Ioasaph receives half the kingdom and rules it justly, while the other half ruled by King Abennir becomes "as smoke vanishing." Ioasaph takes the vow of chastity, converts the sinners at Court, and is given the whole kingdom to rule. At last, wearying of kingship, he appoints a successor and wanders into the desert in search of Barlaam, "his heart wounded with a marvelous longing and divine love for Christ." For two years, tormented by thirst and tempted by the devil, he wanders through the desert. Sometimes the devil leaps on him with a drawn sword, but Ioasaph knows exactly how to deal with him. In the end a hermit leads him to Barlaam's cave:

The Prince stood at the door of the cave and knocked, saying: "*Benedicite*, father, *benedicite!*" When Barlaam heard the voice, he came out and recognized Ioasaph by the spirit, for otherwise it would have been impossible to recognize him, for a marvelous change had altered his appearance from its former youth; for now Ioasaph was black with the sun's heat, and overgrown with hair, and his cheeks were sunken, and his eyes were deep in their sockets, and the eyelids burned with tears, and there was anguish of hunger written there. But Ioasaph recognized his spiritual father, whose features were as he remembered them. The old man stood there facing the East and offering a prayer; and after the prayer, when they had said Amen, they embraced and kissed, and for a long time slaked their joy in one another.

[*Barlaam and Ioasaph*, XXXVIII, 346]

Soon afterward Barlaam died, and Ioasaph buried the body. He never returned to his kingdom, but lived in holiness and peace in the desert. When Ioasaph died, he was buried beside Barlaam, and later the two bodies were removed to the city. Miracles took place at the tomb, and the memories of Barlaam and Ioasaph were held in honor by the faithful.

John Damascene died about 750, having long outlived Cosmas. The iconoclastic controversy was still raging, and shortly after his death, following the Great Council of Constantinople in 752 he was solemnly anathematized:

Anathema to Mansur, cursed favorer of the Saracens;
Anathema to Mansur, image worshiper and author of falsehoods;
Anathema to Mansur who denied Christ and plotted against his
  Emperor;
Anathema to Mansur, teacher of impiety and perverter of the Holy
  Scriptures.

It was the last blow struck by the Iconoclasts. John Mansur, known as St. John Damascene, remains, and no one knows or cares what happened to the 338 prelates who attended the pseudo-Council in Constantinople. The Syrian in his cave not far from Jerusalem was almost the last of the Fathers of the Eastern Church. There remained one more, and when these two had perished there was an end to the long story of Greek philosophy, which had begun with the school of Miletus about 600 B.C., had surged forward with Plato and finally marched across the world with Christianity at its side.

Gregory Palamas

During the six hundred years following John Damascene, the Eastern Church seemed to sink into a long slumber. The doctrine was established, the ancient ceremonies remained unchanged, the precise rituals were determined, and the great Fathers of the Church, remembered in the liturgies and endlessly commented upon by scholars, seemed to walk by the side of the worshipers. For century upon century no breath of new wind blew through Hagia Sophia. A rigid formalism descended upon the Eastern Church, as it descended upon the Byzantine Court. Emperor followed Emperor; the gold vessels blazed; the mosaics glittered; vast processions formed across the Augusteum; and the Church was dying. It did not seem to be dying. The old Hellenic leaven was still working. Men still lived the Christian life. Neither Athanasius nor Basil nor Chrysostom was dead, though sometimes they seemed to be submerged under mountains of commentators; but they were more vigorous than their commentators, and without too great difficulty they could be seen clear, heroic men of a heroic age; and the very tones of their voices, as they delivered their sermons, could be heard down the centuries. Once, orthodoxy meant risk, exile, martyrdom; it did so no longer. John Damascene had placed his seal on dogma. In the eyes of the worshipers the Eastern Church had achieved its final perfection: there was no need to inquire further.

Religions are like men: they grow old and die unless they are renewed, unless the seed perishes and is born again. There was need of a new wind, a wave of freshness, a sudden flare of the spirit. A thousand commentators had been at work. Every word spoken by Jesus had been commented upon until the earth grew heavy with the volumes of the commentators. Dogma became intricate; only a few scholars could understand it. There was need once more of a simple faith, as simple as the prayer of an old peasant in his dying days.

In the West this need was known and answered by St. Francis, who laughed at dogma and hurled the commentators out of the window: it was enough to love God and live in simple charity. He forbade the reading of books and sang songs to his sister the Moon, being the first Pierrot. He danced through the fields of Umbria and offered prayers to his wounds when he was cauterized, and he showed no abiding respect for high ecclesiastical officials. There were periods when he was afraid of being accused of heresy, and perhaps burnt at the stake; yet there were people who believed, and still believe, that of all men he was closest to Christ. In the East such gaiety had appeared among the Desert Fathers: there are times when Antony speaks with a voice like Francis'. In the West Francis shook the dust from the Church; in the East this service was performed by Gregory Palamas, Archbishop of Thessalonica.

At a time when the Byzantine Empire was reeling from the blows of the invaders, and already half betrayed, Gregory upheld the doctrine of *hesychia*—quietness. It was not a negative doctrine; it went back to the earliest origins of Christianity. In its context, and in its vast implications, it was a doctrine of surprising boldness, for it cut through the complicated rituals of the Church. "Men ought always to pray," said Jesus, "and not to faint" (*Luke* 18:1). In a sense it was as simple as that, and as demanding. Offices, dogmas, ceremonies—in Gregory's eyes none of these was so important as the ceaseless stream of prayer mounting upward to God. Only by prayer could a man see God and bathe in the light of the Transfiguration. Only by prayer could his wounds be healed and his salvation be assured. In the quietness of his chamber, in absolute isolation and silence, a man could enjoy the spiritual life to the full, serving God in perpetual contemplation of His glory. By "the care of the heart," by becoming detached from all created things, losing consciousness of himself and being wholly absorbed in the contemplation of God, a man could make the leap into the infinite, passing altogether beyond the world and its cares, wholly losing himself in the blessedness of the divine image. At the end of the road was God, and man had only to hurl himself along the road of prayer to see God's face.

Such a belief in the efficacy of prayer was not new. What was new was the temper of Gregory's mind, his concept of prayer as a kind of glory, a beam of light joining the divine image in man to the divine image in God. In the darkest depths of contemplation, when a man has withdrawn completely from the world into a perfect ecstasy of the spirit, then, according to Gregory, God makes Himself known, the darkness falls away, there is only the beckoning light of God framed in dark fire. Gregory believed that this light which a man sees when he dives deep within himself—that glittering treasure chest, jewel-encrusted and sparkling with blinding rays—was God Himself. If a man prayed with perfect simplicity of heart, repeating over and over the words: "Lord Jesus Christ, have mercy on me; Son of God, help me!" then he was performing the supreme act for which he was created, for he found himself at last within the same light which shone on Mount Tabor during the Transfiguration.

By granting once more the primacy to prayer, Gregory subtly altered the course of the development of the Eastern Church. Origen believed that at the heart of the mystery lay the Incarnation. Many Fathers believed that the Passion lay at the heart of the mystery. For Gregory the heart of the mystery was revealed at that moment, in time and eternity, when the Transfiguration took place. At that moment, comparable to the moment when Moses ascended Mount Sinai, the Word was revealed, for Jesus showed himself for the first and last time in the pure and perfect light of His divinity.

Long ago, at the time of Chrysostom, Cassian of Marseilles had introduced the idea that holiness attended upon the ceaseless repetition of the prayer from the *Psalms:* "O God, make speed to save: O Lord, make haste to help me." He wrote at great length upon the virtues of this prayer, with such grace and eloquence that the Church still begins every office with this versicle. In the sixth century St. John of the Ladder spoke of those prayers which are summoned by the divine fire: "When the fire descends into the heart, then prayer is revived, and when the prayer has risen and ascended to heaven, then the descent of the fire takes place in the chamber of the soul" (*Scala,* XXVIII, 45). The mystics examined the intricacies of prayer; they discussed at what hours of the day, and in what position a man might best pray. They inquired into the techniques of prayer with immense penetration and great learning, until prayer like ritual seemed in danger of losing its innocence. It was left to a remarkable mystic and visionary known as St. Symeon the New Theologian, born about A.D. 949 in Paphlagonia, to crystallize a form of prayer adopted by the monks of Mount Athos. It was a very simple form of prayer. It consisted of sitting in the dark, breathing lightly, head bowed, saying over and over again: "Lord Jesus, Son of God, have mercy upon me."

In the *Logos* of St. Symeon the New Theologian there is a discussion on the nature of the vision between the master and his pupil, remarkable for an astonishing impression of authenticity:

"My child, tell me what you saw there."
"I saw a light, my father, and very sweet."
"Sweet, was it? Can you explain it?"
"I have no skill to explain it, father," he said, and as he spoke his heart leaped, and he was on fire with the things he had seen. Hot tears were falling down his cheeks.

"O my father," he went on, "when this light came to me, the space of my cell was lifted away, and the world also, and it seemed to me I was left alone in this light, and I did not know, my father, where my body was, or whether I was still in the cell. I did not know whether I still wore my body. I knew only that I was wrapped around in a nameless joy, and love and immense desire were within me, and that is why I am weeping. I said to this light: 'Are you my God?' And the light said: 'Yes, I am God who became man for your sake, and I have made you and I shall make you into a God.' Then I said: 'Have pity on me, Son of God, and open the eyes of my soul, so that I shall see the light of the world and become a son of the divine day, and do not let me, dear God, be unworthy of a part of your divinity. Show yourself to me, so that I know you love me, O Lord, for having kept the sacraments; and send to me too, O merciful One, the Paraclete, so that He may teach me the knowledge of God and tell me the secrets that lie hidden in all things, and let the true light shine on me, so that I may see the glory, that glory which was there before the world began, and deign, O invisible One, to take shape within me, so that seeing your incomprehensible beauty, I shall possess your image and forget all the visible world; and grant me the glory the Father granted unto you, so that I can become like unto you, as are your servants, becoming myself a God by divine grace; and let me be with you always and in all the ages to come.'"

St. Symeon the New Theologian spoke with the authority of a mystic too much in love with God to abide theologians. For centuries there had been earnest discussions into the nature of God. St. Symeon simply laughed at them: it was only necessary to know God; to inquire into the mysteries of His Being was "not only rash, but excessively stupid." "Possess God," he wrote once, "and you will need no books." And to those theologians who denied the body, he answered by announcing the essential corporeal unity of man with Christ.

St. Symeon summed up the whole mystical tradition which derived from the more mysterious statements of Jesus and St. Paul. Clement of Alexandria and Origen had spoken of the mystical communion, by which man could become God. Gregory of Nyssa had spoken of man's supreme endowments before the Fall, as though in the twinkling of an eye man could resume the supreme, godlike powers he once enjoyed. Evagrius Pontus, a student of Gregory of Nyssa, had celebrated the honor of being a man, and Maximus the Confessor, in *The Centuries of Love*, had commented at length upon the text: "Ye are the body of Christ, and members in particular" (*I Cor.* 12:27). Maximus the Confessor went further, for he wrote in his commentary on Dionysius the Areopagite: "We are made gods and sons of God and the body and limbs and the members of God" (P.G. XCI, 1092). All that St. Symeon did was to collect the existing mystical traditions and announce them in a language of great power, devotion and authority, and perhaps borrowing from the East some details of mystical practices. Sitting in the dark room, his lips closed, continually repeating the prayer of Jesus, the monk was bidden to lean forward with his eyes directed toward the navel; then with his mystical eye he was urged to follow the entrails upward toward "the place of the heart." Somewhere in the region of the heart he would find the white-hot center:

> Then let the spirit, having tasted of the goodness of the Saviour, know that it will never again be expelled from the place of the heart, for as the apostle Matthew declared: "It is good to remain here," and so remaining, the spirit gazes about these interior places and strikes out at any enemy who is bold enough to appear. So Ecclesiastes says: "Rejoice, young man, in your youth and march on the wings of the heart."   [*Methodos* 11, 9]

Since the time of St. Symeon these practices had been the commonplace of the monks on the Holy Mountain of Athos. Practices very similar to these had perhaps been performed for centuries. Had not St. Paul said: "Pray without ceasing"? (*I Thess.* 5:17). Soon after the Ascension, Peter declared: "It shall come to pass, that whosoever shall call on the name of the Lord shall be saved" (*Acts,* 2:12). The name of Jesus, which so many millions of men have spoken at the last moments of their lives, possessed a peculiar sanctity. For St. Symeon the word itself was like a beacon leading to the Divine Light. Saying this word, the pure see God on earth, "for God is light and contemplation is like unto light"—φῶς ὁ θέος, και ὡς φῶς ἡ θέα αὐτοῦ. And that light which a man sees in the inmost chamber of his heart is the uncreated light of the Transfiguration, which the apostles on Mount Tabor contemplated with their physical eyes.

Such were the beliefs of the monks of the Holy Mountain, who lived their separate lives in quiet cells, remote from the orthodoxy of Constantinople. Orthodoxy might disapprove, but orthodoxy was not prepared to do battle with the monks, who lived in their *hesychasteria,* those small caves carved out of the precipitous rocks in obscure valleys of Cappadocia and Macedonia, and on the islands of the Aegean. They had put the world behind them. "He who is a monk," said St. Symeon, "keeps himself apart from the world and walks forever with God alone" (P.G. CXX, 516b). It was one of the great classic phrases of Byzantine mysticism, and it struck at the heart of the communal worship of the Orthodox Church. The mystic always lives behind the barricades, his devotion suspect, the violence of his efforts to see the face of God at odds with the calm ritual of the orthodox. But the mystic lives his precarious life alone, and is not usually dangerous to the established order. These monks might have been allowed to live their secluded lives alone and uninterruptedly if there had not come from Calabria a monk called Barlaam or Barlaamo who questioned their practices and denounced them as heretics. Against Barlaamo, Gregory Palamas, a monk of Mount Athos, arose with astonishing skill to defend the mysticism of the East against the rationalism of the West. He was to become the last of the Fathers. Nine years after his death, he was proclaimed "the greatest among the Fathers of the Church."

Gregory Palamas was born A.D. 1292 in Constantinople. His father and mother came originally from Anatolia. At the time of his birth his father was a member of the Senate, a close friend and adviser of the Emperor Andronicus II Paleologus. His mother, who entered a nunnery, died when he was seven. She was a gifted and highly intelligent woman, of a deeply religious character, and Gregory seems to have remembered her vividly for the rest of his life, his worship of the Virgin colored by the memory of her grace and beauty. At her death, the boy became the ward of the Emperor, who supervised the education of the five children, three boys and two girls, of the old Senator. Like his younger brothers, he was destined to become a high official at Court. The highest offices of the land were open to him through his father. The family seems to have lived in close intimacy with the gently and pious Emperor, Andronicus II Paleologus, of whom it was remarked that he was an incompetent ruler, though he would have made an admirable professor of divinity. The Emperor was charming, well-read, generous, and wholly under the influence of his second wife, Yolande de Montferrat.

The great Byzantine Empire had already perished; what remained were a few outposts in Asia Minor, a few islands, and a wide swath of land stretching across what is now southern Yugoslavia and northern Greece. The French were in Athens and Thebes; the Venetians ruled Crete and Euboea; the Ottoman Turks had already swallowed nine-tenths of Asia Minor; and the Serbs were threatening to pour through the mountain defiles on all the European territories of the Empire. Constantinople was an old and venerable city, ruled by intrigue.

In the capital of an Empire falling into ruins, Gregory spent his childhood. The old Church rituals were still being performed in Hagia Sophia, but the most beautiful Church in Christendom was falling into decay. The Emperor, descended from four imperial families, went through the motions of reigning, attired in imperial vestments. He gave orders to his generals to attack the enemies of the Empire, but he had no interest in war and seemed not to know that the frontiers were being breached. A contemporary historian said he gave the appearance "of being asleep or else of being dead." Against the doddering Emperor there arose a band of desperate men, led by John Cantacuzene, who were determined not to allow the Empire to perish through the Emperor's inactivity, Suddenly, in 1328, they captured Constantinople, deposed the Emperor, placed his grandson on the throne under the title of Andronicus III, and attempted, though rarely successfully, to stem the tide. Andronicus II disappeared into a monastery, where he was known as "the monk Antony."

Gregory Palamas took no part in the wars against Andronicus II. At some early period in his life he met John Cantacuzene, and they liked each other and remained close friends to the end. When he thought of those early days in Constantinople, Gregory remembered how empty it was in summer and autumn; then the great imperial city was abandoned, while the people worked in the fields, harvesting and wine making. He studied deeply, especially in the works of Aristotle, but neither Aristotle nor court life pleased him. When he was twenty—or according to some records twenty-two—he abruptly left Constantinople and settled among the communities of monks on Mount Athos, which Andronicus II in a golden bull had described as "the second paradise, starry heaven and refuge of all virtues." With Gregory went his two brothers Macarius and Theodore.

On Mount Athos the monks lived lives of serene contemplation. No women were allowed on the mountain; no female animals. The life of the monks was strenuous and masculine. The three brothers put themselves under the monk Theoleptus, later to become Metropolitan of Philadelphia. There, for eight years they remained, training themselves in the practice of unceasing prayer. John Cantacuzene, who refers to Gregory admiringly in his *History,* says that two of Gregory's teachers died and on the death of the second the brothers left Mount Athos as abruptly as they left Constantinople. They went to live, like the hermits of old, in a high mountain cave at Berea, on the frontiers of Macedonia and Thrace. Gregory's austerities in the harsh Macedonian winters impaired his health, and he never completely recovered from an intestinal disease acquired during those early years of self-mortification. After ten years of living in mountain caves he returned to Mount Athos, where he was soon recognized as a spiritual leader, devoted to the Virgin and the name of Jesus. During this period he began to write the homilies and sermons on the Light of the Transfiguration which brought him into the forefront of the doctrinal battle which broke out a few years later.

We have no portrait of him made in his lifetime. Shortly after his death, when his memory was still fresh, an unknown artist painted him on an icon. The painting shows him dark-skinned, like most Anatolians, with enormous eyes deep-set beneath arching brows, a rounded forehead, a nose which is long and thin like a knife blade, and the small lips are pressed together as though in suffering. There is about the grave face within the golden halo a suggestion of wonder caught on the wing, as though the artist depicted him at the moment when he was describing to himself those visions which he described so often in his works. The painting shows him wearing the *omphorion* and *sakkos* of an archbishop, his right hand is raised in blessing, his left holds a jewel-studded Gospel. An inscription reads: "Our Father among the holy names."

Alone in his cell on Mount Athos, he wrote angelically. He seems to have written with immense speed, the pen hardly touching the paper. And always there is that awareness of light, that light which the Greeks worshiped from the early beginnings. That adoration of

the light of God and of the sun and of definition he shared with
Homer and Pindar and Gregory Nazianzen:

ποίησον δ' αἴθρην, δὸς δ' ὀφθαλμοῖσιν ἰδέσθαι
ἐν δε φάει καὶ ὄλεσσον—

*Make the sky clear, and grant us to see with our eyes.
In the light be it, though thou slay us.*

So Ajax prays to Zeus in the *Iliad*, and it wells up from the very
depths of the Greek consciousness. But for Gregory Palamas the
supreme light was that which shone on Mount Tabor, the same light
which streams in radiance across Heaven. Listen to him as he describes the Virgin standing beside Her Son in the shining Heavens:

The death of the Virgin was for her the beginning of life, bringing her to a heavenly and immortal life. Now the whole heavens
are her abiding place, a palace worthy of her dignity. There she
was removed from the earth and took her place on the right hand
of the Emperor of All, wearing her many-colored and golden robe,
according to the Psalmist who has spoken of these things. And
this golden robe is no more than her body gleaming with divine
lights, and decorated with the flowers of her virtue. And she together with her Son are now the only ones to live in the glory of
Heaven.

For neither the earth, nor the sepulcher, nor death itself had
power to hold her body, which is the fountain of life and the dwelling place of the divine, a place more joyful than Heaven or the
Heaven of Heavens. . . . So the body of the Mother is glorified
with the same glory which falls about the body of the Son. . . .
And for her it was not necessary that she should live on earth for
a little while after death, and so she was removed instantly to the
Heavens, leaving behind her the clothes she wore in the tomb.

[*In Dormitionum Deiparae,* P. G. CLI, 464-68]

In the works of Gregory Palamas the words *beauty, splendor, glory,
light, the light of lights* are continually repeated. Like Athanasius, he
sees the universe charged with the energy of the Incarnation, but he also
sees it charged with the beauty of the Virgin. The earth is a divine
place, the beauty of it is almost too much to be borne. The light of the
Transfiguration did not cease; it continues always. "Certain saints," he
wrote, "after the Coming of Christ in the flesh see this light like an

endless sea flowing miraculously from a single sun, which is the adored Body of Christ." For him "the Holy Name contains within itself that divine energy which penetrates and changes a man's heart when it is diffused throughout his body." He believed that men are endowed with a divine breath which moves within their physical bodies, and the body acquires holiness by this divine breath pouring into it. The body is not evil; and even the Fall of Man was not entirely evil, for there would have been no Christ without the sin of Adam. He believed that from the first moment of His existence on earth Christ lived within the beatific vision, and he believed that the Virgin died only because it was neces- sary that she should share the suffering of Her Son. He saw no reason to disbelieve in angels, and in his devotional works dedicated to the Virgin he describes how from the age of three she lived in the Holy of Holies of the Temple in Jerusalem, fed by the angels. For him God was not merely essence; He was also energy; and though the essence re- mained incommunicable, the energy could be perceived by human eyes, in exactly the same way that no man can stare at the sun, but he is aware of its light.

Again and again Gregory Palamas celebrates man. Like many Fathers he believed the human body to be a divine image, a simulacrum of divinity. "The name of man is not given separately to the body and the soul," he wrote, "but to both together, for together, they have been created in the image of God."[1] Like Cyril of Jerusalem, born nearly a thousand years before, he refused to believe the body was the cause of sin:

> Tell me not that the body is the cause of sin. For if the body is the cause of sin, then why does not a dead body sin? Put a sword in the right hand of a man just dead; no murder takes place. Let the most beautiful woman pass before a youth just dead; no desire arises in him. And why is this? It is because the body does not sin of itself, but the soul sins through the body. The body is an instru- ment, and as it were a garment and robe of the soul. . . . Be

[1] I suspect that Gregory Palamas and William Blake would have agreed on many things. Blake preached that the only way to the spirit was through the body, and regarded it with as much reverence as the soul because the body is part of the soul. "Man has no body apart from his soul," Blake wrote, "for that called body is a part of the soul discerned by the five senses, the chief inlets of soul in this age." And again: "If the doors of perception were cleansed, everything would appear to man as it is, infinite."

tender therefore to thy body, as being a temple of the Holy Ghost.
[Cyril of Jerusalem, *Catechetical Lectures,* IV, 22]

Gregory Palamas rejoiced in comparing man to light: "Man being
himself a light, he holds up his light to see the Light, and looking into
himself, he looks upon the Light, and if he looks further, then also he
sees the Light, and always he sees by virtue of the Light, and therefore
there is communion, and all is one." The word *light* is so often repeated
in his pages that they seem to dance and quiver with the beams of light
he saw in his cell in the Holy Mountain.

No one, not even Pico della Mirandola, "the earl of Mirandolle and
lord of Italy," the young and handsome Renaissance humanist who
wrote a *Very Elegant Speech on the Dignity of Man,* celebrated man so
highly. The phrase for which Gregory Palamas was to become most
famous was one of breathtaking simplicity: "Man, by virtue of the
honor of the body created in the likeness of God, is higher than the
angels."

The theology of Gregory Palamas did not spring fully armed from
his contemplative spirit alone; it had its roots in the long history of
Eastern Christianity. He was not the first to say that man occupies a
place of unexampled splendor and importance: otherwise Christ would
not have assumed the flesh of man. Athanasius in *De Incarnatione* had
hinted at the supreme importance of man. St. Macarius, a hermit living
in the Nitrian desert during the lifetime of Athanasius, declared it
openly:

Look how mighty are the heavens and earth, the sun and the
moon! But it was not in these that the Lord rested. Man therefore
is of more value than all creatures, and I dare to say he is more
valuable than any creature, visible or invisible, more valuable than
the ministering angels. When God said: "Let us make man in our
image, after our likeness," he was not speaking of the Archangels
Michael and Gabriel; he was speaking about the spiritual substance
of man, his immortal soul.   [*Fifty Spiritual Homilies,* XV, 22]

Gregory Palamas said that man, body and soul, was higher than the
angels. From the soul came a divine energy which was continually
being poured into the body; and the incorporeal angels, though closer
to God, are deprived of that vessel into which the divine energy is
poured. "Man," said St. Basil, "is a creature who has received the order
to become a god." Gregory Palamas answers that he becomes a god

when he practices meditation and sees in the place of the heart the blazing light of the Transfiguration.

In Gregory Palamas the long debate which revolved around the question whether God could or could not be comprehended came to an end. The question had plagued the Eastern Church through all its history. Because the grace of God is made visible in the uncreated Light which wells up in "the place of the heart," and because the monks, and most especially the saints, enjoy this grace in their deepest meditations, Gregory concluded that God was indeed visible, for He was this Light, but in another sense. He remained eternally invisible, for the greatest saints never claimed they had seen the essence of God. The face of God remained veiled by its own shining, and no mortal man had ever seen His face. The classic statement in which Gregory Palamas resolved the quarrel reads simply:

> We may not participate in the divine nature, and yet in a certain sense we may readily participate in His nature; for we enter into this communion with God, and at the same time God remains entirely inaccessible. So we affirm these two contrary things at one and the same time, and we rejoice in this antinomy as a criterion of truth.   [P.G. CL, 932 D]

Though the statement is simple, he did not come to it by any easy path. By long meditations on the glory of the Virgin, by long reading of the Bible and the Fathers, Gregory Palamas came to a conclusion which threatened the established Church, for he placed the Transfiguration above all the acts of Jesus—even above the Eucharist. "The light of Tabor," he wrote once, "is the Kingdom of God." It was not a sudden light: it was without end or beginning, uncircumscribed in time and place, and imperceptible to the ordinary senses; and yet it was known; and men who were living had seen it, and been deified by it, because they had partaken of the energy of God. So the disciples, standing on Mount Tabor, had seen the Light and become celestial beings, for their flesh, as they gazed on the Light, was transmuted into spirit. This blinding Light was seen by St. Paul at Damascus, by Elijah when he was lifted up in a chariot of fire and by Moses when he stood beside the burning bush. And how shall one seek this Light? Above all, by repentance, by calling upon the Name of Jesus and demanding pity of the Holy Name:

> This Light shines already in the darkness, in the night and the day, in our hearts, in our spirits. It shines down on us, this Light

without turning or change or any decline, unalterable, never eclipsed. It speaks and acts and lives and gives forth life, and whatever it touches it transforms into Light. God is Light, and those who are worthy to set eyes on Him see Him as Light; and those who have received Him receive Him as Light. The Light of His glory streams from His face, and therefore it is not possible to see Him otherwise than as Light, and those who have never seen this Light have never seen God, for God is indeed this Light. And those who have not seen this Light have not yet received God's grace, for on receiving the grace we receive the divine grace. . . . Those who do not receive this Light remain in the world of shadows and images, and are still enslaved. Kings and patriarchs, bishops and priests, princes and attendants, monks and laymen, they all live in the darkness and walk among shadows until they have shown a contrite heart. For Contrition is the gate which leads from darkness into Light, and those who have not yet passed worthily through the gate have not yet entered into the Light.

[Symeon the New Theologian, *Hom.* LXXIX, 2]

Throughout the work of Gregory Palamas and St. Symeon the New Theologian one is made aware of an extraordinary sense of exaltation. As they speak of the Light of God, the *illuminatio divina,* it becomes almost tangible; it gleams, shines, bursts into a thousand separate particles; and the world is clothed with it. The monks of the Eastern Empire seem to have passed through one of those rare periods when joy seems to have come down to earth, and we are reminded of the Fujiwara epoch in Japan, the Gupta epoch in India which saw the birth of the caves of Ajanta, and those days when St. Francis was walking through the fields of Assisi and all over France cathedrals were rising "like flowers."

Something of this same exaltation can be seen in the works of Nicholas Cabasilas, originally an opponent and later a close friend of Gregory Palamas. Two years younger than Gregory, a close friend of John Cantacuzene, he was at once a man of action and a man of contemplation; and though a profound theologian, he remained a layman to the end. Among a host of books, mostly remaining in manuscript, he wrote two books of immense importance: *The Life in Christ,* and *An Interpretation of the Sacred Liturgy.* Both are filled with that sense of soaring exaltation which is characteristic of Byzantine theology in the years before the fall of the Byzantine Empire. Hear him as he describes the infinite love of God for mankind:

God pours Himself out in an ecstasy of love. He does not remain in the Heavens and call to Himself the Servant He loves. No, He Himself descends and searches out for such a servant, and comes near, and lets His love be seen, as He seeks what is like Himself. From those who despise Him He does not depart; He shows no anger toward those who defy Him, but follows them to their very doors, and endures all things, and even dies, in order to demonstrate His love. All this is true, but we have not yet declared the highest thing of all: for not merely does God enter into close fellowship with His servants and extend to them His hand, but He has given Himself wholly to us, so that we are become temples of the living God, and our members are the members of Christ. The Head of these members is worshiped by the Cherubim, and these hands and feet are joined to that heart.

[*Sacrae liturgiae interpretatio*, II, 132]

The music is more somber than Gregory's, and yet there is a piercing joy in it. He shares with Gregory a profound belief in the dignity of man, and where Gregory sees the torrent of light falling on Mount Tabor, Cabasilas is more likely to see the beauty of Christ under the Heavenly Light. "Christ by His beauty overcame the world," Cabasilas wrote once; and the phrase summed up many of his meditations. Listen to him again as he describes Christ after the Ascension, still wearing His royal wounds:

Not only did He suffer the most terrible torments and receive agonizing wounds, but when He had returned to life and stolen His body away from corruption, he kept His wounds and wore their scars on His flesh; and with them He showed Himself to the angels, so that His wounds were like an adornment, and He was pleased to show the marks of His suffering. And all this happened when His body was glorified, without weight or dimension or any corporeal accident; and yet He never desired to put His wounds away or renounce His scars, believing He should preserve them by reason of His love for mankind, by Him regained by virtue of those wounds, because these deathly hurts allowed Him to conquer the object of His love. How otherwise can we explain the presence on His glorified body of wounds which nature or the art of medicine have sometimes been able to remove from mortal and corruptible bodies? One might almost say He wanted to suffer again and again for our sakes; but since this became impossible when His body was removed from all corruptibility, and also to spare his executioners, he decided to keep on His body the proofs of His sacrifice and always to preserve the scars of those wounds, received once on the Tree of Crucifixion. So, in glory, He will be recognized after the event as the One who was crucified, whose side was pierced on behalf of slaves, and He will wear those scars eternally as a royal ornament.   [De Vita in Christo, VI, 1]

So often in reading the Eastern Fathers we are aware of veils which have suddenly vanished, revealing the entire mystery. A word, a phrase, a juxtaposition of texts—and we are suddenly transposed into a region where everything is comprehensible and the most secret mysteries are suddenly made plain. Sometimes Cabasilas says simple things simply, in a way which illuminates whole landscapes. "There was need," he wrote in The Life in Christ, "that God and man should form an alliance in a single person, one to fight, the other to conquer. And so it happened: God took the part of man, for He was man; and man, free of all sin, triumphed over sin, for he was God; and therefore sin was destroyed and man received the crown of victory." With such simplicities Cabasilas described the Kingdom of Heaven.

At the beginning of The Life in Christ Cabasilas announced his aim: to show that "to live in Christ is the very union with Christ," and nothing less than union with Christ is desirable:

For Christ gives men life and growth and nourishment and light and breath, and opened their eyes, and gave them light and the power to see. He gives men the bread of life, and this bread is nothing else than Himself; He is life for those who are living and perfume for those who breathe; He clothes those who desire to be clothed; He upholds the wayfarer, and He is the Way; He is at once the inn upon the road and the end of the journey. When we fight, He fights by our side. When we dispute, He is the arbiter. And when we win the victory, He is the prize.
     [De Vita in Christo, I, 1]

Here the wheel turns full circle, for Gregory's God "who is seen and not seen" is the same as the God of Cabasilas, who "is at once the inn upon the road and the end of the journey."

These quiet meditations of the Byzantine theologians might have continued uninterruptedly, if there had not arrived in Constantinople about 1327 a Calabrian monk who threw the Byzantine Church into a violent quarrel with itself. The Church split. There were those who were on the side of Gregory Palamas and those who opposed him. The opponents of Gregory were led by this strange monk, whose purposes remained obscure to the end.

Bernardo Barlaamo was born, apparently of Greek parentage, in Seminara in Calabria, in southern Italy. He lived for a while at the Papal Court in Avignon, where he met Petrarch, who studied Greek under him. In a letter Petrarch wrote: "Barlaamo is most excellent in Greek eloquence, and very poor in Latin; rich in ideas, and quick in mind. When he spoke in Latin, you could see from the expression on his face that he hated being unable to express himself." He did not teach Petrarch for long, and the poet never succeeded in reading Greek literature in the original. Boccaccio, who encountered Barlaamo during his travels, reported that he was "a man with a small body but enormous knowledge, an author deeply versed in history, philosophy and the Greek language, and he understood Euclid, Aristotle and Plato perfectly." Boccaccio's recommendation appears in his book *The Genealogy of the Gods,* but it is not clear how Boccaccio, who knew very little Greek, arrived at his judgment of the man.

Barlaamo was excellently connected, his erudition was well-known and on his arrival in Constantinople he was treated royally. He spoke often of his affection for the Greek Church, and wrote books against the doctrinal errors of the West. The Grand Domestic and the Emperor were both impressed by his eloquence, his quick mind, his immense learning.[1] They obtained for him the position of abbot in the

[1] Writing toward the end of his life, John Cantacuzene remembered the arrival of Barlaamo:

"A certain monk named Barlaamo, a native of Calabria (brought up among the customs and habits of the Latins), a small man of great promptness in understanding and a considerable eloquence, well-known for his studies of Euclid, Aristotle and Plato, came to this earth to our misery, sowing the seeds of disturbance in our peaceful church. He pretended to be obedient to our discipline, and to show us how completely he had renounced the Latins, he wrote books which claimed to demonstrate their errors, and he did this so well that he earned the affection of the Emperor [Andronicus III] and the Grand Domestic [John Cantacuzene]."

[*Hist.* I, ii, 39]

Church of the Holy Ghost, and there he remained, studying earnestly, continually moving in court circles, a small wizened friendly man who gave all the appearance of being a convert from the Roman faith to the faith of Byzantium. He might have remained there indefinitely if he had not engaged in an argument with the powerful scholar, Nicephorus Gregoras. Defeated in the argument, he decided to leave Constantinople, and he next appears in Thessalonica. There, in 1330, he opened a school and taught logic, astronomy, mathematics, Platonism and Aristotelian dialectics.

According to the Greek historians, Barlaamo was a man who desired power above all things, and was bitterly incensed because he had not received high preferment in Constantinople. It was the time when the doctrine of *hesychia* was being widely discussed, and Barlaamo seems to have decided that by attacking the doctrine he might be able to assume a position of leadership in the Church. He paid a short visit to Mount Athos, and returned to his school, where he delivered a sweeping condemnation of the contemplative practices of the monks, saying that the monks were defying accepted church doctrine and claiming that they could see with their corporeal eyes the uncreated light which shone on Mount Tabor. According to Barlaamo, the monks rested their beards on their chests, settled their eyes on their navels and went into a profound sleep. Afterward they talked of nothing else but "the separations and reunions of the soul, the soul's commerce with demons and the differences between white and pink lights." Barlaamo was deliberately attempting to reduce a contemplative practice to nonsense, and there was some danger that a few monks might be won over to his position. Gregory Palamas, who was then on Mount Athos, sailed for Thessalonica and arranged a meeting with Barlaamo in 1337. The meeting seems to have been friendly. Gregory Palamas explained the doctrine at some length. He told Barlaamo: "The greater part of mankind regards you as a famous scholar, and everyone praises you. So cultivate learning and writing, teach philosophy and the profane wisdom you know well, and then there will be no one who will not listen to you and follow you, and there will be no disagreement with you, and you will enjoy ever-increasing fame." He told Barlaamo bluntly that he must have gotten his information on the doctrine from a monk of quite astonishing naïveté. Later John Cantacuzene said the monk who taught Barlaamo must have been "completely mad, and not very far from being an animal." Barlaamo thereupon agreed to make no further attacks upon the doctrine of *hesychia*.

Two years later, in 1339, Barlaamo headed a mission to Pope Benedict XII in Avignon. He was charged to arrange with the Pope the sending of military assistance against the Turks and the forming of an ecumenical council to settle the doctrinal differences between East and West. It was an important charge. Barlaamo went to Avignon with the blessing of the Emperor Andronicus III and the Grand Domestic, John Cantacuzene, and though the mission was a failure, he returned to the school in Thessalonica with his missionary zeal unimpaired and his reputation untarnished.

At this point the controversy might have died down. There seemed no reason why it should continue. Suddenly, in a number of tracts which followed quickly one after another, Barlaamo bitterly attacked the doctrine of *hesychia* all over again. He could hardly have chosen a worse time. The monks closed their ranks behind Gregory Palamas, who issued a counterstatement in three parts, answering all Barlaamo's charges. Barlaamo appealed directly to the Emperor, and was summoned to Constantinople. There, in Hagia Sophia, at a synod attended by the Emperor and the Patriarch John Kalekas, Barlaamo and Gregory faced each other.

It was a confrontation of quite unusual importance. An ancient teaching had emerged in a new dress; thousands of monks believed this teaching to represent a continual tradition in the Eastern Church. A cleric, trained in the courts of the West, was singlehandedly attempting to destroy a doctrine which represented the deep-lying mysticism of the East. The small Calabrian was opposed by the heavy-built monk from Athos, who bore no title except that of presbyter but already was recognized as the spokesman and leader of the monastic movement throughout the Empire.

The synod met on a sweltering hot day in June. The Emperor attended in tiara and gold vestments. He announced that a decision must be rendered that same day.

Barlaamo was allowed to speak against the errors of Gregory. He attacked the doctrine mercilessly, employing the same brutally concise arguments he had employed in his tracts. Then Gregory rose to address the assembly. He answered Barlaamo's argument point by point. He explained that theology was not dependent upon logic or geometry, those two sciences in which Barlaamo was an adept. "Those human sciences no longer apply in these divine matters which are so far beyond our knowing," Gregory said. "We must go to the Fathers, those holy men who are filled with the holy spirit and who have penetrated the mysteries of God." Then he went on to deny the primacy of science in all respects. What has Euclid to say concerning the nature of God? Shall we listen to Aristotle when we have the Gospel before us? And then he went on to talk once again about the uncreated Light which shone on the face of Christ at Mount Tabor—"that Light which is the glory of God, without end, and the splendor of divinity, divine and eternal, uncreated, being itself the majesty of God." Then he presented the Emperor with a book written by the monks of the Holy Mountain, filled with quotations from the Fathers refuting the doctrines of Barlaamo. Barlaamo turned to the Grand Domestic and appealed for advice. "It would be better if you were humble and acknowledged the merit of the monks," John Cantacuzene answered. Barlaamo seems to have been afraid he would be punished. He announced that he accepted Gregory's arguments: the Light of the Transfiguration was indeed the uncreated and eternal Light, and theology was indeed incapable of scientific interpretation. Then Gregory embraced him, pardoned him and praised him. But in their hurry to bring the synod to an end, the Emperor and the bishops in council forgot, or perhaps deliberately refrained, from passing any formal judgment on Barlaamo. Gregory was annoyed: he had expected a complete repudiation of Barlaamo's arguments. Instead they were merely condemned in a halfhearted manner, and to sweeten the condemnation Barlaamo was sent on another embassy to Benedict XII.

For a moment—for a very brief moment—the battle between Gregory and Barlaamo had been won. Barlaamo went abroad, the monks continued their contemplative practices, and the Empire, though threatened on all sides, was at peace. Suddenly the blow fell. Four days after the meeting of the synod, on June 15, 1341, Andronicus III, who had been in excellent health, died. He seems to have died naturally, of a heart attack, for no one ever suggested that he was poisoned or murdered. His death was like the stroke of an ax which sets an avalanche in motion. With him the Empire perished, though the ghostly remnant of it survived until the final assault by Mahomet II in 1453.

With the death of Andronicus III, the quarrel broke out afresh. With Barlaamo absent, the battle was fought between Greek and Greek; and in the highest circles of the Court, and in the army, and among the Zealots of Thessalonica, there were people who opposed the Prayer of Jesus.

According to the Emperor's will, his ten-year-old son, John V Paleologus, was to be reared by the Grand Domestic, who was to have complete charge of his education. The boy was intelligent, and divided his affections between his mother and his father's closest adviser. For the last eight or nine years the Grand Domestic, John Cantacuzene, with complete control over internal and foreign affairs had ruled the Empire in the Emperor's name. Andronicus III was weak and vacillating. He liked hunting and leading his armies to battle, but took little delight in the day-to-day management of an empire. He was gay, pleasure-loving and possessed little interest in the theological disputes which accompanied the emergence of the doctrine of *hesychia* as part of the recognized cult of the Byzantine Church. He sided at all times with the Grand Domestic, but he did little to discourage his mother and his second wife, Anne of Savoy, from forming a cabal against his chief minister. When he died at the age of forty-five, John Cantacuzene found himself surrounded by enemies at court. In fear of his life, he slipped out of Constantinople, raised an army and proclaimed himself Emperor in Thrace. Shortly afterward the boy Emperor John V Paleologus was solemnly crowned in Constantinople. Then there were two Emperors, and the country was plunged into civil war.

The fine-drawn ascetic features of John Cantacuzene, with his soaring forehead, deep-set eyes and small pointed beard stare out of the Byzantine miniatures of the time. They do not suggest a man with an overriding obsession for power. Gregory Palamas speaks of him as a friend who was deeply religious and contemplative, gentle and unassuming, faithful to the Church. John Cantacuzene wrote later that he was compelled to draw the sword in honor of Byzantine traditions. He argued that he had no alternative but to proclaim himself Emperor, to save the country from the malice of Anne of Savoy, who had been brought up in the Latin Church. He claimed that she was surrounded by sycophants, and that her reign, as regent of the boy Emperor, would have been disastrous for Byzantine civilization. At this late date we cannot judge the moral issues. Yet it is certain that by plunging the country into civil war John Cantacuzene signed the death warrant of the thousand-year-old Empire founded by Constantine. From this time onward the Eastern Empire ran swiftly to its decline.

The civil war lasted for five and a half years. In 1342 the Zealots, who practiced a form of communism, expelled the nobles and the church dignitaries from Thessalonica, and proclaimed the republic. The Turks pressed on the frontiers, and Stephen Dushan at the head of his Serbian armies was overrunning Macedonia. John Cantacuzene was in urgent need of assistance. Stephen Dushan demanded the whole of the Byzantine Empire west of Thessalonica as a reward for his assistance. The eagle was dying. Serbs, Turks and Bulgarians were feeding on it, and each of them wanted the largest share of the spoils.

Gregory Palamas was living on Mount Athos when the civil war broke out. Summoned by the Patriarch John Kalekas to Constantinople, he was asked to repeat his doctrinal beliefs. It was Easter, a time of great processions, the boy Emperor solemnly parading through the streets to Hagia Sophia, where the blessing of God was asked for the Paleologi. John Kalekas knew the close friendship which bound Gregory to Cantacuzene. He knew, too, that the Empire was split between the followers of Barlaamo and the followers of Gregory. So he bade Gregory be silent on all doctrinal matters, and ordered him to remain for the duration of the war in a nearby convent. Gregory rejected both these commands. Then he was placed under a solemn interdiction to keep silent, and John Kalekas added that the order for his house arrest had been signed by the Empress. Until June Gregory lived quietly in the suburbs. He wrote no letters, made no attempt to communicate with Cantacuzene and seemed to be withdrawn completely from the world. Suddenly, early in June, he was visited by two church dignitaries sent by the Patriarch with orders to summon him to a council in which his doctrines would be examined. Once again Gregory rejected the command, explaining that he could not defend himself without the help of the monks of Mount Athos. If he stood alone before the council, he would be defeated. He needed books, papers, documents, all the works of the Fathers. Then knowing that he was about to be arrested and perhaps put on trial, he slipped away to Heraclea in Thrace. The police discovered his hiding place in the autumn. He was brought back to Constantinople and kept under house arrest. He was not alone. Thousands of hesychast monks were also being arrested and imprisoned. In May, 1343, he was ordered by the Patriarch to live in the Monastery of the Incomprehensibility, an ironic choice, for in the eyes of the Patriarch he had spoken too often of God's comprehensibility. At some later period he was thrown into prison.

The civil war was being fought vigorously. In 1346, in the hope of making him an ally, John Cantacuzene had offered the Ottoman Emir Orkhan the hand of his daughter Theodora. The Emir Orkhan accepted her, and gave military assistance—six thousand Ottoman troops entered Thrace. For the first time the Turks poured into Europe. With this marriage and this small army the way was prepared for the final invasion of Turkish armies a hundred years later.

In that same year the Patriarch of Constantinople attempted a reconciliation between Anne of Savoy and John Cantacuzene. The Empress was incensed, and turned against the Patriarch, who had hitherto been her loyal supporter. Suddenly she gave orders that Gregory Palamas and all the monks who had been imprisoned should be released. In February, 1347, she convened a synod in her own palace, determined to dethrone the Patriarch. The Empress and the boy Emperor presided over the assembly of bishops, which solemnly deposed the Patriarch for anathematizing Gregory Palamas. The synod deliberated over the whole question of the doctrine of *hesychia*, and for the second time the doctrine received the imperial authority.

Immediately after the synod, while a banquet to celebrate the doctrine was being held in the great Blachernae Palace, rumors reached Constantinople that John Cantacuzene was drawing close to the capital at the head of his armies. For some reason the Empress believed the rumors were invented by the deposed Patriarch, as a ruse to avoid punishment. She ordered that no one pay heed to the rumors. In fact, John Cantacuzene was a day's march away, and he had already arranged with soldiers within the walls to open the Golden Gate when he gave the signal. He appeared outside the walls of Constantinople the following day, the monks streamed into the streets to welcome him and the Empress and the boy Emperor barricaded themselves in the palace. Among those who were sent to assure the Empress that no harm would come to her if she surrendered was the great theologian, Nicholas Cabasilas.

It was a time of terror and riot, of ambush and intrigue. The Empress was afraid John Cantacuzene would sack the city. Instead he made overtures of peace. He announced that he and the boy Emperor would reign as co-Emperors. The coronation took place on the Feast of Constantine and Helena, on May 13, 1347. Eight days later John Cantacuzene announced the marriage of his daughter Helena to the Emperor John V Paleologus. Helena was thirteen, John was fifteen. Now there were two Emperors and three Empresses on the throne. With a galaxy of imperial rulers the Byzantine Empire saluted its decline. One more shattering blow was reserved for the following year: the Black Death, emerging out of Central Asia, reached Constantinople.

Though Gregory Palamas played no part in the war, he ruled the spiritual empire of the monks, who regarded themselves as the allies of Cantacuzene, the representative of the East, against the Empress Anne, who represented the West. He spent the years of the war under house arrest or in prison, but there was a sense in which the war was being fought in defense of his doctrines. The new Patriarch Isidore appointed him to the vacant archbishopric of Thessalonica, but the city was still in the hands of the Zealots, and when Gregory traveled to Thessalonica to take over his see, he was refused admittance. During the following year the city was captured, and then for the first time he sat on the episcopal throne.

Twice there had been synods at which the doctrines of Barlaamo were repudiated, but there were still Greeks who were prepared to launch attacks against the mystical practices of the monks. The most bitter and the most resourceful were Akindynos, the translator of the *Summa* of St. Thomas Aquinas into Greek, and Nicephorus Gregoras, the author of an immense history of the Roman Empire and one of the greatest scholars of his time. Both had been close friends and defenders of Gregory Palamas: during the time of the first synod, Gregory Palamas had been a guest in the house of Akindynos in Constantinople. Gradually they turned against Gregory. Now once again the issue was to be decided. The third and last synod to decide upon the doctrine of *hesychia* met in August, 1351. The two Emperors, the Patriarch and thirty-seven bishops examined the evidence, and found in favor of the Hesychasts. It is possible that they came to this conclusion for reasons which were not entirely connected with doctrinal matters. The Empire was surrounded by enemies. There was desperate need of some spiritual center, around which the defense of the Empire could be justified. The doctrine of *hesychia* represented a last daring attempt to assert the supremacy of Greek doctrine over the West. Gregory Palamas was an Anatolian, belonging to the *terra irridenta* under the control of the Turks; his birth and upbringing in the Court made him in a sense a symbol of the times. Against him were ranged Barlaamo, who came from Italy; Nicephorus Gregoras, who was also an Italian; Akindynos, who was trained in the methods of Western scholasticism and was by origin a Slav.

On August 15, 1351, the decree against Barlaamo's "blasphemies" was proclaimed, and the acts of the synod were solemnly placed on the altar of Hagia Sophia in the presence of the Patriarch, the co-Emperors and the bishops. It was decreed that Barlaamo must be cut off from intercourse with Christians forever "as much for his numerous private faults as for the fact that he described the Light of the Transfiguration of the Lord, which appeared to the blessed disciples ascending the mountain, as created and describable and differing in nothing from the light per-

ceived by the senses" (P.G. CLI, 718-19). To Gregory Palamas the
Light of the Transfiguration was uncreated, beyond all description and
was perceived not by the senses but by "the eyes of the heart." Barlaamo
may not have been aware that he had been anathematized. He had long
ago left Constantinople, and with the help of Petrarch he had been
appointed Bishop of Geraci, in Italy.

Gregory Palamas was now nearly sixty, a man worn thin by illness
and austerities. The doctrinal quarrels had been astonishingly violent,
with no quarter given on either side. The claim that a monk in the
solitude of his cell might enjoy communion with the uncreated Light
of the Transfiguration was greeted by the followers of Barlaamo with
bitter scorn. Nicephorus Gregoras described the contemplative monks:
"They eat more than pigs, drink more than elephants, and when they
have awakened out of their stupor and recovered their senses, they
say they have penetrated the deepest mysteries and possess the gift of
prophecy." Now the war of words and doctrines and spiritual forces
was over, and Gregory Palamas may have looked forward to spending
his remaining years in peaceful contemplation. He was to have little
rest in the few years left to him.

From the Synod of Constantinople, he made his way to Thessalonica,
arriving there when Thrace was being threatened with invasion by
armies of Bulgarians, Albanians and Turks. He turned back and sailed
for Mount Athos. He had put everything behind him: episcopal power,
his friendship with the two Emperors, his keenness in debate, his sense
of his place in history. From Mount Athos he watched, as from an
immense distance, the stormy career of the Emperor John VI Cantacuzene, who had elected to be a co-Emperor on condition that "the
younger must always defer to the elder." The two Emperors quarreled.
Suddenly John Cantacuzene deposed John Paleologus and proclaimed
his own son Matthew co-Emperor and heir, and Matthew was crowned
in Hagia Sophia. In 1353, when Gregory Palamas was ill on Mount
Athos, there came news of a reconciliation between John Cantacuzene
and John Paleologus. Gregory Palamas was overjoyed, rose from his
sickbed and made his way to Constantinople to offer his gratitude to the
Emperors for composing their differences peacefully. On the way his
ship was attacked and captured by Ottoman pirates. He was put in
chains, starved and beaten. At last he was taken to the Turkish capital
in Asia Minor and brought before the Emir's eldest son and cruelly
treated, but shortly afterward he was allowed to live quietly in the
Monastery of St. Hyacinth in Nicaea until money could be raised for

his ransom. Nicaea, only a few miles from Constantinople, was now within the frontiers of the Turkish Empire.

Late the next year, when the money for his ransom was being raised by friendly Serbs, the Byzantine Empire was once more in convulsions. John Cantacuzene had come to power by wars of maneuver and surprise. Suddenly John Paleologus began to employ the same methods. In December, 1354, he secretly entered the arsenal at Constantinople at night with the co-operation of the Genoese, who had maintained trading posts and shipbuilding yards in Constantinople since the Crusade of 1204. Then at last John Cantacuzene, after a reign of thirteen years, was compelled to abdicate. The former Grand Domestic, the most superbly intelligent of Byzantine Emperors and the one most responsible for the ruin of the Empire, became a monk, taking the name of Ioasaph Christodule, Joseph the Servant of Christ, while his Empress Irene entered a nunnery under the name of Eugenia. For a few months Matthew continued the war, but at last on the advice of his father he swore an oath of loyalty to John V Paleologus. Matthew and John were nearly the same age; they became close friends. And the long quarrel between the Cantacuzenes and the Paleologi came to an end.

Gregory Palamas entered Constantinople a few days after its capture. There was no rejoicing over his safe arrival, for John V Paleologus had issued stern orders against the Hesychast monks, believing them to have been among the faithful supporters of Cantacuzene. It is possible that he was placed under arrest, for nothing about his life during the following year is known. At last in 1356 he made his way to Thessalonica and resumed the care of his see. There, after months of severe illness, he died on November 14, 1359. Nine years later a special council was convened in Constantinople, at which he was canonized and proclaimed "the greatest among the Fathers of the Church."

The doctrine, which he had celebrated so fervently, did not die with him. It continues to this day, altered and enriched by the theologians who came after him. In the nineteenth century the doctrine especially appealed to the Russian Orthodox Church; the figures of Father Zosima and Alyosha Karamazov in *The Brothers Karamazov* are colored by *hesychia*. On the Sunday of Orthodoxy, when the list of those anathematized by the Greek Church is read, the name of Barlaamo still comes first; and that Sunday the name of Gregory Palamas is praised.

He was the last of the Greek Fathers, the last of those who set their seal imperishably on the mind of the Eastern Church. Like Basil and Athanasius, he stood out at a time of crisis, living violently in two worlds—the world of the spirit and the world of human warfare. Less than a hundred years after his death the great Empire, which once stretched from Spain to Persia, fell before the twenty-five-year-old Sultan Mahomet II, "the precursor of Antichrist and the second Sennacherib." The Emperor Constantine XI, the grandson of John V Paleologus, died heroically, defending his capital at the Roman Gate. The Turks rode into Hagia Sophia and despoiled the altars, ravished and murdered and desecrated until the streets ran with blood and the sky was lit with the bonfires of sacred books.

The earthly beauty perished. How beautiful it had been we know from the accounts of the Fathers and the chroniclers. When a Russian embassy led by Prince Vladimir of Kiev visited Constantinople A.D. 987, the official chronicler reported:

> The Greeks led us to the places where they worship their God, and we knew not whether we were in Heaven or on earth. For on earth there is no such splendor or such beauty, and we are at a loss how to describe it. We know only that God dwells there among men, and the service is fairer than the ceremonies of other nations. For we cannot forget that beauty.[2]

But now it was over, and there were some who said there was no more beauty left on the earth because Hagia Sophia had fallen to the enemy. The center of Eastern Christianity perished, but its death was only the beginning of a new life. In the shuddering silence that followed the fall of Constantinople, it was as though the forces of the Kingdom of God, eternally charged with the energy of the Incarnation, became even vaster, more terrible, more majestic; the Eastern Church was never so strong as when its worshipers and priests were in full flight and its churches were no more than the stableyards of Turkish horses. The time of the martyrs had come back again. "Christ by His beauty overcame the world": and that beauty did not perish before a Sultan's sword. The earthly empire falls, the spiritual empire endures.

And there is a sense in which nothing had perished. The ceremonies remained, and the doctrine, and the Fathers, and the love of God. Long ago Cassiodorus had spoken of the Fathers as "those who have fashioned the ladder by which the angels ascend and descend, and on the Fathers the Lord depends as He stretches His hands to the weary and heavy-laden as they climb toward Him" (*Div. Hist.* P.L. LXX, 1107). Their

[2] S. H. Cross, *The Russian Primary Chronicle* (Cambridge: Harvard University Press, 1930), p. 199.

books had not perished: some were brought to the West long before the fall of Constantinople, others were smuggled out, more remained in the libraries of obscure monasteries. Today, among the papyri buried in the sands of Egypt, still more of their sayings are being discovered.

But it is not their books only that are important. They shed a radiance on the world by the example of their lives. They lived righteously, in superb holiness, at peace with God. They took their stand beyond the earthly hierarchies, aware of the nothingness of the self and the plenitude of God. For them Christ depended on man as much as man depended on Christ: therefore the love between them, and therefore the nothingness of the human creature was made into majesty. They did not so much worship the whole man as the highest part of him, the fierce summit of a man's inmost self, the "place of the heart." In awe and majesty and contrition they developed their theories of the nature of God; and where the Western Church fixed its eyes on the Atonement, the Greek Church saw its highest desire in the Incarnation and the Transfiguration. In the West men wanted to be saved; in the more contemplative East, it was a small thing to be saved if one could meet God face to face. From the Greek Fathers we derive almost all the great doctrines of the Church, and we are their children whether we like it or not.

So they pass before us, the gentle Clement, the stern Origen, the steel-hard Athanasius, the three great Cappadocian Fathers somehow combining into a single figure, fulfilling one another, then the golden stream pouring from the mouth of Chrysostom, and afterward the dark cell where Dionysius the Areopagite stands before the beckoning light; dark-faced John Damascene in his eagle's eyrie; Gregory Palamas striding across the marble floors of the palaces of Constantinople, then vanishing to Mount Athos, the eternal repetition of the Name of Jesus and the ceaseless vigil before the Light of the Transfiguration; and as we watch them, all of them seem to be bathed in the blinding light that shone on Mount Tabor.

To these Fathers is due a portion of the glory in raising the habitations of God; and to them we owe, more than we can guess or ever repay, the strength of our faith.

Chronological Table

A.D.

c. 30	Death of Christ
c. 54-64	Missionary activity of Paul
c. 70-95	Three Gospels written
70	Jerusalem destroyed by Titus
c. 100	Death of St. John the Evangelist
c. 107	Martyrdom of Ignatius
c. 150	Birth of Clement of Alexandria
156	Martyrdom of Polycarp
c. 180	Clement arrives in Alexandria
c. 185	Birth of Origen
c. 190	Clement succeeds Pantaenus as head of catechetical school
202	Persecution of Christians by Severus
203	Origen takes charge of catechetical school
212	Caracalla confers Roman citizenship on all freeborn citizens of the Empire
215	Death of Clement of Alexandria
235	Persecutions by Maximin Thrax
250-51	Decian Persecution
253	Death of Origen in Tyre
257-58	Persecutions by Valerian
270	Death of Plotinus
c. 293	Birth of Athanasius
303	Constantine becomes Emperor
c. 309	St. Anthony founds monachism in Egypt
319	Emergence of Arianism
325	Council of Nicaea
c. 329	Birth of Basil in Caesarea
330	Constantinople formally dedicated as capital of the Empire
c. 330	Gregory Nazianzen born
335	First exile of Athanasius
c. 335	Birth of Gregory of Nyssa
337	Death of Constantine at Nicomedia
339	Birth of Ambrose at Treves

A.D.

340–46 Second exile of Athanasius

342 Birth of Jerome at Strido
Pope Julius holds council in Rome and pronounces innocence of Athanasius

347 John Chrysostom born in Antioch

349–52 Athanasius writes *Apology against the Arians*

c. 351 Basil enters University of Athens

356–61 Third exile of Athanasius

c. 358 Basil's first retirement to Pontus

360 Basil ordained deacon

361 Julian the Apostate becomes Emperor

362 Edict by Julian against Athanasius

363 Death of Julian

364 Death of Jovian
Basil ordained priest

368 Disasters in Cappadocia

370 Basil becomes Bishop of Caesarea

371 Valens divides Caesarea into two sees
Gregory consecrated Bishop of Nyssa

372 Modestus interrogates Basil

373 Death of Athanasius in Alexandria

375 Valentinian II proclaimed Emperor
Goths cross the Danube

378 Valens dies at Adrianople

379 Death of Basil
Gregory Nazianzen appears in Constantinople

381 Gregory of Nyssa attends council in Constantinople

386 John Chrysostom's Five Sermons on the Incomphensibility

387 Baptism of Augustine
Death of Monnica
Riots in Antioch
Chrysostom delivers sermons on the Statues

389 Death of Gregory Nazianzen

396 Death of Gregory of Nyssa

397 Death of Ambrose

398 John Chrysostom becomes Patriarch of Constantinople

399 Death of Eutropius

403 Theophilus arrives in Constantinople
Synod of the Oak Tree

404 John Chrysostom exiled

407 Death of John Chrysostom

c. 420 Anglo-Saxons begin invasion of Britain

420 Death of Jerome

A.D.

430   Death of Augustine
438   Relics of John Chrysostom transferred to Church of Apostles in Constantinople
527–65   Reign of Justinian
529   Closing of the Schools in Athens
537   Rededication of Hagia Sophia
546   Rome taken by Goths
560   Byzantine Empire at its greatest extent
570   Birth of Mahomet
602   Fall of Emperor Maurice and coronation of Phocas
632   Death of Mahomet
634   Moslems capture Syria and Jerusalem
c. 676   Birth of John Mansur (John Damascene) in Damascus
717–18   Siege of Constantinople
720   Arabs in Narbonne
726   Leo III the Isaurian issues edict against images
730   Second edict against images
732   Arabs defeated by Charles Martel
735   John Damascene ordained for priesthood
741   Leo III dies
        Constantine Copronymous comes to the throne
c. 750   Death of John Damascene
787   At Second Council of Nicaea Gregory of Nyssa proclaimed "Father of Fathers"
789   Irene restores images
800   Coronation of Charlemagne at Rome
827   Embassy from the Emperor Michael the Stammerer to Louis the Pious, King of the Franks
843   End of Iconoclastic controversy
880   Death of John Scotus Erigena
c.1025   Death of Symeon the New Theologian
1066   Normans capture England
1096–99 First Crusade
1147–49 Second Crusade
1182   Birth of St. Francis
1189–92 Third Crusade
1204   Crusaders besiege Constantinople
1226   Death of Francis of Assisi
1265   Birth of Dante
c.1290   Birth of Nicholas Cabasilas
1292   Birth of Gregory Palamas in Constantinople
c.1292   Birth of John Cantacuzene
1327   Barlaamo arrives in Constantinople

A.D.

1328   Emperor Andronicus II Paleologus deposed

1331   Barlaamo settles in Thessalonica

1337   Confrontation of Gregory Palamas with Barlaamo

1341   Stephen Dushan overruns Macedonia

1342   Zealots expel nobles from Thessalonica

        Barlaamo made Bishop of Geraci

1343   Gregory Palamas arrested

1347   Coronation of Co-Emperors John VI Cantacuzene and John V Paleologus

        Helena Cantacuzene marries John V

1348   Black Death in Constantinople

1350   Thessalonica captured by John VI Cantacuzene

1351   Barlaamo anathematized

        The Eastern Church adopts the Hesychast view

1354   Abdication of John VI Cantacuzene

1359   Death of Gregory Palamas

1368   Gregory Palamas canonized and proclaimed "the greatest among the Fathers of the Church"

1383   Death of John VI Cantacuzene

1430   Ottoman Turks capture Thessalonica

1453   Fall of Constantinople

1461   Last outposts of Byzantine Empire captured by the Turks

Bibliography

The handiest collection of most of the available Greek Fathers is to be found in the monumental *Patrologia Graeca* (Paris, 1857) edited by Abbé Jacques Paul Migne, comprising 161 enormous volumes. Only comparatively small fragments of the *Patrologia Graeca* have been translated.

In English the *Ante-Nicene Fathers,* edited by Alexander Roberts and James Robinson (New York, Charles Scribner's, 1899) and *The Nicene and Post-Nicene Fathers,* edited by Philip Schaff (New York, Christian Literature Company, 1899) remain the most comprehensive of all available compilations. All the extant works of Clement of Alexandria and Origen are included in the former. The latter devotes six volumes to St. John Chrysostom, one each to St. Athanasius, St. Gregory of Nyssa and St. Gregory Nazianzen. St. Basil shares a volume with St. John Damascene. The literary quality of these translations is exceptionally high, but they were based on texts which had not been subjected to modern textual criticism.

More exact translations of a number of important works have recently been produced in *The Library of Christian Classics,* now issuing from Westminster Press, Philadelphia, under the general editorship of John Baillie, John T. McNeill, and Henry P. Van Dusen. The first volumes include the *Letters of Ignatius,* the *Letter of Polycarp, Martyrdom of Polycarp, The Teaching of the Twelve Apostles,* and the *Letter of Diognetus.* The second volume includes extracts from the *Stromateis* of Clement of Alexandria, Origen's *On Prayer* and *Exhortation to Martyrdom* and his recently discovered *Dialogue with Heracleides.* A third volume includes St. Athanasius' *On the Incarnation,* the *Theological Orations* of St. Gregory Nazianzen, and the *Address on Religious Instruction* by St. Gregory of Nyssa. These translations are accurate and pedantic: one misses the fluency of the original Greek.

Few, if any, of the existing English translations compare with the scholarly and exceedingly well-written series known as the *Sources Chrétiennes,* published by Les Editions du Cerf in Paris. I have relied heavily on these translations, which include many important writings of the Fathers. Many of these have not yet appeared in English.

I have added here a short list of useful works on the Fathers. Those marked with an asterisk I have found especially revealing.

CLEMENT OF ALEXANDRIA

BIGG, CHARLES. *The Christian Platonists of Alexandria.* Oxford, Clarendon Press, 1913.
BUTTERWORTH, G. W. (tr.) *Clement of Alexandria.* Loeb Classical Library. Cambridge, Harvard University Press, 1953.
*TOLLINGTON, R. B. *Clement of Alexandria: A Study in Christian Liberalism.* 2 vols., London, Williams and Norgate, 1914.

ORIGEN

*CADOUX, RENÉ. *Origen: His Life at Alexandria.* St. Louis, Herder, 1944.
DANIÉLOU, JEAN. *Origen.* New York, Sheed and Ward, 1955.
DE FAYE, EUGÈNE. *Origen and His Work.* London, George Allen and Unwin, 1926.
LEWIS, GEORGE (tr.). *The Philocalia of Origen.* Edinburgh, T. & T. Clark, 1911.
O'MEARA, JOHN J. (tr.). *Prayer: Exhortation to Martyrdom.* Westminster, The Newman Press, 1954.
TOLLINGTON, R. B. (tr.). *Selections from the Commentaries and Homilies of Origen.* London, S.P.C.K., 1929.

ST. ATHANASIUS

BRIGHT, WILLIAM (tr.). *Historical Writings of St. Athanasius according to the Benedictine Text.* Oxford, Clarendon Press, 1881.
——. *The Orations of St. Athanasius against the Arians.* Oxford, Clarendon Press, 1873.
HOUGH, LYNN HAROLD. *Athanasius the Hero.* New York, Eaton and Maino, 1906.
*NEWMAN, JOHN HENRY. *The Arians of the Fourth Century.* London, Longmans, Green, 1888.
—— (tr.). *St. Athanasius: Select Treatises in Controversy with the Arians.* London, Longmans, Green, 1897.
SHAPLAND, C. R. B. (tr.). *The Letters of St. Athanasius.* New York, Philosophical Library, 1953.

ST. BASIL

ALLARD, PAUL. *St. Basile.* Paris, V. Lecoffre, 1903.
CLARKE, W. K. L. *The Ascetic Works of St. Basil.* London, S.P.C.K., 1925.
——. *St. Basil the Great: A Study in Monasticism.* Cambridge, Cambridge Univ. Press, 1913.
COURTONNE, YVES. *Sainte Basile et l'hellénisme.* Paris, Firmin-Didot, 1934.
DEFERRARI, ROY J. (tr.). *St. Basil: The Letters.* 4 vols. Loeb Classical Library. London, William Heinemann, 1926-34.
FOX, SISTER MARGARET MARY. *The Life and Times of St. Basil the Great*

as Revealed in His Works. Washington, Catholic University of America, 1939.

MORISON, E. F. *St. Basil and His Rule: a Study in Early Monasticism.* Oxford, Clarendon Press, 1912.

WAY, SISTER AGNES CLARE. *The Language and Style of the Letters of St. Basil.* Washington, Catholic University of America, 1927.

ST. GREGORY OF NYSSA

*DANIÉLOU, JEAN. *Platonisme et théologie mystique: Essai sur la doctrine spirituelle de St. Grégoire de Nysse.* Paris, Aubier, 1944.

GAÏTH, JÉRÔME. *La Conception de la liberté chez Grégoire de Nysse.* Paris, J. Vrin, 1953.

GOGGIN, SISTER THOMAS AQUINAS. *The Times of St. Gregory of Nyssa as Reflected in the Letters of the Contra Encomium.* Washington, Catholic University of America, 1947.

GRAEF, HILDA C. (tr.). *The Lord's Prayer, The Beatitudes.* Westminster, The Newman Press, 1954.

*KEENAN, SISTER MARY EMILY. *A Study of the Ascetical Doctrine of St. Gregory of Nyssa.* Dumbarton Oaks Papers No. 5. Cambridge, Harvard Univ. Press, 1950.

SRAWLEY, J. H. (tr.). *The Catechetical Oration of St. Gregory of Nyssa.* London, S.P.C.K., 1917.

ST. GREGORY NAZIANZEN

BENOÎT, ALPHONSE. *Saint-Grégoire de Nazianze, sa vie, ses oeuvres et son épopée.* Marseille, 1876.

PLAIGNIEUX, JEAN. *Saint-Grégoire Nazianze, théologien.* Paris, Editions franciscaines, 1952.

ST. JOHN CHRYSOSTOM

JURGENS, W. A. (tr.) *The Priesthoood.* New York, Macmillan, 1955.

MOORE, HERBERT (tr.). *The Dialogue of Palladius concerning the Life of Chrysostom.* London, S.P.C.K., 1921.

NEWMAN, JOHN HENRY CARDINAL. *Historical Sketches.* Vol. 2. London, Longmans, Green, 1899.

The Riot of A.D. 387 in Antioch: Journal of Roman Studies, XLII. London, 1952.

ROBERTSON, J. N. W. B. (ed.). *The Divine Liturgies of Our Fathers among the Saints, John Chrysostom and Basil the Great.* London, D. Nutt, 1894.

STEPHENS, R. W. R. *Saint John Chrysostom: His Life and Times.* London, J. Murray, 1883.

ST. JOHN DAMASCENE

LUPTON, J. H. *St. John of Damascus.* London, S.P.C.K., 1882.
WOODWARD, G. R. and HAROLD MATTINGLY (tr.). *Barlaam and Ioasaph.*
Loeb Classical Library. London, William Heinemann, 1914.

DIONYSIUS THE AREOPAGITE

DARBOY, MGR. (tr.). *Oeuvres de Saint Denys, l'Aréopagite.* Paris, Sagnier
et Bray, 1932.
DE GANDILLAC, MAURICE (tr.). *Oeuvres Complètes du Pseudo-Denys,
l'Aréopagite.* Paris, Aubier, Editions Montaignes, 1943.
PALMIERI, F. A. "Two Masters of Byzantine Mysticism: Dionysius the
Areopagite and Maximus the Confessor," *American Catholic Quarterly
Review,* XLI. Philadelphia, 1916.
ROLT, C. E. (tr.). *On the Divine Names and the Mystical Theology.*
London, S.P.C.K., 1940.

SYMEON THE NEW THEOLOGIAN

HUSSEY, JOAN M. *Church Learning in the Byzantine Empire.* London,
Oxford Univ. Press, 1937.
PECTORATUS, NIKETAS. *Un grand mystique byzantin. Vie de Symeon le
Nouveau Théologien.* Irénée Hausherr, tr. Orientalia Christiana,
XII, 45.

ST. GREGORY PALAMAS

BRIANCHINOV, IGNATIUS. *On the Prayer of Jesus,* Father Lazarus, tr.
London, Johns Watkins, 1952.
COUSIN, LOUIS (tr.). *Histoire de Constantinople.* Paris, D. Foucault, 1685.
*HAUSHERR, IRÉNÉE. *La Méthode d'Oraison Hésychaste.* Orientalia Chris-
tiana, XXXVII, 1927.
KADLOUBOVSKY, E. and G. E. H. PALMER (tr.). *Early Fathers from the
Philocalia.* London, Faber and Faber, 1954.
KIPRIAN, ARKHIMANDRIT. *Antropologia Sv. Grigoriya Palami.* Paris,
Y.M.C.A., 1950.
TAFRALI, ORESTE. *Thessalonique au Quatorzième Siecle.* Paris, P. Gueth-
ner, 1912.
*Also articles by M. Jugie on St. Gregory Palamas and the Palamite Con-
troversy in A. Vacant. *Dictionaire de Théologie Catholique,* v. 11 (1).
Paris, Librairie Letouzey et Ane, 1913.

GENERAL

AYER, J. C. *A Source Book of Ancient Church History.* New York, Charles
Scribner's Sons, 1952.
BACKHOUSE, EDWARD. *Early Church History.* London, Headley Brothers,
1899.

Bigg, Charles. *Neoplatonism.* London, S.P.C.K., 1895.

Campbell, John Marshall. *The Greek Fathers.* New York, Longmans, Green, 1929.

Cochrane, C. N. *Christianity and Classical Culture.* Oxford, Clarendon Press, 1940.

Farrar, F. W. *The Lives of the Fathers.* 2 vols. London, Adam and Charles Black, 1907.

Gilson, Étienne. *History of Christian Philosophy in the Middle Ages.* New York, Random House, 1955.

Grant, Robert M. *Miracle and Natural Law in Graeco-Roman and Early Greek Christian Thought.* Amsterdam, North Holland Publishing Co., 1952.

Hannay, J. O. *The Spirit and Origin of Christian Monasticism.* London, 1903.

Harnack, Adolf. *History of Dogma.* Neil Buchanan, tr. 7 vols. London, Williams and Norgate, 1894.

Hodges, George. *The Early Church.* Boston, Houghton, Mifflin, 1915.

Jackson, F. J. Foakes. *An Introduction to the History of Christianity, A.D. 590-1314.* New York, Macmillan, 1921.

Kidd, B. J. *A History of the Church to A.D. 461.* 3 vols. London, Clarendon Press, 1922.

Labriolle, Pierre de. *History and Literature of Christianity from Tertullian to Boethius.* New York, Knopf, 1925.

*Lossky, Vladimir. *Essai sur la théologie mystique de l'église d'Orient.* Paris, Aubier, 1944.

Macarius, St. *Fifty Spiritual Homilies.* A. J. Mason, tr. London, S.P.C.K., 1921.

Mackinnon, James. *From Christ to Constantine.* New York, Longmans, Green, 1936.

Palanque, J. R. *The Church in the Christian Roman Empire.* New York, Macmillan, 1953.

Prestige, G. L. *God in Patristic Thought.* London, William Heinemann, 1936.

Stanley, Arthur Penryn. *Lectures on the History of the Eastern Church.* New York, Dutton, 1924.

Stone, James S. *Readings in Church History.* Philadelphia, Porter and Coates, 1889.

Streeter, Burnett. *The Primitive Church.* New York, Macmillan, 1929.

Underhill, Evelyn. *Mysticism.* New York, Noonday Press, 1955.

———. *The Mystic Way.* New York, Dutton, 1913.

Vasil'yev, A. A. *History of the Byzantine Empire, 325-1453.* Madison, University of Wisconsin Press, 1952.

Wells, Charles L. *Manual of Ecclesiastical History.* Sewanee, The University Press, 1912.

WERNLE, PAUL. *The Beginnings of Christianity.* 2 vols. London, Williams and Norgate, 1904.

Readers who may wish to pursue one or another theme intensively will find ample clues in the following manuals and bibliographies:

ALTANER, BERTHOLD. *Patrologie: Leben, Schriften und Lehre der Kirchenväter.* 2nd ed. Frieburg im B., Herder, 1951.
BARDENHEWER, OTTO. *Geschichte der altkichlichen litteratur.* 5 vols. Frieburg im B., Herder, 1902-32.
————. *Patrology,* tr. from the second German edition. St. Louis, Herder, 1908.
CAYRÉ, F. *Patrologie et histoire de la théologie.* 4th ed. 3 vols. Paris, Société de Jean L'Évangeliste, Desclée de Brouwer, 1944-47.
KRUMBACHER, K. *Geschichte der byzantinische* [Evangeliste] *Litteratur.* Stuttgart, W. Kohlhammer, 1955.
LIETZMANN, HANS. *A History of the Early Church.* Bertram Lee Woolf, tr. 4 vols. New York, Charles Scribner's Sons, 1949-1952.
PUECH, AIMÉ. *Histoire de la littérature grecque chrétienne.* 3 vols. Paris, Société d'edition Les Belles Lettres, 1928-30.
QUASTEN, JOHANNES. *Patrology.* 2 vols. Utrecht, Spectrum Publishers, 1950-53.
VON CAMPENHAUSEN, HANS FREIHERR. *Die Griechieschen Kirchenväter.* Stuttgart, W. Kohlhammer, 1955.

Index

Greek - xii

Hymns - 10

Clement's simplicity - 42

     also xvii "panegyris hagia"

Origen - _all_ receive grace

       (animals -- all)

   50
   55

  Athanasius and Augustine - 105

St. Anthony's joy - 105

Gregory (Nyssa)'s writing - a nature
   lover like 18th cent. romantics - 142
 - a universalist - 146

Gregory Nazianzen - the orations
   on the trinity - 187 ff
    birds, peacocks, fishes 188
    Jesus - 189 (the paradoxes)